Bass C[harrington]
World [Cup]
Handb[ook] [19]75

Compiled by Brian Glanville

Name: Graham

Coopre

G
246
A

A Playfair Publication

© Brian Glanville 1974

Also published by Queen Anne Press
Goalkeepers are Crazy and other stories   45p

Cover photo and inside photos courtesy of Colorsport

Published by The Queen Anne Press Limited
12 Vandy Street, London EC2A 2EN

Made and printed in Great Britain by C. Nicholls & Company Ltd,
The Philips Park Press, Manchester

Contents

	Introduction	5
1	The 1974 World Cup	6
	The Final Rounds	14
	The Qualifying Rounds	22
2	The European Cup 1973-74	35
3	The European Cup-Winners' Cup 1973-74	42
4	UEFA Cup 1973-74	50
5	Intercontinental and Super Cups 1973-74	64
6	British International Championship 1973-74	66
7	Friendly Internationals Against Foreign Teams 1973-74	69
8	Friendly Internationals Between Foreign Teams 1973-74	75
9	English and Scottish Cups 1973-74	78
10	English and Scottish Leagues 1973-74	80
11	Fifty World Stars	85
12	World Cup History	97
13	European Football Championship History	168
14	World Club Championship History	173
15	European Cup History	181
16	European Cup-Winners' Cup History	207
17	Fairs Cup and UEFA Cup History	226
18	South American Championship and Cup History	248
19	Olympic Games	250
20	England and Great Britain v The Rest	252
21	UEFA and the Lobo Affair	254

INTRODUCTION

Havelange Wins FIFA Presidency

In Frankfurt, on 11 June, 1974, João Havelange of Brazil became the new president of FIFA, the international body, beating Sir Stanley Rous on the second ballot. On the first, he won by 62 to 56, which did not give him the required threequarters majority. On the second, he won by 68 to 52. So Rous' distinguished if sometimes controversial reign ended after 13 years. The future seemed ominously stormy.

Africa speaks, one might have said, and Europe is obliged to listen Havelange came to power through the votes of the African nations. whom he had spent so much time, money, and assiduity to cultivate. There was much resentment in Europe about the nature of his electoral campaign, whispers – nay, more than whispers – of passages paid from Africa to Frankfurt, of little brown envelopes going into large black hands. Rous insisted that Havelange had promised him he would not stand against him so long as he wished to continue in office. In the event, Rous was fobbed off with the honorary presidency of FIFA; little consolation for being displaced, as it must have seemed to him, by an upstart, with little real background in football.

For Havelange was, in fact a water polo player, who grew rich (though no one is quite sure really how rich) in the transport business. Rich enough, it appears, to have spent in access of half a million dollars and the best part of 10 months electioneering; though much of that money may well have been provided by the Brazilian Sports Confederation of which he has long been president. And detached enough, certainly, from football to fly straight home after the FIFA election, with the World Cup due to start in two days, on the grounds that he had business interests to attend to.

At the Congress, African delegates chattered endlessly and repetitively on political themes, particularly the admission or otherwise of Red China. Many observers felt that all this should have come after, rather than before, the election, and might have cost Rous votes. He stood firmly on principle, refusing to bow to Red China's demand that Formosa be thrown out before they deign to come into FIFA. As Rous sturdily pointed out, Formosa had done nothing wrong. To eject them would be deeply cynical. Whether Havelange is of the same opinion remains to be seen.

'Havelange', wrote Keith Botsford, in *The Sunday Times*, 'is a creature of the Too Much. His career shows an almost erotic ambition. World football has enough disciplinary, economic, and political problems without turning in a wobbly pivot.'

Indeed, it has. But then, if it comes to that, what could be a wobblier pivot than UEFA, tarnished almost beyond redemption by the Lobo Affair? The future seems uncertain and unprepossessing.

CHAPTER ONE

The 1974 World Cup

West Germany, after 20 years, regained the World Cup, beating a brilliant but fallible Dutch team 2-1 in the final in Munich. Thus, by a weird irony, Scotland became the only unbeaten team in the competition, although they failed to reach the second round!

As in 1954, the West Germans lost a match on the way to the title; but this time it could hardly be said that they lightly let it go. Their conquerors were East Germany, in Hamburg; but the defeat may have been a disguised boon. In the first place, it galvanised the West Germans. In the second place, it induced them to make productive changes. In the third, as Franz Beckenbauer himself pointed out, it sent them into the weaker of the two qualifying groups for the final.

The Netherlands might well have won the World Cup had they not lost Barrie Hulshoff, their powerful Ajax centre-half, with a knee injury before the tournament. This led them to pull Arie Haan, one of their best midfield players, into the back four as notional 'sweeper'. Behind these, unexpectedly, they chose the veteran 33-year-old goalkeeper Jongbloed, who had been thought by most to have gone along merely for the ride. Van Beveren, the first-choice 'keeper, and another brilliant midfield player in Gerry Muhren, were also absent. But no one could have played better than did the big inside-left, Wim Van Hanegem, in the final.

The Dutch, who had made heavy weather of their passage to the finals, and whose players till then seemed a bunch of mercenary individualists, were pulled together by a fine manager in Rinus Michels, the former Ajax coach, now with Barcelona. He it was who turned them into the great team their talents suggested they could be. He it was who healed the breach between Cruyff, his protégé, and the rest. But Holland's superb attacking play was not supported by a sound defence. Indeed, it was a tournament full of defensive error, often surprisingly unpunished by the attacks. The most glaring and expensive instance was Johnny Rep's first-half miss in the final, when he and Cruyff were through with only Beckenbauer between them and Sepp Maier. Cruyff passed to Rep, Maier stopped his shot, and West Germany went on to score the next, the decisive, goal.

The World Cup this time had neither quarter- nor semi-finals. Under a new dispensation, the two top teams in four qualifying groups went into two further groups of four teams, run on a league basis. The winner of each group met in the final, which was all well and good. Less satisfying was the fact that the second team in each group was left to play out a perfectly meaningless third-place match. Though the group system fortunately did not lead to the manic defence that some people feared, it did deprive the competition of an exciting semi-final stage.

The first stage produced its quota of dramatic surprises. Italy were eliminated, East Germany beat West Germany, the Netherlands exploded, Sweden went through.

Scotland went out with credit, and a large measure of ill fortune. Some insisted that it was their own fault; for playing so cautiously against feeble Zaire. They scored only twice, whereas the Yugoslavs got nine and the Brazilians, in their last match, three. The third goal, the one that knocked Scotland out of the competition on a basis – such a dubious basis – of 'goal difference', came from a shot by Valdomiro that crept between the goalkeeper's body and the near post. Kazadi had previously been injured in a harsh challenge by Mirandinha.

So Scotland went out without losing a game, having drawn a bruising match 0–0 with Brazil, then drawing 1–1 in Frankfurt with Yugoslavia. Billy Bremner, after an indifferent start against Zaire, was Scotland's chief hero, playing with such inspirational fire that Pelé praised him to the skies, calling him 'a true captain'.

Scotland certainly finished the stronger in a bruising match against Brazil and deserved to win in the last stages. The Brazilians, Pereira and Rivelino in particular, were often displeasingly violent. The Scots might also have won against Yugoslavia. After an uneasy beginning, they took a strong grip on events, and Peter Lorimer, in incisive form, almost scored in the second half when he hooked over Maric, only for Buljan to clear from the line. So it was the Yugoslavs, in a breakaway, who took the first goal. Dragan Dzajic, on the right, cleverly pulled the ball inside his man, crossed elegantly with his left foot, and Karasi, the substitute, headed past the excellent Harvey. With Tommy Hutchison on for the disappointing Dalglish, Scotland fought back for a fine equaliser. Hutchison beat his man in classical winger's style on the left, went to the line, pulled the ball back, and after one Scot had swung and missed, Joe Jordan collected it to tuck it inside the far post with his left foot.

The World Cup was opened with the traditional goalless draw; the third in succession. There might, however, have been several goals in the match in Frankfurt between Yugoslavia and Brazil. The Brazilians might have scored in the first half, Yugoslavia should certainly have done so in the second.

Significantly, all Brazil's best chances came from dead-ball kicks. Maric made excellent saves from thundering shots by the blond Francisco Marinho and Rivelino, and a cleverly worked free kick on the edge of the box almost gave Jairzinho a goal. But Brazil were fragile in midfield, modest in attack. You cannot lose Pelé, Tostão, and Gerson – not to mention Clodoaldo, who dropped out injured on the very eve of the World Cup – and be remotely the same team. With Dzajic gliding effortlessly past Nelinho, a young reserve for Zé Maria, Yugoslavia took up the running, Petkovic missed an easy chance from Dzajic's cross, Oblak hit the post, Katalinski's mighty header beat Leao but was stopped by his opposite number, Pereira. Oblak's superb run to the by-line gave Acimovic an open goal, but Leao saved with his legs. So the new, diminished Brazil survived.

After bringing a couple of splendid saves from Harvey, they virtually survived against Scotland, too. Yugoslavia thrashed Zaire, the 'mattress team', 9–0, after which the Zaireans wanted to go straight home and had to be talked out of it by Vidinic, their coach. Their individual talent was as plain as their total lack of organisation. Brazil beat them 3–0 and thus joined Yugoslavia in the next round.

In Group 1, the West Germans played three indifferent games, won the first two, lost the third. There was unrest at their training camp in Malente, outside Hamburg; the regimen was too severe, they complained. Günter Netzer, out of form and hurt into the bargain, the ghost of himself after a bad season in Spain, missed the first two matches, played 20 anonymous minutes against East Germany, and had to yield the palm to the hero of 1970, Wolfgang Overath.

A spectacular goal by Paul Breitner won the game against a resilient Chilean team in Berlin. The dominating Elias Figueroa and the decisive Quintano bolstered a strong defence. The attack, motivated by Reinoso, sharpened by Caszely – sent off, after being warned, for a retaliatory foul on Vogts – could have scored a couple of breakaway goals. I thought Caszely, who'd been cautioned by the Turkish referee, Babacan, unlucky to go. Had Babacan blown for what was certainly a foul by Vogts, retaliation would not have taken place, but even then, it wasn't worth expulsion.

The limited but courageous Australians acquitted themselves well. The East Germans, playing a harsh game, were rather lucky to beat them 2–0. There was a touch of offside about their first goal – diverted past his own 'keeper by Curran – though Streich took the second well. Against the West Germans, in Hamburg, Australia might well have scored twice in the second half, especially when Abonyi hit the post. Tighter marking might have prevented Overath's first goal, from outside the box; Cullmann's, from a right-wing cross; Gerd Müller's, from a near-post header. But the Australians covered themselves with glory when they held Chile 0–0 in their last match.

The East Germans did still better, in Hamburg. Playing West Germany for the first time, they now eschewed an attacking midfield, put only two men up, defended forcefully, broke dangerously. The West Germans might have scored two first-half goals when Müller twice slipped Weise, once to give Grabowski a chance, once to hit the post. But by the same token, Kreische missed the simplest of chances bang in front of goal for East Germany, and Lauck too might have scored. Eight minutes from time, after dominating the second half, the West German defence at last paid for its failings. Sparwasser took a good pass from the substitute, Hamann, forced his way past Vogts, and beat Maier to win the day.

In Group 3, the Dutch began brilliantly against Uruguay, stumbled against Sweden, then easily despatched the Bulgarians to establish themselves as favourites. No one had ever doubted their potential. The question was whether they could express it, after their indifferent qualifying form, and the endless bickering about money. But Rinus Michels, licked them into shape, and with Johan Cruyff, everything was possible.

Playing with sinuous irresistibility, dynamic and even majestic, Cruyff quickly established himself as the best player in the competition. The cynical Uruguayans did their best to kick him, but couldn't. Demanding money for every statement they made, bringing to Germany Garisto, who had put Australia's Ray Baartz out of the tournament with a karate chop, they were a wretched crew. The Dutch might have had six against them; probably would, had they not been fearful for their legs. As it was, Johnny Rep scored twice for them, and that was enough. Forlan's display was vicious, but it was Montero Castillo who was sent off; for punching Rensenbrink in the stomach.

Using their midfield star, Arie Haan, in the back four, the Dutch then proceeded to draw 0-0 with the surprising Swedes, who had themselves drawn their first match with Bulgaria. Sweden, discounted by everybody, in fact showed their old World Cup resourcefulness, under the able managership of Eriksson. Ralf Edstroem, so elegant on the ground and splendid in the air, resumed his old Atvidaberg partnership with the busy Sandberg, the defence crystallised solidly around Nordqvist and in front of Ronnie Hellstroem: and after the opening match, a more ambitious style was used.

It was good enough to smite the Uruguayans 3-0 in the third match, when the Sandberg-Edstroem combination produced all three goals; Grahn and Larsson making the bullets to be fired, after Hellstroem had made fine saves in the first half. The Bulgarians, in Dortmund, made a number of chances and scored an (own) goal against the Dutch, but could never begin to fathom Cruyff. They gave away two first-half penalties, both converted by Neeskens, and the Dutch were shooting in for much of the second half. They missed many chances, but eventually Rep, with a neat volley, and the substitute, De Jong, a couple more away.

Italy, among the favourites when the tournament started, went out ignominiously, howling all the way back to Milan. There was abundant trouble in the camp, first with Juliano, then Re Cecconi, and finally and most cataclysmically with Giorgio Chinaglia. Furious at being substituted in the first game against Haiti, in Munich, he made a vulgar gesture at Ferruccio Valcareggi, the manager, as he left the field, smashed six mineral water bottles in the dressing-room, and finally made a public attack on the Italian manager and directors. His Lazio manager, Maestrelli, flew by private plane to West Germany and managed to stop the officials sending him home. Wine and rolls were brought out; Chinaglia actually played in (part of) the final game.

The Haitians, of all people, put an end to Dino Zoff's amazing record, after 1,144 unbeaten minutes. It was the rapid centre-forward Sanon, who was responsible, and who gave Italy brief nightmares of another North Korea. Taking a pass from Vorbe, he slipped Spinosi with ease, swerved outside Zoff, and scored. The stunned Italians then pulled themselves together, and replied three times, despite the excellence of Francillon, the Haitian 'keeper, who was later signed by Munich 1860.

The Haitians were happy as larks at the zoo next morning, but shadows hung over them. Jean Joseph, the red-haired mulatto centre-half, was found guilty of taking a stimulant after the dope test. In vain he protested it was a drug he took for asthma. Even his own, French, team doctor disavowed him, and he was suspended from international football for a year. The Haitians, faithful to the traditions of the Ton Ton Macoutes, then forcibly abducted him from the Grunwald Sports School where the team was staying, incarcerated him in the Sheraton Hotel, and next morning flew him back to Port Au Prince and the condign wrath of President Baby Doc Duvalier. A sinister episode: but Jean Joseph had enough publicity to survive.

Haiti lost 7-0 in Munich to the rampant Poles, 4-1 to the Argentinians, and did little more than Zaire to suggest they had any right to be there.

The Poles were the revelation of the group, winning all three matches and finally despatching a stunned Italian team. In their first game, they opened furiously against Argentina, who deployed a weird formation, with Perfumo an uneasy sweeper behind a line of three, Bargas floating about in front of them. Only when Houseman and then Telch came on in the second half did they get to grips with things. Yet they might have scored in the third minute when Brindisi's lovely ball sent Kempes clear through; to miss. Two banal errors in the seventh minute then cost them two goals. First Carnevali inexplicably dropped Gadocha's corner for Lato to score. Then Lato's pass utterly breached a slack defence for Szarmach, a fine new centre-forward, to make it 2-0. Heredia came up to reduce the margin, after half-time; but then Carnevali, after a fine save, threw the ball straight out to Lato, who promptly cantered in from the right to make it 3-1. Babington's subsequent goal was not enough.

Against Italy, however, Carlos Babington was one of the two finest players on the field. The other was little René Houseman, who danced rings around the Italians, while Babington coolly and elegantly ran the show from midfield. Obsessed to a bizarre fault by tactics, Valcareggi convinced himself that Houseman, a natural winger, would play in midfield, and marked him with Capello. This cost him a good inside-forward and gave him an indifferent fullback.

Not for a full 25 minutes, in which Houseman had splendidly exploited Babington's pass to score, did the penny drop. Then Valcareggi swopped Benetti for Capello. Houseman continued to run riot, despite Benetti's many and ugly fouls, but Italy survived. A silly own goal by Perfumo, diverting Benetti's cross from the left past Carnevali, lost them a lead they never won back. But Telch played a limp Rivera out of the game, the talismanic Riva did nothing, and both were dropped from the match against Poland.

The Poles, thumping seven past the Haitians, were much too lively for the demoralised Italians. Well judged crosses by Kasperczak gave goals to Szarmach, a glorious header, and Deyna, a glorious volley. Italy might have had an early penalty, and did get a late goal through

Capello, but they were simply not in the hunt. They went home, vowing as always that they'd change everything, train their players harder, and turn their backs on negative *catenaccio* with a fixed sweeper.

Hardly had the Italians returned home, however, than they were involved in another sensation. A few days after the World Cup final, the Polish team manager, Gorski, alleged in a newspaper interview that attempts had been made by Italians to bribe his team to allow Italy to draw – and so qualify. Gorski withdrew the allegations, but stories circulating in Warsaw suggested they had strong foundation; that attempts had even been made by Italian Players to bribe the Poles on the field.

Now the tournament divided itself into two final groups of four, and contrived to produce the 'ideal' final. Holland, stronger and more adventurous with every game, won all their matches without conceding a goal; though there were times when their undermanned defence trembled. West Germany, rising from the ashes of the East German defeat, won all three of their matches, too, though Sweden gave them a fright in Dusseldorf.

For the Dutch, Johan Cruyff seemed to reach greater heights with every game. If the Brazilians succeeded in subduing him, by fair means and foul, in the first half of their decisive match in Dortmund, he played havoc with them in the second, making one goal and scoring another.

Holland's first opponents were Argentina, severely weakened by the absence of the immaculate Babington. He had been booked three times, and must bitterly have regretted his idiocy in twice handling the ball in the Italian game. Without him, Argentina had neither the craft nor the pace to withstand a superb Dutch performance. Already 4–1 victors over Argentina in a friendly match, they showed even greater superiority in Gelsenkirchen.

Chances were made in profusion and thrown away with prodigality, till Cruyff neatly lobbed Carnevali after 11 minutes. Fourteen minutes later, the goalkeeper was beaten again by a bullet from Krol on the edge of the box. Only heavy rain in the second half prevented the Dutch running up a great score. Nor did a brutal foul by Perfumo on Neeskens deter them. Rep headed the third from Cruyff's measured centre, and just on time, with Argentina down to 10 men, Cruyff got the fourth, after Carnevali had gallantly saved from Van Hanegem.

The East Germans played a dourly negative game on the same ground, Weise marking Cruyff diligently. The Dutch, who were rather subdued in the first half after a dazzling first 10 minutes, scored in nine from a left-foot shot by Neeskens, from a chance made by Rensenbrink. Rensenbrink himself scored the second goal, after a movement begun by Cruyff and carried on by Neeskens and Van Hanegem.

So the Dutch needed only a draw in their third match, against Brazil, to qualify on goal difference. A cunning free kick, struck by Rivelino, with Jairzinho ducking in the 'wall', brought victory against the East Germans. The Argentinians were beaten 2–1 at Hanover in a game that might have gone either way; though at least the Brazilians did score

11

twice in other than dead-ball situations. Argentina should have had a penalty when Marinho brought down Babington, but they didn't get it, and nine minutes later, Brazil scored. Rivelino's clever, swerving shot beat Carnevali. The Brazilians, ironically, were to concede their first goal of the tournament . . . from a free kick, Brindisi cleverly lobbing a baffled Leao. But a surging run by Zé Maria, after tackling Babington, a cross from the by-line, and a header by Jairzinho after 49 minutes won the match for Brazil.

Against the Dutch, Brazil's performance was frankly shameful. True, the Dutch defenders fouled frequently, and incurred several bookings, but it was the Brazilians who cynically began it, the Brazilians who cold-bloodedly sustained it till, in the end, Luis Pereira was sent off for chopping Neeskens. Neeskens, previously, had been knocked cold by Mario Marinho of Santos, a foul the unimpressive West German referee, Herr Tschencher, couldn't see.

Yet Brazil might have won. The Dutch defence was incredibly thin and presumptuous in the first half, when Paulo César and Jairzinho missed easy chances. As against that, only a wonderful save by Leao stopped Holland scoring an early goal when Zé Maria pushed the ball straight to Cruyff's feet. In the second half, however, the Brazilians had shot their bolt. Neeskens, working an electric one-two with Cruyff, lobbed over Leao for the first goal. Cruyff himself, with a superb volley, scored the second, from Krol's left-wing cross. The Brazilians, in keeping Rivelino so deep, allowed Neeskens to attack forcefully.

West Germany ploughed on to the final, given a hard run for their money by Poland. Indeed, the decisive third match, in Frankfurt, might have gone the other way had there not been torrential rain, and had Poland not lacked Szarmach. The game was held up for over half an hour, and some thought it should still not have been played. As it was, the drenched conditions favoured West Germany's strength. The Poles were the better team in the first half, when only a marvellous double save by Sepp Maier from Lato and Gadocha, after Beckenbauer's mistake, prevented a goal. In the second half, Maier's opposite number, Jan Tomaszewski, saved a penalty after Holzenbein was brought down. But he had no chance when a shot by Hoeness was deflected to Gerd Müller, who swooped and scored.

Though Lato and Gadocha were superb throughout, Poland did not have an easy passage in their previous two games. In Stuttgart, it was only Sweden's carelessness that prevented them winning. Playing a clever, counter attacking game, with Grahn and Larsson shrewd in midfield, Sandberg and Edstroem a fine spearhead, well supported from behind, they twice split Poland in the first half. First Tapper, then Grahn, missed his chance, while in the second half, Tomaszewski (moving before the kick?) saved Tapper's penalty.

So it was that the Lato and Gadocha combination produced the only goal, in the first half; a cross from Gadocha on the right, a header by Szarmach, another by Lato.

Poland then beat Yugoslavia at Frankfurt, but again were fortunate.

Yugoslavia were without Dragan Dzajic, officially because he had a heavy cold (which he did have), allegedly because he had severely criticised the tactics of Miljan Miljanic, the manager, against West Germany. Moreover, a stupid aberration by Karasi, flooring Szarmach, gave Poland a penalty and a goal by Deyna to open the score. Just before half-time, Karasi spun through for a clever equaliser. Poland won with yet another Lato-Gadocha goal; Gadocha's left-wing corner, Lato's shrewd header on the near post, after 63 minutes; just when Yugoslavia seemed to be calling the tune.

This the Yugoslavs never did against West Germany. They were quite simply overplayed, and might have lost by much more than 2–0. A spectacular drive from Paul Breitner, Germany's attacking fullback, produced the first goal, after 38 minutes. Uli Hoeness got to the line and pulled the ball back for Müller to swoop and get the second, 12 minutes from time. Franz Beckenbauer had a majestic game.

Sweden gave the Germans much more trouble, in rainy Dusseldorf, and might have given more, had Larsson not had to go off, injured, in the second half. Edstroem, with a fine volley after Schwarzenbeck's weak header, scored the opening goal. But West Germany, with Bonhof again making a great difference with his powerful midfield play, fought back. Five minutes after half time, their pressure paid at last when, after Hoeness' run, Müller found Overath, who equalised. A minute later, the irrepressible Hoeness struck again, Müller breasted his cross back to Bonhof, whose shot was reached by Hellstroem, hit both posts, and went in.

Sweden, however, had not given up. They broke away, the German defence missed Edstroem's pass, Sandberg pounced on it and scored. Then West Germany took over. Holzenbein neatly laid the ball off for Grabowski, on as substitute, to score after 79 minutes. A penalty by Hoeness, after Müller was knocked down, made it 4–2; a vibrant game.

Sweden went on to beat Yugoslavia 2–1 to take third place. In the other group, the Argentinians and East Germans drew 1–1 in their last match, each ending with a single point, but with the DDR ahead on goal difference.

The third-place match was the usual tired fiasco between two disappointed teams, though it did give Brazil's Ademir Da Guia, son of the famous Domingas, the chance to make his only World Cup appearance; and a pleasing one. Lato won it with a second-half goal, after running the legs off Alfredo; and he missed a much easier chance in the last minutes.

So to the final, and that astonishing first goal. Not a single West German player had touched the ball between the Dutch kick-off and the moment that Cruyff, spurting into the penalty area, was brought down by Hoeness. Neeskens scored from the spot as Maier dived the wrong way.

For 25 minutes, the Netherlands dominated the game but made no more scoring chances. So it was that the West Germans were able to equalise: from another penalty. Young Holzenbein, who played a lively game, cut boldly inside, was brought down by Jansen, and Paul Breitner scored.

Rep missed his chance, and after 43 minutes, West Germany scored their winner. Grabowski cleverly sent the powerful Bonhof, who had given the German midfield new drive, up the right. Bonhof beat Haan for pace, crossed, the Dutch failed to clear, and Gerd Müller shot home. After the final, Müller would announce his retirement from international football.

There were no goals in the second half, though Holland came out vigorously to play, and Maier had to make a splendid stop from Neeksen's volley. They were obliged to put on Van de Kerkhoff for Rensenbrink, who had passed a very late fitness test after pulling a muscle, and eventually replaced the injured, highly effective, Rijsbergen with De Jong. But the truth of it was that the early goal was a snare and a delusion. Cruyff was never allowed to run riot; and West Germany regained the Cup.

GROUP 1

Berlin, 14 June 1974
   West Germany (1) 1   Chile (0) 0
   Breitner

West Germany: Maier; Vogts, Breitner, Schwarzenbeck, Beckenbauer, Cullmann, Grabowski, Hoeness, Müller, Overath (Holzenbein), Heynckes.
Chile: Vallejos; Garcia, Quintano, Arias, Figueroa, Rodriguez (Lara), Caszely, Valdes (Veliz), Ahumada, Reinoso, Paez.

Hamburg, 14 June 1974
   East Germany (0) 2   Australia (0) 0
   Curran (o.g.), Streich

East Germany: Croy; Kische, Bransch, Weise, Waetzlich, Irmscher, Pommerenke, Sparwasser, Loewe (Hoffmann), Streich, Vogel.
Australia: Reilly; Utjesenevic, Wilson, Schaefer, Curran, Richards, Rooney, Mackay, Warren, Alston, Buljevic.

Hamburg, 18 June 1974
   West Germany (2) 3   Australia (0) 0
   Overath, Cullmann, Müller

West Germany: Maier; Vogts, Breitner, Schwarzenbeck, Beckenbauer, Cullmann (Wimmer), Grabowski, Heynckes (Holzenbein), Overath, Müller, Hoeness.
Australia: Reilly; Utjesenevic, Wilson, Schaefer, Curran, Richards, Rooney, Mackay, Campbell (Abonyi), Alston, Buljevic (Ollerton).

West Berlin, 18 June 1974
   East Germany (0) 1   Chile (0) 1
   Hoffmann   *Ahumada*

East Germany: Croy; Bransch, Kische, Weise, Waetzlich, Irmscher, Seguin (Kreische), Sparwasser, Hoffmann, Streich, Vogel (Ducke).

Chile: Vallejos; Garcia, Figueroa, Quintano, Arias, Paez, Valdes (Yavar), Reinoso, Socias (Farias), Ahumada, Veliz.

Hamburg, 22 June 1974
 East Germany (1) 1 West Germany (0) 0
 Sparwasser
East Germany: Croy; Kurbjuweit, Bransch, Weise, Kreische, Waetzlich, Lauck, Sparwasser, Irmscher (Hamann), Kische, Hoffmann.
West Germany: Maier; Vogts, Schwarzenbeck (Hottges), Beckenbauer, Breitner, Hoeness, Overath (Netzer), Cullmann, Grabowski, Müller, Flohe.

Berlin, 22 June 1974
 Chile (0) 0 Australia (0) 0
Chile: Vallejos; Garcia, Quintano, Figueroa, Arias, Paez, Valdes (Farias), Caszely, Ahumada, Reinoso, Veliz (Yavar).
Australia: Reilly; Utjesenovic, Wilson, Schaefer, Curran (Williams), Richards, Rooney, Mackay, Abonyi, Alston (Ollerton), Buljevic.

	P	W	D	L	F	A	Pts
East Germany	3	2	1	0	4	1	5
West Germany	3	2	0	1	4	1	4
Chile	3	0	2	1	1	2	2
Australia	3	0	1	2	0	5	1

GROUP 2
Frankfurt, 13 June 1974
 Brazil (0) 0 Yugoslavia (0) 0
Brazil: Leao; Nelhinho, Luis Pereira, M. Marinho, F. Marinho, Wilson Piazza, Rivelino, Paulo César Lima, Valdomiro, Jairzinho, Leivinha.
Yugoslavia: Maric; Buljan, Katalinski, Bogicevic, Hadziabdic, Muzinic, Oblak, Acimovic, Petkovic, Surjak, Dzajic.

Dortmund, 14 June 1974
 Scotland (2) 2 Zaire (0) 0
 Lorimer, Jordan
Scotland: Harvey; Jardine, McGrain, Bremner, Holton, Blackley, Dalglish (Hutchison), Hay, Lorimer, Jordan, Law.
Zaire: Kazadi; Mwepu, Mukombo, Buhanga, Lobilo, Kilasu, Mayanga (Kembo), Mana, Ndaye, Kidumu (Kiwonge), Kakodo.

Frankfurt, 18 June 1974
 Brazil (0) 0 Scotland (0) 0
Brazil: Leao; Nelinho, Luis Pereira, M. Marinho, F. Marinho, Wilson Piazza, Rivelino, Paulo César Lima, Jairzinho, Mirandinha, Leivinha (Paulo César Carpegiani).
Scotland: Harvey; Jardine, McGrain, Holton, Buchan, Bremner, Hay, Dalglish, Morgan, Jordan, Lorimer.

Gelsenkirchen, 18 June 1974
   Yugoslavia (6) 9   Zaire (0) 0
   Bajevic (3), *Dzajic, Surjak,*
   Katalinski, Bogicevic, Oblak,
   Petkovic
Yugoslavia: Maric; Buljan, Katalinski, Hadziabdic, Bogicevic, Petkovic, Oblak, Acimovic, Surjak, Bajevic, Dzajic.
Zaire: Kazadi (Tubilandu); Mwepu, Mukombo, Bwanga, Lobilo, Kilasu, Ndaye, Mana, Kembo, Kidumu, Kakoko (Mayanga).

Frankfurt, 22 June 1974
   Scotland (0) 1   Yugoslavia (0) 1
   Jordan   *Karasi*
Scotland: Harvey; Jardine, McGrain, Holton, Buchan, Bremner, Dalglish (Hutchison), Hay, Morgan, Jordan, Lorimer.
Yugoslavia: Maric; Buljan, Hadziabdic, Oblak, Katalinski, Bogicevic, Petkovic, Acimovic, Bajevic (Karasi), Surjak, Dzajic.

Gelsenkirchen, 22 June 1974
   Brazil (1) 3   Zaire (0) 0
   Jairzinho, Rivelino,
   Valdomiro
Brazil: Leao; Nelinho, Luis Pereira, S. Marinho, F. Marinho, Wilson Piazza (Mirandinha), Rivelino, Leivinha (Valdomiro), Paulo César Lima, Jairzinho, Edu.
Zaire: Kazadi; Mwepu, Mukombo, Bwanga, Lobilo, Kibonge, Tshinabu (Kembo), Mana, Ntumba, Kidumu (Kilasu), Mayanga.

	P	W	D	L	F	A	Pts
Yugoslavia	3	1	2	0	10	1	4
Brazil	3	1	2	0	3	0	4
Scotland	3	1	2	0	3	1	4
Zaire	3	0	0	3	0	14	0

GROUP 3
Hanover, 15 June 1974
   Netherlands (1) 2   Uruguay (0) 0
   Rep 2
Netherlands: Jongbloed; Suurbier, Rijsbergen, Haan, Krol, Jansen, Neeskens, Van Hanegem, Cruyff, Rep, Rensenbrink.
Uruguay: Mazurkiewicz; Jauregui, Masnik, Forlan, Pavoni, Esparrago, Montero Castillo, Rocha, Cubilla (Milar), Morena, Mantegazza.

Dusseldorf, 15 June 1974
   Sweden (0) 0   Bulgaria (0) 0
Sweden: Hellstroem; Olsson, Karlsson, Bo Larsson, Andersson, Kindvall (Magnusson), Tapper, Grahn, Torstensson, Sandberg, Edstroem.
Bulgaria: Goranov; Velitchkov, Kolev, Penev, Voinov (Mikhailov), Bonev, Denev, Panov (M. Vassilev), Nikodimov, Z. Vassilev, Ivkov.

Dortmund, 19 June 1974
 Netherlands (0) 0   Sweden (0) 0
Netherlands: Jongbloed; Suurbier, Haan, Krol, Rijsbergen, Jansen, Neeskens, Van Hanegem (De Jong), Rep, Cruyff, Keizer.
Sweden: Hellstroem; Olsson (Grip), Andersson, Karlsson, Nordqvist, Bo Larsson, Ejderstedt, Tapper (Persson), Edstroem, Grahn, Sandberg.

Hanover, 19 June 1974
 Bulgaria (0) 1   Uruguay (0) 1
 Bonev   *Pavoni*
Bulgaria: Goranov; Velitchkov, Ivkov, Kolev, Z. Vassilev, Penev, Voinov, Bonev, Denev, Panov, Nikodimov (Mikhailov).
Uruguay: Mazurkiewicz; Jauregui, Forlan, Pavoni, Esparrago, Morena, Rocha, Garisto (Masnik), Mantegazza (Cardaccio), Milar, Corbo.

Dortmund, 23 June 1974
 Netherlands (2) 4   Bulgaria (0) 1
 Neeskens 2 (*2 pens*), *Rep*,   *Krol* (*o.g.*)
 De Jong
Netherlands: Jongbloed; Suurbier, Haan, Rijsbergen, Krol, Neeskens (De Jong), Van Hanegem (Israel), Jansen, Rep, Cruyff, Rensenbrink.
Bulgaria: Staikov; Velitchkov, Ivkov, Penev, Z. Vassilev, Stoyanov (Mikhailov), Bonev, Kolev, Voinov, Panov (Borisov), Denev.

Dusseldorf, 23 June 1974
 Sweden (0) 3   Uruguay (0) 0
 Edstroem 2, *Sandberg*
Sweden: Hellstroem; Andersson, Grip, Karlsson, Nordqvist, Bo Larsson, Grahn, Kindvall (Torstensson), Edstroem, Magnusson (Ahlstroem), Sandberg.
Uruguay: Mazurkiewicz; Jauregui, Forlan, Pavoni, Garisto (Masnik), Esparrago, Rocha, Mantegazza, Milar, Morena, Corbo (Cubilla).

	P	W	D	L	F	A	Pts
Netherlands	3	2	1	0	6	1	5
Sweden	3	1	2	0	3	0	4
Bulgaria	3	0	2	1	2	5	2
Uruguay	3	0	1	2	1	6	1

GROUP 4
Munich, 15 June 1974
 Italy (0) 3   Haiti (0) 1
 Rivera, Benetti, Anastasi   *Sanon*
Italy: Zoff; Spinosi, Morini, Burgnich, Facchetti, Mazzola, Capello, Rivera, Benetti, Chinaglia (Anastasi), Riva.
Haiti: Francillon; Bayonne, Jean Joseph (Barthelemy), Nazaire, Auguste, Antoine, Desir, Vorbe, Francois, G. Saint-Vil, Sanon.

Stuttgart, 15 June 1974
  Poland (2) 3   Argentina (0) 2
  Lato 2, *Szarmach*   *Heredia, Babington*
Poland: Tomaszewski; Gorgon, Szymanowski, Zmuda, Musial, Kasperczak, Deyna, Maszczyk, Lato, Szarmach (Domarski), Gadocha (Cmikiewicz).
Argentina: Carnevali; Perfumo, Wolff, Heredia, Sa, Bargas (Telch), Babington, Brindisi (Houseman), Kempes, Ayala, Balbuena.

Stuttgart, 19 June 1974
  Argentina (1) 1   Italy (1) 1
  Houseman   *Perfumo (o.g.)*
Argentina: Carnevali; Wolff (Glaria), Perfumo, Heredia, Sa, Telch, Houseman, Babington, Ayala, Kempes, Yazalde (Chazarreta).
Italy: Zoff; Spinosi, Facchetti, Benetti, Morini (Wilson), Burgnich, Mazzola, Capello, Anastasi, Rivera (Causio), Riva.

Munich, 19 June 1974
  Poland (5) 7   Haiti (0) 0
  Lato 2, *Deyna, Szarmach 3,*
  Gorgon
Poland: Tomaszewski; Szymanowski, Gorgon, Zmuda, Musial (Gut), Deyna, Kasperczak, Lato, Maszczyk (Cmikiewicz), Szarmach, Gadocha.
Haiti: Francillon; Auguste, Bayonne, Vorbe, Nazaire, Antoine, André (Barthelemy), Francois, R. Saint-Vil (Racine), Desir, Sanon.

Munich, 23 June 1974
  Argentina (2) 4   Haiti (0) 1
  Yazalde 2, *Houseman, Ayala*   *Sanon*
Argentina: Carnevali; Wolff, Heredia, Perfumo, Sa, Babington, Telch, Houseman (Brindisi), Yazalde, Ayala, Kempes (Balbuena).
Haiti: Francillon; Ducoste, Bayonne, Vorbe, Desir, Antoine, G. St Vil (F. Leandre), Racine, Nazaire (M. Leandre), Sanon, Louis.

Stuttgart, 23 June 1974
  Poland (2) 2   Italy (0) 1
  Szarmach, Deyna   *Capello*
Poland: Tomaszewski; Szymanowski, Gorgon, Musial, Zmuda, Kasperczak, Deyna, Maszczyk, Gadocha, Szarmach (Cmikiewicz), Lato.
Italy: Zoff; Spinosi, Facchetti, Benetti, Morini, Burgnich (Wilson), Causio, Mazzola, Capello, Anastasi, Chinaglia (Boninsegna).

	P	W	D	L	F	A	Pts
Poland	3	3	0	0	12	3	6
Argentina	3	1	1	1	7	5	3
Italy	3	1	1	1	5	4	3
Haiti	3	0	0	3	2	14	0

GROUP A
Hanover, 26 June 1974
  Brazil (0) 1   East Germany (0) 0
  Rivelino
Brazil: Leao; Zé Maria, Luis Pereira, M. Marinho, F. Marinho, Paulo César Carpegiani, Rivelino, Dirceu, Valdomiro, Jairzinho, Paulo César Lima.
East Germany: Croy; Kurbjuweit, Bransch, Weise, Streich, Waetzlich, Lauck (Loewe), Sparwasser, Hamann (Irmscher), Kische, Hoffmann.

Gelsenkirchen, 26 June 1974
  Netherlands (2) 4   Argentina (0) 0
  Cruyff 2, Krol, Rep
Netherlands: Jongbloed; Suurbier (Israel), Haan, Rijsbergen, Krol, Jansen, Neeskens, Van Hanegem, Rep, Cruyff, Rensenbrink.
Argentina: Carnevali; Perfumo, Sa, Wolff (Glaria), Telch, Heredia, Balbuena, Yazalde, Ayala, Squeo, Houseman (Kempes).

Gelsenkirchen, 30 June 1974
  Netherlands (1) 2   East Germany (0) 0
  Neeskens, Rensenbrink
Netherlands: Jongbloed; Suurbier, Haan, Rijsbergen, Krol, Jansen, Neeskens, Van Hanegem, Rep, Cruyff, Rensenbrink.
East Germany: Croy; Kische, Bransch, Weise, Kurbjuweit, Pommerenke, Schnuphase, Lauck (Kreische), Loewe (Ducke), Sparwasser, Hoffmann.

Hanover, 30 June 1974
  Brazil (1) 2   Argentina (1) 1
  Rivelino, Jairzinho   *Brindisi*
Brazil: Leao; Zé Maria, Luis Pereira, M. Marinho, F. Marinho, Paulo César Carpegiani, Rivelino, Dirceu, Valdomiro, Jairzinho, Paulo César Lima.
Argentina: Carnevali; Glaria, Heredia, Bargas, Sa (Carrascosa), Brindisi, Squeo, Babington, Balbuena, Ayala, Kempes (Houseman).

Dortmund, 3 July 1974
  Netherlands (0) 2   Brazil (0) 0
  Neeskens, Cruyff
Netherlands: Jongbloed; Suurbier, Haan, Rijsbergen, Krol, Neeskens (Israel), Van Hanegem, Jansen, Rep, Cruyff, Rensenbrink (De Jong).
Brazil: Leao; Zé Maria, Luis Pereira, M. Marinho, F. Marinho, Paulo César Carpegiani, Rivelino, Dirceu, Paulo César Lima (Mirandinha), Jairzinho, Valdomiro.

Gelsenkirchen, 3 July 1974
  Argentina (1) 1   East Germany (1) 1
  Houseman   *Streich*

Argentina: Fillol; Wolff, Heredia, Bargas, Carrascosa, Brindisi, Telch, Babington, Houseman, Ayala, Kempes.
East Germany: Croy; Kurbjuweit, Bransch, Weise, Schnuphase, Pommerenke, Loewe (Vogel), Streich (Ducke), Sparwasser, Kische, Hoffmann.

	P	W	D	L	F	A	Pts
Netherlands	3	3	0	0	8	0	6
Brazil	3	2	0	1	3	3	4
East Germany	3	0	1	2	1	4	1
Argentina	3	0	1	2	2	7	1

GROUP B

Stuttgart, 26 June 1974
Poland (1) 1   Sweden (0) 0
Lato

Poland: Tomaszewski; Szymanowski, Gorgon, Zmuda, Gut, Deyna, Kasperczak, Maszczyk, Lato, Szarmach (Kmiecik), Gadocha.
Sweden: Hellstroem; Karlsson, Grip, Nordqvist, Andersson (Augustsson), Grahn, Tapper (Ahlstroem), Bo Larsson, Torstensson, Sandberg, Edstroem.

Dusseldorf, 26 June 1974
West Germany (1) 2   Yugoslavia (0) 0
Breitner, Müller

West Germany: Maier; Vogts, Schwarzenbeck, Beckenbauer, Breitner, Bonhof, Wimmer (Hoeness), Holzenbein (Flohe), Overath, Müller, Herzog.
Yugoslavia: Maric; Buljan, Hadziabdic, Muzinic, Katalinski, Oblak (Jerkovic), Popivoda, Acimovic, Surjak, Karasi, Dzajic (Petkovic).

Frankfurt, 30 June 1974
Poland (1) 2   Yugoslavia (1) 1
Deyna(pen), Lato   *Karasi*

Poland: Tomaszewski; Szymanowski, Gorgon, Zmuda, Musial, Kasperczak, Maszczyk, Deyna (Domarski), Lato, Szarmach (Cmikiewicz), Gadocha.
Yugoslavia: Maric; Buljan, Hadziabdic, Bogicevic, Katalinski, Oblak (Jerkovic), Petkovic (V. Petrovic), Karasi, Bajevic, Acimovic, Surjak.

Dusseldorf, 30 June 1974
West Germany (0) 4   Sweden (1) 2
Overath, Bonhof, Grabowski,   *Edstroem, Sandberg*
Hoeness(pen)

West Germany: Maier; Vogts, Schwarzenbeck, Beckenbauer, Breitner, Hoeness, Overath, Bonhof, Holzenbein (Flohe), Müller, Herzog (Grabowski).
Sweden: Hellstroem; Olsson, Augustsson, Karlsson, Nordqvist, Bo Larsson (Ejderstedt), Torstensson, Tapper, Edstroem, Grahn, Sandberg.

Dusseldorf, 3 July 1974
 Sweden (1) 2   Yugoslavia (1) 1
 Edstroem, Torstensson   *Surjak*
Sweden: Hellstroem; Olsson, Karlsson, Nordqvist, Augustsson, Tapper, Grahn, Persson, Torstensson, Edstroem, Sandberg.
Yugoslavia: Maric; Buljan, Hadziabdic, Katalinski, Bogicevic, Pavlovic (Peruzovic), V. Petrovic (Karasi), Jerkovic, Surjak, Acimovic, Dzajic.

Frankfurt, 3 July 1974
 West Germany (0) 1   Poland (0) 0
 Müller
West Germany: Maier; Vogts, Schwarzenbeck, Beckenbauer, Breitner, Bonhof, Overath, Hoeness, Grabowski, Müller, Holzenbein.
Poland: Tomaszewski; Szymanowski, Gorgon, Zmuda, Musial, Kasperczak (Cmikiewicz), Deyna, Maszczyk (Kmiecik), Lato, Domarski, Gadocha.

	P	W	D	L	F	A	Pts
West Germany	3	3	0	0	7	2	6
Poland	3	2	0	1	3	2	4
Sweden	3	1	0	2	4	6	2
Yugoslavia	3	0	0	3	2	6	0

THIRD PLACE MATCH
Munich, 6 July 1974
 Poland (0) 1   Brazil (0) 0
 Lato
Poland: Tomaszewski; Szymanowski, Gorgon, Zmuda, Musial, Maszczyk, Deyna, Kasperczak (Cmikiewicz), Lato, Szarmach (Kapka), Gadocha.
Brazil: Leao, Zé Maria, Alfredo, M. Marinho, F. Marinho, Paulo César Carpegiani, Rivelino, Ademir da Guia (Mirandinha), Valdomiro, Jairzinho, Direu.

FINAL
Munich, 7 July 1974
 West Germany (2) 2   Netherlands (1) 1
 Breitner(pen), Müller   *Neeskens(pen)*
West Germany: Maier; Vogts, Schwarzenbeck, Beckenbauer, Breitner, Bonhof, Hoeness, Overath, Grabowski, Müller, Holzenbein.
Netherlands: Jongbloed; Suurbier, Rijsbergen (De Jong), Haan, Krol, Jansen, Van Hanegem, Neeskens, Rep, Cruyff, Rensenbrink (R. Van der Kerkhof).

LEADING SCORERS
7 – Lato (Poland); 5 – Szarmach (Poland), Neeskens (Netherlands); 4 – Rep (Netherlands), Edstroem (Sweden), Müller (West Germany); 3 – Bajevic (Yugoslavia), Rivelino (Brazil), Deyna (Poland), Cruyff (Netherlands), Houseman (Argentina), Breitner (West Germany).

Qualifying Tournament

EUROPEAN SECTION

Group 1

A group that culminated in an exciting play-off at Gelsenkirchen, where Sweden, the dark horses of the group, having failed to win in Malta by a margin of at least two goals to qualify, very nearly came to grief. Austria rose far above their recent, feeble form and were unlucky to lose.

It is always hard to play in Malta's dusty, grassless conditions; nor did a riot by the crowd, which held up the game for eight minutes, assist the Swedes. Sweden could have made an official protest, but generously refrained. Malta actually took the lead in a 20th-minute breakaway, Camilleri cleverly beating two men in a tight dribble to score. But Ove Kindvall headed in Bo Larsson's corner to equalise, and when Kindvall was tripped, it was Larsson who scored the winning penalty goal. After that, the excellent goalkeeping of Debono kept Sweden out.

In Gelsenkirchen, on a snow-bound pitch, the Swedes had the greater subtlety, thanks largely to the midfield trio of Nordqvist-Larsson-Kindvall. Playing on the break, Sweden went ahead when Kindvall sent through the young Sandberg after 11 minutes, and after 28 minutes Kindvall himself was put through by the towering Edstroem. Rettenstein, the Austrian 'keeper, pulled him down, and Bo Larsson struck in the penalty. Three minutes later, Austria's pressure was at last recompensed when Hattenberger scored, but when the splendid Hasil went off, exhausted, on the hour, Austria lost their poise in midfield. Sweden, with Hellstroem a fine goalkeeper, held on to make sure they would return to West Germany.

11.11.73   Malta (1) 1   Sweden (2) 2
                Camilleri   *Kindvall, Larsson (pen)*

	P	W	D	L	F	A	Pts
Sweden	6	3	2	1	15	8	8
Austria	6	3	2	1	14	7	8
Hungary	6	2	4	0	12	7	8
Malta	6	0	0	6	1	20	0

Play-off Gelsenkirchen, 28.11.73

     Sweden (2) 2   Austria (1) 1
     Sandberg,   *Hattenberger*
     Larsson (pen)

Group 2

Italy, the 1970 runners-up, qualified, but not before the Swiss had given them a fright in Rome. Until Gigi Riva gave them the lead six minutes from half-time with a penalty, Italy were at sixes and sevens against a Swiss team that fought vigorously; sometimes too vigorously, as witness Muller's dreadful foul on Rivera, who went off with a gashed left knee in consequence. Later, after another incident – Anastasi retaliating violently on Hasler – Muller himself was knocked down by Morini's elbow. Doubted by some, the penalty was in fact a just decision, Schild clearly crooking his hand round Riva's shoulder. Not till the last 20 minutes did the brave Swiss run out of steam. Italy now went over to the assault, and Riva headed a second goal nine minutes from time from Causio's corner.

In their last game, the Swiss were far less incisive, losing 2–0 to a combative Turkey.

20.10.73 Italy (1) 2   Switzerland (0) 0
          Riva (2) (1 pen)
18.11.73 Turkey (0) 2   Switzerland (0) 0
          Mehmet, Metin

	P	W	D	L	F	A	Pts
Italy	6	4	2	0	12	0	10
Turkey	6	2	2	2	5	3	6
Switzerland	6	2	2	2	2	4	6
Luxembourg	6	1	0	5	2	14	2

Group 3

The Netherlands, perhaps the most talented international team in Europe, duly won through to their first World Cup finals since 1938, but what a laborious business it was! In the end they survived only on goal-difference, failing twice to beat, or score against, their old rivals, Belgium. The decisive match in Amsterdam was a dreadful, negative, cynical affair that reflected no credit on either team. The Belgians, though they had to win to qualify, played an eight-man defence. The Dutch seemed indifferent to the huge bonuses awaiting them – thanks to commercial firms – if they succeeded. Perhaps their Czech-born manager, Fahdrhronc, had failed to appeal to their mercenary dispositions. Even the return of Johan Cruyff from Barcelona for the match failed to galvanise their team.

So it was that the Netherlands owed their qualification to the 17 goals they scored in two games against Norway and Iceland.

Having thrashed the Icelanders – in Deventer by agreement after a 5–0 win in Amsterdam – the Dutch could only squeeze through 2–1 in Oslo. It was a very different affair from the first 9–0 match, though a repetition seemed likely when Brokamp made a headed goal for Cruyff after only seven minutes. The Dutch, however, then took things too casually, and with 15 minutes left an error by their 'keeper Van Beveren allowed Hestad to equalise. It was only two minutes from time that Barry Hulshoff, the stopper, came upfield to get the winner.

Belgium, well under strength, then beat Norway 2–0 in Brussels with a penalty in each half; and the stage was set for Amsterdam. Alas, the performance was unworthy. The wonder of it was that only Raoul Lambert, Belgium's centre-forward, should be cautioned by the permissive Russian referee, Kasakov; and that merely for dissent! A shabby conclusion to what should have been an outstanding group tournament.

	P	W	D	L	F	A	Pts
Netherlands	6	4	2	0	24	2	10
Belgium	6	4	2	0	12	0	10
Norway	6	2	0	4	9	16	4
Iceland	6	0	0	6	2	29	0

Group 4

The solid East German team won their key, home match against Romania, who'd beaten them the previous May, to qualify. It was, however, a rough affair, and cost them their best player, the inside-right Hans-Jurgen Kreische, whose badly damaged knee needed an operation after his collision with the huge 'keeper, Raducanu.

A crowd of 95,000 watched this match in Leipzig. Romania were without two stars in Nunweiler VI and Dobrin, but they defended well. It took two unexpected goals from the German sweeper Bernd Bransch, from a free kick in each half, to unblock the result. Bransch had never before scored for East Germany.

Albania then won their only match, beating Finland by a penalty 1–0; the Romanians thrashed Finland 9–0; but East Germany had a decisive 4–1 win in Albania, like the Romanians themselves, to qualify. Even without Kreische, the German forwards were too strong for the Albanians, two of the goals going to Streich.

26.9.73	East Germany (1) 2 *Bransch (2)*	Romania (0) 0
10.10.73	Albania (0) 1 *Ragamiin (pen)*	Finland (0) 0
14.10.73	Romania (5) 9 *Dumitru, Marcu (2), Mircea (2), Dumitrache (2), Pantea, Georgescu*	Finland (0) 0
3.11.73	Albania (1) 1 *Dika*	East Germany (2) 4 *Streich (2), Lowe, Sparwasser*

	P	W	D	L	F	A	Pts
East Germany	6	5	0	1	18	3	10
Romania	6	4	1	1	17	4	9
Finland	6	1	1	4	3	21	3
Albania	6	1	0	5	3	13	2

Group 5

For the first time since they entered the competition in 1950, England failed to qualify for the finals of the World Cup. For the first time since 1938, Poland reached them: at the expense of Wales as well as England.

The myriad near misses, the thousand natural shocks, the infinite narrow escapes of the decisive match at Wembley between Poland and England, on 17 October 1973, could not obscure the fact that England dug their own grave. More precisely, there was reason to believe it was dug for them by inept selection and mistaken tactics. These could scarcely have been better symbolised than by Sir Alf Ramsey's decision to bring on Kevin Hector of Derby for the flaccid Martin Chivers 90 *seconds* before the end of the match at Wembley! Afterwards, Ramsey limply explained that he had lost track of the time. Those less charitable among us reflected that he had always been curiously slow and maladroit in his use of substitutes, whether in León, Katowice, or at Wembley.

Indeed, there was good reason to believe that it was at Chorzow in Katowice rather than at Wembley that England were eliminated. It was in Poland the previous June that Ramsey, having promised to play an attacking game, chose a cautious 4–4–2 team without his best striker, Mike Channon, whom he inexplicably failed to send on, even after England were two goals behind. Stubbornly, he protested that England had played well.

The following September, Wales went to Chorzow and were beaten 3–0 in a bloodthirsty match. After being harried out of the match at Cardiff 2–0, the Poles were out for revenge. The game had scarcely started when Gadocha cold-bloodedly kicked Rodrigues; later he would add butting to kicking. Leighton James, the young Burnley winger, was so cruelly kicked that he carried a 'dead' leg for much of the match. Trevor Hockey, a marked man since his ferocity at Cardiff, foolishly allowed himself, like Alan Ball the previous June, to be provoked into getting sent off by the cunning Cmikiewicz.

Perhaps things would have been different under a braver referee, for Wyn Davies appeared to head a perfectly good early goal. The ball was already in the net when he came down to earth, collided with the 'keeper, and was penalised. A foolishly miscued pass back by Thomas on the half hour allowed Gadocha through to score, and that was effectively that. Though without the brilliant Lubanski, whose knee injury would also keep him out of the return match with England, Poland's forwards were formidable. Deyna came into his own in midfield while Lato, a right winger who headed the second and made the third, was vastly dangerous.

At Wembley, the Poles had small recourse to violence. England had had a recent, illusory 7–0 win over feeble Austria, but their forwards lacked the invention and the sharpness to breach Poland's defence. Poor selection played its part again. It was as unfair to the burly Chivers as it was to England to pick him at a moment when he was so obviously out of form. Afterwards, people spoke of bad luck. It might have been more correct to talk of good luck; that enjoyed by the reckless, brave, but hopelessly disorganised Polish 'keeper, Jan Tomaszewski, whose wild sorties from goal were blessed by some guardian angel. He was beaten only once, by Allan Clarke's penalty in the 63rd minute, given dubiously for an obstruction on Peters.

But Poland were already ahead, Hunter's maladroit, right-footed interception on the touchline allowing Lato to burst through down the left and make a goal for Domarski. Curiously, it was the kind of strange lapse one had associated with Bobby Moore, the very man Hunter had replaced. In fairness to Hunter himself, let it be said that it was only his dramatic equaliser against Wales that had kept England in the competition.

Breaking cleverly against a desperate opponent, Poland might have scored two other goals. McFarland cynically and deplorably dragged Lato back when he would otherwise have gone clean through the middle; then Lato did get through, only to throw the chance away as Shilton cleverly contained him. It was an immensely exciting game, but England's deficiencies – rather than their misfortunes – would be reemphasised when Italy came to Wembley; and won.

Chorzow, 26.9.73

    Poland (2) 3   Wales (0) 0
    Gadocha, Lato,
    Domarski

Poland: Tomaszewski; Szymanowski, Gorgon, Musial, Bulzacki, Kasperczak, Cmikiewicz; Lato, Deyna, Domarski, Gadocha.

Wales: Sprake (Leeds United); Rodrigues (Sheffield Wednesday), Thomas (Swindon Town); Mahoney (Stoke City [sub. Phillips (Cardiff City)], England (Tottenham Hotspur), Roberts (Birmingham City); B. Evans (Hereford United) [sub. Reece (Cardiff City)]; Yorath (Leeds United), W. Davies (Blackpool), Hockey (Aston Villa), James (Burnley)

Wembley, 17.10.73

    England (0) 1   Poland (0) 1
    Clarke(pen)   *Domarski*

England: Shilton (Leicester City); Madeley (Leeds United), Hughes (Liverpool); Bell (Manchester City), McFarland (Derby County), Hunter (Leeds United); Currie (Sheffield United), Channon (Southampton), Chivers (Spurs) [sub. Hector (Derby County)], Clarke (Leeds United), Peters (Spurs).

Poland: Tomaszewski; Szymanowski, Gorgon, Musial, Bulzacki, Kasperczak, Cmikiewicz, Deyna; Lato, Domarski, Gadocha.

	P	W	D	L	F	A	Pts
Poland	4	2	1	1	6	3	5
England	4	1	2	1	3	4	4
Wales	4	1	1	2	3	5	3

Group 6

Bulgaria somewhat unimpressively won this group, making one wonder what might have happened had the dice not been so severely loaded against Northern Ireland – the inability to play in Belfast, the antics of George Best, the unfortunate schism between Dougan and Neill, the team manager. There's no question that Northern Ireland improved as the competition unfurled, little doubt that dubious refereeing played a part in their disastrous loss in Cyprus.

What Bulgaria had was the best individual player in the group; Christo Bonev. He it was who saw to it that Bulgaria drew their decisive game in Lisbon, which Portugal needed to win 3–0 to qualify. In fact Bulgaria drew 2–2 and very nearly won, both their goals going to Bonev. Against a Portuguese side without Jorge and Baptista, which recalled the tall veteran striker Torres, and lost Eusebio, injured, after half an hour, Bonev was formidable. Six minutes after Simões headed the first goal, he equalised after a marvellous run of more than half the field. After 65 minutes, he gave Bulgaria the lead, Quaresma equalising only in the last minute.

Previously, Northern Ireland, obliged to play at a deserted Hillsborough, Sheffield, held Bulgaria to 0–0. Might they have won in a more committed Belfast? Bulgaria wanted a point and got it in a fearfully dull game, using a *catenaccio* defence and seldom bothering to break. Might Dougan have made the difference? The question was relevant, given his fine form in the League for Wolves.

At least George Best came back for Northern Ireland's last, irrelevant, match, in Portugal; and played well. Indeed, it was from his corner kick that Bertie Lutton headed an equaliser to Jordão's goal; which may have been offside. It was a good, encouraging result for Northern Ireland; yet disappointing, too, in terms of what might have been. Bulgaria then went through the formality of beating Cyprus 2–0.

Hillsborough, 26.9.73
    Northern Ireland (0) 0   Bulgaria (0) 0

Northern Ireland: McFaul (Newcastle United); Rice (Arsenal), Craig (Newcastle United); O'Kane (Nottingham Forest), Hunter (Ipswich Town), Clements (Everton); Hamilton (Ipswich Town), Jackson (Nottingham Forest) [sub. Cassidy (Newcastle United)], Morgan (Aston Villa), Anderson (Manchester United), O'Neill (Nottingham Forest) [sub. Coyle (Sheffield Wednesday)].
Bulgaria: Goranov; Zasirov, Itkov, Aladjov, Jetchev, Kolev, Aleksandrov (Borisov), Bonev, Miljanov, Stajanov, Denev.

13.10.73	Portugal (0) 2	Bulgaria (0) 2
	Simões, Quaresma	*Bonev 2*
14.11.73	Portugal (1) 1	Northern Ireland (0) 1
	Jordão	*Lutton*

Portugal: Damas; Pietra, Humberto, Alhinho, Adolfo, Fraguito, Octavio, Toni, Nene, Jordão, Diniz.
Northern Ireland: Jennings (Spurs); Rice (Arsenal), Craig (Newcastle United); Lutton (West Ham United), O'Kane (Nottingham Forest), Clements (Everton); Jackson (Nottingham Forest), O'Neill (Nottingham Forest), Morgan (Aston Villa), Anderson (Manchester United), Best (Manchester United).

Bulgaria (1) 2   Cyprus (0) 0
Kolev, Denev

	P	W	D	L	F	A	Pts
Bulgaria	6	4	2	0	13	3	10
Portugal	6	2	3	1	10	6	7
Northern Ireland	6	1	3	2	5	6	5
Cyprus	6	1	0	5	1	14	2

Group 7

The second European group to go to a play-off. Spain and Yugoslavia finished level not only on points but on goals as well, and so met in February at Frankfurt.

Yugoslavia were expected to settle things when the two played at Zagreb, but with Dzajic in the Army, Petkovic in France, and the brilliant 18-year-old Petrovic left out, they weren't good enough to outwit a combative, wily Spanish team. Spain, counter-attacking cleverly, would have won but for some fine saves by Maric, who was lucky when Martinez hit the post. Valdez, Spain's Argentinian-born winger, was too quick for a clearly unfit Krivocuka, twice forcing Maric to a dazzling save. Iribar, in the Spanish goal, looked just as safe.

Spain were expected now to qualify, since Yugoslavia had to win by at least two goals against a Greek team formidable at home in order to force a play-off. Inducements purportedly offered by the Spanish Tourist Office to the Greek players led to their punishment by the Greek FA and an official FIFA inquiry. In the event, Yugoslavia, recalling Dzajic and Petkovic, won 4–2, even though their centre-forward, Bajevic, was contentiously sent off. Petkovic, the first 'exile' to be used by Yugoslavia in memory, had an excellent game, centreing for Bajevic to head the first goal. A blunder by the fallible Greek 'keeper, Kelessidis, allowed Karasi to make it 2–0, but the Greeks stormed back and were level by half-time through a long drive by Eleftherakis and a sad own goal by Katalinski.

With Bajevic off, things looked bleak for the Slavs, but they recovered magnificently, Suriac and Karasi getting the goals they vitally needed, despite an attempt by the Greeks to 'close up' the game at 3–2.

Yugoslavia, despite the fact that they were in the middle of their winter hiatus, convincingly won a sometimes bruising play-off, permissively refereed by Belgium's Vital Loraux. But Spain looked a mediocre side, the more so when Amancio was hurt and left the field.

The single goal came after 14 minutes from the big stopper, Katalinski, when his header from Buljan's free kick was only blocked by Iribar (a fine goalkeeper, like Maric) and he drove in the rebound. Dzajic, given Army leave, had a few moments on the Yugoslav left wing, but was largely invisible, and the decisive part was played by the fine Yugoslav midfield, with Oblak outstanding.

	P	W	D	L	F	A	Pts
Spain	4	2	2	0	8	5	6
Yugoslavia	4	2	2	0	7	4	6
Greece	4	0	0	4	5	11	0

Play-off Frankfurt, 13.2.74
    Yugoslavia (1) 1   Spain (0) 0
    Katalinski

Group 8

Scotland, vigorously and exhilaratingly – unexpectedly, too, let it be confessed – qualified for the World Cup finals for the first time since 1958. They did so at the expense of a Czech team whose recent improvement had made them solid favourites; and thanks to the boldness of a manager who had taken over in midstream and had radically changed the team.

Scotland, under Tommy Docherty, had beaten Denmark twice, while the Czechs had dropped an invaluable point. But Scotland's first match under Willie Ormond in February 1973 was a traumatic 5–0 home defeat by England. Ormond, far from being demoralised, exploited the result to build his own team, rejecting Graham and Colquhoun on the grounds of slowness and Buchan for weakness in the air. He also had the courage, in the vital home game against the Czechs, to give a first cap to Coventry's long-legged outside-left, Tommy Hutchison, who repaid him abundantly with his speed and skill; and his capacity to prevent Pivarnik overlapping.

Physically, it was a very harsh game, the Czech defenders wading in ruthlessly from the first, the Scots, predictably, giving as good as they got; perhaps better when it's recalled that they lamed the irreplaceable midfield half-back Kuna, who had to go off. Scotland's morale was more impressive than for a long while. After 33 minutes Hunter's ineptitude allowed Nehoda's first time lob to float over him into goal. But it took Scotland only seven minutes to equalise. The 33-year-old Denis Law, enjoying a remarkable Indian summer, forced Viktor to turn his free kick round the post, and Hutchison's corner was headed in by the massive centre-half, Jim Holton.

With Bremner in galvanic form, well abetted by both backs, Hay and Morgan, Scotland now forced the pace, Joe Jordan, the Leeds reserve, replaced Dalglish after 64 minutes, and after 75, he won the match; plus Scotland a ticket to West Germany. Bremner's shot, from Morgan's rolled free kick, rebounded from the inside of the far post,

Morgan crossed again, and Jordan headed past Viktor. Delirium!

The match in Bratislava thus became no more than a futile exercise. Ormond picked a depleted team, his chief preoccupation being to avoid suspensions from the competition proper. In this he succeeded. For what it mattered, the Czechs won 1–0. Nehoda was again the scorer, this time from a first half penalty, awarded when he beat Forsyth and the defender handled the ball on the ground.

Hampden Park, 26.9.73

   Scotland (1) 2   Czechoslovakia (1) 1
   Holton, Jordan   *Nehoda*

Scotland: Hunter (Celtic); Jardine (Rangers), McGrain (Celtic); Bremner (Leeds United), Holton (Manchester United), Connelly (Celtic); Morgan (Manchester United), Hay (Celtic), Law (Manchester City), Dalglish (Celtic) [sub. Jordan (Leeds United)], Hutchison (Coventry City).

Czechoslovakia: Viktor; Pivarnik, Samek, L. Zlocha, Bendl, Bicovsky, Kuna (Dobias), Adamec, Nehoda, Stratil, Panenka.

Bratislava, 17.10.73

   Czechoslovakia (1) 1 Scotland (0) 0
   Nehoda (pen)

Czechoslovakia: Viktor; Pivarnik, Samek, Dovrak, Hagara, Bicovsky, Pollak, Gajdusek, Frantisek, Vesely (Klement), Nehoda, Capkovic (Panenka).

Scotland: Harvey (Leeds United); Jardine (Rangers), McGrain (Celtic); Forsyth (Rangers), Blackley (Hibernian), Hay (Celtic); Morgan (Manchester United), Jordan (Leeds United), Law (Manchester City) [sub. Ford (Hearts)], Dalglish (Celtic), Hutchison (Coventry City).

	P	W	D	L	F	A	Pts
Scotland	4	3	0	1	8	3	6
Czechoslovakia	4	2	1	1	9	3	5
Denmark	4	0	1	3	2	13	1

Group 9

	P	W	D	L	F	A	Pts
Russia	4	3	0	1	5	2	6
Eire	4	1	1	2	4	5	3
France	4	1	1	2	3	5	3

Russia qualified to play off against Chile, winners of South American Group 3.

SOUTH AMERICAN SECTION
Group 1

Uruguay's qualification on superior goal difference was rather hard luck on Colombia, who sensationally beat Uruguay 1–0 in Montevideo and didn't give a goal away against them; nor lose a single game.

	P	W	D	L	F	A	Pts
Uruguay	4	2	1	1	6	2	5
Colombia	4	1	3	0	3	2	5
Ecuador	4	0	2	2	3	8	2

Group 2

The Argentinians, under the diligent managership of the old Juventus inside-left, Omar Sivori, qualified for the finals for the first time since 1966. Sivori made a very good job of a team that had outstanding forwards in Brindisi and Ayala, but fell foul of officials, Press, and big clubs alike. Consequently his demise was certain; and duly followed in December, despite his reported friendship with Peron. He wouldn't speak to the Press, did not disguise his contempt for the officials, and kept his players in training camp at great expense for 93 days to the fury of the clubs. He even had a special side training at altitude to play Bolivia, who in fact lost every game!

2.9.73	Bolivia (1) 1 *Morales*	Paraguay (1) 2 *Escobar, Insfran*
9.9.73	Argentina (2) 4 *Brindisi 2, Ayala 2*	Bolivia (0) 0
16.9.73	Paraguay (1) 1 *Arrua*	Argentina (1) 1 *Ayala*
23.9.73	Bolivia (0) 0	Argentina (1) 1 *Fornari*
30.9.73	Paraguay (3) 4 *Insfran, Barreiro, Osorio, Arrua*	Bolivia (0) 0
7.10.73	Argentina (1) 3 *Ayala 2, Guerini*	Paraguay (1) 1 *Escobar*

	P	W	D	L	F	A	Pts
Argentina	4	3	1	0	9	2	7
Paraguay	4	2	1	1	8	5	5
Bolivia	4	0	0	4	1	11	0

Group 3

Venezuela withdrew, leaving only Chile and Peru, who were favourites after their fine 1970 World Cup. But the Chileans, thanks to the opportunism of such as the lively Caszely, the cool authority of their centre-half Figueora, surprised them. After losing 2–0 in Lima, they won 2–0 in Santiago and took the play-off in Montevideo 2–1.

This meant that they still had another high mountain to climb before they came upon the promised land of West Germany; they must beat Russia, winners of the European Group 9.

Play-off (European Group 9 v South American Group 3)
1st Leg. Moscow, 26.9.73
Russia (0) 0   Chile (0) 0

The Chileans played dourly for a draw in Moscow, and got it, with a bleakly defensive performance. Clearly they were set on winning the return on 21 November in Santiago; but it did not take place. The Russians refused to play in the national stadium, in protest against its use as a virtual concentration camp for victims of the right-wing coup against Allende's Marxist government.

The spectacle of Soviet Russia, pioneers of the labour camp and mass 'liquidation', recoiling in horror from playing a football match on such tainted ground, was enough in itself to turn the stomach. It was compounded, however, by the fact that the protest was made only *after* the drawn game in Moscow, which made the Chileans strong favourites to win in Santiago. Had the Russians made their stand before that result, they might have been heard more seriously.

FIFA, in any case, had no alternative under their own rules but to disqualify them when they failed to turn up in Santiago. Russia insisted that the match be played on neutral ground, and would not listen even to the suggested compromise of some other Chilean venue. They appealed to the FIFA World Cup Committee, but their appeal was turned down on 6 January in Frankfurt. Altogether, a shabby episode. Shabby, too, was the Committee's decision to make the winners of the two groups play-off in the first place.

ASIAN GROUP

The Australians, a polyglot amalgam of Scots, Slavs, and others, did wonderfully well to win a protracted qualifying tournament in which the likes of Israel, qualifiers in 1970, and North Korea, heroes of 1966, fell by the wayside. Coached by a determined Yugoslav, Rale Rasic, they won a group that included Iraq, New Zealand, and Indonesia, then beat Iran, and finally, in a Hong Kong play-off, eliminated South Korea, conquerors of Israel.

Australia had so little trouble with Iran in Sydney, where Utjesenovic's clever free kicks produced the first two goals, that they may have been over confident in Teheran. Iran scored twice in the first half hour, but then Australia's determined, straightforward, long-passing team settled, and held them at bay.

At home to South Korea, they faltered badly, unrecognisably sterile in a 0–0 draw. In Seoul, they again went two down, but fought back gallantly to draw 2–2. So to Hong Kong, where a massive 25-yard shot by the midfield player Jim Mackay gave them victory.

Australia (winners Group B1) v Iran (winners B2)
18.8.73	Australia (1) 3 *Alston, Abonyi, Wilson*	Iran (0) 0
24.8.73	Iran (2) 2 *Gelichkhani 2 (1 pen)*	Australia (0) 0
	Australia won 3–2 on aggregate	

28.10.73	Australia (0) 0	South Korea (0) 0
10.11.73	South Korea (2) 2	Australia (1) 2
	Kim Jae Han,	*Buljevic, Baartz*
	Koh Jae Wook	
13.11.73	**Play-off In Hong Kong**	
	Australia (0) 1	South Korea (0) 0
	Mackay	

AFRICAN SECTION

An extraordinary double for the former Yugoslav international goalkeeper, Blagoje Vidinic. In 1970 he got Morocco through to the World Cup finals as winners of the first ever separate African qualifying section. This time, having been dismissed by Morocco, he did the same, at their expense, for Zaire (otherwise Congo Kinshasha). The furious Moroccans, well beaten in the first leg of the final eliminator in Kinshasha, cried foul and petulantly refused to play the return, appealing to FIFA against the refereeing in the first (and only) leg. But there was no chance they would be given a hearing. The stars of a talented Zaire team were chiefly Bwanga, a polished young centre-half, African Player of the Year, Kazadi, a spectacular 'keeper, and the swift striker, Kakoko.

In the third round of the long tournament, Zaire went down to old rivals, Ghana, losing 1–0 in Accra to a penalty by Amankwa. This was Zaire's second defeat of the competition, for they had been beaten by the Cameroons 1–0 in Kinshasha, only to then win 2–0 in the play-off, again in Kinshasha, two days later. The same venue saw a 4–1 victory for Zaire in the return against Ghana, Kakoko scoring twice.

Meanwhile, Zambia and Morocco joined them in the final pool. Zambia got away to a splendid start, thrashing Morocco 4–0, to become favourites. But Zaire went to Lusaka and boldly beat the Zambians 2–0. A superb individual goal by Kakoko gave Zaire another victory in Kinshasha after Zambia had fought back well to equalise Kembo's goal. Finally, Morocco, after an even first half in Kinshasha, were thrashed 3–0, with goals from Chaoui, Kembo, and Mbungu.

Final Group

21.10.73	Zambia (2) 4	Morocco (0) 0
	Sinyangwe 2, Simwala,	
	Chanda	
4.11.73	Zambia (0) 0	Zaire (2) 2
		Mayanga, Kakoko
18.11.73	Zaire (1) 2	Zambia (1) 1
	Kembo, Kakoko	*Chitalu*
25.11.73	Morocco (1) 2	Zambia (0) 0
	Maghfour, Faras	
23.12.73	Zaire (0) 3	Morocco (0) 0
	Chaoui, Kembo,	
	Mbungu	

	P	W	D	L	F	A	Pts
Zaire	3	3	0	0	7	1	6
Zambia	4	1	0	3	5	6	2
Morocco	3	1	0	2	2	7	2

CONCACAF SECTION

Usually regarded as an easy stepping stone for Mexico, who had not missed a World Cup since the war, the group was surprisingly won by Haiti; who were given the advantage of playing on their own ground, and at least one bizarre performance by a referee.

The Mexicans were shattered by their 4-0 thrashing at the hands of the obscure Trinidad and Tobago team. Televised direct, it was to leave the streets of Mexico City almost deserted. A little raw but lively and enterprising, the West Indians overwhelmed a Mexican team which had thought itself invincible; and had after all reached the 1970 quarter-finals. Trinidad would have probably beaten Haiti, too, but for the outrageous refereeing of the El Salvadorian, Enriquez, who disallowed four Trinidadian goals! He refereed no more games.

This was a serious blemish on Haiti's achievement. But despite this, and the fact that they lost to Mexico, they unquestionably surpassed themselves. Under the managership of Antoine Tassy, they often played well, and had several accomplished players such as Emmanuel Sanon, their chief bombardier, and Claude Desire, in midfield.

This was the first time that the whole tournament had been played within a brief period, on the soil of one of the competitors, and the opposition towards the idea by such countries as Mexico was to a great extent borne out. Haiti, after all, would scarcely have qualified without home advantage, and the episode of their match with Trinidad left an unpleasant taste.

In the Group 1 preliminary round, one of the salient features was the remarkable improvement of Canada, who took three points from the United States and lost twice by only the odd goal to Mexico, whose five-point margin was somewhat deceptive.

Final Group (Port Au Prince, Haiti)

29.11.73	Honduras 2, Trinidad 1
30.11.73	Mexico 0, Guatemala 0
1.12.73	Haiti 3, Netherland Antilles 0
3.12.73	Honduras 1, Mexico 1
4.12.73	Haiti 2, Trinidad 1
5.12.73	Netherland Antilles 2, Guatemala 2
7.12.73	Haiti 1, Honduras 0
8.12.73	Mexico 8, Netherland Antilles 0
10.12.73	Trinidad 1, Guatemala 0
12.12.73	Honduras 2, Netherland Antilles 2
13.12.73	Haiti 2, Guatemala 1
14.12.73	Trinidad 4, Mexico 0

15.12.73 Honduras 1, Guatemala 1
17.12.73 Trinidad 4, Netherland Antilles 0
18.12.73 Mexico 1, Haiti 0

	P	W	D	L	F	A	Pts
Haiti	5	4	0	1	8	3	8
Trinidad	5	3	0	2	11	4	6
Mexico	5	2	2	1	10	5	6
Honduras	5	1	3	1	6	6	5
Guatemala	5	0	3	2	4	6	3
Neth. Antilles	5	0	2	3	4	19	2

CHAPTER TWO

European Cup 1973-74

For the first time in the history of the competition, a final had to be replayed, and for the first time in its history, a West German club – Bayern Munich – took the title. Their splendid 4–0 win in the replay at Brussels not only properly rewarded a brilliantly endowed team, but properly punished one that should never have been in the final. If Atlético Madrid had won the Cup, after their savage excesses against Celtic in the semi-final in Glasgow, it would have been a blow to the very future of football. Alas, it was one more instance of UEFA's inability to discipline properly the tournaments they run.

Celtic once again reached the semi-final, where they lost in deeply unsatisfactory circumstances. Liverpool went out in the second round, but there was no disgrace in being eliminated by a team in such superb form as Red Star, Belgrade.

Celtic's was a very different story. A team once again in the process of rebuilding, by no means the force of the latter 1960s, they had made somewhat limping progress through the earlier rounds and had certainly benefited from a benign draw. Even so, they had needed extra time to overcome the far from irresistible Swiss team, Basle, in the return leg at Celtic Park.

Atlético Madrid arrived there after disposing of Red Star. Their 2–0 victory in Belgrade, an immense surprise, had been the fruit of good luck and opportunism. They were under pressure for most of the game; the woodwork of their goal was struck half-a-dozen times; yet twice they broke away to score, even though without their most dangerous forward, Ruben Ayala. In Madrid, they were content with a goalless draw.

The manager of Atlético was none other than the notorious Juan Carlos Lorenzo, whose ruthless Argentinian World Cup team had been accused by Sir Alf Ramsey in 1966 of 'acting as animals'. In 1970, he was personally and violently involved in the Lazio players' attack on Arsenal after a Fairs Cup match banquet in Rome. Now he brought to Glasgow a team that never at any moment elected to play football but treated the Celtic players with cynical brutality. Jimmy Johnstone, in particular, was monstrously abused, largely by Diaz, the very player who had so ill-used him when Celtic played Racing Club in the black Intercontinental series of 1967.

Eventually the courageous, unlucky Turkish referee, Babacan, sent off three Spaniards, all in the second half. They were Diaz, Quique, and Ayala – who was transformed for the evening from exciting striker into mere hatchet man. All three, plus three who were cautioned, were suspended from the return game. But despite the premeditated violence – which had its sequel when one of the expelled players attacked Johnstone at the final whistle – the return went on in Madrid.

As the Spanish Press behaved as accessories after the fact, there was a predictably ferocious hostility in the air; both outside and inside the stadium. Celtic resisted as bravely as they could, but in the closing minutes Garate, after a centre by Irureta, and Adelardo, with an admirable chip, beat Connachan to take Madrid through. Jock Stein, Celtic's manager, bitterly and justifiably attacked UEFA's decision to play the return in Madrid.

Bayern Munich's path to the final was less controversial, though they did reel at Atvidaberg, in Sweden, in the first round return leg. There, a missile from the crowd broke the shin of poor Breitner, the West German international left-back; the lively Torstensson scored twice for Atvidaberg; and Bayern survived only on penalty kicks.

They then, adhering to the old principle that, if you can't beat them, join them, proceeded to sign Torstensson, whom the somewhat permissive rules of the European Cup allowed them to use with great success in the quarter- and semi-finals, not to mention the final. He scored in both matches against Ujpest, and his opportunism in the opening quarter-final was the undoing of CSKA, Sofia, previously and surprisingly the conquerors of Ajax.

For Ajax it was a disappointing season, giving fresh life to the belief that one man can, in fact, make a team. When Johan Cruyff went, for a king's ransom, to rejoin his old manager, Rinus Michels, in Barcelona (and succeed brilliantly), Ajax waned. Their new manager, George Knobel, did his best, but he found a factious team, lost patience with them in the spring, and was sacked for his pains.

CSKA, in the second round, went down only 1–0 in Amsterdam, where Mulder missed a penalty; a contrast to their trouncing by Ajax the previous season. In Sofia, they attacked, scored in the second half after a piece of carelessness by Keizer, and prevailed in extra time with a fulminating long shot by Mikhailov. They beat Bayern there, too; but Breitner's penalty goal had put the Germans three ahead on aggregate, and there was obviously no hope of survival.

One of the most fascinating ties of the competition involved Bayern with the East German champions, Dynamo Dresden; distinguished conquerors of Juventus in the first round.

With Hans-Jurgen Kreische, the outstanding figure of the game, in magnificent form at inside-right, Dresden were worth more than their 2–0 win at home. Juventus, hardly assisted by the fact that their Championship had not yet officially begun, were helped at least by the absence of Kreische from the second leg. He had been injured playing for East Germany against Romania, but though Juventus built up a 3–1 half-time lead, a goal by Sachse was the only one of the second half, and Dresden went through.

They gave Bayern a very hard fight of it, and it was chiefly the rediscovered opportunism of Gerd Müller that kept them afloat, when, in the return, he exploited a fine pass from Uli Hoeness. Young Hoeness scored the first two goals of the game himself in a two-minute spell, virtually guaranteeing Bayern's passage into the semi-final. Between them, these two splendidly exciting German games produced no fewer than 13 goals!

Liverpool caught a true Tartar in Red Star; at a time when their own form was shaky. In Belgrade, they were overplayed in the first half, but gave away only one goal, a glorious angled shot from Jankovic. Early in the second half the ultra-versatile Bogicevic got another when Liverpool's offside trap moved out too slowly. But then Red Star seemed to run out of steam. Liverpool should have had a penalty when Toshack's leg was grasped by the 'keeper, but eventually Lawler's shot crept home after a corner, and they were still in with a chance.

That chance disappeared at Anfield where Red Star played much beautiful football; and belied the old myth about Continental shooting by scoring two fulminating goals. The first, after an hour, came from a searing, right-footed, swerving shot by the veteran centre-forward, Lazarevic; the second, just before time, a crashing drive to the top corner from Jankovic's free kick. In between, intense Liverpool pressure at last brought a goal by Lindsay, but it was not enough.

Ujpest, till their fall in Munich, had another successful run, unearthing on the way a gifted young forward in the 19-year-old Fekete, fast and strong, who had never played a full game before materially helping to put out Benfica, in Budapest.

In the final, at Brussels, Atlético behaved themselves almost impeccably in the first match, showing they had no need of violence to master even an attack as clever as Bayern's. Their own fault was perhaps that they put two men to watch Müller, thus giving Hoeness too much scope.

There was no score in ordinary time, and in the extra half-hour it looked as though Bayern's greater stamina might turn the trick. Instead, six minutes from the end, an enormously skilful free kick by Luis from the edge of the penalty box curled past Maier to put Atlético ahead; and apparently give them the Cup. Instead, with virtually the last kick of the match, Schwarzenbeck, the big German stopper, thundered upfield to equalise with a spectacular 30-yard shot. So the final had to be replayed, two days later.

This was an almost schizophrenically different story. Bayern, deciding to be more bold in attack, now fairly riddled what had seemed a solid Atlético defence and won with derisory ease. Uli Hoeness, who with Müller played ducks and drakes with the Spaniards, should have put Bayern ahead early when Müller sent him splendidly through alone – to round the goalkeeper but shoot over the bar. Müller himself headed sharply against the bar, but finally Breitner's fine pass breached the defence again, and this time Hoeness cheekily shot home through Reina's legs.

Three more splendid goals came in the second half, when the injured Adelardo had to be substituted. When Kapelmann resourcefully beat his man down the left, Müller smashed his long cross in from the far post, and then exquisitely lobbed over Reina from Zobel's pass. Finally, when Melo slipped, Hoeness coolly took the ball on, evaded another tackle, went wide of Reina, and this time put the ball, inexorably, in the net. A distinguished victory for a team on which Franz Beckenbauer had stamped his unique personality.

ROUND BY ROUND RESULTS

First Round

Jeunesse Esch (0) 1　　　　　　Liverpool (1) 1
Dussier　　　　　　　　　　*Hall*

Jeunesse: R. Hoffmann; Schaul, Schmit (Mond), Morocutti, Da Grava, Hnatow, Langer, Zwalli (Dussier), J. P. Hoffmann, Reiland, Di Genova
Liverpool: Clemence; Lawler, Thompson; Smith, Lloyd, Hughes; Keegan, Hall, Heighway, Boersma, Callaghan.

Liverpool (0) 2　　　　　　　Jeunesse Esch (0) 0
Monel (o.g.), *Toshack*

Liverpool: Clemence; Lawler, Lindsay; Smith, Lloyd, Hughes; Keegan, Hall, Heighway, Toshack, Callaghan.
Jeunesse: R. Hoffmann; Schaul, Schmit, Morocutti, Da Grava, Mond, Langer, Zwalli, J. P. Hoffmann, Reiland, Di Genova.

TPS Turku (1) 1　　　　　　Celtic (2) 6
Andelmin (pen)　　　　　　*Callaghan 2, Hood, Johnstone, Connelly, Deans*

Turku: Enckelman (Kokkonen); Kymalainen, Saari, Nummi, Nummelin, Toivanen, Salama, Lindholm, Haittu, Andelmin, Suhonen.
Celtic: Hunter: McGrain, Brogan; Murray, McNeill, Connelly; Johnstone, Hay, Hood (Deans), Callaghan, Wilson (Davidson).

Celtic (2) 3　　　　　　　　TPS Turku (0) 0
Deans, Johnstone 2

Celtic: Hunter; McCluskey, Brogan; Murray, McNeill, Connelly; Johnstone, Davidson, Deans, Dalglish (McNamara), Wilson.
Turku: Enckelman; Kynatainer, Saari, Numm, Salonen, Toivanen, Salama, Lindholm, Haittu, Andelmin, Saarinan.

Crusaders (0) 0

Dynamo Bucharest (4) 11
Georgescu 4, *Dumitrache*,
Dinu, *Nunweiler* 4,
Beckett (o.g.)
Benfica (1) 1
Messias
Olympiakos Piraeus (0) 0

Waterford (1) 2
Kirby, O'Neill
Ujpest (1) 3
A. Dunai, Fazekas, Nagy
Dynamo Dresden (2) 2
Kreische, Schade
Juventus (3) 3
*Furino, Altafini,
Cuccureddu*
Vejle (Denmark) (2) 2
Markussen, Lund
Nantes (0) 0

Bayern Munich 3
Muller 2, *Olsson* (o.g.)
Atvidaberg 3
Torstensson 2, *Wallinder*
Bayern won on penalties
Zaria Voroshilovgrad 2
Apoel Nicosia (0) 0

Red Star Belgrade (1) 2
Petrovic, Karasi
Stal Mielec (0) 0

Bruges (5) 8
Lambert 3, *Lefèvre*, *Carteus* 2,
Houwaert, Russmann
Floriana (0) 0

Atlético Madrid (0) 0
Galatasaray (0) 0

after extra time
Viking Stavanger (0) 1
Kvia
Spartak Trnava (1) 1
Martinkovic

Dynamo Bucharest (1) 1
Cooke (o.g.)
Crusaders (0) 0

Olympiakos Piraeus (0) 0

Benfica (1) 1
Nene
Ujpest (1) 3
Zambo, Fazekas, Nagy
Waterford (0) 0

Juventus (0) 0

Dynamo Dresden (1) 2
Capello (o.g.), *Sachse*

Nantes (1) 2
Rampillon, Couécou
Vejle (0) 1
Norregaard
Atvidaberg 1
Durnberger (o.g.)
Bayern Munich 1
Hoeness

Apoel Nicosia (0) 0
Zaria (0) 1
Kuznetzov
Stal Mielec (0) 1
Lato
Red Star (1) 1
Lazarevic
Floriana (Malta) (0) 0

Bruges (0) 2
Thio, Houwaerts
Galatasaray (0) 0
Atlético Madrid (0) 1
Falceto

Spartak Trnava (2) 2
Adamec, Martinkovic
Viking Stavanger (0) 0

Frem Reykjavik (0) 0   Basle (2) 5
Cubillas, Balmer 2,
Hasler, Demarmels

(1*st leg played in Basle*)
Basle (3) 6   Frem Reykjavik (0) 2
Tanner 2, *Cubillas, Wampfler,*   *Leifson, Eliasson*
Stohler, Geirsson (o.g.)
(2*nd leg played in Olten, Switzerland*)
CSKA Sofia (3) 3   Wacker Innsbruck (0) 0
Maraschliev, Denev, Shekov
Wacker Innsbruck (0) 0   CSKA Sofia (0) 1
Shekov

Second Round

Red Star Belgrade (1) 2   Liverpool (0) 1
Jankovic, Bogicevic   *Lawler*
Red Star: O. Petrovic; Krivocuka, Bogicevic, Pavlovic, Dojcinovski, Baralic; Jankovic (Kery), Karasi, Lazarevic, Acimovic (Jovanovic), V. Petrovic.
Liverpool: Clemence; Lawler, Lindsay; Smith, Lloyd, Hughes; Keegan, Cormack, Toshack, Callaghan, Heighway.

Liverpool (0) 1   Red Star Belgrade (0) 2
Lindsay   *Lazarevic, Jankovic*
Liverpool: Clemence; Lawler, Lindsay; Thompson, Lloyd, Hughes; Keegan, McLaughlin (Hall), Heighway (Boersma), Toshack, Callaghan.
Red Star: O. Petrovic; Jovanovic, Bogicevic, Pavlovic, Dojcinovski, Baralic, Jankovic, Karasi, Lazarevic, Acimovic, V. Petrovic.

Celtic (0) 0   Vejle (0) 0
Celtic: Hunter; McGrain, Hay, Murray, Connelly, McCluskey, Johnstone, Hood (Wilson), Dalglish, Callaghan, Lennox.
Vejle: Wodsku; J. Jensen, S. Hansen, Serritslev, G. Jensen, Sorensen, T. Hansen, Markussen, Huttel, Pedersen, Norregaard (Johansen).

Vejle (0) 0   Celtic (1) 1
         Lennox
Vejle: Wodsku; J. Jensen, F. Hansen, Serritslev, G. Jensen, Sorensen, Norregaard, T. Hansen, Markussen, Fritsen, Andersen.
Celtic: Hunter; McGrain, Brogan, McCluskey, McNeill, Connelly, Lennox, Murray, Deans, Hay, Dalglish.

Benfica (0) 1   Ujpest (0) 1
Eusebio   *Toth*
Ujpest (0) 2   Benfica (0) 0
Bene, Kolar
Bayern Munich (2) 4   Dynamo Dresden (3) 3
Hoffman, Duernberger,   *Sachse* 2, *Heidler*
Roth, Müller
Dynamo Dresden (1) 3   Bayern Munich (2) 3
Waetzlich, Schade, Haefner   *Hoeness* 2, *Müller*

Ajax (1) 1
Mulder
CSKA (0) 2
Maraschliev, Mikhailov
after extra time
Dynamo Bucharest (0) 0

Atlético Madrid (1) 2
Ayala, Capon
Spartak Trnava (0) 0
Zaria (0) 0

Bruges (1) 2
Carteus, Thio
Basle (3) 6
Hasler, Balmer,
Wampfler 2,
Hitzfeld 2 (1 *pen*)

CSKA Sofia (0) 0
Ajax (0) 0

Atlético Madrid (1) 2
Becera, Eusebio
Dynamo Bucharest (2) 2
Lucescu, Georgescu
Zaria (0) 0
Spartak Trnava (0) 1
Martinkovic
Basle (1) 1
Odermatt
Bruges (2) 4
Lambert 3 (1 *pen*),
Carteus

Quarter-Finals
Basle (2) 3
Hitzfeld 2 (1 *pen*),
Odermatt

Celtic (1) 2
Wilson, Dalglish

Basle: Laufenburger; Mundschin, Fischli, Rahmen, Demarmels, Odermatt (Wampfler), Hasler, Stohler, Balmer, Hitzfeld, Wenger (Tanner).
Celtic: Williams; McGrain, McNeill, Connelly, Brogan; Hay, Murray, Dalglish; Hood, Deans (Callaghan), Wilson.

Celtic (2) 4
Dalglish, Deans,
Callaghan, Murray
after extra time

Basle (2) 2
Mundschin, Balmer

Celtic: Connachan; Hay, Brogan, Murray, McNeill, Connelly (McCluskey), Johnstone, Hood, Deans, Callaghan, Dalglish.
Basle: Laufenburger (Kunz); Rahmen, Stohler, Hasler, Fischli, Mundschin, Balmer, Odermatt, Hitzfeld, Wampfler, Tanner.

Bayern Munich (2) 4
Torstensson 2,
Beckenbauer, Müller
CSKA Sofia (1) 2
Kolev (*pen*), *Denev*
Red Star Belgrade (0) 0

Atlético Madrid (0) 0
Spartak Trnava (1) 1
Kabat
Ujpest (1) 1
Fekete

CSKA Sofia (1) 1
Maraschliev

Bayern Munich (1) 1
Breitner (*pen*)
Atlético Madrid (1) 2
Luis, Garate
Red Star Belgrade (0) 0
Ujpest (0) 1
Toth (*pen*)
Spartak Trnava (1) 1
Adamec

after extra time; Ujpest won on penalties.

Semi-Finals

Celtic (0) 0   Atlético Madrid (0) 0

Celtic: Connachan; Hay, McNeill, McCluskey, Brogan; Murray, Dalglish, Hood; Johnstone, Deans (Wilson), Callaghan.

Atlético Madrid: Reina; Mela, Diaz, Benegas, Ovejero, Eusebio, Heredia, Adelardo, Garate (Quique), Irureta (Alberto), Ayala.

Atlético Madrid (0) 2   Celtic (0) 0
Garate, Adelardo

Atlético Madrid: Reina; Benegas, Capon, Adelardo, Heredia (Bemejo), Eusebio, Ufarte, Luis (Cabrero), Garate, Irureta, Becerra.

Celtic: Connachan; McGrain, Brogan; Hay, McNeill, McCluskey; Johnstone, Murray, Dalglish, Hood, Lennox.

Ujpest (0) 1   Bayern Munich (0) 1
Fazekas   *Torstensson*
Bayern Munich (1) 3   Ujpest (0) 0
Torstensson, Müller 2

Final Brussels, 15 May, 1974

Atlético Madrid (0) 1   Bayern Munich (0) 1
Luis   *Schwarzenbeck*
after extra time

Atletico Madrid: Reina; Melo, Capon, Adelardo, Heredia, Eusebio, Ufarte (Becerra), Luis, Garate, Irureta, Salcedo (Alberto).

Bayern Munich: Maier; Hansen, Breitner, Schwarzenbeck, Beckenbauer, Roth, Torstensson (Durnberger), Zobel, Müller, Hoeness, Kappelmann.

Replay Brussels, 17 May, 1974

Bayern Munich (1) 4   Atlético Madrid (0) 0
Hoeness 2, Müller 2

Bayern Munich: Maier; Hansen, Breitner, Schwarzenbeck, Beckenbauer, Roth, Torstensson, Zobel, Müller, Hoeness, Kappelmann.

Atlético Madrid: Reina; Melo, Capon, Adelardo (Benegas), Heredia, Eusebio, Salcedo, Luis, Garate, Alberto (Ufarte), Becerra.

CHAPTER THREE

European Cup-Winners Cup 1973-74

The tournament was won only for the second time by a team from an Iron Curtain country, and for the first by an East German club. Magdeburg, recently crowned East German champions, well deserved their victory in the final over Milan, whose success against Leeds in the 1973 final had a cloud of suspicion over it. Nor, indeed, had the refereeing of their semi-final return leg away to Borussia Mönchengladbach, by the Spaniard Martinez, been without its sharp critics.

Milan reached the final at a moment when their morale was fragile, their record in the League poor, and their best striker, Chiarugi, suspended. They very badly needed an early goal; the very last thing they needed was to fall behind, as they did, to an own goal. Thereafter, the less technically gifted, but quicker, stronger, more decisive, more confident East Germans took control and well deserved to score their second goal. A mere 5,000 saw the match, in Rotterdam, partly explicable by the fact that East German supporters aren't allowed, for obvious reasons, to travel, but also a sign that this is not precisely the cup that cheers – or draws.

It was not a distinguished season for British clubs. Sunderland began well but, as a Second Division team, inevitably lacked experience. Rangers went out to powerful Borussia Mönchengladbach, and brave little Glentoran – reviving memories of their 1967 European Cup run – eventually were swamped by them in turn.

There is some reason to believe that Sunderland were undone by the problem of boredom, one of which Sir Alf Ramsey has long been well aware. The players complained, after their defeat in Lisbon by Sporting, that they had been out there too long before the match with too little to do.

Yet Sunderland had made a flying start. To win their first match ever in European competition 2–0 on the ground of as experienced a team as Vasas was no small achievement. Their second goal was a marvellous individual one by Dennis Tueart, who beat four men before he scored. Jim Montgomery, in goal, also made a large contribution to the win. In the return, played on a ghastly night on a slippery pitch, Tueart scored the solitary goal half an hour from time from a penalty, given for hands. An irony, this, since Sunderland had failed with numerous chances, often being thwarted by the goalkeeping of Meszaros.

A freakish goal helped Sunderland to another narrow home win in the second round against Sporting Lisbon. Damas, Sporting's usually impeccable international goalkeeper, caught a shot by Bobby Kerr; then inexplicably stepped back over his line! After 64 minutes, Kerr got round the back of the Lisbon defence, and crossed for Mick Horswill to head the second goal. It looked a better ending to the evening than had ever seemed likely until the prolific Argentinian, Yazalde, was left unmarked to head past Montgomery.

One goal was a slender lead to take to Lisbon, and it did not prove enough. After 25 minutes, Sporting took the lead through Yazalde after an error by Montgomery, and 50 minutes later scored again through Fraguito after a missed interception by Dave Watson. It was their second British victim, for they had narrowly beaten Cardiff City in the previous round.

Rangers, back after a year's suspension in the competition they had won in 1972, comfortably defeated Ankaragucu, who had given Leeds some trouble the previous year, 2–0 in Turkey and 4–0 at home, where their veteran defender John Greig scored two of the goals, and two Turks were sent off. Borussia Mönchengladbach, even without the transferred Netzer, were too good for them, however.

In the first leg, Borussia beat them 3–0 in Germany, Peter McCloy, their international 'keeper, giving away the first goal but going on to play splendidly. The game was exciting but hard, two Scots and a German being booked. In the return, Rangers played vigorously and were in sight of success when Jensen, the Danish winger, scored his second goal of the match and made qualification sure for Borussia.

Glentoran did wonderfully well till they, too, foundered on the rock of Münchengladbach in particularly unhappy circumstances. Chimia Vilcea, the Romanians, were their first victims. Twice behind in the away leg, Glentoran twice equalised, then won the return 2–0 in Belfast. They were again behind in the first, away, leg against Brann, the Norwegians, but again equalised, to win the return by a two-goal margin.

The home leg against Borussia Mönchengladbach, in the quarter-finals, was ill-starred to a degree. After 35 minutes, Walker, the Glentoran centre-half, broke a leg, but the Irishmen fought well, losing only 2–0. That night, a much worse disaster befell them when their midfield player, Roy Stewart, died from a heart attack. They lost the return leg, unsurprisingly, 5–0.

Milan's passage to a final they'd won in such controversial circumstances the year before was an unusual one. In a state of chronic crisis all season, losing two managers – Nereo Rocco and his successor, Cesare Maldini – within a few months, they still managed to raise their game on the occasion of each European Cup-Winners' Cup match. The most remarkable occasion was for the home leg against powerful Borussia, which they won despite the fact that Maldini had resigned, in protest against their feeble show at Verona, only three days earlier, and despite the absence of the incomparable Gianni Rivera.

Trapattoni, their new manager and former left-half, managed to lift their morale, and a goal scored after 18 minutes by Bigon from a corner lifted it still higher. The Germans almost equalised through Heynckes, might have had a penalty when Rupp was brought down by Lanzi, but fell further behind after 51 minutes. Bigon's dribble opened the defence, Bergamaschi's shot was not held by Kleff, and Chiarugi scored. Milan, whose rivals, Inter, had been involved in a notorious European Cup serial with Borussia in 1971, were the better side on the night, Maldera keeping a firm grip on Wimmer.

The return was a bruising affair, Kulik and Milan's own German, Schnellinger, being carried off after bad fouls. Though they had four reserves playing, Borussia forced the pace almost throughout, yet scored only once, when Sabadini, under pressure from Koppel, headed through his own goal, after 27 minutes. So they went through, materially helped by the curious refereeing of the Spaniard, Martinez.

Magdeburg, the East Germans, encouraged by winning their Championship, beat Sporting Lisbon 2–1 that night to join them.

In the final, at Rotterdam, a fine save by Schulze from the clever little Tresoldi prevented Milan getting the first goal they so badly needed. Magdeburg scored it instead when Raugust broke fast down the left, evaded Schnellinger in the two-on-two situation, and put over a fast cross which Lanzi, in his desperate attempt to stop the ball reaching Sparwasser, put past his own goalkeeper.

Before half-time, it looked as if Magdeburg could also have had a penalty after a foul in the right-hand corner of the box, but a permissive Dutch referee let it go. The East Germans began the second half with panache, on one occasion having a series of three shots successively blocked, Hoffmann and Sparwasser, their most dangerous men, being responsible for two of them. Milan did briefly ignite hope when Rivera's strong header was in turn headed off the line by Abraham and when Benetti cleverly made space for a left-foot shot, saved by Schulze.

Magdeburg finally put them out of their misery when Hoffmann broke away again on the left, laid bare the defence with his fast cross, and Seguin, running in, beat first his man, then Pizzaballa.

ROUND BY ROUND RESULTS

First Round

Vasas (0) 0   Sunderland (0) 2
Hughes, Tueart
Vasas: Meszaros; Torok, Fabian, Kantor, Lakinger (Gass), Vidats, Muller, Toth, Varadi, Kovacs, Sipoez.
Sunderland: Montgomery; Malone, Guthrie; Horswill, Watson, Pitt; Kerr, Hughes, Halom (Young), Porterfield, Tueart.

Sunderland (0) 1   Vasas (0) 0
Tueart (pen)
Sunderland: Montgomery; Malone, Guthrie; Horswill, Watson, Young, Kerr, Hughes, Halom, Porterfield, Tueart.
Vasas: Torok; Fabian, Kantor, Toth, Vidats, Muller, Kamjati (Foldi), Gass, Lakinger, Varadi (Szoke).

Ankaragucu (0) 0   Rangers (1) 2
Conn, McClean
Ankaragucu: Baskin; Remzi, Ismail, Mehmet, Mujdat, Selcuk, Metin, Zafer, Melih, Ali Osman, Tahsin.
Rangers: McCloy; Jardine, Mathieson; Greig, Jackson, Smith; McLean, Forsyth, Parlane, Conn, Young.

Rangers (1) 4   Ankaragucu (0) 0
Greig 2, O'Hara,
Johnstone
Rangers: McCloy; Jardine, Mathieson; Greig, Johnstone, MacDonald; McLean, Forsyth, O'Hara, Conn, Houston.
Ankaragucu: Baskin; Remzi, Ismail, Errian, Mujdat, Zafer, Mehmet, Metin, Melih, O. Coskun, Tahsin.

Cardiff City (0) 0   Sporting Lisbon (0) 0
Cardiff City: Irwin; Dwyer, Bell; Smith, Murray, Phillips; Villars (King), McCulloch, Woodruff, Vincent, Anderson.
Sporting: Damas; Manaca, Pereira, Fraguito, Laranjeira, Alhinho, Marinho, Nelson, Yazalde, Wagner, Dinis.

Sporting Lisbon (1) 2   Cardiff City (1) 1
Yazalde, Fraguito   *Villars*
Sporting: Damas; Manaca, Laranjeira, Alhinho, Carlos Pereira, Fraguito, Nelson, Marinho, Tome (Chico), Yazalde, Dinis.
Cardiff City: Irwin; Dwyer, Bell, Woodruff, Murray, Phillips, Villars (Reece), McCulloch, Showers, Vincent, King.

Chimia Vilcea (2) 2   Glentoran (1) 2
Gijgaru 2   *McCreary, Jamison*
Glentoran (1) 2   Chimia (0) 0
Jamison, Craig
Banik (Czech) (1) 1   Cork Hibernian (0) 0
Albrecht
Cork Hibernian (0) 1   Banik (1) 2
Humphries   *Albrecht, Tondra*
Reipas (Finland) (0) 0   Lyon (0) 0
Lyon (1) 2   Reipas (0) 0
Di Nallo 2
Gzira United (Malta) (0) 0   Brann Bergen (1) 2
                                  Blinhaern 2 (1 pen)
Brann Bergen (1) 7   Gzira United (0) 0
Espeseth 2, Hauge, Osland, Blindheim, Oeyaseater, Larsen
Milan (2) 3   Dynamo Zagreb (0) 1
Bigon 2, Chiarugi   *Lalic*
Dynamo Zagreb (0) 0   Milan (1) 1
                                  Chiarugi
Pezoporikos (Cyprus) (0) 0   Malmö (0) 0
Malmö (6) 11   Pezoporikos (0) 0
Cervin 4, Tapper 3, Kristensson, Olsberg, Andersson, Bo Larsson
Anderlecht (0) 3   Zurich (2) 2
Rensenbrink 3   *Stierli, Jeandupeux*
Zurich (1) 1   Anderlecht (0) 0
Rutschmann
Vestmannaeyia (Iceland) (0) 0   Borussia Mönchengladbach (3) 7
                                  Heynckes 3, Kulik 2, Sigurgerisson (o.g.), Finnbogason (o.g.)
Borussia Mönchengladbach (6) 9   Vestmannaeyia (0) 1
Wimmer 2, Simonsen 3, Koppel 2, Rupp, Valtyrsson (o.g.)
Torpedo Moscow (0) 0   Atlético Bilbao (0) 0

Altético Bilbao (1) 2   Torpedo Moscow (0) 0
Astrain, Lasa
NAC Breda (0) 0   Magdeburg (0) 0
Magdeburg (0) 2   NAC Breda (0) 0
Tyll, Hoffmann
Randers Freja (Denmark) (0) 0   Rapid Vienna (0) 0
Rapid Vienna (1) 2   Randers Freja (0) 1
Krankl, Lorenz
Legia Warsaw 1   PAOK Salonica 1
Pieszko   *Terzenidis*
PAOK Salonica (0) 1   Legia Warsaw (0) 0
Parides
Fola Esch (Luxembourg) (0) 0   Beroe (Bulg) 7
                                Petkov 3, Bonchev 2,
                                Stoyanov, Todorov
Beroe (1) 4   Fola Esch (0) 1
Petkov, Belchev,   *Melda*
Todorov, Kirov
(*Both games at Stara Zagora*)

Second Round

Sunderland (1) 2   Sporting Lisbon (0) 1
Kerr, Horswill   *Yazalde*
Sunderland: Montgomery; Malone, Bolton; Horswill, Watson, Young; Kerr, Hughes, Halom, Porterfield, Tueart.
Sporting: Damas; Manaca, Pereira, Fraguito, Laranjeira, Alhinho, Chico, Nelson, Yazalde, Wagner, Nando.

Sporting Lisbon (1) 2   Sunderland (0) 0
Yazalde, Fraguito
Sporting: Damas; Manaca, Carlos Pereira, Fraguito, Laranjeira, Alhinho, Chico, Nelson, Yazalde (Tome), Wagner, Marinho (Nando).
Sunderland: Montgomery; Malone, Bolton; Horswill (Lathan), Watson, Young, Kerr, Hughes (Guthrie), Porterfield, Tueart.

Borussia Mönchengladbach (1) 3 Rangers (0) 0
Heynckes 2, Rupp
Borussia: Kleff; Vogts, Bonhof, Sieloff, Danner, Koppel, Wimmer, Kulik, Jensen, Rupp, Heynckes.
Rangers: McCloy; Jardine, Johnstone, Forsyth, Mathieson, Greig, MacDonald, Houston, McLean, Parlane (O'Hara), Conn.

Rangers (2) 3   Borussia Mönchengladbach (1) 2
Conn, Jackson, MacDonald   *Jensen 2*
Rangers: McCloy; Jardine, Mathieson, Greig, Jackson, MacDonald, McLean, Forsyth (Young), O'Hara, Conn, Houston.
Borussia: Kleff; Danner, Bonhof, Kulik, Sieloff, Vogts, Jensen, Koppel, Rupp, Wimmer, Heynckes.

Brann Bergen (1) 1   Glentoran (0) 1
Jensen   *Feeney*

Glentoran (2) 3 | Brann Bergen (0) 1
Feeney, Jamison 2 | *Oxland*
Milan (0) 0 | Rapid Vienna (0) 0
Rapid Vienna (0) 0 | Milan (2) 2
| *Bigon 2*
Zurich (0) 0 | Malmö (0) 0
Malmö (1) 1 | Zurich (0) 1
Malmberg | *Katic*
Beroe (1) 3 | Atlético Bilbao (0) 0
Dimitrov, Zhelev, Bonchev
Atlético Bilbao (1) 1 | Beroe (0) 0
Lasa
Lyon (1) 3 | PAOK Salonica (1) 3
Lacombe, Di Nallo, | *Aslanidis, Terzanidis,*
Ravier | *Sazafis*
PAOK Salonica (2) 4 | Lyon (0) 0
Paridis 2, Aslanidis (pen),
Terzanidis
Banik Ostrava (1) 2 | Magdeburg (0) 0
Albrecht, Klement
Magdeburg (1) 3 | Banik Ostrava (0) 0
Abraham (pen), Hoffmann,
Sparwasser
after extra time

Quarter-Finals

Magdeburg (0) 2 | Beroe (0) 0
Hermann, Mewes
Beroe (0) 1 | Magdeburg (0) 1
Vutov (pen) | *Hermann*
Milan (2) 3 | PAOK Salonica (0) 0
Bigon, Benetti, Chiarugi
PAOK Salonica (1) 2 | Milan (0) 2
Sarafis 2 | *Bigon, Tresoldi*
Glentoran (0) 0 | Borussia Mönchengladbach (1) 2
| *Heynckes, Koppel*
Borussia Mönchengladbach (2) 5 | Glentoran (0) 0
Wimmer, Heynckes 2,
Koppel, Vogts
Sporting Lisbon (0) 3 | Zurich (0) 0
Nelson, Marinho, Yazalde (pen)
Zurich (1) 1 | Sporting Lisbon (1) 1
Botteron | *Baltasar*

Semi-Finals

Milan (1) 2 | Borussia Mönchengladbach (0) 0
Bigon, Chiarugi
Borussia Mönchengladbach (1) 1 | Milan (0) 0
Sabadini (o.g.)

Sporting Lisbon (0) 1
Manaca
Magdeburg (1) 2
Pommerenke, Sparwasser

Magdeburg (0) 1
Perera (o.g.)
Sporting Lisbon (0) 1
Marinho

Final Rotterdam, 8 May, 1974
Magdeburg (1) 2 Milan (0) 0
Lanzi (o.g.), *Seguin*
Magdeburg: Schulze; Enge, Zapf, Gaube, Abraham, Tyll, Pommerenke, Seguin, Raugust, Sparwasser, Hoffmann.
Milan: Pizzaballa; Anquilletti, Sabadini, Lanzi, Schnellinger, Maldera, Tresoldi, Benetti, Bigon, Rivera, Bergamaschi. sub: Turini.

CHAPTER FOUR

UEFA (European Union) Cup 1973-74

For the first time for seven years, an English club failed to win this competition when Spurs, former victors, were well beaten in Rotterdam by Feyenoord. It was particularly unfortunate that the match was disturbed by the deplorable violence of young Spurs fans, who ignored appeals from the club chairman and manager and fought with the police.

So Spurs' long, surprising run in the Cup came to an end; surprising because they showed form in it which completely belied their poor showing in the League. This was never so starkly apparent as when they went to Cologne, and won against a team riding high in the Bundesliga – and this just after a pathetic exhibition away to Queen's Park Rangers. Ipswich, who beat Real Madrid, Twente, and Lazio in a dazzling run – their first appearance in Europe since 1962 – then fell to Locomotive Leipzig, were immeasurably more impressive in the First Division. Yet where they failed, Spurs succeeded, beating Leipzig not only at home but away; a feat beyond the powers of Wolves, too.

To explain Spurs' Jeykll and Hyde persona is most difficult. Tony Waddington, Stoke's manager, attributed it to the fact that they could build up more slowly in Europe. Tottenham's own players admitted, in puzzlement, that they seemed to bring out something extra for the UEFA Cup games. Certainly there was an edge to their play, an enthusiasm so often missing in the Championship, even if there were special cases, such as that of Dynamo Tblissi, where they exploited failing not to be found in English teams. Dynamo's ineptitude in the air allowed Spurs to head a cascade of more or less easy goals after they'd had a somewhat embarrassing first half.

The competition was scarred by the viciousness of Lazio's players in their second round return leg against Ipswich in Rome. Their behaviour was so outrageous, so wildly brutal, that some speculated about the fact that in Italian *League* games, anti-doping control is automatic.

Thrashed 4–0 at Portman Road, where the young inside-forward Trevor Whymark scored all four – the last, it is true, with assistance from his hand – Lazio went berserk at the Olympic Stadium. They kicked and chased the Ipswich players on the field; especially after Ipswich had scored from a penalty. Worst of all, in the tunnel, as the players left the field, Giuseppe Wilson, Lazio's Darlington-born captain, hacked David Best, the Ipswich 'keeper, to the ground and kicked him ferociously until Cyril Lea, Ipswich's coach, managed to intervene. Bobby Robson, Ipswich's manager, describing Lazio as 'human beings gone berserk', felt they 'should be thrown out of Europe for ever'. The one-year ban UEFA placed on Lazio for European competitions seemed a disgracefully inadequate punishment; till ironically Lazio won the

Italian Championship and thus found themselves banned from the European Cup for 1974-75.

Ipswich, a young, lively, progressive team, always ready to blood young reserves, lost 4-2 that night, but went into the third round on aggregate. In the first round, they had been splendid against a waning Real Madrid, attacking for most of the match at Portman Road, though it was only a belated own goal by Rubinan, diverting Mills' shot past the excellent Garcia-Remon, that gave them victory.

Astonishingly, Ipswich were still more superior in Madrid, where Real might have been expected to attack in waves, even though Nezter and Amancio were missing, and Pirri went off on a stretcher. Instead, Ipswich carried the game to them, should have been well ahead at half-time, and were poorly rewarded by a goalless draw.

Against Twente, the Dutchmen, in the third round, Ipswich continued their attacking policies. Things looked bleak for them when, in the first leg at Portman Road, their pressure on a frosty night brought but one goal – when Woods hit the post, and Whymark scored. In Holland, however, they again showed that to attack away from home can pay handsomely. Missing chances in the first half, under pressure for 10 minutes of the second, they scored at last after 57 minutes. Whymark pulled the ball back from the line for Morris to shoot home. After 71 minutes Bryan Hamilton, who had previously been struck and knocked down by Achterberg, scored the second from the clever Viljoen's pass, again from the line.

But Leipzig, till Spurs toppled them, were the bane of English teams. Wolves were their first victims, though their 3-0 defeat in Leipzig was an odd one. They dominated the first half, hit the wood twice in the second, yet lost heavily, giving away two goals in the last 10 minutes. Matoul, East Germany's leading scorer, got two of Leipzig's three, the second from a disputed penalty when Munro brought him down.

At Molineux, Wolves thrashed Locomotive 4-1, but Lowe's breakaway goal was enough to put his club into the next round. Fine goalkeeping by Werner Friese saved Leipzig from heavier defeat.

At Ipswich, in the quarter-finals, the East Germans were a much tighter unit. Ipswich had all the play, but only a very late goal driven home splendidly by their fine young halfback, Kevin Beattie, gave them victory. They would probably have qualified had not Mills been provoked by Lowe in Leipzig. Retaliating, he was sent off, and Ipswich, reduced to 10 men, lost 1-0. And when the previously immaculate Hunter missed one of their series of penalties, their glorious run had ended.

Leeds United's attitude to the competition was, not for the first time, tepid. They beat Hibernian at Easter Road only on penalties, surviving a petulant protest that the result should be annulled because Leeds had coaches on the field at the time. But the team they sent to Vitoria Setubal in the next round was full of reserves and was predictably beaten.

Spurs, too, defeated a Scottish team in the second round. They drew away with Aberdeen, then beat them 4-1 at Tottenham, a score unkind to an Aberdeen side who played much good football. but paid for missed chances and defensive errors. Spurs came to life when, in the second half, the young Irish forward Chris McGrath came on as substitute. Running exuberantly at the defence, McGrath scored twice, and Tottenham had clearly found a new star.

In the first round, they had twice beaten Grasshoppers of Zurich by comfortable scores, though their 5–1 away win was a parody of play. Pat Jennings, indeed, had to make some remarkable saves.

Dynamo Tblissi, the Georgians, captained by the old warhorse Khurtsilava, hero of many Russian international matches, looked a fearsome opponent. But Spurs again raised their game. In Georgia, four days after a home League defeat by Wolves, they took the lead through Ralph Coates. His allegedly weaker left foot drove the ball fiercely in after Chivers had touched it back. Dynamo's skilful team, inactive in recent weeks, gradually found its touch, attacked solidly, and equalised after 75 minutes through Asatian. Jennings had another excellent game

At White Hart Lane, Dynamo's weakness in the air undid them after they'd had the better of the early play. The only goal of the first half was neatly headed by McGrath, though Dynamo had threatened several times to score. Then the high crosses started to come over; Gogia, in the Tblissi goal, was just not sufficient, and by the end Spurs were virtually playing head tennis. Coates made a goal for the forceful Chivers, Ebralidze scored for Dynamo, then Peters, twice, and Chivers headed goals for Spurs.

Next, Cologne – Overath and all – were beaten on their own ground, despite intense pressure. Cologne had sent observers to White Hart Lane to see Spurs play ineptly against Manchester City. They were worse still four days before the tie at Queen's Park Rangers, where Martin Chivers had a dreadful game. In Cologne, he was transformed. He has a German mother and always wants to do well on German soil. Playing little Dillon as an extra defender, Spurs still contrived to take an early lead through – once more – McGrath, after Chivers' burst and shot. Nine minutes after half-time Muller equalised, but Spurs would not be put down. A quarter-hour from time, Peters scored the winner, heading in after a break down the right by Naylor.

The return at White Hart Lane was virtually no contest. Spurs simply walked over a passive Cologne. Chivers scored from Naylor's centre, made a second for Coates, and a third, just after half-time, for Peters. One of the Bundesliga's strongest teams had been annihilated by one of the First Division's least impressive.

So it was no surprise when Spurs, in Leipzig, showed Wolves and Ipswich how it should be done. Locomotive were too cautious, giving the first half initiative to Spurs and conceding two goals in consequence. Martin Peters, with characteristic opportunism, scored the first after 15 minutes. As Neighbour shaped to control England's long clearance, at the edge of the box, Peters nipped in and drove it past Friese. The second came when Evans overlapped down the left and pulled the ball back for Coates to get another of his UEFA Cup goals. It would have been three had Chivers not had abominable luck. His header from Neighbour's cross beat Friese, hit the post, then bounced to safety off the goalkeeper's head! On the hour, Lowe was therefore able to head a goal for Leipzig; though their previous away form hardly suggested they would overhaul Spurs.

Nor did they, though at Tottenham Spurs took half-an-hour to get into their stride and gave Leipzig some displeasingly harsh treatment. Lowe, through all alone, missed a wonderful chance to give Locomotive the lead, and that was that; even though Jennings had to make two splendid saves from headers in the second half. Tottenham swarmed over Leipzig, McGrath headed the first goal from Coates' right wing centre, placing it coolly wide of Friese, and late in the game Chivers converted Perryman's pass from the left to make it 2–0.

Feyenoord qualified to meet them; not the team that once had won the European Cup, but still a formidable one with a keen opportunist in Schoenmaker. He it was who scored both goals that night at Stuttgart, whose scourge he had also been in the previous leg, which Feyenoord won.

Indeed, Spurs at last caught a Continental Tartar when Feyenoord came to Tottenham for the first leg of the final. The match was drawn 2–2, Spurs twice having the lead, but the score was a parody of play, so far were Feyenoord ahead in the arts of the game. England, thundering in to free-kicks from the right by Evans, precipitated both Spurs goals, splendidly heading the first himself, causing confusion and an own goal for the second. But before he scored, the cool, incisive Feyenoord team had missed a couple of easy chances through Schoenmaker and De Jong, who broke so powerfully from midfield.

Van Hanegem, loping about at quarter pace, struck a marvellous left-footed free-kick in off the bar to equalise the first goal. Spurs' second seemed to have come late enough to give them the game, but a splendid one-two between De Jong and Kristensen, the clever Dane, brought a very late, deeply deserved equaliser.

In Rotterdam, Spurs' often physical methods in defence were not enough to hold at bay the Feyenoord attack, still clever and impressive despite the absence of the suspended Van Hanegem. Additionally, their players may well have been perturbed by the behaviour of their own fans: to whom they uselessly appealed at half-time.

Fine saves by Jennings from Kristensen – with a foot – and Schoenmaker kept Tottenham for a time in the game; both Peters and Perryman might have scored. But, untypically, it was an error by Jennings that led to the first Dutch goal a minute from half-time. His punch did not fully connect with Ramljak's centre, and Rijsbergen headed into the far corner: the signal for the Spurs fans to riot. The second goal was scored by Ressel; a shot from the edge of the box into the far corner. It was all a depressing anti-climax to Spurs' achievements in the previous rounds.

ROUND BY ROUND RESULTS
First Round

Strömsgodset (1) 1   Leeds United (1) 1
Amundsen   *Clarke*

Strömsgodset: Thun; Wolner, Pedersen, Nostdahl, S. Andersen, Amundsen, Olsen, B. Andersen (Aarseth), Presberg, S. Pettersen, I. Pettersen (Halvorsen).
Leeds United: Sprake; Madeley, Cherry; Yorath, McQueen, Bates; F. Gray, Liddell, Clarke, Jones, E. Gray.

Leeds United (3) 6   Strömsgodset (1) 1
Clarke 2, Jones ñ,   *S. Petterson*
F. Gray, Bates

Leeds United: Harvey; Reaney (O'Neill), Cherry; Bremner, Ellam, Yorath; Lorimer, Clarke (McGinley), Jones, Bates, F. Gray.
Strömsgodset: Thun; Wolner (Aarseth), Pedersen, Nostdahl, S. Andersen, Amundsen, Olsen, B. Andersen, Presberg, S. Pettersen, I. Pettersen (Halvorsen).

Ipswich Town (0) 1   Real Madrid (0) 0
Rubinan (o.g.)

Ipswich Town: Best; Mills, Harper; Collard, Hunter, Beattie; Hamilton, Viljoen, Johnson, Whymark, Lambert (Miller).
Real Madrid: Garcia-Remon; Luis, Rubinan, Benito, Tourino; Pirri, Amancio, Grosso; Planelles, Netzer, Mas.

Real Madrid (0) 0   Ipswich Town (0) 0

Real Madrid: Garcia-Remon; Luis, Benito, Tourino, Pirri, Zoco, Aguilar, Grosso, Planelles, Del Bosque, Mas.
Ipswich Town: Best; Mills, Harper; Collard, Hunter, Beattie; Hamilton, Viljoen, Johnson, Whymark, Lambert.

Grasshoppers (1) 1   Tottenham Hotspur (2) 5
Noventa   *Chivers 2, Gilzean 2, Coates*

Grasshoppers: Deck; Staudenmann, Malzacher, H. Niggl, T. Niggl, Meyer, Grahn, Ohlhauser, Becker, Elsener, Noventa.
Spurs: Jennings; Evans, Knowles; Perryman, England, Beal; Peters, Pratt, Chivers, Coates (Holder), Neighbour (Gilzean).

Tottenham Hotspur (0) 4   Grasshoppers (1) 1
Lador (o.g.), Peters 2,   *Elsener*
England

Spurs: Daines; Evans, Knowles; Pratt, England, Beal, Perryman, Gilzean, Chivers, Peters, Coates.
Grasshoppers: Deck; Staudenmann, Malzacher, H. Niggl, T. Niggl, Meyer, Grobli, Lador, Capro, Becker, Elsener.

Aberdeen (3) 4   Finn Harps (0) 1
Miller, Jarvie 2, Graham   *Harkin*

Aberdeen: Clark; Hair, Hermiston, Thomson, Young, W. Miller, Willoughby, Graham, Taylor, Jarvie, R. Miller.

Finn Harps: Murray; McGroary, Hutton, McDowall, Sheridan, McDermott, Smith, Nicholl, Bradley, Harkin, Ferry.

Finn Harps (0) 1   Aberdeen (2) 3
Harkin   *Robb, Graham, Miller*

Finn Harps: Murray; McDowell, Hutton, O'Doherty, Sheridan, McDermott, Smith, Nicholl, Bradley, Harkin, Ferry (McGrory).
Aberdeen: Clark; Hair, Hermiston, Thomson (Smith), Young, W. Miller, Willoughby, Robb, Graham (Purdie), Harvie. R. Miller.

Hibernian (1) 2   Keflavik (0) 0
Black, Higgins

Hibernian: Robertson; Bremner, Schaedler, Stanton, Black, Blackley Edwards, O'Rourke, Higgins, Cropley, Munro (Duncan).
Keflavik: Olafsson; G. Jonsson, A. Gunnarsson, E. Gunnarsson, Kjartansson, Zakariasson, Juliusson, Hermansson, Johansson, Torfason, J. Jonsson.

Keflavik (1) 1   Hibernian (0) 1
Zakariasson   *Stanton*

Keflavik: Olafsson; G. Jonsson, A. Gunnarsson, E. Gunnarsson, Kjartansson, Zakariasson, Juliusson, Hermansson, Johansson, Torfason, J. Jonsson.
Hibernian: Robertson; Bremner, Schaedler; Stanton, Black, Blackley; Edwards, O'Rourke, Gordon, Cropley, Duncan.

Ards 3   Standard Liège 2
Cathcart, McAvoy (pen),   *Bukal 2*
McAteer (pen.)

Standard Liège (3) 6   Ards (1) 1
Henrotay, Bukal 4, Covaert   *Guy*

Dundee (0) 1   Twente Enschede (1) 3
Stewart   *Achterberg, Jeuring 2*

Dundee: Allan; Wilson, Johnston, Ford, Stewart, Gemmell, Robinson (Pringle), Gray (I. Scott), Wallace, J. Scott, Lambie.
Twente: Ardesch; Oranen, Drost, De Vries, Van Jerssel, Van Der Valk, Achterberg, Thijssen, Notten, Jeuring, Pahlplatz (Ziedema.)

Twente Enschede (2) 4   Dundee (1) 2
Vandervall, Achterberg,   *Johnson, J. Scott*
Zuidema 2

Twente: Ardesch; Van Jerssel, De Vries, Drost (Zuidema), Oranen, Thijssen, Achterberg, Van Der Vall, Notten, Schwemmle, Pahlplatz.
Dundee: Allan; Wilson, Pringle, Gemmell, Johnston, Ford, Robinson, Lambie (Anderson), Gray (Semple), I. Scott, J. Scott.

Belenenses (0) 0   Wolverhampton Wanderers (1) 2
                               Richards, Dougan

Belenenses: Mourinho; Murça, Calado, Feritas, Pietra, Quaresma, Eliseu, Godinho, Quinito, Carlos, Gonzalez.
Wolves: Pierce; Taylor, Parkin; Bailey (Hegan), Munro, McAlle; McCalliog, Hibbitt, Richards, Dougan, Wagstaffe.

Wolverhampton Wanderers (1) 2 Belenenses (1) 1
Eastoe, McCalliog *Murça*
Wolves: Pierce; Taylor, Parkin, Sunderland, Munro, McAlle, McCalliog, Hibbitt, Eastoe, Dougan, Wagstaffe.
Belenenses: Mourinho; Murça, Calado, Freitas, Cardoso, Quaresma, Quinito (Toninho), Eliseu, Carlos, Godinho, Gonzalez.

Nice (1) 3 Barcelona (0) 0
Van Dijk, Molitor 2
Barcelona (1) 2 Nice (0) 0
Sotil, Juanito
Union Luxembourg (0) 0 Marseilles (3) 5
  Hardt (o.g.), Kuzowski 3, Buigues
Marseilles (4) 7 Union Luxembourg (0) 1
Magnusson, Skoblar 3, *Hoffmann (pen)*
Kuzowski, Bracci (pen),
Trésor
Fiorentina (0) 0 Universitatea Craiova (0) 0
Universitatea Craiova (0) 1 Fiorentina (0) 0
Oblemenco
Admira Wacker (1) 1 Internazionale (0) 0
Swojanowsky
Internazionale (0) 2 Admira Wacker (0) 1
Moro, Boninsegna *Kaltenbrunner*
after extra time
Torino (0) 1 Locomotive Leipzig (0) 2
Bui *Loewe, Mozzini (o.g.)*
Locomotive Leipzig (2) 2 Torino (0) 1
Lisiewicz, Matoul *Sala*
Lazio (3) 3 Sion (0) 0
Chinaglia 3 (2 pen)
Sion (1) 3 Lazio (1) 1
Isoz 2, Barberis *Garlaschelli*
Fredrikstad (0) 0 Dynamo Kiev 1
  Docinko
Dynamo Kiev (2) 4 Frederikstad (0) 0
Trohskin, Kolotov, Buryak,
Blokhin
Ruch Chorzow (1) 4 Wuppertal (0) 1
Bula, Marks, Herisz, Maszczyk *Kohl*
Wuppertal (2) 5 Ruch Chorzow (3) 4
Stoebl, Cremer 2, Propper, *Beniger, Kopecera, Marks,*
Reichart *Bon*
BK 1903 Copenhagen (2) 2 AIK Stockholm (1) 1
Nielsen, Thorn *Zetterlund*
AIK Stockholm (0) 1 BK 1903 Copenhagen (0) 1
Aaslund *Kristensson*

Carl Zeiss Jena (2) 3
Brausch, Schlutter, Scheitler
Mikkelin (0) 0

Fortuna Dusseldorf (0) 1
Hesse
Naestved (0) 2
Olsen, Ottosen
Oesters (1) 1
Svensson
Feyenoord (1) 2
Kristenssen, De Jong
Espanol (0) 0

Racing White (1) 1
Polleunis
Vitoria Setubal (2) 2
Torres 2
Beerschot (0) 0

Ferencvaros (0) 0

Gwardia Warsaw (2) 2
Wisnieski, Szymczak
VfB Stuttgart (5) 9
*Enternmamm 3, Ettmayer 2,
Brenninger, Ohlicher, Mall,
Weidmann*
Olympiakos Nicosia (0) 0

(Second leg played in Stuttgart)
Tatran Presov (3) 4
Novak, Turcanyi, Sobota, Cabala
Velez (0) 1
Colic
Dynamo Tblissi (2) 4
Slavia Sofia (0) 2
Panathinaikos (0) 1
Antoniadis
OFK Belgrade (0) 0

Fenerbahce 5
Cemil 3, Osman, Mustapha
Arges Pitesti (1) 1
Dobrin
VSS Kosice 1
Pollak

Mikkelin (0) 0

Carl Zeiss Jena (2) 3
Irmscher, Ducks 2
Naestved (0) 0

Fortuna Dusseldorf (1) 2
Seel, Hertzog
Feyenoord (0) 3
Van Hanegem 2, Wery
Oesters (0) 1

Racing White (2) 3
Koen, Polleunis, Teuguels
Espanol (1) 2
Amiano, Martinez
Beerschot (0) 0

Vitoria Setubal (1) 2
José Maria 2
Gwardia Warsaw (1) 1
Szymczak
Ferencvaros (0) 1
Mate
Olympiakos Nicosia (0) 0

VfB Stuttgart (2) 4
*Ohlicher, Martin, Muller,
Ettmayer*

Velez (2) 2
Kvesic 2
Tatran Presov (1) 1
Sobota
Slavia Sofia (0) 1
Dynamo Tblissi (0) 0
OFK Belgrade (1) 2
Lukic 2
Panathinaikos (1) 1
Demelo
Arges Pitesti 1
Resu
Fenerbahce (1) 1
Cemil
Honved (0) 0

Honved (2) 5 VSS Kosice (2) 2
Pinter 2, Szucs, Fule (o.g.), *Pollak, Stafura*
Bortak

Eskisehirspor (0) 0 Cologne (0) 0
Cologne 2 Eskiserhirspor (0) 0
Lauscher, Lohr

Panachaiki (1) 2 GK Graz (0) 1
Michalopoulos, Spentzopoulos *Koleznik*
GK Graz (0) 0 Panachaiki (0) 1
  Spentzopoulos
Sliema Wanderers (0) 0 Locomotive Plovdiv (2) 2
  Vassilev, Camilleri (o.g.)
Locomotive Plovdiv (1) 1 Sliema Wanderers (0) 0
Vassilev

Second Round

Ipswich Town (2) 4 Lazio (0) 0
Whymark 4

Ipswich Town: Best; Mills, Harper; Morris, Hunter, Beattie (Hammond); Hamilton, Viljoen, Johnson (Woods), Whymark, Lambert.
Lazio: Pulici; Facco, Martini, Wilson, Oddi, Nanni (Manservisi), Garlaschelli (D'Amico), Re Cecconi, Chinaglia, Frustalupi, Petrelli.

Lazio (2) 4 Ipswich Town (0) 2
Garlaschelli, Chinaglia 3 (1 pen) *Viljoen (pen), Johnson*

Lazio: Pulici; Facco, Martini, Wilson, Oddi, Nanni, Garlaschelli, Re Cecconi, Chinaglia, Frustalupi, D'Amico (sub. Petrelli.)
Ipswich Town: Best; Mills, Harper (Hammond); Morris, Hunter, Beattie; Hamilton, Viljoen, Woods (Johnson), Whymark, Miller.

Leeds United (0) 0 Hibernian (0) 0

Leeds United: Harvey; Cherry, Madeley; Bremner, Ellam, Yorath; Lorimer, Clarke, Jones (Jordan), Bates, Gray (O'Neill).
Hibernian: McArthur; Bremner, Schaedler; Stanton, Black, Blackley; Smith (Hazel), Higgins, Gordon, Cropley, Duncan.

Hibernian (0) 0 Leeds United (0) 0

Hibernian: McArthur; Bremner, Schaedler; Stanton, Black, Blackley; Edwards, Higgins (Hazel), Gordon, Cropley, Duncan.
Leeds United: Shaw (Letheren); Reaney, Cherry; Bremner, Ellam, Yorath; Lorimer, Clarke, Jordan, Bates, Gray.
Leeds won on penalties.

Aberdeen (0) 1 Tottenham Hotspur (1) 1
Hermiston (pen) *Coates*

Aberdeen: Clark; Hair, Hermiston; Thomson (R. Miller), Young, W. Miller; Graham, Robb, Jarvie, Smith, Taylor.
Spurs: Daines; Evans, Kinnear (Naylor); Pratt, England, Beal; Gilzean, Perryman, McGrath, Peters, Coates (Neighbour).

Tottenham Hotspur (2) 4   Aberdeen (0) 1
Peters, Neighbour, McGrath 2   *Jarvie*
Spurs: Jennings; Evans, Knowles; Pratt, England, Beal; Gilzean, Perryman, Chivers, Peters, Neighbour (McGrath).
Aberdeen: Clark; Hair, Hermiston (Mitchell); Thomson, Young, W. Miller (R. Miller); Willoughby, Robb, Jarvie, Smith, Graham.

Locomotive Leipzig (1) 3   Wolverhampton Wanderers (0) 0
Matoul 2 (1 pen), Koeditz
Locomotive: Friese; Sekora, Grobner, Giessner, Fritsche, Geisler, Moldt, Frenzel (Koditz), Liesewicz, Matoul, Loewe.
Wolves: Parkes; Palmer, Parkin, Hegan, Munro, McAlle, McCalliog, Hibbitt, Sunderland (Eastoe), Dougan, Daley.

Wolverhampton Wanderers (0) 4   Locomotive Leipzig (0) 1
Kindon, Munro, Dougan, Hibbitt   *Loewe*
Wolves: Parkes; Palmer, Parkin; Powell, Munro, McAlle; Hibbitt, Sunderland, Kindon, Dougan, Wagstaffe.
Locomotive: Friese; Sekora, Grobner, Giessner, Fritsche, Geisler, Moldt, Frenzel, Lisiewicz, Matoul, Loewe.

Nice (2) 4   Fenerbahce (0) 0
Molitor 4
Fenerbahce (1) 2   Nice (0) 0
Osman 2 (1 pen)
Marseilles (0) 2   Cologne (0) 0
Lopez, Kuzowski
Cologne (4) 6   Marseilles (0) 0
Flohe, Muller 2, Overath (pen),
Lohr 2
VfB Stuttgart (0) 3   Tatran Presov (1) 1
Muller, Brenninger, Ohlicher   *Skorupa*
Tatran Presov (1) 3   VfB Stuttgart (1) 5
Turcanyi 2, Skorupa   *Ohlicher 2, Handschuh 2,*
                              Turcanyi

after extra time
Admira Wacker (1) 2   Fortuna Dusseldorf (0) 1
Budde   *Kaltenbrunner 2*
Fortuna Dusseldorf (3) 3   Admira Wacker (0) 0
Brei 2, Geye
Vitoria Setubal (0) 1   Racing White (0) 0
Vicente
Racing White (1) 2   Vitoria Setubal (0) 1
Depireux, Veenstra   *Vicente*
Lokomotiv Plovdiv (2) 3   Honved (3) 4
Georgiev, Ivanov, Bonev   *Kozma 2, Kocsis, Pal*
Honved (1) 3   Lokomotiv Plovdiv (0) 2
Kozma 2, Pinta   *Ivanov, Vasiliev*
Feyenoord (0) 3   Gwardia Warsaw (1) 1
Schoenmaker 2, De Jong   *Szymczak*

Gwardia Warsaw (1) 1   Feyenoord (0) 0
Szymczak
Dynamo Kiev (0) 1   BK 1903 Copenhagen (0) 0
Buryak
BK 1903 Copenhagen (0) 1   Dynamo Kiev (0) 2
Kristensen   *Kolotov, Troshkyn*
Dynamo Tblissi (2) 3   OFK Belgrade (0) 0
OFK Belgrade (0) 1   Dynamo Tblissi (3) 5
Stojanovic   *Chelidze, Nodia, Kipiani 2,
    Tsereteli*

Standard Liège (1) 2   Universitatea Craiova (0) 0
Bukal 2 (1 pen)
Universitatea Craiova (1) 1   Standard Liège (0) 1
Balan   *Henrotte*
Ruch Chorzow (1) 3   Carl Zeiss Jena (0) 0
Bennigen, Kepicha, Bula
Carl Zeiss Jena (0) 1   Ruch Chorzow (0) 0
Brausch
Panachaiki (1) 1   Twente (1) 1
Davourlis(pen)   *Tissel*
Twente (0) 7   Panachaiki (0) 0
*Pahlplatz 4, Zuidermi,
Van der Vaal (pen), Van Ierssel*

Third Round

Dynamo Tblissi (0) 1   Tottenham Hotspur (1) 1
Asatiani   *Coates*
Dynamo: Gogia; Dzodzuashvili, Chelidze, Khurtsilava, Kanteladze, Ebralidze (Tsereteli), Asatiani, Machaidze, Kipiani, G. Nodia, I. Nodia.
Spurs: Jennings; Evans, Knowles; Pratt, England, Beal; Naylor, Perryman, Chivers, Peters, Coates.

Tottenham Hotspur (1) 5   Dynamo Tblissi (0) 1
McGrath, Chivers 2, Peters 2   *Ebralidze*
Spurs: Jennings; Evans, Naylor; Pratt, England, Beal; McGrath, Perryman, Chivers, Peters, Coates.
Dynamo: Gogia; Dzozuashvili, Chelidze, Khurtsilava, Kinchagashvili, Ebralidze; Machaidze, Asatiani, Kutsaev, G. Nodia, Kipiani.

Ipswich Town (0) 1   Twente Enschede (0) 0
Whymark
Ipswich Town: Sivell; Hammond, Mills; Morris, Keeley, Beattie; Hamilton (Gates), Viljoen (Collard), Johnson, Whymark, Woods.
Twente: Schrijvers; Notten, De Vries, Van Ierssel, Oranen, Thijssen, Van der Vall, Achterberg, Schwemmel, Zuidema, Pahlplatz.

Twente Enschede (0) 1   Ipswich Town (0) 2
Struer   *Morris, Hamilton*

Twente: Schrijvers; Notten, De Vries, Van Ierssel, Oranen, Thijssen, Van der Vall (Struer), Achterberg, Schwemmle (Brinks), Zuidema, Pahlplatz.
Ipswich Town: Best; Hammond, Mills; Morris, Hunter, Beattie; Hamilton, Viljoen, Johnson, Whymark, Woods.

   Leeds United (0) 1   Vitoria Setubal (0) 0
   Cherry
Leeds United: Harvey; Reaney (Davey), Cherry; Bremner, McQueen, Hunter; Lorimer, Clarke, Jordan, Bates, Yorath (Gray).
Vitoria Setubal: Joaquim Torres; Rebelo, Cardoso; Mendes, Carrico, Octavio; Maria, Matine, Vicente, Duda (José Torres), João.

   Vitoria Setubal (0) 3   Leeds United (0) 1
   Duda 2, José Torres   *Liddell*
Vitoria Setubal: Joaquim Torres; Rebelo, Cardoso; Mendes, Carrico, Machado; Maria, Matine (Vicente), José Torres (Arcanjo), Duda, João.
Leeds United: Harvey; Reaney, Cherry; Yorath, McQueen (Liddell), Ellam; Lorimer, Mann, Hampton, Jordan, F. Gray.

Nice (0) 1	Cologne (0) 0
Eriksson	
Cologne (2) 4	Nice (0) 0
Muller, Flohe 2, Lohr	
Standard Liège (0) 3	Feyenoord (0) 1
Piot (pen), Lambrechts, Thissen	*Kristensen*
Feyenoord (0) 2	Standard Liège (0) 0
Schoenmacher, Van Hanegem	
Honved (1) 2	Ruch Chorzow (0) 0
Pusztai 2	
Ruch Chorzow (1) 5	Honved (0) 0
Kopicera 2, Bon, Marks, Bula	
Fortuna Dusseldorf (0) 2	Locomotive Leipzig (1) 1
Brei, Herzog	*Matoul (pen)*
Locomotive Leipzig (1) 3	Fortuna Dusseldorf (0) 0
Lisiewicz, Lowe, Frenzel	
Dynamo Kiev (1) 2	VfB Stuttgart (0) 0
Verameyev, Troshkin	
VfB Stuttgart (1) 3	Dynamo Kiev (0) 0
Ohlicher, Handschuh, Martin	

Quarter-Finals
   Cologne (0) 1   Tottenham Hotspur (1) 2
   Muller   *McGrath, Peters*
Cologne: Weiz; Knopka, Hein, Weber, Cullmann, Simmet, Glowacz, Flohe, Muller, Overath, Lohr.
Spurs: Jennings; Evans, Naylor; Pratt, England, Beal; McGrath, Perryman, Chivers, Peters, Dillon.

Tottenham Hotspur (2) 3　　　　Cologne (0) 0
Chivers, Coates, Peters
Spurs: Jennings; Evans, Naylor; Pratt, England, Beal; McGrath, Perryman, Chivers, Peters, Coates.
Cologne: Schumacher; Knopka, Hein, Weber, Cullmann, Simmet, Glowacz, Flohe, Muller, Overath, Lauscher (Neumann).

Ipswich Town (0) 1　　　　Locomotive Leipzig (0) 0
Beattie
Ipswich Town: Sivell; Burnley, Mills; Morris, Hunter, Beattie; Hamilton, Talbot, Johnson, Whymark, Woods.
Locomotive: Friese; Sekora, Grobner, Giessner, Fritsche, Altmann, Hammer, Frenzel, Lisiewicz, Matoul, Loewe.

Locomotive Leipzig (0) 1　　　　Ipswich Town (0) 0
Giessner
after extra time; Leipzig won 4–3 on penalties.
Locomotive: Friese; Giessner, Sekora, Groebner, Fritsche, Altmann, (Moldt), Hammer, Frenzel, Lisiewicz, (Geisler), Matoul, Loewe.
Ipswich Town: Sivell; Burnley, Mills; Morris, Hunter, Beattie; Hamilton, Talbot, Johnson, Whymark, Woods (Osborne).

Ruch Chorzow (1) 1　　　　Feyenoord (1) 1
Maszczyk　　　　*Schoenmaker*
Feyenoord (0) 3　　　　Ruch Chorzow (1) 1
Schoenmaker 2 (1 pen), Jensen　　　　*Marx*
after extra time; full-time 1–1.
VfB Stuttgart (0) 1　　　　Vitoria Setubal (0) 0
Stickel
Vitoria Setubal (2) 2　　　　VfB Stuttgart (0) 2
Martin (o.g.), José Maria　　　　*Ochlicher, Stickel*

Semi-Finals
Locomotive Leipzig (0) 1　　　　Tottenham Hotspur (2) 2
Loewe　　　　*Peters, Coates*
Locomotive: Friese; Sekora, Groebner, Giessner, Geisler, Hammer, Moldt (Altmann), Frenzel, Lisiewicz, Matoul, Loewe.
Spurs: Jennings; Evans, Naylor; Pratt, England, Beal; Neighbour, Perryman, Chivers, Peters, Coates.

Tottenham Hotspur (0) 2　　　　Locomotive Leipzig (0) 0
McGrath, Chivers
Spurs: Jennings; Kinnear, Naylor; Pratt (Holder); England, Beal; McGrath, Perryman, Chivers, Peters, Coates.
Locomotive: Friese; Sekora, Groebner, Giessner, Geisler, (Hammer), Altmann; Moldt, Frenzel, Lisiewicz (Koditz), Matoul, Loewe.

Feyenoord (0) 2　　　　VfB Stuttgart (1) 1
Schoenmaker 2　　　　*Brenninger*
VFB Stuttgart (0) 2　　　　Feyenoord (1) 2
Brenninger 2　　　　*Schoenmaker 2*

Final
Tottenham, 22 May, 1974
   Tottenham Hotspur (1) 2   Feyenoord (1) 2
   England, Israel (o.g.)   *Van Hanegem, De Jong*
Tottenham Hotspur: Jennings; Evans, England, Beal (Dillon), Perryman, Pratt, Coates; McGrath, Chivers, Coates.
Feyenoord: Treytel; Rijsbergen, Van Daele, Israel, Vos; Van Hanegem, De Jong, Jansen; Ressel, Schoenmaker, Kristensen.

Second Leg Rotterdam, 29 May, 1974
   Feyenoord (1) 2   Tottenham Hotspur (0) 0
   Rijsbergen, Ressel
Feyenoord: Treytel; Ramljak, Israel, Van Daele, Vos, Rijsbergen (Boscamp), De Jong, Jansen, Ressel, Schoenmaker, Kristensen.
Tottenham Hotspur: Jennings; Evans, Naylor, Pratt (Holder), England, Beal, McGrath, Perryman, Chivers, Peters, Coates.

CHAPTER FIVE

Intercontinental and 'Super' Cups 1973-74

WORLD CLUB (INTERCONTINENTAL) CHAMPIONSHIP

The so-called Intercontinental Championship took another long step backwards. Ajax, after their bruising experiences against Independiente in 1972, once again refused to compete. The Argentinians, however, South American Cup winners again, were as eager as before to repair their finances. At first the European Cup runners-up, Juventus, also refused to meet them, but when they had unexpectedly been knocked out in the first round of the European Cup, they changed their minds and agreed to play: on a one match basis, in Rome. It was the first time the competition had not been played over two legs.

Juventus, in the event, took the match as light-heartedly as Independiente took it with deadly seriousness. Capello, the Juve tactician, was left out, though he could probably have played; Furino was missing, too. Nevertheless Juventus hit both post and bar, missed a (dubiously awarded) penalty through Cuccureddu just after half-time, and might still have survived if their manager, Vycpalek, hadn't inexplicably taken off their best forward, Roberto Bettega. So it was that a goal beautifully engineered by Bertone and 19-year-old Bocchini, who beat two men before shooting past Zoff, won the game for Independiente.

Buenos Aires went wild with joy, and it was said that each member of the victorious Independiente team would be given a plot of land on which to build a house! The Argentinians had looked tactically inferior; individually, as so often, far superior.

Olympic Stadium, Rome, 28 November 1973
Juventus (0) 0   Independiente (0) 1
Bocchini
Juventus: Zoff, Spinosi (Longobucco), Marchetti, Gentile, Morini, Salvadore, Causio, Cuccureddu, Anastasi, Altafini, Bettega (Viola).
Independiente: Santoro; Lopez, Pavoni, Comisso, Raimondo, Sa, Balbuena, Galvan, Maglione, Bocchini, Bertone (Semenewicz).

'SUPER' CUP
This loosely and grandiosely named trophy was put up for competition between the winners of the European and the European Cup-Winners' Cups by a Dutch newspaper; ignoring all implicit anomalies. After all, the 'super' teams are those that win their national championships and thus compete in the European Cup. The Cup-Winners' Cup is, by definition, a kind of distinguished second division.

Joe Jordan heads Scotland into the World Cup finals, where they were unbeaten in their group yet failed, on goal difference, to qualify for the next round.

Luis Pereira, the powerful centre-back, was one of few Brazilians to emerge with credit in a side which had seemingly replaced attacking brilliance with defensive cynicism.

Robert Gadocha, excellent in Poland's World Cup qualifying matches, continued to excel in West Germany, where the Poles silenced their critics with the quality and attractiveness of their winning displays.

A star of three World Cups, Franz Beckenbauer captained the
West Germans in 1974, but his side, disappointing in their early
matches, required his authority as much as his graceful,
poised 'detachment' in their bid for the World Cup.

Paul Breitner, Maoist and attacking fullback, scored the first goal of the 1974 World Cup with his magnificent long-range shot against Chile.

Inspired, inspirational, and infuriating . . . Johan Cruyff was all of these as he led his talented Dutch side through the World Cup finals and showed why so many consider him the finest footballer in the world today.

The fulminating shot of Johan Neeskins, strong, dynamic midfield star of Ajax and the Netherlands.

Another time, another place . . . but 'Gigi' Riva could well be expressing the frustration of all Italy at their team's failure to qualify for the second series of group matches in the World Cup.

Inaugurated in season 1972-73, the trophy was first won by Ajax at the expense of Rangers. In 1973-74, Ajax, still reeling from the loss of Cruyff, lost the first leg most undeservedly in Milan to a piece of opportunism by Chiarugi. In Amsterdam, however, they played as brilliantly as they ever had with Cruyff and simply overwhelmed an ineptly defensive Milan.

San Siro, Milan, 9 January 1974
Milan (0) 1   Ajax (0) 0
Chiarugi
Milan: Vecchi; Sabadini, Maldera III, Anquilletti, Schnellinger, Turone, Turini (Bergmaschi), Benetti, Rivera, Biasiolo, Chiarugi.
Ajax: Stuy; Suurbier, Blankenburg, Hulshoff, Krol, Haan, Neeskens, Mulder, Rep, G. Muhren, Keizer.

Amsterdam, 16 January 1974
Ajax (2) 6   Milan (0) 0
Mulder, Keizer,
Neeskens, Rep,
G. Muhren (pen.),
Haan
Ajax: Stuy; Suurbier, Hulshoff, Blankenburg, Kroll, Haan, Neeskens, G. Muhren, Rep, Mulder, Keizer.
Milan: Vecchi; Anquilletti, Maldera III, Dolci, Schnellinger, Turone, Sabadini, Benetti, Rivera, Biasiolo, Chiarugi.

FOOTBALL DAY

A strangely aberrational, quite fatuous, initiative by FIFA gave us Football Day, and the sublime non-event of a dreary match between Europe and South America. Predictably, no one cared, least of all the Europeans, and the crowd was suitably and insultingly small. For what it mattered, South America 'won' on penalties, 3-2.

Barcelona, 31 October 1973
Europe (0) 0   South America (0) 0
Europe: Viktor (Czechoslovakia) [Iribar (Spain)]; Krivokuca (Yugoslavia) [Dimitriu (Greece)], Sol (Spain) [Kapsis (Greece)], Pavlovic (Yugoslavia), Facchetti (Italy); Asensi (Spain), Bene (Hungary) [Pirri (Spain)], Keita (Mali) [Nene (Portugal)], Cruyff (Netherlands), [Oldermatt (Switzerland)], Eusebio (Portugal) [Edstroem (Sweden)] Jara (Austria).
South America: Santoro (Argentina) [Carnevali (Argentina)]; Wolf (Argentina) [Arrua (Paraguay)], Pereira (Brazil), Chumpitaz (Peru), Marco Antonio (Brazil); Esparrago (Uruguay), Brindisi (Argentina) [Lasso (Ecuador)]; Paulo César (Brazil) [Caszely (Chile)], Cubillas (Peru) [Borga (Mexico)], Sotil (Peru) [Ortiz (Colombia)], Rivelino (Brazil).

CHAPTER SIX

British International Championship 1973-74

Two factors gave the International Championship particular piquancy this time: the dismissal of Sir Alf Ramsey when he had already announced the England players, and Scotland's qualification for the World Cup. In the event, Scotland rose above their previous performances to beat England soundly at Hampden for the first time for 10 years, and share the Championship. Northern Ireland, again obliged to play all their matches away from Belfast, won at Hampden and did well at Wembley. Wales scored their first goal in the Championship for four years and it was enough to give them victory in their final match, against Ireland. Appropriately, the scorer, on his home ground of Wrexham, was David Smallman, who had played such a large part in the Third Division club's splendid Cup run.

The sacking of Ramsey was so clumsily and belatedly done that it ran the risk of making him look a martyr. In fact, he could not reasonably claim much sympathy, having scarcely attempted to conceal his scorn for FA councillors during his years of office. This was legitimate enough if he realised, which perhaps he did, that only continued success could guarantee him his job. In the event, he was lucky to last as long as he did, the mere statistics of his record concealing the fact that England had consistently lost most of the matches that counted since their World Cup success of 1966. And if he was the first manager to win England the World Cup, he was equally the first to fail to qualify England for the finals.

Ramsey's place was taken by the Coventry City general manager, Joe Mercer, as a stopgap. Mercer called Weller and Nish into the party and won his first two matches. Poor goalkeeping by Phillips helped England off the hook in Cardiff, where Mercer's decision to play without a centre-forward seemed likely to prove fatal till Phillips made a hash of Weller's low cross and Bowles scored.

Against Northern Ireland, the same fault was sadly evident, till Mercer brought on Frank Worthington for his first cap. Worthington, who replaced Bowles, was an instant success. With an initial pass and eventual header, he made the only goal for Weller. Next day, Bowles walked out of the England team's hotel and was eventually discovered at the White City dog track. The pity of it was that after three chances, he had still failed to show the marvellous form displayed with Queen's Park Rangers.

Scotland, meanwhile, lost 1–0, ineptly, at home to a tightly organised Northern Ireland team, in which 19-year-old Chris McGrath of Spurs showed marvellous temperament during the series. Cassidy scored the only goal, taking a return from Hamilton and squeezing the ball out of the grasp of Harvey. The Scots then sensibly moved Dalglish back into midfield, but they were far from majestic when they beat Northern Ireland 2–0. A series of headers by Morgan, Ford, and finally Dalglish brought the first goal. The second, two minutes from half-time, was a penalty by Jardine after Page brought down Dalglish on the edge of the box. Wales themselves should certainly have had a penalty rather than an indirect free-kick when Buchan fouled Reece. There might have been another Scottish goal from Ford, late on, but Sprake saved superbly.

For their third match, the Scots had to do without Tommy Hutchison, badly gashed in a tackle with Roberts, against Wales. Willie Ormond boldly gambled with two established right wingers, the impish Johnstone and the hard-shooting Lorimer. The gamble paid. As early as the fifth minute, Worthington lost the ball to Bremner who put through Lorimer on the left. Shilton could only block the shot; Jordan, a great success, directed it back towards the goal where Pejic, desperately, diverted it home.

England's defence, in which Norman Hunter was unwisely chosen for centre-half after McFarland had been badly hurt against Ireland, was porous. By the time Watson came on for the second half, there were two goals in Scotland's bag. The second was also touched with fortune, for when Lorimer, receiving from Johnstone, and Dalglish moved the ball swiftly from the right, it took a deflection by Todd to beat Shilton. The goalkeeper made wonderful saves from Hay in the first half, and Jordan and Dalglish in the second. By the end, the match, so to speak, had grown to fit the score.

Scotland's fire and commitment were too much for an England team whose four-man midfield was inferior to Scotland's three, galvanised as it was by Bremner. The replacement of Worthington by Macdonald midway through the second half seemed particularly inept, when what was needed was so clearly an extra striker, not a substitute one. It was, however, manifestly Scotland's day, and their crowd gave them sustained, delirious support.

Cardiff, 11 May, 1974

Wales (0) 0 England (1) 2

Wales: Phillips (Chelsea); P. Roberts (Portsmouth) [Cartwright (Coventry City)], J. Roberts (Birmingham City), D. Roberts (Oxford City), Thomas (Derby County); Mahoney (Stoke City), Villars (Cardiff City), Yorath (Leeds United); James (Burnley), Davies (Portsmouth) [Smallman (Wrexham)], Reece (Cardiff City).

England: Shilton (Leicester City); Nish (Derby County), McFarland (Derby County), Todd (Derby County), Pejic (Stoke City); Hughes (Liverpool), Bell (Manchester City), Weller (Leicester City); Keegan (Liverpool), Channon (Southampton), Bowles (Queen's Park Rangers).
Scorers: Bowles, Keegan for England.

Glasgow, 11 May, 1974
    Northern Ireland (1) 1   Scotland (0) 0
Northern Ireland: Jennings (Spurs); Rice (Arsenal), O'Kane (Nottingham Forest), Hunter (Ipswich Town), Nelson (Arsenal); Hamilton (Ipswich Town) [Jackson (Nottingham Forest)], Cassidy (Newcastle United), Clements (Everton); McIlroy (Manchester United), Morgan (Aston Villa), McGrath (Spurs).
Scotland: Harvey (Leeds United); Jardine (Rangers), Holton (Manchester United), Buchan (Manchester United), Donachie (Manchester City [J. Smith (Newcastle United)]; Bremner (Leeds United), Hay (Celtic), Hutchison (Coventry City); W. Morgan (Manchester United), Law (Manchester City) [Jordan (Leeds United)], Dalglish (Celtic).
Scorer: Cassidy for Northern Ireland.

Glasgow, 14 May, 1974
    Scotland (2) 2   Wales (0) 0
Scotland: Harvey (Leeds United); Jardine (Ragers), Holton (Manchester United), Buchan (Manchester United) [McGrain (Celtic)], Hay (Celtic); Bremner (Leeds United), Dalglish (Celtic), Hutchison (Coventry City) [J. Smith (Newcastle United)]; Johnstone (Celtic), Jordan (Leeds United), Ford (Hearts).
Wales: Sprake (Cardiff City); Thomas (Derby County), J. Roberts (Birmingham City), D. Roberts (Oxford United), Page (Birmingham City); Mahoney (Stoke City), Villars (Cardiff City), Yorath (Leeds United); James (Burnley), Reece (Cardiff City) [Smallman (Wrexham)], Cartwright (Coventry City).
Scorers: Dalglish, Jardine (pen) for Scotland.

Wembley, 15 May, 1974
    England (0) 1   Northern Ireland (0) 0
England: Shilton (Leicester City); Nish (Derby County), McFarland (Derby County) [Hunter (Leeds United)], Pejic (Stoke City); Bell (Manchester City), Hughes (Liverpool), Weller (Leicester City); Keegan (Liverpool), Channon (Southampton), Bowles (Queen's Park Rangers) [Worthington (Leicester City)].
Northern Ireland: Jennings (Spurs); Rice (Arsenal), O'Kane (Nottingham Forest), Hunter (Ipswich Town), Nelson (Arsenal) [Jackson (Nottingham Forest)]; Hamilton (Ipswich Town) [O'Neill (Nottingham Forest)], Cassidy (Newcastle United), Clements (Everton); McIlroy (Manchester United), Morgan (Aston Villa), McGrath (Spurs).
Scorer: Weller for England.

Hampden Park, 18 May, 1974
    Scotland (2) 2   England (0) 0
Scotland: Harvey (Leeds United); Jardine (Rangers), Holton (Manchester United), Blackley (Hibernian), McGrain (Celtic); Bremner (Leeds United), Dalglish (Celtic), Hay (Celtic); Johnstone (Celtic), Lorimer (Leeds United), Jordan (Leeds United).

England: Shilton (Leicester City); Nish (Derby County), Todd (Derby County), Hunter (Leeds United) [Watson (Sunderland)], Pejic (Stoke City); Hughes (Liverpool), Peters (Spurs), Weller (Leicester City), Bell (Manchester City); Worthington (Leicester City) [Macdonald (Newcastle United)], Channon (Southampton).
Scorers: Pejic (o.g.), Todd (o.g.) for Scotland.

Wrexham, 18 May, 1974
 Wales (1) 1   Northern Ireland (0) 0
Wales: Sprake (Leeds United); Thomas (Derby County), Roberts (Birmingham City), Yorath (Leeds United), Page (Birmingham City); Phillips (Cardiff City), Mahoney (Stoke City), Cartwright (Coventry City); James (Burnley), Smallman (Wrexham) [Villars (Cardiff City)], Reece (Cardiff City).
Northern Ireland: Jennings (Spurs); Rice (Arsenal), O'Kane (Nottingham Forest), Hunter (Ipswich Town), Dowd (Glentoran); Hamilton (Ipswich Town) [Jackson (Nottingham Forest)], Clements (Everton), Cassidy (Newcastle United), O'Neill (Nottingham Forest), McGrath (Spurs), McIlroy (Manchester United).
Scorer: Smallman for Wales.

Final Table

	P	W	D	L	F	A	Pts
Scotland	3	2	0	1	4	1	4
England	3	2	0	1	3	2	4
N. Ireland	3	1	0	2	1	2	2
Wales	3	1	0	2	1	4	2

Scotland and England share the Championship.

CHAPTER SEVEN

Friendly Internationals Against Foreign Teams

A programme necessarily restricted during the season by the demands of the World Cup nevertheless had many intriguing aspects: Italy's first win in England after 39 years, seven misleading English goals against Austria, a fine performance by Scotland against West Germany, Argentina's first appearance at Wembley since the notorious quarter-final of 1966, an East European tour by England.

The Austrian friendly, coming as it did a few weeks before the 'real' thing against Poland, was a snare and a delusion. Austria, after briefly exposing flaws in England's defence in the opening phases, were inept beyond belief, their defence a joke, their goalkeeper a liability. Channon, Clarke, and Currie ran riot, Bell was able to forget about defence; and

England were able to forget the ominous and more significant fact that Chivers, at centre-forward, had done so little in a 7-0 win.

After the Italian defeat, Sir Alf Ramsey confessed absolute bewilderment, again invoking the threadbare vindication of hard luck. In fact the Italians, playing well within their powers, had steadily snuffed out the unimaginative, predictable England attack, though they did need several glorious saves by the superb Zoff – especially from Currie – to do it. They would probably have won more easily had Riva not been so preoccupied with stopping Madeley overlapping. As it was, the only goal came three minutes from the end. Bobby Moore, recalled to the team, was too cumbersome to prevent Giorgio Chinaglia breaking past him from a standing start, on the right-hand goalline. Chinaglia shot hard and right-footed, Shilton couldn't hold the ball, and Capello was there to put it in. For Chinaglia, at 19 a free-transfer player with Swansea, it was an ecstatic return. The Italian defence, very strong in the air, easily gobbled up the traditional high crosses to which England's forwards were gradually reduced.

In Glasgow, on the same night, Scotland were giving a vastly more imaginative performance, beating away at a West German defence that was very lucky to concede only one goal. Had Bremner not had his penalty saved by Maier a quarter-hour from time, after Beckenbauer pushed over Dalglish, the Scots must have won. At that point they were leading by an early goal headed by the inevitable Holton, but Hoeness's header on the far post to Flohe's long, left-wing cross equalised nine minutes from the end. Though Germany lacked Müller, they did have Netzer, and the Scots had every right to feel pleased with such a lively, well balanced display.

The return game, in Frankfurt the following March, was altogether less pleasing. Ormond was obliged to field a skeletal team, getting minimal cooperation from several clubs; notably Leeds. This team was quite outplayed by the West Germans, who should have won by many more goals. Franz Beckenbauer was in magisterial form, the absence of both Overath and Netzer being insignificant. The Germans' passing and combination was often a delight. When Jardine tripped Wimmer, Breitner scored the penalty. When Stanton lost the ball to Hoeness, he put through Grabowski to score the second. Hutchison dribbled elegantly but to a fault, Bremner was badly missed, and Allan made three fine saves. Kenny Dalglish's late goal, when he may have been offside as he exploited Hutchison's pass, turned the score into a fiasco.

In Lisbon, England's rain soaked match with Portugal, a week later, was watched by only 10,000 or so; an occasion with no significance now that both teams had been eliminated. England had to put out as *ersatz* a team as Scotland, a crop of injuries (all genuine?) and a clash with an FA Cup semi-final replay forcing Ramsey to cap six new players.

Of these, Parkes made a wonderful save from Octavio in the second half, all the better for the fact that he was 'cold', Dave Watson settled well at centre-half after three early errors, and Trevor Brooking was a force in midfield. The pick of the team, however, were Colin Todd, amnestied at last after his controversial suspension from international football, Mike Channon, and Martin Peters, who had his best international for many moons.

Portugal seemed none too interested, but they brightened for a while in the second half when they brought on three substitutes. England might have won the game in the early stages, when Channon headed against the post and Macdonald's immediate shot was blocked on the line. So there were no goals.

Argentina came to Wembley for the first time since the notorious World Cup quarter-final of 1966, when Ramsey, much put upon, said he hoped England's next opponents wouldn't 'act as animals'. The Argentinians insisted on having their own referee, who gave them a very late, much disputed but probably just penalty, from which Kempes (the man who'd been brought down) equalised. Certainly it wasn't a just result. After early stutterings and evident inferiority in technique to an Argentinian team in which the long-haired Ayala was brilliantly elusive, England took a strong grip on the game. Immediately before half-time, the excellent Dave Watson came upfield, found Bell with an excellent pass, and Bell shrewdly sent through Channon, who rounded Carnevali to score. The goal was followed by a clash between Hughes, whose impetuousness displeased Joe Mercer, and two Argentinians, one of whom, Glaria, knocked him down and blacked his eye.

Glaria was diplomatically removed for the second half, which soon saw England score again, Bell hitting the bar after a corner and Worthington sweeping the ball home. But Hughes, getting in the way of Shilton as Ayala centred, gave Kempes an easy goal. Argentina recovered morale and finally equalised. Deplorable fouls by Perfumo – the one survivor of 1966 – and a general cynicism in defence suggested that the leopards had scarcely changed their spots. England's midfield played well, but the lack of a real wing-half was manifest when Argentina attacked; rarely but insidiously.

England's summer tour began with a splendid display against East Germany in Leipzig. Had they not struck the post and bar four times – twice through Channon, once through Brooking and Bell – they must have won impressively. As it was, the vigorous, fit, but somewhat predictable East Germans came back into the game, and actually took the lead after half time when Lindsay missed his header and the forceful Streich scored. In the very next minute, Mike Channon struck a glorious low shot from a free kick into the right-hand corner, and England were deservedly level.

The East Germans risked an all-attacking midfield and were caught unawares when England dictated the game from the first, playing football of very high quality. Dobson, the ideal wing-halfback, gave the midfield new quality, Bell was tirelessly excellent, Brooking most fluent.

Frank Worthington was formidable both in the air and on the ground, while Clemence, replacing Shilton in goal, made half a dozen fine saves.

Another fine performance came in Sofia against Bulgaria, beaten 1–0 by Frank Worthington's beautifully struck left-foot goal, two minutes from half-time, when Keegan flicked him through. There could have been, once more, several other goals – notably for Dobson, Worthington, and Channon, who again hit the post. The same post was hit by a remarkable free-kick from Bonev in the first half, but the Bulgarians, short of morale, fell away badly, were whistled by their crowd, and were finally dominated by this powerful and elegant England team. The defence, in which Watson and Lindsay were outstanding, was formidable; the midfield again excellent; the three-man attack splendidly confident, fast, and incisive. Scotland, that same evening, lost disappointingly in Belgium.

England completed their tour with a meritorious 2–2 draw in Belgrade against Yugoslavia. On arrival, Kevin Keegan was brutally dragged off and beaten by the airport police, in a ludicrously unnecessary incident which I witnessed. Quite innocently, he was sitting on the wrong side of the luggage conveyor belt. Alec Lindsay, on the same side, walked on the rollers, was brusquely ordered out by an official, and went. The policeman then pushed the unfortunate Keegan in the back, pushed him again, and, after a short altercation, the Liverpool man was grabbed round the neck by another, enormous policeman and arrested. Ironically, it would probably never have happened but for a bizarre error in the party's itinerary, the travel agency having made no allowance for the change in the hour. Thus England arrived early, with no Yugoslav officials to meet them.

It must have been a particular satisfaction for Keegan, who recovered quickly from his maltreatment, to head England's late equaliser. They had gone ahead quickly when Maric flapped feebly at Keegan's inswinging corner, Brooking's shot was blocked, and Channon drove the ball in. Yugoslavia equalised when Colin Bell, who otherwise played superbly, headed straight to one of their players, the lively Surjak crossed from the right, and Petkovic headed in. Oblak put Yugoslavia ahead seven minutes into the second half with an astonishing 30-yard left-foot shot to the far top corner, but England, despite the sapping pitch and clammy heat, recovered for Hughes, Lindsay, and Macdonald cleverly to make Keegan's equaliser.

Wembley, 26 September, 1973
England (3) 7   Austria (0) 0

England: Shilton (Leicester City); Madeley (Leeds United), Hughes (Liverpool); Bell (Manchester City), McFarland (Derby County), Hunter (Leeds United); Currie (Sheffield United), Channon (Southampton), Chivers (Spurs), Clarke (Leeds United), Peters (Spurs).

Austria: Koncilia; Sara, Krieger, Schmidradner, Eigenstiller (Kriess), Hattenberger (Gombasch), Starek, Ettmayer, Kreuz, Krankl, Jara.

Scorers: Channon 2, Clarke 2, Chivers, Currie, Bell for England.

Wembley, 14 November, 1973
  England (0) 0   Italy (0) 1
England: Shilton (Leicester City); Madeley (Leeds United), Hughes (Liverpool); Bell (Manchester City), McFarland (Derby County), Moore (West Ham United); Currie (Sheffield United), Channon (Southampton), Osgood (Chelsea), Clarke (Leeds United) [Hector (Derby County)], Peters (Spurs).
Italy: Zoff; Spinosi, Facchetti, Bellugi, Burgnich, Benetti, Causio, Capello, Rivera, Chinaglia, Riva.
Scorer: Capello for Italy.

Hampden Park, 14 November, 1973
  Scotland (1) 1   West Germany (0) 1
Scotland: Harvey (Leeds United); Jardine (Rangers), McGrain (Celtic); Bremner (Leeds United), Holton (Manchester United), Connelly (Celtic); Morgan (Manchester United), Smith (Newcastle United) [Lorimer (Leeds United)], Law (Manchester City) [Jordan (Leeds United)], Dalglish (Celtic), Hutchison (Coventry City).
West Germany: Kleff (Maier); Vogts, Hottges, Beckenbauer, Weber, Wimmer (Cullmann), Grabowski, Hoeness, Held (Flohe), Netzer, Kremers, E. (Heynckes).
Scorers: Holton for Scotland; Hoeness for West Germany.

Frankfurt, 27 March, 1974
  West Germany (2) 2   Scotland (0) 1
West Germany: Maier; Vogts, Schwarzenbeck, Beckenbauer, Breitner, Hoeness, Wimmer, Cullmann, Grabowski, Müller, Herzog.
Scotland: Allan (Dundee); Jardine (Rangers), Stanton (Hibernian), Buchan (Manchester United), Schaedler (Hibernian), Hay (Celtic), Burns (Birmingham City) [Robinson (Dundee)], Hutchison (Coventry City), Morgan (Manchester United), Law (Manchester City) [Ford (Hearts)], Dalglish (Celtic).
Scorers: Breitner (pen), Grabowski for West Germany; Dalglish for Scotland.

Lisbon, 3 April, 1974
  Portugal (0) 0   England (0) 0
Portugal: Damas; Rebelo, Humberto Coelho, José Mendes, Artur; Octavio, Arnaldo (Vitor Pereira), Toni (Walter); Jordão, Vitor Baptista (Romeu), Jacinto Joao.
England: Parkes (Queen's Park Rangers); Nish (Derby County), Pejic (Stoke City); Dobson (Burnley), Watson (Sunderland), Todd (Derby County); Bowles (Queen's Park Rangers), Channon (Southampton), Macdonald (Newcastle United) [Ball (Arsenal)], Brooking (West Ham United), Peters (Spurs).

Wembley, 22 May, 1974
  England (1) 2   Argentina (0) 2

73

England: Shilton (Leicester City); Hughes (Liverpool), Watson (Sunderland), Todd (Derby County), Lindsay (Liverpool); Bell (Manchester City), Weller (Leicester City), Brooking (West Ham United); Keegan (Liverpool), Channon (Southampton), Worthington (Leicester City).
Argentina: Carnevali; Glaria (Wolff), Perfumo, Bargas, Sa; Telch, Brindisi (Houseman), Balbuena; Kempes, Squeo, Ayala.
Scorers: Channon, Worthington for England; Kempes 2 (1 pen) for Argentina.

Leipzig, 29 May, 1974
East Germany (0) 1　　　　　　England (0) 1
East Germany: Croy; Fritsche, Bransch, Weise, Watzlich, Pommerenke, Irmscher, Loewe, Streich, Sparwasser, Vogel (Hoffmann).
England: Clemence (Liverpool); Hughes (Liverpool), Lindsay (Liverpool), Todd (Derby County), Watson (Sunderland), Dobson (Burnley), Keegan (Liverpool), Channon (Southampton), Worthington (Leicester City), Bell (Manchester City), Brooking (West Ham United).
Scorers: Streich for East Germany; Channon for England.

Sofia, 1 June, 1974
Bulgaria (0) 0　　　　　　England (1) 1
Bulgaria: Goranov; Zafirov, Jetchev, Velitchkov, Kolev, Penev, Volnov, Bonev, Michailov, Borisov, Denev.
England: Clemence (Liverpool); Hughes (Liverpool), Todd (Derby County), Watson (Sunderland), Lindsay (Liverpool), Dobson (Burnley) Brooking (West Ham United), Bell (Manchester City), Keegan (Liverpool), Channon (Southampton), Worthing (Leicester City).
Scorer: Worthington for England.

Bruges, 1 June, 1974
Belgium (1) 2　　　　　　Scotland (1) 1
Belgium: Piot; Van Binst, Dewalque, Vanderdaele, Martens, Van Moer, Verheyen, Van Himst, Van Herp, Lambert, Henrotay.
Scotland: Harvey (Leeds United); Jardine (Rangers), McQueen (Leeds United), Blackley (Hibernian), McGrain (Celtic), Bremner (Leeds United), Dalglish (Celtic) [Hutchison (Coventry City)], Hay (Celtic), Johnstone (Celtic) [Morgan (Manchester United)], Jordan (Leeds United), Lorimer (Leeds United).
Scorers: Henrotay, Lambert (pen) for Belgium; Johnstone for Scotland.

Belgrade, 5 June, 1974
Yugoslavia (1) 2　　　　　　England (1) 2
Yugoslavia: Maric; Buljan, Krivokuca, Muzinic (Bajevic), Katalinski, Bogicevic, Petkovic, Oblak, Surjak, Acimovic, Dzajic.
England: Clemence (Liverpool); Hughes (Liverpool), Todd (Derby County), Watson (Sunderland), Lindsay (Liverpool), Dobson (Burnley), Bell (Manchester City), Brooking (West Ham United), Keegan (Liverpool), Channon (Southampton), Worthington (Leicester City) [Macdonald (Newcastle United)].
Scorers: Petkovic, Oblak for Yugoslavia; Channon, Keegan for England.

Oslo, 6 June, 1974
Norway (1) 1   Scotland (0) 2
Norway: Karisen; Wormdal, Birklund, Kordal, Grondalan, Berg (Thunsbeg), Johansen, Kvia, Skuseth, Lund, Hestad.
Scotland: Allen (Dundee); Jardine (Rangers), McGrain (Celtic), Holton (Manchester United), Buchan (Manchester United), Bremner (Leeds United), Hay (Celtic), Johnstone (Celtic), Lorimer (Leeds United), Jordan (Leeds United), Hutchison (Coventry City) [Dalglish] (Celtic),.
Scorers: Lund for Norway; Jordan, Dalglish for Scotland.

CHAPTER EIGHT

Friendly Internationals Between Foreign Teams

1973

5 August:	Russia (0) 0	Sweden (0) 0
29 August:	Finland (1) 1 *Suhanen*	Sweden (0) 2 *Torstensson, Svensson*
8 September:	France (1) 3 *Jouve, Berdoll, Chiesa*	Greece (0) 1 *Aidiniou*
20 September:	Mexico (1) 1	Chile (0) 2
29 September:	Italy (0) 2 *Anastasi, Riva*	Sweden (0) 0
10 October:	Netherlands (1) 1 *De Jong*	Poland (1) 1 *Deyna*
10 October:	West Germany (2) 4 *Müller 2, Weber, E. Kremers*	Austria (0) 0
13 October:	Denmark (1) 2 *Jensen, Stendahl*	Hungary (2) 2 *Fazekas 2*
13 October:	West Germany (0) 2 *Müller 2 (1 pen)*	France (0) 1 *Trésor*
16 October:	Mexico (1) 2	USA (0) 0
17 October:	East Germany (1) 1 *Streich*	Russia (0) 0
17 October:	Turkey (0) 0	Spain (0) 0
21 October:	Eire (1) 1 *Dennehy*	Poland (0) 0
31 October:	Algeria (1) 2	Morocco (0) 1
4 November:	Luxembourg (1) 2 *Monacelli, Langers*	Norway (1) 1 *Sunde*
13 November:	Israel (2) 3	USA (1) 1
15 November:	Israel (2) 2	USA (0) 0
21 November:	Hungary (0) 0	East Germany (1) 1 *Loewe*

21 November:	France (2) 3 *Bereta, P. Revelli, Papi*	Denmark (0) 0
24 November:	West Germany (2) 2 *Heynckes 2*	Spain (0) 1 *Claramunt*

1974

23 February:	Spain (1) 1 *Asensi*	West Germany (0) 0
26 February:	Italy (0) 0	West Germany (0) 0
1–14 March:	AFRICAN NATIONS CUP (in Egypt)	

Group A
Egypt 2, Uganda 1
Zambia 1, Ivory Coast 0
Egypt 3, Zambia 1
Uganda 2, Ivory Coast 2
Egypt 2, Ivory Coast 0
Zambia 1, Uganda 0

Group B
Congo 2, Mauritius 0
Zaire 2, Guinea 1
Congo 2, Zaire 1
Guinea 2, Mauritius 1
Congo 1, Guinea 1
Zaire 4, Mauritius 1

Semi-Finals (9 March)
Zaire 3, Egypt 2
Zambia 4, Congo 2 (after extra time)

Final (Cairo, 12 March)
Zaire (0) 2   Zambia (1) 2
Ndaye 2   *Kaushi, Syniangwe*
after extra time

Replay (14 March)
Zaire (1) 2   Zambia (0) 0
Ndaye 2

13 March:	East Germany (0) 1 *Streich*	Belgium (0) 0
23 March:	France (0) 1 *Bereta*	Romania (0) 0
24 March:	Haiti (0) 0	Uruguay (0) 1 *Morena*
26 March:	Haiti (0) 0	Uruguay (0) 0
27 March:	Netherlands (1) 1 *Krol*	Austria (1) 1 *Krankl*
27 March:	East Germany (1) 1 *Streich*	Czechoslovakia (0) 0
31 March:	Hungary (2) 3 *Fazekas 2, Bene*	Bulgaria (0) 1 *Bonev*
1 April:	Brazil (0) 1 *Jairzinho*	Mexico (0) 1 *Manzo*
7 April:	Brazil (0) 1 *Marinho*	Czechoslovakia (0) 0
7 April:	Morocco (0) 2 *Ahmed, Haddad*	Algeria (0) 0
14 April:	Bulgaria (0) 0	Czechoslovakia 1
17 April:	Brazil 2 *Edu, Leivinha*	Romania (0) 0

17 April:	West Germany (1) 5 *Wimmer, Holzenbein,* *Kremers, Müller 2*	Hungary (0) 0
17 April:	Belgium (1) 1 *Van Moer*	Poland (0) 1 *Deyna*
17 April:	Yugoslavia (0) 0	Russia (0) 1 *Kipiani*
20 April:	Indonesia (1) 2 *Kadir, Asmara*	Uruguay (0) 1 *Silva*
21 April:	Brazil (2) 4 *Paulo Cesar, Rivelino,* *Vorbe (o.g.), Edu*	Haiti (0) 0
21 April:	Indonesia 2	Uruguay 3
22 April:	Argentina (0) 2 *Houseman, Kempes*	Romania (1) 1 *Kun*
25 April:	Australia (0) 0 Haiti (0) 0	Uruguay (0) 0 Chile (0) 1 *Garcia*
27 April:	Haiti (0) 0	Chile (0) 0
27 April:	Australia (0) 2 *Baartz, Ollerton*	Uruguay (0) 0
28 April:	Brazil (0) 0	Greece (0) 0
28 April:	Czechoslovakia (2) 3 *Pivarnik, Byscovsky,* *Panenka*	France (2) 3 *Chiesa, Lacombe 2*
1 May:	Brazil (0) 0	Austria (0) 0
1 May:	West Germany (0) 2 *Heynckes 2*	Sweden (0) 0
1 May:	Switzerland (0) 0	Belgium (0) 1 *Vanherp*
5 May:	Brazil 2 *Leivinha, Rivelino*	Eire 1 *Mancini*
8 May:	Uruguay (2) 2 *Morena 2*	Eire (0) 0
8 May:	Bulgaria 5 *Bonev, Zetchev, Denev,* *Penev, Grigorov*	Turkey 1
12 May:	Chile (0) 1 *Valdez*	Eire (1) 2 *Hand, Conway*
12 May:	Brazil (2) 2 *Marinho (pen), Rivelino*	Paraguay (0) 0
12 May:	Algeria (1) 1 *Gamouh*	Tunisia (0) 2 *Malki (pen), Temime*
15 May:	Poland (1) 2 *Lato, Jacobczak*	Greece (0) 0
18 May:	France (0) 0	Argentina (1) 1 *Kempes*
20 May:	Russia 0	Czechoslovakia 1

21 May: Indonesia 1   Australia 2
23 May: East Germany 1   Norway 0
26 May: Netherlands 4   Argentina 1

CHAPTER NINE

English and Scottish Cups 1973-74

FA CUP 1974

A tournament full of the customary and classical surprises ended with Liverpool's second victory at Wembley; an extremely one-sided conquest of Newcastle United, who went to pieces in the second half.

Newcastle, in fact, were most lucky to be at Wembley – where they'd never previously lost a final – at all. In the quarter-finals, they were 3-1 down to Nottingham Forest, a lively Second Division team, at St James' Park when their stopper, Howard, was sent off, at which some 300 supporters invaded the pitch, attacked some of the Forest players, and had the match temporarily abandoned. When it was resumed, a petrified Forest lost 4-3. The bewildered Football Association, with no precedents to deal with such situations, ordered the game to be replayed on a neutral ground. This time it was a draw, but Newcastle won at the third attempt and did well to beat Burnley in the semi-final. Malcom Macdonald's opportunism was their trump card, but they had struggled horribly to beat the amateurs, Hendon, and Scunthorpe, both of whom held them to a draw on Tyneside.

Among the surprises was Aston Villa's conquest of Arsenal in a replay in Birmingham, Bristol City's splendid win at Elland Road in another replay against Leeds before going down at home to Liverpool. Shankly's team played admirably in the semi-final against Leicester at Old Trafford, deserved to thrash them, had to replay, and did the job then.

The final was moderately even till the last minutes of the first half, when the electric Steve Heighway and Kevin Keegan began to use the flanks. In the second half, Keegan scored twice, each time from centres by the veteran right-back Tommy Smith, and John Toshack headed Steve Heighway through for an excellent second goal. It was an embarrassingly convincing victory.

Final Wembley, 4 May, 1974

Liverpool (0) 3   Newcastle United (0) 0
Keegan 2, Heighway

Liverpool: Clemence; T. Smith, Lawler; Cormack, Thompson, Hughes; Keegan, Callaghan, Toshack, Hall, Heighway.
Newcastle United: McFaul; Clark, Kennedy; McDermott, Howard, Moncur; J. Smith (Gibb), Tudor, Macdonald, Cassidy, Hibbitt.

FOOTBALL LEAGUE CUP 1974

Though producing, as always, a suspiciously high quota of 'surprises', the League Cup at least gave us a decent final this time. Wolves and

78

Manchester City provided much excitement and many turns of fortune. City's inept marking in midfield allowed Mike Bailey to exert a great influence on the game, but the only goal of the first half, just before the interval, came when Hibbitt's miskick deceived MacRae. An uncharacteristic error by Munro, who allowed the ball to skim his head, gave Bell the equaliser, but later when Bell beat the excellent Pierce it was to shoot against the bar. So Richards, two minutes later and six from time, was able to hit the winning goal, when Sunderland's cross came to him off the unlucky Marsh. Richards, with an injured groin, had previously made little contribution to the game.

In the earlier rounds, Plymouth Argyle of the Third Division had eliminated both promoted First Division teams, Burnley and Queen's Park Rangers, on their own grounds, and given Manchester City a fine run for their money, while Tranmere had beaten Arsenal at Highbury.

Final Wembley, 2 March, 1974
Wolverhampton Wanderers (1) 2   Manchester City (0) 1
Hibbitt, Richards   *Bell*
Wolves: Pierce; Palmer, Munro, McAlle, Parkin; Bailey, Hibbitt, Sunderland; Richards, Dougan, Wagstaffe (Powell).
Manchester City: MacRae; Pardoe, Doyle, Booth, Donachie; Towers, Bell, Marsh; Summerbee, Lee, Law.

SCOTTISH CUP 1974
Celtic won this, too, beating Dundee in the semi-final 1–0; Dundee United, more easily, in the final. United had done well to defeat Hearts on a replay, in their semi-final, but they were no match for Celtic at Hampden. Gray, a lively young forward, gave Celtic's defence some trouble, but goals from Murray (21 minutes) and Hood (25) settled the game. Dalglish ran irresistibly from deep positions and Deans added a third in the last seconds.

Final Hampden Park, 5 May, 1974
Celtic (2) 3   Dundee United (0) 0
Murray, Hood, Deans
Celtic: Connaghan; McGrain, Brogan; Murray, McNeill, McCluskey; Johnstone, Hood, Deans, Hay, Dalglish.
Dundee United: Davie; Gardner, Kopel; Copland, D. Smith, W. Smith; Payne, Fleming, Houston, Knox, Gray.

SCOTTISH LEAGUE CUP 1973
A brave and bold effort by Dundee prevented Celtic from bringing off the treble. But only 27,974 fans saw Dundee's notable conquest in the final; a victory in which the former Celtic attacking fullback Tommy Gemmell, had the satisfaction of taking part.

Final Hampden Park, 15 December, 1973
Dundee (0) 1   Celtic (0) 0
Wallace

Dundee: Allan; R. Wilson, Gemmell; Ford, Stewart, Phillip; Duncan, Robinson, Wallace, J. Scott, Lambie.
Celtic: Hunter; McGrain, Brogan; McCluskey, McNeill, Murray; Hood (Johnstone), Hay (Connelly), Wilson, Callaghan, Dalglish.

CHAPTER TEN

English and Scottish Leagues 1973-74

FOOTBALL LEAGUE

A fascinating season, though blemished by the mild imbecility of three-up, three-down at the very moment when the gap between the divisions is at its widest in the history of the competition — and is certain to grow still wider.

The power crisis, the three-day week, the forbidding of floodlight football, though partly compensated for by Sunday football, made an already difficult economic situation harder still. But there was much drama. Leeds United won the Championship far less easily than they for long threatened. Their first defeat came only on 23 February, at Stoke, when they were threatening to equal Burnley's famous 30-match unbeaten record. But for some time before they had lived dangerously, Birmingham and Queen's Park Rangers being among the clubs that threatened to beat them.

Leeds, at their best, early in the season, were a splendid team, but a dreadful plethora of injuries to such as Giles, Bates, and Eddie Gray eventually undermined them. A fine late burst by Liverpool almost allowed them to keep the Championship. Then they faltered, finally losing a midweek match at home to Arsenal; and Leeds, deservedly, had done it. Billy Bremner had a magnificent season for them, both as propulsive force in midfield and as opportunist, while David Harvey was a superb goalkeeper.

At the other end, Norwich fell out of the First Division, though appointing John Bond in place of Ron Saunders; who set up some sort of unenviable record by being sacked in turn by Manchester City, after only four months. Manchester United accompanied them, despite vivid improvement in the last few weeks; the first time the team had slid out of the First Division since the war. George Best came back, plump and much slower, glimmered briefly, then retired again; this time, it seemed, definitively, a wretched loss to football. Southampton went down too; rather unluckily.

Derby County, champions of 1972, lost their manager Brian Clough in torrid circumstances when he resigned and failed to exert leverage from outside, his place going to Dave Mackay. Chelsea's manager Dave Sexton had a struggle for power that ended in his transferring two stars, Alan Hudson to Stoke and Peter Osgood to Southampton. Queen's Park Rangers and Burnley, the promoted teams, thoroughly distinguished themselves, with Rangers' Stan Bowles being perhaps the most exciting forward in the division.

Jackie Charlton had an astonishing first season with Middlesbrough, who virtually strolled away with the Second Division; from which, alas, his brother Bobby's Preston were relegated. Luton and Carlisle struggled up with 'Borough; far and faint in the rear.

Bristol Rovers flagged after setting a killing pace in the Third Division, owing much, perhaps too much, to the finishing of Warboys and Bannister. Peterborough United, under Noel Cantwell, came through forcefully in Division Four.

First Division

	P	W	D	L	F	A	Pts
Leeds Utd.	42	24	14	4	66	31	62
Liverpool	42	22	13	7	52	31	57
Derby County	42	17	14	11	52	42	48
Ipswich Town	42	18	11	13	67	58	47
Stoke City	42	15	16	11	54	42	46
Burnley	42	16	14	12	56	53	46
Everton	42	16	12	14	50	48	44
Queen's Park Rangers	42	13	17	12	56	52	43
Leicester City	42	13	16	13	51	41	42
Arsenal	42	14	14	14	49	51	42
Tottenham Hotspurs	42	14	14	14	45	50	42
Wolverhampton W.	42	13	15	14	49	49	41
Sheffield United	42	14	12	16	44	49	40
Manchester City	42	14	12	16	39	46	40
Newcastle United	42	13	12	17	49	48	38
Coventry City	42	14	10	18	43	54	38
Chelsea	42	12	13	17	56	60	37
West Ham United	42	11	15	16	55	60	37
Birmingham City	42	12	13	17	52	64	37
Southampton	42	11	14	17	47	68	36
Manchester United	42	10	12	20	38	48	32
Norwich City	42	7	15	20	37	62	29

Second Division

	P	W	D	L	F	A	Pts
Middlesbrough	42	27	11	4	77	30	65
Luton Town	42	19	12	11	64	51	50
Carlisle United	42	20	9	13	61	48	49
Orient	42	15	18	9	55	42	48
Blackpool	42	17	13	12	57	40	47
Sunderland	42	19	9	14	58	44	47
Nottingham Forest	42	15	15	12	57	43	45
West Bromwich Albion	42	14	16	12	48	45	44

Hull City	42	13	17	12	46	47	43
Notts County	42	15	13	14	55	60	43
Bolton Wanderers	42	15	12	15	44	40	42
Millwall	42	14	14	14	51	51	42
Fulham	42	16	10	16	39	43	42
Aston Villa	42	13	15	14	48	45	41
Portsmouth	42	14	12	16	45	62	40
Bristol City	42	14	10	18	47	54	38
Cardiff City	42	10	16	16	49	62	36
Oxford United	42	10	16	16	35	46	36
Sheffield Wednesday	42	12	11	19	51	63	35
Crystal Palace	42	11	12	19	43	56	34
Preston North End	42	9	14	19	40	62	31
Swindon Town	42	7	11	24	36	72	25

One point deducted from Preston for including unregistered player.

Third Division

	P	W	D	L	F	A	Pts
Oldham Athletic	46	25	12	9	83	47	62
Bristol Rovers	46	22	17	7	65	33	61
York City	46	21	19	6	67	38	61
Wrexham	46	22	12	12	63	43	56
Chesterfield	46	21	14	11	55	42	56
Grimsby Town	46	18	15	13	67	50	51
Watford	46	19	12	15	64	56	50
Aldershot	46	19	11	16	65	52	49
Halifax Town	46	14	21	11	48	51	49
Huddersfield Town	46	17	13	16	56	55	47
Bournemouth	46	16	15	15	54	58	47
Southend United	46	16	14	16	62	62	46
Blackburn Rovers	46	18	10	18	62	64	46
Charlton Athletic	46	19	8	19	66	73	46
Walsall	46	16	13	17	57	48	45
Tranmere Rovers	46	15	15	16	50	44	45
Plymouth Argyle	46	17	10	19	59	54	44
Hereford United	46	14	15	17	53	57	43
Brighton	46	16	11	19	52	58	43
Port Vale	46	14	14	18	52	58	42
Cambridge United	46	13	9	24	48	81	35
Shrewsbury Town	46	10	11	25	41	62	31
Southport	46	6	16	24	35	82	28
Rochdale	46	2	17	27	38	94	21

Fourth Division

	P	W	D	L	F	A	Pts
Peterborough	46	27	11	8	75	38	65
Gillingham	46	25	12	9	90	49	62
Colchester United	46	24	12	10	73	36	60

Bury	46	24	11	11	81	49	59
Northampton Town	46	20	13	13	63	48	53
Reading	46	16	19	11	58	37	51
Chester	46	17	15	14	54	55	49
Bradford City	46	17	14	15	58	52	48
Newport County	46	16	14	16	56	65	45
Exeter City	45	18	8	19	58	55	44
Hartlepool	46	16	12	18	48	47	44
Lincoln City	46	16	12	18	63	67	44
Barnsley	46	17	10	19	58	64	44
Swansea City	46	16	11	19	45	46	43
Rotherham United	46	15	13	18	56	58	43
Torquay United	46	13	17	16	52	57	43
Mansfield Town	46	13	17	16	62	69	43
Scunthorpe United	45	14	12	19	47	64	42
Brentford	46	12	16	18	48	50	40
Darlington	46	13	13	20	40	62	39
Crewe Alexandra	46	14	10	22	43	71	38
Doncaster Rovers	46	12	11	23	47	80	35
Workington	46	11	13	22	43	74	35
Stockport County	46	7	20	19	44	69	34

Scunthorpe v Exeter was not played. Scunthorpe were awarded two points. One point deducted from Newport for including unregistered player.

SCOTTISH LEAGUE

Another win, their ninth in succession, for Celtic, whose preeminance is a continuing tribute to the excellent of Jock Stein. Nevertheless, they can scarcely be said this time to have run away with the title. Rangers and Hibernian, traditional foes, chased them hard to the end, while they sometimes had trouble with such 'lesser' teams as Arbroath, whose striker, Sellers, had a wonderfully prolific season.

Though Kenny Dalglish continued to grow in stature as a midfield player, Deans to knock in the goals, and Jimmy Johnstone returned vivaciously to form late in the season, it was not the mighty Celtic of a few years ago. Murray, from Aberdeen, succeeded Bobby Murdoch, who went south on a free transfer to play splendidly for Middlesbrough. Hay settled down after seeming on the point of going to Spurs, and Connelly had the bad luck to break an ankle playing against Basle in the European Cup. There were also problems in goal.

Rangers, with new faces such as Fyfe and Young in attack, had a satisfactory season – so far as that is consonant with finishing behind Celtic – while Aberdeen did surprisingly well considering they had sold several stars.

First Division

	P	W	D	L	F	A	Pts
Celtic	34	23	7	4	82	27	53
Hibernian	34	20	9	5	75	42	49
Rangers	34	21	6	7	67	34	48
Aberdeen	34	13	16	5	46	26	42
Dundee	34	16	7	11	67	48	39
Hearts	34	14	10	10	54	43	38
Ayr United	34	15	8	11	44	40	38
Dundee United	34	15	7	12	55	51	37
Motherwell	34	14	7	13	45	40	35
Dumbarton	34	11	7	16	43	58	29
Partick Thistle	34	9	10	15	33	46	28
St Johnstone	34	9	10	15	41	60	28
Arbroath	34	10	7	17	52	69	27
Morton	34	8	10	16	37	49	26
Clyde	34	8	9	17	29	65	25
Dunfermline	34	8	8	18	43	65	24
East Fife	34	9	6	19	26	51	24
Falkirk	34	4	14	16	33	58	22

Second Division

	P	W	D	L	F	A	Pts
Airdrieonians	36	28	4	4	102	25	60
Kilmarnock	36	26	6	4	96	44	58
Hamilton Academicals	36	24	7	5	68	38	55
Queen of the South	36	20	7	9	73	41	47
Raith Rovers	36	18	9	9	69	48	45
Berwick Rangers	36	16	13	7	53	35	45
Stirling Albion	36	17	6	13	76	50	40
Montrose	36	15	7	14	71	64	37
Stranraer	36	14	8	14	64	70	36
Clydebank	36	13	8	15	47	48	34
St Mirren	36	12	10	14	62	66	34
Alloa Athletic	36	15	4	17	47	58	34
Cowdenbeath	36	11	9	16	59	85	31
Queen's Park	36	12	4	20	42	64	28
Stenhousemuir	36	11	5	20	44	59	27
East Stirling	36	9	5	22	47	73	23
Albion Rovers	36	7	6	23	38	72	20
Forfar Athletic	36	5	6	25	42	94	16
Brechin City	36	5	4	27	33	99	14

CHAPTER ELEVEN

Fifty World Stars

AYALA, Ruben (Atlético Madrid and Argentina). Exciting, goal-scoring centre-forward – especially from the left – who had much to do with Argentina's qualification for the 1974 World Cup. Ayala, whose shoulder-length hair and drooping moustache make him a doubly unusual figure on the football field, made his name with San Lorenzo de Almagro, but after finishing the qualifying series with Argentina in September 1973, he went straight to Atlético Madrid, where his manager, Juan Carlos Lorenzo, had preceded him. He made an instant impact both in the Spanish League and the European Cup, though he was one of those sent off in the disgraceful display against Celtic in the 1974 semi-final. A fine ball player, he is very fast, with an excellent left foot.

BARGAS, Hugo (Nantes and Argentina). This extremely skilled and resourceful stopper came to Nantes from Chacarita Juniors half-way through season 1972–73, when he was 26. He made an immediate impression with his calm efficiency, resolute tackling, and, though he is not tall, his excellence in the air. Moreover, his use of the ball is exceptional. In France, they think him more of a European than a classically South American player, though he has the Argentinian mastery of technique. Played a large part in Argentina's qualification for the 1974 World Cup.

BECKENBAUER, Franz (Bayern Munich and West Germany). A world star since the 1966 World Cup, Beckenbauer has developed since then from a splendid attacking right-half into a player of huge versatility perhaps seen at his best as West Germany's 'attacking sweeper' in the 1972 European Championship. Graceful, absolutely relaxed, a fine ball player with a strong right-foot shot and surprising acceleration, he took over from Uwe Seeler as German football's 'ego ideal'. He was a schoolboy and youth international, winning his first cap for West Germany in 1965, when 20. But for his shoulder injury in Mexico City against Italy, in the semi-final, his country would surely have reached the World Cup final of 1970. But he was still there in 1974.

BENE, Ferenc (Ujpest and Hungary). This little striker, whose ball control, pace, and shot make him so consistent a scorer at all levels, made a name in the Olympic Tournament of 1964 in Tokyo. There, as 19-year-old centre-forward of the victorious Hungarian team, he scored a spectacular goal in the final having previously put six past Morocco. Two years later he had a splendid World Cup in England, playing largely on the right wing and scoring a vital goal against Brazil, while in 1972 he helped Hungary to reach the European Championship semi-finals. Meanwhile he had done much to make Ujpest the most successful club in Hungary and a power in the European Cup.

BENETTI, Romeo (Milan and Italy). Tough, blond, skilful inside-forward or halfback who has been used as both by Milan and Italy. Born in Albaredo d'Adige, province of Verona, on 20 October 1945, Benetti took a suprisingly long time to affirm himself. He began with nearby Bolzano in Division D, went on to Siena, Taranto, and Palmermo, and played his initial First Division match only when Juventus signed him in 1968. He stayed there a season, moving on to Sampdoria. But he did so well in Genoa that Milan snapped him up, and he has been with them since 1970. First capped as substitute against Mexico at Genoa in September 1971.

BONEV, Christo (Lokomotiv Plovdiv and Bulgaria). Outstandingly the best Bulgarian footballer of his generation, Bonev might be described as a classical inside-forward in the 'W' formation manner. He is certainly far more than just a midfield player, though his stamina is immense, his distribution excellent, and he seems always to be on hand to help defenders in possession. Besides this, he has a turn of speed, splendid control, and an excellent shot. He has seldom shown these to better advantage than when scoring twice against Portugal in Lisbon in October 1973 to make sure Bulgaria would qualify for the 1974 World Cup. He had already played in 1970 in Mexico.

BREITNER, Paul (Bayern Munich and West Germany). A tall, attacking fullback with a mop of curly hair, and unusual political views. (He's a Maoist, whose ambition it is finally to retire at about 30 and open a school for handicapped children). Born 3 September 1951, Breitner played for the youth team of his native Freilassing, a small Bavarian town near the Austrian border; went to Bayern on leaving school, and at 20 became West Germany's outstanding left-back in the European Championship team of 1972, winning a medal in the final. He recovered quickly from a wretched injury at Atvidaberg in a European Cup match early in season 1973–74 when his shin was broken by a missile thrown from the crowd.

BREMNER, Billy (Leeds United and Scotland). Little, red-haired, attacking right-half of huge dynamism, under whose captaincy both Leeds United and Scotland have flourished. His contribution to the Scots' qualification for the 1974 World Cup was perhaps decisive. Born in Stirling, he went to Leeds as a 15-year-old outside-right, modulating into an inside-right, then a halfback famous for his combination with Johnny Giles. Has been intimately involved with all Leeds' successes in Championship, FA Cup, and Fairs Cup, not to mention their other forays in Europe. A hard tackler with a right-foot shot remarkable in so small a man, he is a splendid opportunist. First capped for Scotland against England at Hampden Park in 1966.

BRINDISI, Miguel (Huracan and Argentina). Inside-right or attacking right-half who was the chief propelling force of the Argentinian team that qualified for the 1974 World Cup. Brindisi was soon afterwards given the Medal of National Reconstruction by President Perón to show appreciation for his refusal to leave Argentina for the lusher pastures of Europe – unlike most of his colleagues. Brindisi, an excellent penalty taker, was leading scorer in the 1972 Championship, scoring 22 goals for Huracan and making many of the 17 scored by his colleague Avallay, who finished second. By the time the 1974 World Cup finals arrived, he'd already been an international for five years, having first been capped as a teenager.

CASZELY, Carlos (Levante and Chile). Striking inside-forward who emerged as an international star, in a flurry of goals, early in 1973. It was then that his consistent scoring helped his club, Colo Colo of Santiago, to reach the final of the South American Cup, where they gave Independiente a hard run. He then helped Chile to overcome Peru and qualify for the World Cup finals. Shortly after this, Caszely left for Spain to play for the Second Division club, Levante – a racehorse pulling a plough – and perhaps it was not surprising that he did **not** easily settle down. A very accomplished ball player, he is small, lean, very quick, and never intimidated. 'When I come on to the field,' he says, 'I refuse to think about defeat.'

CHANNON, Mike (Southampton and England). Striking inside-right who uses the whole right flank with skill, pace, and success. He has an admirable right-foot shot, and is strong in the air besides. A countryman, from Wiltshire, who keeps horses, Channon has been with Southampton since he left school. His first cap for England came, very successfully, against Yugoslavia at Wembley in October 1972, after which he was mysteriously dropped. But he forced his way back into the side even if his controversial exclusion in Katowice was thought by some to have cost England that vital World Cup game against Poland. A few days later, in Moscow, Channon established himself as a major international forward.

CLODOALDO (Santos and Brazil). Coloured midfield right half who made his debut for Brazil against England in Rio at the age of 19 in June 1969. A year later, in Mexico, strong, skilled, and quick, he emerged as the best linking halfback Brazil had had since Zito, getting better with every game; even if his slip did give Italy their goal in the final. An orphan, born 25 September 1949 in the North of Brazil at Aracaju, he came to the city of Santos when he was five and at first played football up against the wall of the Santos stadium.

CRUYFF, Johan (Barcelona and Netherlands). The living evidence that one man *can* make a team. When this tall, slim centre-forward left Ajax for Barcelona early in season 1973–74, the Dutch team were promptly knocked out of a European Cup they'd held for three years – while the Spanish team dazzlingly took wing. Born in Amsterdam on

25 April 1947 near the Ajax ground, to a mother who once worked there as a cleaner, Cruyff became European Footballer of the Year for the second time in December 1973. He first played for Ajax as a 19-year-old in season 1965–66, and had barely made his debut for the Netherlands when he was suspended for a year after an incident in a match against Czechoslovakia. His relationship with the national team has always been brittle, but he helped the Dutch qualify for the 1974 World Cup. No player did more to make Ajax's 'total football' possible. With his glorious control, technique, flair, and finishing power, Cruyff made the whole team tick, now in the centre, now burning up his favourite left wing. He scored both goals in Ajax's second successful European Cup final in 1972, against Inter in Rotterdam, and was a major cause of their renewed success in 1972–73, though much troubled by ankle injuries. After reported dissension with this fellow Ajax players, he demanded to leave Ajax for Barcelona – at a king's ransom. And in the Autumn of 1973, after initial resistance by both club and Dutch Federation, he had his way. His instant adaptation and immediate triumph in Spanish football is not the least remarkable feature of an extraordinary career.

DEYNA, Kazimierz (Legia Warsaw and Poland). Injury to Lubanski, the dominant figure in Polish football, allowed the then 26-year-old Deyna to come into his own in the autumn of 1973 with splendid midfield performances against Wales in Katowice and England at Wembley. A forward of great skill, fine balance, and a splendid vision of play, he also has a strong right-foot shot with which he has scored many goals for club and country. Though he plays for a Warsaw team, he was born near the port of Gdansk at Starogard Gdanski. He scored both Poland's goals in the 1972 Olympic final.

DUMITRACHE, Florean (Dynamo Bucharest and Romania). At once golden boy and prodigal son of Romanian football, the fair-haired Dumitrache is a centre-forward of outstanding gifts but unpredictable temperament. In the Mexico World Cup of 1970, still only 21, he was outstanding, even though his team manager criticised him for excessive individualism. Having assured Romania's qualification with a magnificent goal against Portugal, he proceeded to score a penalty against the Czechs and a skilful goal against Brazil. A player who, though not fragile, prevails through technical excellence, pace, and flair.

DZAJIC, Dragan (Red Star and Yugoslavia). An outside-left who has been the outstanding Yugoslav player of his generation, above all perhaps in the 1968 European Championship final. Then, aged 22, he scored the only goal of the semi-final against England in Florence, and the Yugoslav goal in Rome against Italy in the drawn final. He was deservedly picked to play for the Rest of the World the following season. A strong, clever, elusive, incisive player with absolute mastery of the ball and a fine left foot, he was born in Belgrade on 30 May, 1946 and made his debut for Red Star on 4 June 1963. Club and country missed him badly when he first broke a leg then went into the army in 1973. In December, he was given leave to play for Yugoslavia in their vital World Cup game in Greece and played a substantial part in their win, though it was his first professional game since the previous March. He himself says Josip Skoblar was his mentor.

EDSTROEM, Ralf (PSV Eindhoven and Sweden). At 6ft 6in, and proportionately dangerous in the air, Edstroem became a European figure when he scored three goals against Russia in August 1972. He went on, with his Atvidaberg club mate Sandberg, to help the club win the Championship, each of them scoring 16 goals. The summer of 1973 saw him transferred to the Netherlands, but he continued to play for the Swedish World Cup team, helping them qualify for Munich. PSV released him for the decisive play-off against Austria in Gelsenkirchen.

FIGUEROA, Elias (Internacional Porto Alegre and Chile). Reckoned the best centre-half in Brazil, Figueroa did much to help Chile qualify, at the expense of Peru and Russia, for the 1974 World Cup. It was his second, for he had represented Chile in England in 1966. In 1970, to their mutual chagrin, he was refused permission by Peñarol of Montevideo, for whom he was then playing, to represent Chile in the eliminators . . . against Uruguay. From Montevideo he passed on to Internacional, where his combination of power and elegance, great skill, and clever positional play at once made him a hero. Still in his mid-20s, he was then able to make up for the disappointments of 1970 by returning to the successful Chilean World Cup team.

GADOCHA, Robert (Legia Warsaw and Poland). Strong, fast left-winger who played a large part in getting Poland to the 1974 World Cup finals. Aged 27 at the time, he gave two fine performances against England, including an excellent, if somewhat over-physical, one in Katowice. Born in Cracow. He had a good understanding with Deyna both in the Legia and Polish teams, while he, too, won a gold medal in the Olympic football tournament of 1972. An excellent left-foot shot.

HAAN, Arie (Ajax and Netherlands). Right flank midfield player who came on as substitute in the European Cup final of 1971 and proceeded to score Ajax's second goal against Panathinaikos. Born 16 November 1948, he joined Ajax as a schoolboy and worked his way up through all the junior teams. Naturally right footed, a mobile, intelligent, and enterprising player, he was a star of the 1972 and 1973 European Cup-winning teams and a member of the Dutch side that qualified for the 1974 World Cup. He has a teacher's diploma and speaks both French and English.

HEYNCKES, Jupp (Borussia Mönchengladbach and West Germany). Originally with Hanover 96, joining Borussia in 1970, Josef Heynckes has become an all-round striker. Born 9 May 1945, he made sporadic appearances for West Germany before winning a regular place in the 1972 European Championship side, helping to make two goals in the final against Russia. Since then he has been one of the few rivals to Gerd Müller as a leading goalscorer in the Bundesliga, getting both Borussia's goals when they won the second leg of the 1973 UEFA Cup final at home to Liverpool. A fast, strong, elusive, determined player who can beat a man or exploit the wall pass with equal adroitness.

HULSHOFF, Barry (Ajax and Netherlands). A strongly built, decisive centre-half, known for his ability to score unexpected goals as well as to prevent them. Born 30 September 1946. He played in all Ajax's European Cup finals; the losing one against Milan in 1969, then the three successful ones of 1971, 1972, and 1973. First capped for the Netherlands against East Germany on 10 October 1971, scoring a goal that proved decisive.

HUTCHISON, Tommy (Coventry City and Scotland). Willie Ormond, Scotland's team manager, had dismissed Hutchison's possibilities when he saw him playing as a youngster for Alloa. But in September 1973 it was to the long-legged Hutchison that Ormond turned, with splendid effect, in his attempt to beat Czechoslovakia and win Scotland a place in the World Cup finals. Hutchison made a debut remarkable in the tense circumstances, materially helping Scotland to win. Signed from Alloa by Blackpool, he displayed excellent form at Bloomfield Road which led to his transfer to Coventry and return to the First Division, when Blackpool were relegated. He has the classical winger's gifts; speed, marvellous control, the readiness and ability to beat defenders. Coventry have used him successfully as a deep-lying player starting his runs from midfield.

JAIRZINHO (Botafogo and Brazil). One of the most effective and exciting forwards of the 1970 World Cup. Jairzinho's immensely forceful, rapid play on the right wing gave Brazil's attack much of its threat. In the final, his unselfish running into the middle – an area he really prefers – made space for Carlos Alberto's deadly overlapping. 1974 was his third World Cup, since he was used in the 1966 tournament at outside-left. He began with Botafogo as a teenage centre-forward – Garrincha was on the right wing – was first capped during the 'Little World Cup' of 1964, and reverted to centre-forward on Brazil's European tour of 1973. Recovered impressively from a severe operation on his leg in 1967.

JARDINE, Sandy (Rangers and Scotland). An accomplished defender in the modern manner; one just as able to go forward with the ball as to destroy. Fast, versatile, and decisive. His lively overlapping was a major factor in Scotland's qualification for the 1974 World Cup. He played in the same position for Rangers when they won the Cup-

Winners' Cup of 1972, beating Moscow Dynamo at Barcelona. In 1967, when Rangers lost the final to Bayern Munich in Nuremberg, he was at right-half. He was first capped against Denmark in 1970-71, coming on as substitute.

JENNINGS, Pat (Tottenham Hotspur and Northern Ireland). Voted British Footballer of the Year in 1973, Jennings is one of the best goalkeepers in the game, with a huge kick, a vast pair of hands, great courage and agility. He could easily have been lost to the game as a youth. No professional club 'discovered' him in his native Newry, and for a time he was felling trees. Then he joined Newry Town, played for the Northern Ireland youth team in the 1963 European Youth Championship, was signed by Watford, and from there joined Spurs. Many times an Irish international, and surely the best since Elisha Scott, he has won FA and UEFA Cup medals with Tottenham.

KEIZER, Piet (Ajax and Netherlands). Tall, fair-haired left-winger who built a splendid understanding with Johan Cruyff. He's is a calmer, more introverted figure; his attitudes and career deeply affected by a severe head injury received in October 1963, when playing against DWS, which necessitated a cranial operation. Keizer, only 18 at the time, was out of football for more than a year, most of it spent in hospital. A forward of great poise and sophistication, an excellent finisher, he has won three European Cup winners medals with Ajax. Like Cruyff, his relationship with the national team has been somewhat stormy, but he helped them reach the 1974 World Cup finals.

KHURTSILAVA, Murta (Dynamo Tbilisi and Russia). This dark, balding, powerfully built Georgian is another stopper – or sweeper – with a penchant for scoring goals. He was Russia's best player, as well as their captain, in the 1972 European Championship final against West Germany in Brussels, having two shots of spectacular power. Born 5 January 1943, he played for Russia in the World Cup finals of 1966 and 1970. He combines strength with excellent positional sense and very sound technique.

KREISCHE, Hans-Jurgen (Dynamo Dresden and East Germany). The best East German player of his time, an inside-right who can play skilfully and creatively in midfield or go up to score goals. He was his League's leading scorer in season 1972–73. Alas, playing the decisive World Cup match against Romania in the autumn of 1973, he was badly injured in a clash with the massive goalkeeper Raducanu, and had to have a knee operation. East German Footballer of the Year for 1973, when he had a superb game against Juventus at Dresden in the European Cup, Dynamo winning 2-0.

KROL, Rudi (Ajax and Netherlands). Overlapping fullback *par excellence*, quite capable of attacking down the right, as well as down his own left flank. Born 24 March 1949, he went to Ajax in 1968 from

Rood Wit, succeeding Van Duivenbode at left-back and playing in the 1972 and 1973 European Cup finals, having missed the 1971 final through a broken leg. A leading member of the Dutch 1974 World Cup team.

KUNA, Ladislav (Spartak Trnava and Czechoslovakia). Tall, dark, strongly built midfield halfback of great creative ability and ball skills, not to mention a fine left foot with which he scores many goals. Even in his own country Kuna, who at 22 played in the 1970 Czech World Cup team, has been criticised for being slow. In fact, he makes his own time and space, using the ball superbly. His injury at Glasgow, which obliged him to go off, may have cost the Czechs their decisive 1973 World Cup tie against Scotland. Has won Championship medals and figured impressively in the European Cup with Trnava.

LUBANSKI, Wlodzimierz (Gornik and Poland). A greatly gifted inside-forward, versatile to a degree, and perhaps the finest Polish player of all time. It was greatly to his country's tribute that they should qualify for the 1974 World Cup finals, beating Wales and drawing with England, after they had lost him through a knee injury after their victory over England at Katowice. Lubanski, born in 1947 in the town of Giliwice, is well used to long, inactive periods. An overdose of tablets prescribed for an illness cost him two years out of the game in his early 20s. First capped for Poland against Norway at the age of 16, he had won 63 other caps up to and including the Katowice game with England, when he scored a memorable, decisive goal. A player of majestic qualities, of subtlety, power, skill, and incision.

MARIC, Enver (Velez Mostar and Yugoslavia). Yugoslavia have produced a seemingly endless line of fine goalkeepers since Beara in the 1950s. The blond Maric is the latest; an acrobatic, spectacular player of great gifts. At 24, he played for Yugoslavia in Brazil in the Independence Cup. The following season, his brilliance enabled them to win in West Germany. A master of the 'impossible' save, he has, like many remarkable goalkeepers, his black days – but his best days are phenomenal. Few were better than his performance against Spain in Zagreb in the important World Cup qualifying match of October 1973, when he virtually saved his team.

MAZZOLA, Sandrino (Internazionale and Italy). A forward for the great occasion, never better than in the European Championship final of 1968 in Rome, against Yugoslavia, or against Brazil in the World Cup final of 1970. In both games he played as a linking inside-forward, making great use of his dribbling ability, his control, his quickness of thought and movement. In fact he played for years as a striker, both for Inter, with whom he won two European Cup and two Intercontinental medals, and Italy, for whom he made his debut against Brazil in Milan on 12 May 1963, scoring from a penalty. Son of Valentino

Mazzola, the captain of Italy who died in the 1949 Superga air crash, Sandro was born in Turin on 8 November 1942. He joined Inter as a boy, making his debut against Juventus when Inter put out their youth side as a protest – and lost 9–1, Mazzola getting the goal. That was in 1961. Two years later he was a regular first team player, as he has been ever since.

MÜLLER, Gerd (Bayern Munich and West Germany). The most extraordinary opportunist of his time, Müller had overhauled Uwe Seeler's German international goalscoring record, which took 12 years to establish, in half the time, scoring more than 60 goals in his first 50 internationals, and becoming European Footballer of the Year for 1972 in the process. With Seeler, he made up a formidable combination in the 1970 World Cup, when he was leading scorer with 10 goals. Müller's prowess, at a time of packed defences when goals are supposedly harder to get than they've ever been, defies analysis. A Bavarian, born 3 November 1945 at Noerdlingen, Müller was signed by Bayern only because their president overruled their then manager, the Yugoslav Cjaicowski! He had already been spurned by TSV Munich and Nuremberg, who must still be kicking themselves.

First capped for Germany in October 1966 against Turkey in Ankara, Müller, dark and thick thighed, has subsequently become a small miracle of sheer effectiveness, able to score with either foot or with neat flicks of the head, anywhere in and around the box. Among his many achievements were three out of West Germany's five goals in the semi-final and final of the 1972 European Championship in Belgium. But the number of his goals is legion.

MUHREN, Gerry (Ajax and Netherlands). Fine left side midfield player with an exceptional left foot, Muhren, whose brother Arnold is also an Ajax man, was born at Volendam on 2 February 1946, and left there for Amsterdam in 1968. He still, he says, feels a provincial, most at home in the fields. A dedicated, self-disciplined professional, he played in Ajax's three consecutive European Cup-winning teams, and in the Dutch team that reached the 1974 World Cup finals.

NEESKENS, Johan (Ajax and Netherlands). Strongly built midfield player of great power and drive, hard in the tackle but also vigorous in attack. Neeskens, born 15 September 1951, was already an Ajax star at 19. As good on the right as on the left, he is an all-round athlete who did well at baseball and basketball, and loves to play in goal in practice games. Went to Ajax from Haarlem; played fullback in their first European Cup success, against Panathinaikos, midfield in the next two. An established Dutch international.

NETZER, Günter (Real Madrid and Spain). Surprisingly transferred to Real Madrid from his original club Borussia Mönchengladbach in the summer of 1973, Netzer continued his alternating pattern of dazzling virtuosity and absence through injury. Perhaps the world's best linking inside-forward, with his flowing fair hair, his huge but precise feet – size 11 – his pace, his extraordinary passing, and his swerving free kicks. Missed the 1970 World Cup finals through injury, but played gloriously in the finals of the 1972 European Championship in Belgium. His right foot is perhaps unique in its virtuosity, whether hitting immaculate long passes, or 'banana' shots. Born 14 September 1944.

OBLAK, Brank (Hajduk and Yugoslavia). Born in 1947: A lineal successor to such fine Yugoslav halfbacks as Cjaicowski and Boskov, Oblak enjoyed a splendid year in 1974. Blond, sturdily built, combative and skilful, he did much to see Yugoslavia through their World Cup play-off against Spain in February and later helped Hajđuk, of Split, regain the Yugoslav championship. In the World Cup itself, he was one of the most industrious and effective midfield players, the possessor of a magnificent shot – as England and Clemence discovered when he unleashed an amazing left-footed diagonal drive into the far top corner from some 30 yards out.

ODERMATT, Karl (Basle and Switzerland). Born in 1943, this blond, well-built inside-forward made his debut for Switzerland 20 years later – in May 1963 – for a team beaten 8-1 at Basle, by England. More than eight years later, Odermatt would have two dazzling games against England, in Basle and at Wembley, in the European Championship, scoring Switzerland's goal in the second game. He has now won over 50 caps, and has refused many offers from abroad. He prefers to stay in Basle, where he began his footballing career with Concordia and owns two restaurants. The highest paid player in Switzerland, he is also noted for his midfield partnership with Kuhn in the international team, for which he made but one World Cup appearance, at outside-right in 1966 against West Germany.

PAULO CÉSAR (Flamengo and Brazil). A *reserve de luxe* for Brazil in the 1970 World Cup, when he made four appearances (two as a substitute) but did not play in the final. Then a deep-lying winger, somewhat after the manner of Zagalo but more spectacular, he was, by 1974, a key midfield player. In the meantime he had expensively left his original Rio club, Botafogo, for Flamengo. Born at Guanabara on 16 June 1949, Paulo César has all the exuberance, both on and off the field, of the black Brazilian footballer; a player fast, skilful, equally good now at beating a man or making a through pass to a colleague.

PELÉ (Santos and Brazil). Still, surely, the greatest player of all time, a veteran of four World Cups (a hero of two) whom every Brazilian wanted to play in a fifth. Born into a poor black family in Três Corações, in the state of Minas Gerais, he was only 17 when he scored three goals in the semi-final and two in the final of the 1958 World Cup. In Chile in 1962 injury put him out in Brazil's second match; in 1966 he was hurt again. But in 1970 he was transcendentally in form, heading one splendid goal and making two in the final in Mexico City. An astonishing compound of masterly control, dynamic force, intelligence, and acrobatics, Pelé has delighted and adorned the world game for over 15 years, retiring from international football in 1971, promising to retire altogether at the end of 1974.

PEREIRA, Luis (Palmeiras and Brazil). Tall, powerful, composed black centre-half who established himself in the national team on their European tour of 1973. When Pereira first went to Palmeiras in 1968 from Salvador de Bahia – he was born at Juazeiro, Bahia, on 21 June 1949 – he at first found the way barred by two centrehalves called Nelson and Baldochi. His debuts were unsuccessful, since he played on his weaker, left side, but in due course he established himself solidly on the right. Originally nicknamed 'Chevrolet' for his wild forays, he is now authoritative and economical and the nickname has fallen into disuse.

RIVA, Luigi (Cagliari and Italy). Had he been transferred to Juventus in the summer of 1973, it would have been for the equivalent of £1½ million – a fact that thoroughly disgusted him. Riva, orphaned in boyhood, has always been his own man; a player of character as well as unusual effectiveness, twice recovering magnificently from a broken leg – the left in 1967, the right in 1970. Born at Leggiuno in the north of Italy on 7 November 1944, he escaped the notice of those big clubs who were later to covet him, joining little Legnano, then transferring in 1963 to Cagliari, who were then in Serie B (Division 2). His superb opportunism, especially with the left foot, helped them in turn to promotion and the Championship. Italy first capped him in June 1965 against Hungary in Budapest, but didn't choose him for the 1966 World Cup. By the 1970 tournament he was an almost Messianic figure, and though he played well and scored in the quarter- and semifinals, he could scarcely hope to live up to expectations. Meanwhile, he had scored against Yugoslavia in the final of the 1968 European Championship in Rome. Six years later, he was still a major force in the Italian team that qualified for the 1974 World Cup.

RIVELINO, Roberto (Corinthians and Brazil). An outstanding forward in the 1970 World Cup, when he played broadly as a deep-lying left winger, making full use of his explosive left-foot shot, Rivelino can create goals too. Born in São Paulo on 19 January 1946, he is stockily built, favouring thick moustache and sideburns. First capped for Brazil against Mexico in 1968, when he also toured Europe with them and was seen as a midfield rival to Gerson. Zagalo neatly solved the problem in Mexico by putting Rivelino on the wing when Gerson played, but by the 1974 World Cup he was firmly established in midfield.

RIVERA, Gianni (Milan and Italy). An infant prodigy who has never betrayed his promise; an inside-forward of consummate technique and skill. Played his first Serie A game for Alessandria at the age of 15, joined Milan for the equivalent of £130,000 in 1960, at 16. Though his game is based on finesse and his remarkable passing is his main asset, he also possesses a formidable shot. The son of an Alessandria railwayman, born on 8 August 1943, he has won Championship, European Cup, Cup-Winners' Cup, and Intercontinental honours with Milan, besides playing in four World Cups and the Olympic tournament of 1960.

SHILTON, Peter (Leicester City and England). *Protégé* of and sucessor to Gordon Banks both in the Leicester and England teams. Shilton's splendid physique ridicules the fact that he once feared he wouldn't be big enough to make a professional goalkeeper. Leicester born and developed, it was perhaps appropriate that his representative debut, for an FA XI against Mexico in Guadalajara in 1969, should be made when Banks had to fly home. Won his first full cap at Wembley in 1971 against East Germany, but took time to settle down in the international side, fully establishing himself only in season 1972–73 with a long series of spectacular performances. A devoted trainer and perfectionist, he combines power and authority with enormous agility and a mastery of angles.

VAN HIMST, Paul (Anderlecht and Belgium). Another boy wonder who successfully matured, Van Himst has been the Belgian record holder of international caps since June 1972. At first a centre-forward, he has modulated over the years into a deeper-lying player, though his strength, control, and dash still bring him frequent goals. Born 2 October 1943, he joined Anderlecht as a boy, and was Belgian Footballer of the Year at 17 and 18. Renowned for his precociously cool temperament, he did much to help Belgium reach the 1970 World Cup finals in Mexico, but once there had one of his few disappointing passages.

WIMMER, Herbert, (Borussia Mönchengladbach and West Germany). Another West German star to make his name in the 1972 European Championship, when he capped his splendid form with a goal in the final against Russia in Brussels. A midfield player who generously avows his debt to Gunter Netzer, his colleague and mentor at Mönchengladbach, Wimmer is an exceptionally good right winger turned midfield man. In the semi-final against Belgium, in Antwerp, he did most of his best work on the right wing. A player of initiative and finesse, he was born 9 November 1944.

ZOFF, Dino (Juventus and Italy). Voted No. 2 in the European Footballer of the Year poll of 1973, Zoff gets better and better as he grows older. After helping Italy to win the 1968 European Championship in Rome he was reduced to Albertosi's reserve in the Mexico World Cup; but he proceeded to win back his place in the national team and to gain Championship medals with Juventus. Moreover, he went for the equivalent of more than 10 games with the Italian team without conceding a goal, thanks in no small measure to his own extraordinary acrobatics, skill, and bravery. Born in the North-East in Gorizia, at Mariano del Friuli, on 28 February 1942, he is another deeply committed professional, whose career has taken him from Udinese (Serie A debut 1961) to Mantova (1963), Naples (1967), then, at a vast fee, to Juventus in 1972. A bulwark of Italy's 1974 World Cup team.

CHAPTER TWELVE

World Cup History

The World Cup – or to give it its proper name, the Jules Rimet Trophy – was first played in Montevideo in 1930, but the principle of it was agreed by FIFA, the Federation of International Football Associations, at their Antwerp Congress of 1920. No man did more to further the idea than Jules Rimet, President of the French Football Federation, who was elected FIFA president in Antwerp, and it was thus that the attractive gold cup came to be given his name.

By 1930 the four British associations had withdrawn from FIFA, and it was not for another 20 years that British teams competed for a World Cup. Whether they would have won it between the wars is open to question. The fact that they did not undergo the test allowed the myth of British superiority in football to last a generation longer than it might otherwise have done. In 1934, just before the Italian version of the World Cup, Hugo Meisl, the brilliant manager of the Austrians, expressed the view that England, had they competed, would not even have reached the semi-final.

Four years later, England were invited to compete in the finals without qualifying, to take the place of Austria, overrun by the Nazis. But the invitation was refused.

In 1930 the competing countries were divided into four pools, the qualifiers going into the semi-finals, which were played on the normal cup-tie basis of 'sudden death'. In 1934 and 1938 the World Cup finals were played as a straight knock-out tournament, but in 1950 the four pools were reconstituted, with one main difference. The four winners went into a further pool to contest the title. It was thus only a matter of chance that the last match between Brazil and Uruguay, one of the most passionate and exciting in the history of the tournament, should also turn out to be the decider.

In 1958 and 1962 four groups were again constituted, but on these occasions, two teams from each went into the quarter-finals after which, as in 1930, the tournament followed the pattern of a straight knock-out contest. In 1966, when the World Cup was played in England, the same dubious formula applied. In 1970, goal 'difference' replaced goal average. In 1974, two further qualifying groups replaced the quarter and semi-finals, and produced the finalists.

WORLD CUP 1930 – Montevideo

Though the tournament was won by a very fine team – Uruguay had previously come to Europe to take the Olympic titles of 1924 and 1928 – it hardly drew a representative entry.

In the 1926 FIFA Congress Henri Delaunay, the French Federation's excellent secretary, expressed the view that football could no longer be confined to the Olympics: 'Many countries where professionalism is now recognised and organised cannot any longer be represented there by their best players.' In 1928, FIFA passed his resolution to hold a World Cup tournament at once. Only the Scandinavian block, and Estonia, voted against it! Odd that Sweden should eventually stage a World Cup and play in the final.

Uruguay got the competition for a variety of reasons: their Olympic success, their promise to pay every competing team's full expenses and to build a new stadium, and the fact that 1930 was their centenary.

But distance and the need to pay their players for a couple of months led to most of the big European powers withdrawing: Italy, Spain, Austria, Hungary, Germany, Switzerland, Czechoslovakia, Britain, of course, were out of FIFA. It was only thanks to King Carol himself that Romania entered; he not only picked the team but got time off for the players from their firms. France, Belgium, and Yugoslavia were the other three: lower middle-class European teams of that era. The stage was set for South American domination.

It was the United States who provided the surprise. Their team, made up largely of ex-British professionals jokingly christened 'the shot putters' by the French, because of their massive physique, showed great stamina and drive and actually qualified for the semi-finals. There, an excellent Argentinian eleven – beaten 2–1 in the replayed 1928 Olympic final by Uruguay – brushed them aside.

Uruguay, however, again proved irresistible. They prepared with the dedication one has come to expect over the past fifteen years from leading South American teams; but then, it was quite new. For two months, their players were 'in concentration' at an expensive hotel in the middle of the Prado park. When Mazzali, the brilliant goalkeeper, sneaked home late one night, he was thrown out of the team.

A splendid half-back line (playing in the old attacking centre-half-back style) was Uruguay's strength: José Andrade, Lorenzo Fernandez and Alvaro Gestido. José Nasazzi, the captain and right-back, was a great force, and in the forward-line Scarone and Petrone (now slightly over the hill) were superb technicians and dangerous goalscorers.

The tournament began on 13 July 1930. France surprised Argentina in an early match, losing only 1–0 after the crowd had invaded the pitch, when the referee blew for time six minutes early – then had to clear the pitch and restart the game. The Argentinians, who had the ruthless but effective Monti at centre-half, and the clever Stabile at centre-forward, duly won that group. Their match with Chile included a violent free-for-all, provoked by Monti.

Yugoslavia, beating Brazil 2–1 in their first match, also qualified.

The brave Americans won their pool without conceding a goal, while Uruguay, too, kept their defence intact, though Peru ran them very close. This was the first match to be played at the new Centenary Stadium, which still wasn't ready when the competition started.

In the semi-finals, Argentina and Uruguay both had 6–1 wins, against the USA and Yugoslavia respectively. In the final, Uruguay had to take the field without their new star, the young centre-forward Anselmo, who was unfit. But Argentina's new man, Stabile, first capped in their opening game, was able to lead their attack.

The match took place on 30 July 1930. Uruguay deservedly won, but their team seemed to lack the confidence it had shown in the two Olympic successes. An argument about the ball led to each side playing one half with a ball of native manufacture. Argentina survived an early goal by Pablo Dorado, the Uruguayan outside-right, to lead 2–1 at half-time, through Peucelle and Stabile. But a splendid dribble by Pedro Cea was crowned by the equaliser, after which Iriarte and Castro made it 4–2. Montevideo went wild – the following day was a national holiday.

POOL 1
France (3) 4, Mexico (0) 1
France: Thépot; Mattler, Capelle; Villaplane (capt), Pinel, Chantrel; Liberati, Delfour, Maschinot, Laurent, Langiller.
Mexico: Bonfiglio; R. Guitierrez (capt), M. Rosas; F. Rosas, Sanchez, Amezcua; Perez, Carreno, Mejia, Ruiz, Lopez.
Scorers: Laurent, Langiller, Maschinot (2) for France; Carreno for Mexico.

Argentina (0) 1, France (0) 0
Argentina: Bossio; Della Torre, Muttis; Suarez, Monti, J. Evaristo; Perinetti, Varallo, Ferreira, (capt), Cierra, M. Evaristo.
France: Thépot; Mattler, Capelle; Villaplane (capt), Pinel, Chantrel; Liberati, Delfour, Maschinot, Laurent, Langiller.
Scorer: Monti for Argentina.

Chile (1) 3, Mexico (0) 0
Chile: Cortes; Morales, Poirer; A. Torres, Saavedra, Helgueta; Ojeda, Subiabre, Villalobos, Vidal, Schneeberger (capt).
Mexico: Sota; R. Guitierrez (capt) M. Rosas; F. Rosas; Sanchez, Amezcua; Perez, Carreno, Ruiz, Gayon, Lopez.
Scorers: Vidal, Subiabre (2) for Chile.

Chile (0) 1, France (0) 0
Chile: Cortes; Ciaparro, Morales; A. Torres, Saavedra, C. Torres; Ojeda, Subiabre, Villalobos, Vidal, Schneeberger (capt).
France: Thepot; Mattler, Capella; Chantrel, Delmer, Villaplane (capt); Liberati, Delfour, Pinel, Veinantie, Langiller.
Scorer: Subiabre for Chile.

Argentina (3) 6, Mexico (0) 3
Argentina: Bossio; Della Torre, Paternoster; Cividini, Zumelzu (capt), Orlandini; Peucelle, Varallo, Stabile, Demeria, Spadaro.
Mexico: Bonfiglio; R. Guitierrez (capt), F. Guiterrez; M. Rosas, Sanchez, Rodriguez; F. Rosas, Lopez, Gayon, Carreno, Olivares.
Scorers: Stabile (3), Varallo (2), Zumelzu for Argentina; Lopez, F. Rosas, M. Rosas for Mexico.

Argentina (2) 3, Chile (1) 1
Argentina: Bossio; Della Torre, Paternoster: J. Evaristo, Monti, Orlandini; Peucelle, Varallo, Stabile, Ferreira, M. Evaristo.
Chile: Cortes; Ciaparro, Morales; A. Torres, Saavedra, C. Torres; Arellanc, Subiabre (capt), Villalobos, Vidal, Aguilera.
Scorers: Stabile (2), M. Evaristo for Argentina; Subiabre for Chile.

	P	W	D	L	F	A	Pts
Argentina	3	3	0	0	10	4	6
Chile	3	2	0	1	5	3	4
France	3	1	0	2	4	3	2
Mexico	3	0	0	3	4	13	0

POOL 2

Yugoslavia (2) 2, Brazil (0) 1
Yugoslavia: Yavocic; Ivkovic (capt), Milhailovic; Arsenievic, Stefanovic, Djokic; Tirnanic, Marianovic, Beck, Vujadinovic, Seculic.
Brazil: Montiero; Costa, Gervasoni; Fonseca, Santos, Guidicelli; Ribeiro, Braga, Patsuca, Neto, Pereira.
Scorers: Tirnanic. Beck for Yugoslavia; Neto for Brazil.

Yugoslavia (0) 4, Bolivia (0) 0
Yugoslavia: Yavocic; Ivkovic (capt), Milhailovic; Arsenievic, Stefanovic, Djokic; Tirnanic, Marianovic, Beck, Vujadinovic, Naidanovic.
Bolivia: Bermudez; Durandal, Civarria; Argote, Lara, Valderama; Gomez, Bustamante, Mendez (capt), Alborta, Fernandez.
Scorers: Beck (2), Marianovic, Vujadinovic for Yugoslavia.

Brazil (1) 4, Bolivia (0) 0
Brazil: Velloso; Gervasoni, Oliveira; Fonseca, Santos, Guidicelli; Meneses, Quieroz, Leite, Neto (capt), Visintainer.
Bolivia: Bermudez; Durandal, Civarria; Sainz, Lara, Valderama; Oritiz, Bustamante, Mendez (capt), Alborta, Fernandez.
Scorers: Visintainer (2), Neto (2) for Brazil.

	P	W	D	L	F	A	Pts
Yugoslavia	2	2	0	0	6	1	4
Brazil	2	1	0	1	5	2	2
Bolivia	2	0	0	2	0	8	0

POOL 3
Romania (1) 3, Peru (0) 1
Romania: Lapuseanu; Steiner, Burger; Rafinski, Vogl (capt), Eisembeisser; Covaci, Desu, Wetzer, Staucin, Barbu.
Peru: Valdivieso; De las Casas (capt), Soria; Galindo, Garcia, Valle; Flores, Villanueva, Denegri, Neira, Souza.
Scorers: Staucin (2), Barbu for Romania; Souza for Peru.

Uruguay (0) 1, Peru (0) 0
Uruguay: Ballesteros; Nasazzi (capt), Tejera; Andrade, Fernandez, Gestido; Urdinaran, Castro, Petrone, Cea, Iriarte.
Peru: Pardon; De las Casas, Maquilon (capt); Denegri, Galindo, Astengo; Lavalle, Flores, Villanueva, Neira, Souza.
Scorer: Castro for Uruguay.

Uruguay (4) 4, Romania (0) 0
Uruguay: Ballesteros; Nasazzi (capt), Mascheroni; Andrade, Fernandez, Gestido; Dorado, Scarone, Anselmo, Cea, Iriarte.
Romania: Lapuseanu; Burger, Tacu; Robe, Vogl (capt), Eisembeisser Covaci, Desu, Wetzer, Rafinski, Barbu.
Scorers: Dorado, Scarone, Anselmo, Cea for Uruguay.

	P	W	D	L	F	A	Pts
Uruguay	2	2	0	0	5	0	4
Romania	2	1	0	1	3	5	2
Peru	2	0	0	2	1	4	0

POOL 4
United States (2) 3, Belgium (0) 0
United States: Douglas; Wood, Moorhouse; Gallacher, Tracey, Brown; Gonsalvez, Florie (capt), Patenaude, Auld, McGhee.
Belgium: Badjou; Nouwens, Hoydonckx; Braine (capt), Hellemans, De Clercq; Diddens, Moeschal, Adams, Voorhoof, Versijp.
Scorers: McGhee (2), Patenaude for United States.

United States (2) 3, Paraguay (0) 0
United States: Douglas; Wood, Moorhouse; Gallacher, Tracey, Auld; Brown, Gonsalvez, Patenaude, Florie (capt), McGhee.
Paraguay: Denis; Olmedo, Miracca; Etcheverri, Diaz, Aguirre; Nessi, Romero, Dominguez, Gonzales, Carceres, Pena (capt).
Scorers: Patenaude (2), Florie for United States.

Paraguay (1) 1, Belgium (0) 0
Paraguay: P. Benitez; Olmedo, Flores; S. Benitez, Diaz, Garcete; Nessi, Romero, Gonzales, Carceres, Pena (capt).
Belgium: Badjou; De Deken, Hoydonckx; Braine (capt), Hellemans, Moeschal; Versijp, Delbeke, Adams, Nouwens, Diddens.
Scorer: Pena for Paraguay.

	P	W	D	L	F	A	Pts
United States	2	2	0	0	6	0	4
Paraguay	2	1	0	1	1	3	2
Belgium	2	0	0	2	0	4	0

SEMI-FINALS
Argentina (1) 6, United States (0) 1
Argentina: Botasso; Della Torre, Paternoster; J. Evaristo, Monti, Orlandini; Peucelle, Scopelli, Stabile, Ferreira (capt), M. Evaristo.
United States: Douglas; Wood, Moorhouse; Gallacher, Tracey, Auld; Brown, Gonsalvez, Patenaude, Florie (capt), McGhee.
Scorers: Monti; Scopelli, Stabile (2), Peucelle (2) for Argentina; Brown for United States.

Uruguay (3) 6, Yugoslavia (1) 1
Uruguay: Ballesteros; Nasazzi (capt), Mascheroni; Andrade, Fernandez, Gestido; Dorado, Scarone, Anselmo, Cea, Iriarte.
Yugoslavia: Yavocic; Ivkovic (capt), Milhailovic; Arsenievic, Stefanovic, Djokic; Tirnanic, Marianovic, Beck, Vujadinovic, Seculic.
Scorers: Cea (3), Anselmo (2), Iriarte for Uruguay; Seculic for Yugoslavia.

FINAL
Uruguay (1) 4, Argentina (2) 2
Uruguay: Ballesteros; Nasazzi (capt), Mascheroni; Andrade, Fernandez, Gestido; Dorado, Scarone, Castro, Cea, Iriarte.
Argentina: Botasso; Della Torre, Paternoster; J. Evaristo, Monti, Suarez; Peucelle, Varallo, Stabile, Ferreira (capt), M. Evaristo.
Scorers: Dorado, Cea, Iriarte, Castro for Uruguay; Peucelle, Stabile for Argentina.
Leading Scorer: Stabile (Argentina) 8.

WORLD CUP 1934 – Italy
The 1934 World Cup was altogether more representative and better attended, even though Uruguay, piqued by the way the European powers had snubbed them, stayed away and Argentina, fearful to lose more of their stars to Italian clubs, did not take part at full strength. Eight FIFA conferences were needed before Italy was chosen as the host. It had been realised that future World Cups could no longer be played in a single city nor could they be put on by any but a wealthy football federation. Italy, whose Fascist government looked on the powerful national team as a fine instrument of propaganda, eagerly put forward her claims. 'The ultimate purpose of the tournament', said General Vaccaro, a political appointment as president of the Italian Federation (FIGC), 'was to show that Fascist sport partakes of a great quality of the ideal'.

'Italy wanted to win', wrote the Belgian referee, John Langenus, 'it was natural. But they allowed it to be seen too clearly.'

Italy's remarkable team manager Vittorio Pozzo drew from the inflated, martial spirit of the times the authority and inspiration to build a fine team. It contained three Argentinians – Monti, Guaita, and Orsi – of Italian extraction, whose inclusion Pozzo justified on the grounds that they would have been eligible to fight for Italy in the first world war. 'If they were able to die for Italy, they could certainly play for Italy.'

His team pivoted round a strong, attacking centre-half in Monti; had a splendid goalkeeper in Combi; a powerful defence, and a clever attack in which Meazza, one of the most gifted Italian forwards of all time, figured as a 'striking' inside-right.

Austria, Italy's great rivals, were a tired team, and their equally gifted manager, Hugo Meisl, was convinced they could not win the tournament. Nevertheless in Seszta, their rugged left-back, Smistik, the roving centre-half, and Sindelar, the brilliantly elusive, ball-playing centre-forward, they had players of world class. The previous February Austria's *wunderteam* had beaten Italy 4–2, in Turin.

Hungary and Spain were the strongest 'outsiders'. Hungary had a fine centre-forward in Dr Georges Sarosi, later to become an attacking centre-half. Their technique was brilliant, but their finishing poor. Both they and the Czechs had beaten England 2–1 on England's May tour of Europe. Spain had their great veteran, Ricardo Zamora, in goal, and the excellent Quincoces at left-back. The Czechs had an equally famous and experienced goalkeeper in Planicka and a smooth, clever forward-line.

Then there was Germany, playing a rigid third-back game, captained by the blond and versatile Franz Szepan.

Italy kicked off in Rome with an easy win against the United States, fielding only three of their 1930 team. The surprise of the first round was France's excellent performance against Austria in Turin. As in 1930, the French rose to the occasion. They nearly scored in the first minute when Seszta's mistake was brilliantly retrieved by Peter Platzer, Austria's goalkeeper, and would probably have won had it not been for an injury to Nicolas, their captain and centre-forward, who had to go on the wing. He scored almost at once, but that was virtually his last contribution. Despite the handicap, France dominated the second half, and it was only a doubtful goal by Schall in extra-time – he looked offside – that really beat them. In later years, Schall himself said it was offside.

Germany, beating Belgium in Florence, looked uninspired; only Szepan, at centre-half, rose above mediocrity. The Czechs were another disappointment, needing two fine saves by Planicka to survive against the Romanians in Trieste; Egypt gave Hungary a fright at Naples, going down 4–2; and both South American challengers went out at once, Brazil to Spain, Argentina to Sweden.

In the second round in Florence, a marvellous exhibition of goal-keeping by Zamora enabled Spain to hold Italy to a 1–1 draw, but so roughly was he handled in a feebly refereed match that he could not take part in the replay. This was still more lamentably refereed, so much so that the Swiss official, Mercet, was suspended by his own Federation. Italy got through, thanks to a goal by Meazza, in a game that left a very nasty aftertaste.

The other match of the second round was that which opposed the classical Danubian rivals, Hungary and Austria. 'It was a brawl', said Meisl, 'not an exhibition of football'. He brought the lively Horwath into his attack, and Horwath rewarded him with a goal after only seven minutes. Markos, Hungary's outside-right, was sent off, soon after Sarosi (on a poor day) had got Hungary's only goal from a penalty. The Austrians just about deserved their 2–1 win. Germany beat a Swedish team reduced for most of the match to 10 men, and the Czechs beat Switzerland 3–2 in Turin in the most thrilling match of the round. Nejedly got the winning goal seven minutes from the end.

The semi-finals pitted Italy against Austria in Milan, Germany against Czechoslovakia in Rome. Italy deservedly got through, on a muddy ground thanks to a goal by Guaita after 18 minutes, showing amazing stamina after their hard replay against Spain only two days before. Austria did not have a shot until the 42nd minute.

The Czechs, surviving the trauma of a ridiculous equalising goal, when Planicka inexplicably let the ball sail over his head, were much too clever for the Germans and beat them 3–1. Thus, they would meet Italy in the final.

Meanwhile, in the third place match, a dejected Austrian team surprisingly went down 3–2 at Naples to the plodding Germans, who scored in 24 seconds.

Fortified by gargantuan presents of food, the Czechs gave Italy a tremendous run for their money in the final. Short passing cleverly, making use of Puc's thrust on the left wing, with Planicka at his best in goal, they had slightly the better of the first half. Twenty minutes from time, Puc took a corner, and when the ball came back to him, drove it past Combi for the first goal.

Czechoslovakia should have clinched it then. Sobotka missed a fine chance, Svoboda hit the post. Then Guaita and Schiavio switched, the Italian attack began to move better, and a freak goal by Orsi equalised. His curling, right-foot shot swerved in the air, and went over Planicka's hands. Next day in practice he tried 20 times, without success, to repeat it.

In the seventh minute of extra time, the injured Meazza got the ball on the wing, centred to Guaita, and the ball was moved on to Schiavio, who scored. Italy had done it, with little to spare. Neutral experts believed that home ground, frenzied support, the consequent intimidation of referees, may have been decisive. Nevertheless, theirs was a fine, splendidly fit and dedicated team.

FIRST ROUND
Italy (3) 7, United States (0) 1 (Rome)
Italy: Combi; Rosetta (capt), Allemandi; Pizziolo, Monti, Bertolini; Guarisi, Meazza, Schiavio, Ferrari, Orsi.

United States: Hjulian; Czerchiewicz, Moorhouse (capt); Pietras, Gonsalvez, Florie, Ryan, Nilsen, Donelli, Dick, Maclean.
Scorers: Schiavio (3), Orsi (2), Meazza, Ferrari for Italy; Donelli for United States.

Czechoslovakia (0) 2, Romania (1) 1 (Trieste)
Czechoslovakia: Planicka (capt); Zenisek, Ctyroky; Kostalek, Cambal, Krcil; Junek, Silny, Sobotka, Nejedly, Puc.
Romania: Zambori; Vogl, Albu; Deheleanu, Cotormani (capt), Moravet; Bindea, Covaci, Depi, Bodola, Dobai.
Scorers: Puc, Nejedly for Czechoslovakia; Dobai for Romania.

Germany (1) 5, Belgium (2) 2 (Florence)
Germany: Kress; Haringer, Schwarz; Janes, Szepan (capt), Zielinksi; Lehner, Hohmann, Conen, Siffling, Kovierski.
Belgium: Van de Weyer; Smellinckx, Joacim; Peeraer, Welkenhuyzen (capt), Klaessens; Devries, Voorhoof, Capelle, Grimmonprez, Herremans
Scorers: Voorhoof (2) for Belgium; Conen (3), Kovierski (2) for Germany.

Austria (1) 3, France (1) 2 (1–1) after extra time (Turin)
Austria: Platzer; Cisar, Seszta; Wagner, Smistik (capt), Urbanek; Zischek, Bican, Sindelar, Schall, Viertel.

France: Thépot; Mairesse, Mattler; Delflour, Verriest, Llense; Keller Alcazar, Nicolas (capt), Rio, Aston.
Scorers: Nicolas, Verriest (pen) for France; Sindelar, Schall, Bican for Austria.

Spain (3) 3, Brazil (1) 1 (Genoa)
Spain: Zamora (capt); Ciriaco, Quincoces; Cillauren, Muguerza, Marculeta; Lafuente, Iraragorri, Langara, Lecue, Gorostiza.
Brazil: Pedrosa; Mazzi, Luz; Tinoco, Zaccone, Canilli; Oliviera, De Britto, Leonidas, Silva, Bartesko.
Scorers: Iraragorri (pen), Langara (2) for Spain; Silva for Brazil.

Switzerland (2) 3, Netherlands (1) 2 (Milan)
Switzerland: Sechehaye; Minelli, Weiler (capt); Guinchard, Jaccard, Hufschmid; Von Kaenel, Passello, Kielholz, Abegglen III, Bossi.
Netherlands: Van der Meulen; Weber, Van Run; Rellikaan, Andeniesen (capt), Van Heel; Wels, Vente, Bakhuijs, Smit, Van Nellen.
Scorers: Kleilholz (2), Abegglen III for Switzerland; Smit, Vente for Netherlands.

Sweden (1) 3, Argentina (1) 2 (Bologna)
Sweden: Rydberg; Axelsson, S. Andersson; Carlsson, Rosen (capt), E. Andersson; Dunker, Gustafsson, Jonasson, Keller, Kroon.

Argentina: Freschi; Pedevilla, Belis; Nehin, Sosa-Urbieta, Lopez; Rua, Wilde, De Vincenzi (capt), Galateo, Iraneta.
Scorers: Bellis, Galateo for Argentina; Jonasson (2), Kroon for Sweden.

Hungary (2) 4, Egypt (1) 2 (Naples)
Hungary: A. Szabo; Futo, Sternberg; Palotas, Szucs, Lazar; Markos, Vincze, Teleky, Toldi, F. Szabo.
Egypt: Moustafa Kamel; Ali Caf, Hamitu; El Far, Refaat, Rayab; Latif, Fawzi, Muktar (capt), Masoud Kamel, Hassan.
Scorers: Teleky, Toldi (2), Vincze for Hungary; Fawzi (2) for Egypt.

SECOND ROUND
Germany (1) 2, Sweden (0) 1 (Milan)
Germany: Kress; Haringer, Busch; Gramlich, Szepan (capt), Zielinski; Lehner, Hohmann, Conen, Siffling, Kobierski.
Sweden: Rydberg; Axelsson, S. Andersson; Carlsson, Rosen (capt), E. Andersson; Dunker, Jonasson, Gustafsson, Keller, Kroon.
Scorers: Hohmann (2) for Germany; Dunker for Sweden.

Austria (1) 2, Hungary (0) 1 (Bologna)
Austria: Platzer; Disar, Seszta; Wagner, Smistik (capt), Urbanek; Zischek, Bican, Sindelar, Horwath, Viertel.
Hungary: A. Szabo; Vago, Sternberg; Palotas, Szucs, Szalay; Markos, Avar, Sarosi, Toldi, Kemeny.
Scorers: Horwarth, Zischek for Austria; Sarosi (pen) for Hungary.

Italy (0) 1, Spain (1) 1 after extra time (Florence)
Italy: Combi (capt); Monzeglio, Allemandi; Pizziolo, Monti, Castellazzi; Guaita, Meazza, Schiavio, Ferrari, Orsi.
Spain: Zamora (capt); Ciriaco, Quincoces; Cillauren, Muguerza, Fede; Lafuente, Iraragorri, Langara, Regueiro, Gorostiza.
Scorers: Regueiro for Spain; Ferrari for Italy.

Italy (1) 1, Spain (0) 0. Replay (Florence)
Italy: Combi (capt); Monzeglio, Allemandi; Ferraris IV, Monti, Bertolini; Guaita, Meazza, Borel, De Maria, Orsi.
Spain: Noguet; Zabalo, Quincoces (capt); Cillauren, Muguerza Lecue, Ventolra, Regueiro, Campanal, Chacho, Bosch.
Scorer: Meazza for Italy.

Czechoslovakia (1) 3, Switzerland (1) 2 (Turin)
Czechoslovakia: Planicka; Zenisek, Ctyroky; Kostalek, Cambal, Krcil; Junek, Svoboda, Sobotka, Nejedly, Puc.
Switzerland: Sechehaye; Minelli, Weiler; Guinchard, Jaccard, Hufschmid; Von Kaenel, Jaeggi IV, Kielholz, Abegglen III, Jaeck.
Scorers: Kielholz, Abegglen III for Switzerland; Svoboda, Sobotka, Nejedly for Czechoslovakia.

SEMI-FINALS
Czechoslovakia (1) 3, Germany (0) 1 (Rome)
Czechoslovakia: Planicka (capt); Burger, Ctyroky; Kostalek, Cambal, Krcil; Junek, Svoboda, Sobotka, Nejedly, Puc.
Germany: Kress; Haringer, Busch; Zielinski, Szepan (capt), Bender; Lehner, Siffling, Conen, Noack, Kobierski.
Scorers: Nejedly (2), Krcil for Czechoslovakia; Noack for Germany.

Italy (1) 1, Austria (0) 0 (Milan)
Italy: Combi (capt); Monzeglio, Allemandi; Ferraris IV, Monti, Bertolini; Guaita, Meazza, Schiavio, Ferrari, Orsi.
Austria: Platzer; Disar, Seszta; Wagner, Smistik (capt), Urbanek; Zischek, Bican, Sindelar, Schall, Viertel.
Scorer: Guaita for Italy.

THIRD PLACE MATCH
Germany (3) 3, Austria (1) 2 (Naples)
Germany: Jakob; Janes, Busch; Zielinski, Muenzenberg, Bender; Lehner, Siffling, Conen, Szepan (capt), Heidemann.
Austria: Platzer; Disar, Seszta; Wagner, Smistik (capt), Urbanek; Zischek, Braun, Horwath, Viertel.
Scorers: Lehner (2), Conen for Germany; Horwath, Seszta for Austria.

FINAL
Italy (0) 2, Czechoslovakia (0) 1 after extra time (Rome)
Italy: Combi (capt); Monzeglio, Allemandi; Ferraris IV, Monti, Bertolini; Guaita, Meazza, Schiavio, Ferrari, Orsi.
Czechoslovakia: Planicka (capt); Zenisek, Ctyroky; Kostalek, Cambal, Krcil; Junek, Svoboda, Sobotka, Nejedly, Puc.
Scorers: Orsi, Schiavio for Italy; Puc for Czechoslovakia.
Leading Scorers: Schiavio (Italy), Nejedly (Czechoslovakia), Conen (Germany) each 4.

WORLD CUP 1938 – France
Italy were the winners again, but this time their win was more convincing. For the first time, indeed, a host nation failed to take the World Cup. Pozzo himself has said that on grounds of pure football, his 1938 side was superior to the team of 1934. Only the inside-forwards Meazza and Ferrari survived from that eleven. Monti's place at centre-half had been taken by another South American, Andreolo from Uruguay. Foni and Rava, fullbacks in the successful Italian Olympic side of 1936, were now in the full national side. Olivieri, an excellent goalkeeper, was a fitting successor to Combi. At centre-forward, the tall, powerful Silvio Piola rivalled Meazza (and overhauled him in 1951!) as the most prolific Italian goalscorer of all time.

Argentina wanted to stage this World Cup, but the claims of France were preferred. Austria and Spain had to withdraw for political reasons, Uruguay, still worried by the crisis of professionalism (another factor in their refusal to compete in 1934) refused again to take part. So did Argentina – whose fans demonstrated their displeasure outside the offices of the Federation.

But Brazil, a much improved side, were there again, with the great Leonidas at centre-forward and Da Guia at fullback. Sarosi was in great form for Hungary, who had not long since beaten the Czechs 8–3, and he had fine support from Szengeller, the 22-year-old inside-left. Planicka, Nejedly, and Puc survived from the Czechs' 1934 team, and Germany, now under Sepp Herberger, was still recovering from a 6–3 home defeat by England. The Swiss, who had beaten England 2–1 a few days later in Zurich, looked strong.

In the first round, the hardest fought tie was that between Germany and Switzerland. The Germans fielded four Austrians in the first match, one of whom, the outside-left, Pesser, was sent off in extra time. Gauchel gave Germany the lead from Pesser's centre. Abegglen headed an equaliser, and extra time brought no more goals. The teams had a good five days to gird themselves for the replay. This time, Germany fielded three Austrians and brought back their talented 1934 captain, Szepan, to play at inside-left. They went into a 2–0 lead – one from Hahnemann, an unlucky own goal by Loertscher, the Swiss left-half – at half-time. Wallaschek made it 1–2 early in the second half, but when the Swiss left-winger Aebi went off injured, the die seemed cast.

Not a bit of it. The Swiss held out till Aebi came back, Bickel equalised and Abegglen, the star of the match, rounded it off with two fine goals.

The greatest surprise was Cuba's defeat of Romania, after a 3–3 draw in Toulouse. Half the Romanian side had previous World Cup experience, three having played in Uruguay. But the Cubans played with great speed and *brio* and were 3–2 ahead in extra time when the Romanians equalised. In the replay, they surprisingly dropped their star goalkeeper, Carvajales, who was brilliantly replaced by Ayra, and won, after being a goal down. The winner, according to the French linesman, was offside, but the German referee allowed it. What has happened to Cuban football since 1938? Obscurely, it has sunk without trace.

The Czechs, with four 1934 men, beat the Netherlands 3–0 in Le Havre, but needed extra time to do it and were fortunate that the Dutch lacked Bakhuijs, their leading scorer. Two of the Czech goals came from their half-backs; the celebrated Nejedly got the other.

At Strasbourg, a marvellous match between Brazil and Poland saw the score at 4–4 after 90 minutes. Poland had had a fine season, culminating with a 6–1 win over Ireland and victory by 4–1 aggregate over Yugoslavia in the eliminators for the World Cup. Their inside-forward, Ernest Willimowski, was one of the most talented in Europe and a notable goalscorer. Brazil had six players making their international debut. Their magnificent centre-forward Leonidas, the Black Diamond, did the hat-trick for them in the first half, but in the second the Polish half-backs took control. In extra time, Leonidas and Willimowski each scored his fourth goal, but another by Romeu for Brazil was decisive – 6–5.

In Marseilles, Italy got the shock of their lives from little Norway. Within two minutes, Ferrari had given Italy the lead, but Norway tightened their grip on Piola and their own centre-forward, the powerful Brunyldsen, gave Andreolo a terrible time of it. Three times the Italian posts and bar were hit; at others Olivieri saved them. In the second half, Brustad, an excellent left-winger, made it 1–1, but Piola eventually got the winner from a rebound.

Pozzo, however, revived his team's morale, and in the next round they won comfortably, 3–1 against France in Paris before 58,000 spectators, the biggest crowd of that World Cup. Foni replaced Monzeglio at right-back, and Biavati, the winger with the fluttering foot, took over from Paserati. For France, Delfour and Mattler were playing their third World Cup. The star was Piola. His two goals in the second half won the game, after France had rashly thrown themselves into attack.

Sweden, exempt from the first round, managed by Nagy, a Hungarian, and smarting from their humiliation by Japan in the last Olympiad, put an end to the Cuban illusion, winning 8–0. Torre Keller, their 35-year-old right-half and captain, was celebrating 14 years of international competition. The fair-haired right-winger, Gustav Wetterstroem, was, however, the chief destroyer. Four of the goals were his.

In Lille, a tired Swiss team lost 2–0 to a technically superior Hungary; the Swiss felt the lack of Minelli and Aebi.

In Bordeaux, where the new municipal stadium was inaugurated, Czechoslovakia, 1934 finalists, played Brazil, the now joint favourites with Italy. It was a holocaust; three players sent off, two Brazilians and a Czech, while Planicka with a broken arm and Nejedly with a broken leg finished in hospital. Zeze, violently kicking Nejedly for no apparent reason – and getting himself sent off – began it. Leonidas gave Brazil the lead, Nejedly equalised from a penalty in the second half, and the depleted Czechs held out against the nine-man Brazilians in extra time.

Curiously enough, the replay was conducted in the mildest of climates. The Brazilians made nine changes, the Czechs six. The Czechs led at half-time through the energetic Kopecky, moved up to the attack, but they badly missed the passing of Nejedly. Worse, Kopecky had to leave the field injured, a shot by Senecky seemed to be over the line before the Brazilian 'keeper cleared it – and Leonidas was at his best. He it was who equalised and Roberto got the winning goal.

In the semi-finals, Brazil paid the penalty for over-confidence, inexplicably omitting Leonidas and the brilliant Tim, against the Italians at Marseilles. Colaussi scored the opening goal and Meazza clinched the game from a penalty after Domingas had rashly fouled Piola. Thus it was 2–0, and Romeu's goal for Brazil had no real significance. For all his folly, Domingas had impressed Pozzo as 'one of the greatest defenders one is likely to meet'.

In the other semi-final, Hungary thrashed Sweden 5–1 in Paris. Nyberg got a 35-second goal for Sweden, but the Hungarians took it in their stride. They were 3–1 up by half-time – two for Szengeller – and he and Sarosi added goals in the second half. There could have been many more.

Sweden again took the lead in the third place match, at Bordeaux, and led 2–1 against Brazil at half-time. Then Leonidas turned it on, scored two goals, and Brazil won 4–2.

On 19 June, at the Stade Colombes, the Hungarians played graceful, short-passing football, the Italians showed rhythm and bite. Again, Colaussi got the first goal. Titkos equalised within a minute – he was Hungary's great hope – but Meazza, getting too much room all the while, made one for Piola, and Italy led 2–1. By half-time Colaussi, put through by Meazza, had scored again – 3–1.

In the second half, Sarosi added Hungary's second in a scramble, but the Italian defence was in control. Colaussi was too fast for Polgar, while Biavati and Piola were too quick for the whole defence when Piola scored from Biavati's ultimate back-heel. A swift, strong, ruthless team had kept the World Cup in Italy.

FIRST ROUND

Switzerland (1) 1, Germany (1) 1 after extra time (Paris)
Switzerland: Huber Minelli (capt), Lehmann; Springer, Vernati, Loertscher; Amado, Wallaschek, Bickel, Abegglen III, Abei.
Germany: Raftl; Janes, Schnaus; Kupfer, Mock (capt), Kitzinger; Lehner, Gellesch, Gauchel, Hahnemann, Pesser.
Scorers: Gauchel for Germany, Abegglen III for Switzerland.

Switzerland (0) 4, Germany (2) 2 Replay (Parc des Princes, Paris)
Switzerland: Huber; Minelli (capt), Lehmann; Springer, Vernati, Loertscher; Amado, Abegglen III, Bickel, Wallaschek, Abei.
Germany: Raftl; Janes, Strietel; Kupfer, Goldbrunner, Skoumal; Lehner, Stroh, Hahnemann, Szepan (capt), Haumer.
Scorers: Hahnemann, Loertscher o.g. for Germany; Wallaschek, Bickel, Abegglen III (2) for Switzerland.

Cuba (0) 3, Romania (1) 3 after extra time (Toulouse)
Cuba: Cavajeles; Barquin, Chorens (capt); Arias; Rodriguez, Berges; Maquina, Fernandez, Socorro, Tunas, Sosa.
Romania: Palovici; Burger, Chiroiu; Vintila, Rasinaru (capt), Rafinski; Bindea, Covaci, Baratki, Bodola, Dobai.
Scorers: Covaci, Baratki, Dobai for Romania; Tunas, Maquina, Sosa for Cuba.

Cuba (0) 2, Romania (1) 1 Replay (Toulouse)
Cuba: Ayra; Barquin, Chorens (capt); Arias, Rodriguez, Berges; Maquina, Fernandez, Socorro, Tunas, Sosa.

Romania: Sadowski; Berger, Felecan; Barbulescu, Rasinaru, Rafinski; Bogden, Moldoveanu, Baratki, Pranzler, Dobai.
Scorers: Socorro, Maquina for Cuba; Dobai for Romania.

Hungary (4) 6, Dutch East Indies (0) 0 (Reims)
Hungary: Hada; Koranyi, Biro; Lazar, Turai, Balogh; Sas, Szengeller, Sarosi (capt), Toldi, Kohut.
Dutch East Indies: Mo Heng; Hu Kom, Sameuls; Nawir, Meng (capt), Anwar; Hang Djin, Soedarmadji, Sommers, Pattiwael, Taihuttu.
Scorers: Kohut, Toldi, Sarosi (2), Szengeller (2) for Hungary.

France (2) 3, Belgium (1) 1 (Colombes, Paris)
France: Di Lorto; Czenave, Mattler (capt); Bastien, Jordan, Diagne; Aston, Heisserer, Nicolas, Delfour, Veinante.
Belgium: Badjou; Pavrick (capt), Sayes; Van Alphen, Stynen, De Winter; Van de Wouwer, Voorhoof, Isemborghs, R., Braine, Byle.
Scorers: Vienante, Nicolas (2) for France, Isemborghs for Belgium.

Czechoslovakia (0) 3, Netherlands (0) 0 after extra time (Le Havre)
Czechoslovakia: Planicka; Berger, Daucik; Kostalek, Boucek (capt), Kopecky; Riha, Simunek, Zeman, Nejedly, Puc.
Netherlands: Van Male; Weber, Caldenhove; Pawae, Anderiesen (capt), Van Heel; Wels, Van der Veen, Smit, Vente, De Harder.
Scorers: Kostalek, Boucek, Nejedly for Czechoslovakia.

Brail (3) 6, Poland (1) 5 after extra time (Strasbourg)
Brazil: Batatoes; Domingas Da Guia, Machados; Zeze, Martin (capt), Alfonsinho; Lopez, Romeu, Leonidas, Peracio, Hercules.
Poland: Madejski; Szcepaniak, Galecki; Gora, Nytz (capt), Dytko; Piec I, Piontek, Szerfke, Willimowski, Wodarz.
Scorers: Leonidas (4), Peracio, Romeu for Brazil; Willimowski (4), Piontek for Poland.

Italy (1) 2, Norway (0) 1 after extra time (Marseilles)
Italy: Olivieri; Monzeglio, Rava; Serantoni, Andreolo, Locatelli; Paserati, Meazza (capt), Piola, Ferrari, Ferraris.
Norway: H. Johansen; R. Johansen (capt), Holmsen; Henriksen, Eriksen, Homberg; Frantzen, Kwammen, Brunylden, Isaksen, Brustad.
Scorers: Ferrari, Piola for Italy; Brustad for Norway.

SECOND ROUND
Sweden (4) 8, Cuba (0) 0 (Antibes)
Sweden: Abrahamson; Eriksson, Kjellgren; Almgren, Jacobsson. Svanstroem; Wetterstroem, Keller, H. Andersson, Jonasson, Nyberg.
Cuba: Carvajeles; Barquin, Chorens; Arias, Rodriquez, Berges; Ferrer, Fernandez, Socorro, Tunas, Alonzo.
Scorers: Andersson, Jonasson, Wetterstroem (4), Nyberg, Keller for Sweden.

Hungary (1) 2, Switzerland (0) 0 (Lille)
Hungary: Szabo; Koranyi, Biro; Szalay, Turai, Lazar; Sas, Vincze, Sarosi (capt), Szengeller, Kohut.
Switzerland: Huber; Stelzer, Lehmann (capt); Springer, Vernati, Loertscher; Amado, Wallaschek, Bickel, Abegglen III, Grassi.
Scorers: Szengeller (2) for Hungary.

Italy (1) 3, France (1) 1 (Colombes, Paris)
Italy: Olivieri; Foni, Rava; Serantoni, Andreolo, Locatelli; Biavati, Meazza (capt), Piola, Ferrari, Colaussi.
France: Di Lorto; Czenave, Mattler (capt); Bastien, Jordan, Diagne; Aston, Heisserer, Nicolas, Delfour, Veinante.
Scorers: Colaussi, Piola (2) for Italy; Heisserer for France.

Brazil (1) 1, Czechoslovakia (1) 1 after extra time (Bordeaux)
Brazil: Walter; Domingas Da Guia, Machados; Zeze, Martin (capt), Alfonsinho; Lopez, Romeu, Leonidas, Peracio, Hercules.
Czechoslovakia: Planicka; Berger, Daucik; Kostalek, Bocek (capt), Kopecky; Riha, Simunek, Ludl, Nejedly, Puc.
Scorers: Leonidas for Brazil; Nejedly (pen) for Czechoslovakia.

Brazil (0) 2, Czechoslovakia (1) 1 Replay (Bordeaux)
Brazil: Walter; Jahu, Nariz; Britto, Brandao (capt), Algemiro; Roberto, Luisinho, Leonidas, Tim, Patesko.
Czechoslovakia: Burket; Berger, Daucik; Kostalek, Bocek (capt), Ludl; Horak, Senecky, Kreutz, Kopecky, Rulc.
Scorers: Leonidas, Roberto for Brazil; Kopecky for Czechoslovakia.

SEMI-FINALS
Italy (2) 2, Brazil (0) 1 (Marseilles)
Italy: Olivieri; Foni, Rava; Serantoni, Andreolo, Locatelli; Biavati, Meazza (capt), Piola, Ferrari, Colaussi.
Brazil: Walter; Domingas, Da Guia, Machados; Zeze, Martin (capt), Alfonsinho; Lopez, Luisinho, Peracio, Romeu, Patesko.
Scorers: Colaussi, Meazza (pen) for Italy, Romeu for Brazil.

Hungary (3) 5, Sweden (1) 1 (Colombes, Paris)
Hungary: Szabo; Koranyi, Biro; Szalay, Turai, Lazar; Sas, Szengeller, Sarosi (capt), Toldi, Titkos.
Sweden: Abrahamson; Eriksson, Kjellgren; Almgren, Jacobsson, Svanstroem; Wetterstroem, Keller (capt), H. Andersson, Johanasson, Nyberg.
Scorers: Szengeller (3), Titkos, Sarosi for Hungary; Nyberg for Seden.

THIRD PLACE MATCH
Brazil (1) 4, Sweden (2) 2 (Bordeaux)
Brazil: Batatoes; Domingas Da Guia, Machados; Zeze, Brandao, Alfonsinho; Roberto, Romeu, Leonidas (capt), Peracio, Patesko.

Sweden: Abrahamson; Eriksson, Nilssen; Almgren, Linderholm, Svanstroem (capt); Berssen, H. Andersson, Jonasson, A. Andersson, Nyberg.
Scorers: Romeu, Leonidas (2), Peracio for Brazil; Jonasson, Nyberg for Sweden.

FINAL
Italy (3) 4, Hungary (1) 2 (Colombes, Paris)
Italy: Olivieri; Foni, Rava; Serantoni, Andreolo, Locatelli; Biavati, Meazza (capt), Piola, Ferrari, Colaussi.
Hungary: Szabo; Polgar, Biro; Szalay, Szucs, Lazar; Sas, Vincze, Sarosi (capt), Szengeller, Titkos.
Scorers: Colaussi (2), Piola (2) for Italy; Titkos, Sarosi for Hungary.

WORLD CUP 1950 – Brazil
The first World Cup for 12 years, the first since the outbreak of war, was in many ways the most vivid and impassioned yet. If Brazil were the moral victors, Uruguay's success was a marvellous anticlimax, emphasising the uncertainties of the game. Certainly the Uruguayans were most fortunate to have their qualifying pool reduced to a single, ludicrous match against Bolivia – but in the final the defensive prowess of Varela, Andrade, and Maspoli, and the counter-attacking of Schiaffino and Ghiggia, were worthy of success.

For the first – and so far last – time the competition was organised on the curious basis of four qualifying pools and a final pool. Again, there were several distinguished absentees; Austria, Hungary, Czechoslovakia, Argentina. The Austrians, who seem to suffer from a periodic inferiority complex (they were to withdraw again in 1962) said quaintly that their team was too inexperienced – and then proceeded to beat Italy in Vienna. Russia stayed out, and Germany were still excluded from FIFA. But the British countries took part for the first time, their own International Championship charitably being recognised as a qualifying group, in which the first two would go through to the finals. Scotland, with baffling insularity and pique, decided that if they did not win the title they would not go to Brazil. England beat them 1–0 at Hampden – and they stayed at home to sulk.

England and Brazil were the favourites; Brazil as talented hosts, England for, presumably, historical reasons. Their chances were diminished by the withdrawal of Neil Franklin, their gifted centre-half, who flew off to play in Bogota, Colombia, then unregistered with FIFA. Injuries had blunted the edge of the gallant Mortensen, a splendid opportunist, but there were still such giants as Matthews, Finney, Williams, Ramsey, Mannion. In retrospect, the team looks better than one felt it to be in prospect.

Brazil approached the tournament with all the intense dedication shown by Uruguay in 1930 – and Italy in 1934. Managed by Flavio Costa, a lean, intense man with the inevitable South American moustache, they took up monastic residence in a house just outside Rio, with vitamin drinks, 10 o'clock curfew, and a ban on wives. Local firms accoutred the house for nothing. There were two doctors, two masseurs, three chefs.

The massive Maraçana Stadium – shades of Uruguay in 1930 – was still being completed (capacity 200,000) when the teams arrived – and when they left. Its seats had been painted blue; allegedly a pacifying colour.

France, angered by the amount of travelling they would have to do, withdrew at the last moment; this, after having been eliminated, then invited to take the place of Turkey, another country that withdrew. Though the French attitude was hardly defensible, there's no doubt that the travelling arrangements strongly favoured Brazil. So did the thin air of Rio.

Brazil kicked off against Mexico in a stadium that was still no more than an ambitious shambles. Brazil won 4–0, two of the goals coming from their lithe and brilliant centre-forward, Ademir. In São Paulo, a brave Swedish team sprang the first surprise of the competition by beating Italy. George Raynor, their clever little Yorkshire coach, had brilliantly rebuilt an Olympic-winning team pillaged of its stars by – the Italians. In Nacka Skoglund and Kalle Palmer, he had unearthed two delicate and subtle inside-forwards, flanking a powerful leader in the fair-haired Hasse Jeppson who completely mastered the great Carlo Parola. Italy had picked a strange team with Campatelli, a veteran left-half, at inside-left – after three years out of the national side. Carapallese, the Italian captain and outside-left, gave them the lead before a crowd that was full of Italo-Brazilians, but the hefty Knud Nordahl dominated Gino Cappello, their centre-forward. Jeppson equalised, Andersson gave Sweden the lead with a long shot, and a mistake in the second half by Sentimenti in goal allowed Jeppson to clinch it. Muccinelli pulled back a goal, Carapallese hit the bar – but that was as near as Italy could get.

In the other matches, the United States roused echoes of 1930 by leading Spain at half-time, fighting gallantly, and going down only by 3–1. Spain, with fine wingers in Basora and Gainza, and a tough centre-forward in Zarra, were greatly surprised. At the hard little Belo Horizonte ground, Yugoslavia easily beat Switzerland. Cjaicowski at right-half and Mitic and Bobek at inside-forward stood out for their skill.

England's win against Chile in Rio was laboured, but in their next match they suffered one of the greatest humiliations in world football history; they were beaten 1–0 by the United States in Belo Horizonte. So casually did the Americans take the game that most of them were up till the small hours. Everything seemed set for England: crisp mountain air; a British mining firm to put them up; a forward line of stars. But gallant defence by Borghi in goal, Colombo at centre-half, and Eddie McIlvenny, a Scotsman discarded 18 months earlier by Third Division Wrexham on a free transfer, held them out; and after 37 minutes America scored. Gaetjens got his head to a cross by Bahr to beat Williams; and all England's pressure could not bring an equaliser. Did Mullen's header from Ramsey's free kick cross Borghi's line? Perhaps; but America deserved their win for their courage.

In São Paulo, Brazil, too, faltered; held to a 2–2 draw by little Switzerland, who equalised two minutes from the end. Costa had picked a team full of *paulistas*, to flatter São Paulo, and the gesture had very nearly been expensive.

Italy beat Paraguay, who had drawn with Sweden, but the die was cast. Brazil, who had to beat Yugoslavia, conquerors of Mexico, in Rio, to qualify, got through by the skin of their teeth. Indeed, had it not been for a wretchedly unlucky head injury to Mitic on a steel girder outside the dressing-room, who knows what might have happened?

In the third minute, Ademir took a pass from the splendid right-half Bauer and opened the score. Yugoslavia, however, gave as good as they got. Cjaicowski II missed a fine chance to equalise, Bauer found the inimitable Zizinho – playing his first game of the tournament – and the inside-right wriggled through to clinch a difficult game. The Brazilians, playing 'diagonal' defence with a wandering centre-half and half-backs on the flanks, had made heavy weather of qualifying. Uruguay, 8–0 conquerors of Bolivia, had no trouble at all.

As for England, they went down 1–0 to Spain (a goal headed by Zarra) in Rio, and that was the end of them. Changes brought in Eddie Baily of Spurs at inside-left, Stanley Matthews on the right wing, Jackie Milburn at centre-forward, but the forward-line was still dogged by bad luck, and when Milburn did get the ball in the net, he was very dubiously given offside. Chile, winning 5–2 against the United States, emphasised England's shame.

In their first matches of the final pool, Brazil played some of the finest football that has ever graced the World Cup. Their inside-forward trio of Zizinho, Ademir, and Jair, with its pyrotechnical ball play, its marvellous understanding, was practically unstoppable, and Bauer gave it marvellous support. Raynor planned for Sweden to get an early goal, but two early chances went begging, and after that Brazil swept them aside. It was sheer execution. A second-half penalty by Andersson was the most Sweden could do against seven Brazilian goals, four of them Ademir's.

Spain went the same way, giving one goal less away. This time Jair and Chico got two each, Ademir did not score. Meanwhile Spain had held Uruguay to a bad-tempered 2–2 draw, Basora getting two more goals, despite the markings of Andrade. It seemed doubtful indeed whether the Uruguayans, bogeys of Brazil though they were, could hold them this time when they were under full sail.

Against Sweden, in São Paulo, the Uruguayans scraped through 3–2, after being a goal down at half-time. Skogland's off day and a bad foul by M. Gonzales on Johnsson – not to mention Uruguay's far easier programme – weighed against Sweden in the second half.

Thus to the deciding match, played before 200,000 impassioned fans at the Maracaña; a match which Brazil had only to draw to take the

World Cup. For three quarters of an hour they pounded a superb Uruguayan defence, brilliantly marshalled by their veteran centre-half, Obdulio Varela. Not till two minutes after half-time did Friaça meet a cross from the left to beat the astonishing Maspoli. Then Uruguay began to hit back, Varela turned to the attack, and after 20 minutes sent the fragile Ghiggia away on the right. Tall, pale, slender Juan Schiaffino controlled his centre unmarked, advanced, shot – and scored. Eleven minutes from time, Ghiggia took a return from Perez, ran on, and scored the winner.

Sweden, beating Spain 3–1 with a sudden late show of life, bravely took third place. And Brazil had to wait another eight years for ultimate satisfaction.

POOL 1
Brazil (1) 4, Mexico (0) 0 (Rio)
Brazil: Barbosa; Augusto (capt), Juvenal; Eli, Danilo, Bigode; Meneca, Ademir, Baltazar, Jair, Friaça.
Mexico: Carbajal; Zetter, Montemajor; Ruiz, Ochoa, Roca; Septien, Ortis, Casarin, Perez, Velasquez (capt).
Scorers: Ademir (2), Jair, Baltazar for Brazil.

Yugoslavia (3) 3, Switzerland (0) 0 (Belo Horizonte)
Yugoslavia: Mrkusic; Horvat, Stankovic; Cjaicowski I (capt), Jovanovic, Djaic; Ognanov, Mitic, Tomasevic, Bobek, Vukas.
Switzerland: Corrodi; Gyger, Rey; Bocquet, Eggimann, Neury; Bickel (capt), Antenen, Tamini, Bader, Fatton.
Scorers: Tomasevic (2), Ognanov for Yugoslavia.

Yugoslavia (2) 4, Mexico (0) 1 (Porto Alegre)
Yugoslavia: Mrkusic; Horvat, Stankovic; Cjaicowski I (capt), Jovanovic, Djaic; Milhailovic, Mitic, Tomasevic, Bobek, Cjaicowski II.
Mexico: Carbajal; Gutierrez, Ruiz; Gomez, Ochoa, Ortiz; Flores, Naranjo, Casarin, Perez, Velasquez (capt).
Scorers: Bobek, Cjaicowski II (2), Tomasevic for Yugoslavia; Casarin for Mexico.

Brazil (2) 2, Switzerland (1) 2 (São Paulo)
Brazil: Barbosa; Augusto (capt), Juvenal; Bauer, Ruy, Noronha; Alfredo, Maneca, Baltazar, Ademir, Friaço.
Switzerland: Stuber; Neury, Bocquet; Lasenti, Eggimann, Quinche; Tamini, Bickel (capt), Antenen, Bader, Fatton.
Scorers: Alfredo, Baltazar for Brazil; Fatton, Tamini for Switzerland.

Brazil (1) 2, Yugoslavia (0) 0 (Rio)
Brazil: Barbosa; Augusto (capt), Juvenal; Bauer, Danilo, Bigode; Maneca, Zizinho, Ademir, Jair, Chico.

Yugoslavia: Mrkusic; Horvat, Brokela; Cjaicowski I (capt), Jovanovic, Djaic; Vukas, Mitic, Tomasevic, Bobek, Cjaicowski II.
Scorers: Ademir, Zizinho for Brazil.

Switzerland (2) 2, Mexico (0) 1 (Porto Alegre)
Switzerland: Hug; Neury, Bocquet; Lusenti, Eggimann (capt), Kerner; Tamini, Antenen, Friedlander, Bader, Fatton.
Mexico: Carbajal; Gutierrez, Gomez; Roca, Ortiz, Vuburu; Flores, Naranjo, Casarin, Borbolla, Velasquez (capt).
Scorers: Bader, Fatton for Switzerland; Velasquez for Mexico.

	P	W	D	L	F	A	Pts
Brazil	3	2	1	0	8	2	5
Yugoslavia	3	2	0	1	7	3	4
Switzerland	3	1	1	1	4	6	3
Mexico	3	0	0	3	2	10	0

POOL 2
Spain (0) 3, United States (1) 1. (Curitiba)
Spain: Eizaguirre; Asensi, Alonzo; Gonzalvo III, Gonzalvo II, Puchades; Basora, Hernandez, Zarra, Igoa, Gainza.
United States: Borghi; Keough, Maca; McIlvenny (capt), Colombo, Bahr; Craddock, J. Souza, Gaetjens, Pariani, Valentini.
Scorers: Basora (2), Zarra for Spain. J. Souza for United States.

England (1) 2, Chile (0) 0 (Rio)
England: Williams; Ramsey, Aston; Wright (capt), Hughes, Dickinson; Finney, Mortensen, Bentley, Mannion, Mullen.
Chile: Livingstone; Faerias, Rolden; Alvarez, Busquez (capt) Carvalho; Malanej, Cremaschi, Robledo, Munoz, Dias.
Scorers: Mortensen, Mannion for England.

United States (1) 1, England (0) 0 (Belo Horizonte)
United States: Borghi; Keough, Maca; McIlvenny (capt), Colombo, Bahr; Wallace, Pariani, Gaetjens, J. Souza, E. Souza.
England: Williams; Ramsey, Aston; Wright (capt), Hughes, Dickinson; Finney, Mortensen, Bentley, Mannion, Mullen.
Scorer: Gaetjens for United States.

Spain (2) 2, Chile (0) 0 (Rio)
Spain: Eizaguirre; Alonzo, Pana; Gonzalvo III, Antunez, Puchades; Basora, Igoa, Zarra, Panizo, Gainza.
Chile: Livingstone; Faerias, Roldon; Alvarez, Brusquez (capt), Valho, Prieto, Cremaschi, Robledo, Munoz, Dias.
Scorers: Basora, Zarra for Spain.

Spain (0) 1, England (0) 0 (Rio)
Spain: Ramallets; Asensi, Alonzo; Gonzalvo III, Antunez, Puchades, Basora, Igoa, Zarra, Panizo, Gainza.

England: Williams; Ramsey, Eckersley; Wright (capt), Hughes, Dickinson; Matthews, Mortensen, Milburn, Baily, Finney.
Scorer: Zarra for Spain.

Chile (2) 5, United States (0) 2 (Recife)
Chile: Livingstone; Machuca, Roldon; Alvarez, Busquez (capt), Faerias; Munoz, Cremaschi, Robledo, Prieto, Ibanez.
United States: Borghi; Keough, Maca; McIlvenny (capt), Colombo, Bahr; Wallace, Pariani, Gaetjens, J. Souza, E. Souza.
Scorers: Robledo, Cremaschi, (3), Prieto for Chile; Pariani, J. Souza (pen.) for United States.

	P	W	D	L	F	A	Pts
Spain	3	3	0	0	6	1	6
England	3	1	0	2	2	2	2
Chile	3	1	0	2	5	6	2
United States	3	1	0	2	4	8	2

POOL 3
Sweden (2) 3, Italy (1) 2 (São Paulo)
Sweden: Svensson; Samuelsson, G. Nilsson (capt); Andersson, K. Nordahl, Gard; Sundqvist, Palmer, Jeppson, Skoglund, S. Nilsson.
Italy: Sentiment IV; Giovannini, Furiassi; Annovazzi, Parola, Magli; Muccinelli, Boniperti, Cappello, Campatelli, Carapallese (capt).
Scorers: Jeppson (2), Andersson for Sweden; Carapellese, Muccinelli for Italy.

Sweden (2) 2, Paraguay (1) 2 (Curitiba)
Sweden: Svensson; Samuelsson, E. Nilsson (capt); Andersson, K. Nordahl; Gard; Johnsson, Palmer, Jeppson, Skoglund, Sundqvist.
Paraguay: Vargas; Gonzalito, Cespedes; Gavilan, Lequizamon, Cantero; Avalos, A. Lopez, Jara, F. Lopez, Unzaim.
Scorers: Sundqvist, Palmer for Sweden; A. Lopez, F. Lopez, for Paraguay.

Italy (1) 2, Paraguay (0) 0 (São Paulo)
Italy: Moro; Blason, Furiassi; Fattori, Remondini, Mari; Muccinelli, Pandolfini, Amadei, Cappello, Carapellese.
Paraguay: Vargas; Gonzalito, Cespedes; Gavilan, Lequizamon Cantero; Avalos, A. Lopez, Jara, F. Lopez, Unzaim.
Scorers: Carapellese, Pandolfini for Italy.

	P	W	D	L	F	A	Pts
Sweden	2	1	1	0	5	4	3
Italy	2	1	0	1	4	3	2
Paraguay	2	0	1	1	1	4	1

POOL 4
Uruguay (4) 8, Bolivia (0) 0 (Recife)

Uruguay: Maspoli; M. Gonzales, Tejera; W. Gonzales, Varela (capt), Andrade; Ghiggia, Perez, Miguez, Schiaffino, Vidal.
Bolivia: Gutierrez I; Achs, Bustamente; Greco, Valencia, Ferrel; Alganaraz, Ugarte, Caparelli, Gutierrez II, Maldonado.
Scorers: Schiaffino (4), Miguez (2), Vidal, Ghiggia for Uruguay.

FINAL POOL

Uruguay (1) 2, Spain (2) 2 (São Paulo)
Uruguay: Maspoli; M. Gonzales, Tejera; W. Gonzales, Varela (capt), Andrade; Ghiggia, Perez, Miguez, Schiaffino, Vidal.
Spain: Ramallets; Alonzo, Gonzalvo II; Gonzalvo III, Parra, Puchades; Basora, Igoa, Zarra, Molowny, Gainza.
Scorers: Ghiggia, Varela for Uruguay; Basora (2) for Spain.

Brazil (3) 7, Sweden (0) 1 (Rio)
Brazil: Barbosa; Augusto (capt), Juvenal; Bauer, Danilo, Bigode; Maneca, Zizinho, Ademir, Jair, Chico.
Sweden: Svensson; Samuelsson, E. Nilsson; Andersson, K. Nordahl, Gard; Sunqvist, Palmer, Jeppson, Skoglund, S. Nilsson.
Scorers: Ademir (4), Chico (2), Maneca for Brazil; Andersson (pen) for Sweden.

Uruguay (1) 3, Sweden (2) 2 (São Paulo)
Uruguay: Paz; M. Gonzales, Tejera; Gambetta, Varela (capt), Andrade; Ghiggia, Perez, Miguez, Schiaffino, Vidal.
Sweden: Svensson; Samuelsson, E. Nilsson; Andersson, Johansson, Gard, Johnsson, Palmer, Melberg, Skoglund, Sunqvist.
Scorers: Ghiggia, Miguez (2) for Uruguay; Palmer, Sunqvist for Sweden,

Brazil (3) 6, Spain (0) 1 (Rio)
Brazil: Barbosa; Augusto (capt), Juvenal; Bauer, Danilo, Bigode; Friaça, Zizinho, Ademir, Jair, Chico.
Spain: Eizaguirre; Alonzo, Gonzalvo II; Gonzalvo III, Parra, Pucades; Basora, Igoa, Zarra, Panizo, Gainza.
Scorers: Jair (2), Chico (2), Zizinho, Parra (o.g.) for Brazil; Igoa for Spain.

Sweden (2) 3, Spain (0) 1 (São Paulo)
Sweden: Svensson; Samuelsson, E. Nilsson; Andersson, Johansson, Gard; Sunqvist, Mellberg, Rydell, Palmer, Johnsson.
Spain: Eizaguirre; Asensi, Alonzo; Silva, Parra, Puchades; Basora, Fernandez, Zarra, Panizo, Juncosa.
Scorers: Johansson, Mellberg, Palmer for Sweden; Zarra for Spain.

Uruguay (0) 2, Brazil (0) 1 (Rio)
Uruguay: Maspoli; M. Gonzales, Tejera; Gambetta, Varela (capt), Andrade; Ghiggia, Perez, Miguez, Schiaffino, Moran.

Brazil: Barbosa; Augusto (capt), Juvenal; Bauer, Danilo, Bigode; Friaça, Zizinho, Ademir, Jair, Chico.
Scorers: Schiaffino, Ghiggia for Uruguay; Friaça for Brazil.

	P	W	D	L	F	A	Pts
Uruguay	3	2	1	0	7	5	5
Brazil	3	2	0	1	14	4	4
Sweden	3	1	0	2	6	11	2
Spain	3	0	1	2	4	11	1

Leading Scorers: Ademir (Brazil) 7, Schiaffino (Uruguay), Basora (Spain) 5.

WORLD CUP 1954 – Switzerland

The 1954 World Cup, which rolled over little, under-organised Switzerland like a tidal wave over some peaceful village, was another instance of the Cup being won, at the last gasp, by the 'wrong' team. This time, the 'wrong' team was Sepp Herberger's cunningly managed Germany, the 'wronged' team, the brilliant Hungarians.

Hungary, who had smashed England's unbeaten home record against foreign teams 6–3 at Wembley the previous November, then beaten them again 7–1 in Budapest, as an aperitif to the World Cup, had the finest team the world had seen since the 1950 Brazilians; and probably the best Europe has ever seen.

The organisation of the tournament settled down into the somewhat hybrid and equally unsatisfactory form it retained until 1970. Four qualifying groups provided two qualifiers each, which then met in the quarter-finals, those finishing first playing those finishing second. Again, the British Championship was charitably designated as a qualifying group, and this time Scotland, again runner-up to England, deigned to enter. Their team paid a heavy penalty for the insularity of their Association in 1950.

Uruguay at last entered a European World Cup; they had yet to lose a match in the competition. Of the victorious 1950 team, still playing with a roving centre-half and 'bolt' defence, Maspoli, Andrade, Varela, Miguez, and Schiaffino all remained. There were splendid new wingers in Abbadie and Borges, and a powerful stopper in the fair-haired Santamaria, later to become a bulwark of Real Madrid.

Even so, Hungary remained favourites with their marvellous attack, pivoting on Boszik, the right-half, and Nandor Hidegkuti, the deep-lying centre-forward; most of their goals scored from the remarkable head of Sandor Kocsis or the matchlessly powerful left foot of the captain, Ferenc Puskas, whose injury was probably to decide the series.

Austria, whose European dominance was ended by Hungary, had the remains of a fine team, a superb half-back in the tall, dark, strong Ernst Ocwirk, formerly their roving centre-half, now a wing-half. Austria had at last abandoned the classic Vienna School for the third back game which Meisl would have loathed.

Sweden, robbed of their stars by Italian clubs and eliminated by Belgium, were not there. Italy, under the management of the Hungarian Lajos Czeizler, basing their defence on the Inter (Milan) block, had a good recent record. Brazil had largely rebuilt their side. The great inside-forward trio had disappeared *en bloc*. Only Bauer and Baltazar remained, but the black Djalma Santos and his elegant namesake Nilton were fine backs, and Julinho came with a forbidding reputation for power and brilliance on the right wing. The defence still clung to the old 'diagonal' system and had not mastered the third-back game. Costa had given way to Zeze Moreira as the manager.

Yugoslavia, with the experience of Mitic, Bobek, and Cjaicowski I, the acrobatic goalkeeping of Beara, the skill and finishing power of the excellent Zebec and Vukas, were obviously good outsiders. One should add that an absurd omission in the rules made it necessary for extra time to be played *whenever* two teams were level at full-time. Each pool included two 'seeded' teams.

The tournament began with France losing by a single goal to Yugoslavia – a goal scored by the young Milutinovic, who was later to play for Racing Club de Paris. Brazil, with Didi directing operations, gobbled up Mexico. Hungary had an even easier task against little Korea in Pool 2. Germany disposed of Turkey without trouble.

Scotland played well against the talented Austrian side in Zürich, and their remodelled defence, with new backs in Willy Cunningham and Aird, looked promisingly solid. In attack, they missed the punch of Lawrie Reilly, who had been ill. Scotland gave Schmied in the Austrian goal much more to do than had their own goalkeeper; their half-backs were excellent, and it was only Schmied's late, daring save from centre-forward Mochan that allowed the Austrians to hang on to Probst's first-half goal.

England, still tottering from the travesty of Budapest, threw away all Matthews' brilliant work in a 4–4 draw with Belgium. Pol Anoul, the fair-haired inside-forward, gave Belgium the lead after only five minutes. Fifteen minutes from time England were 3–1 in the lead thanks to the finishing of Ivor Broadis and Nat Lofthouse, but, over-complacent, they allowed Belgium to wipe out the lead through Anoul again and the talented compact centre-forward, the unpredictable Rik Coppens. That meant – under the farcical rules of the competition – extra time.

For half an hour, England were dominant, but Matthews, the inspiration of the side – here, there and everywhere – pulled a muscle, and two minutes after Lofthouse had crowned a fine inter-passing movement between Broadis and Manchester United's Tommy Taylor, Dickinson headed Dries' free kick past Merrick for the Belgian equaliser.

In the meantime, Italy surprisingly came a cropper at Lausanne against Switzerland. The days of Pozzo, present only in his capacity of journalist, were distant indeed. Bad refereeing by Viana of Brazil unsettled the players and led to a holocaust of fouls and bad temper. Italy had the play, Switzerland got the goals, Hugi, who had switched to outside-right, scoring the winner 12 minutes from time. Two Swiss players were kicked in the stomach, and the Italians chased Viana off the field after he had dubiously ruled out a goal by Benito Lorenzi, who had persistently argued with him. Not for nothing was Lorenzi nicknamed '*Veleno*' – Poison.

The next round of matches included what was perhaps the decisive moment of the competition; the kick, accidental perhaps, with which Germany's centre-half Werner Liebrich injured Ferenc Puskas and put him out of action till a final in which he should not really have taken part. Sepp Herberger cleverly decided to throw away this match, fielding a team which consisted largely of reserves, convinced that Germany would easily dispose of Turkey in the play-off. The Hungarians tore Germany apart, getting eight goals, four of them by Kocsis, whose heading was remarkable. The fact that a team could be thus overwhelmed and still come back to win a *cup* competition was as good a comment on the organisation of this World Cup as one could require. Three of Hungary's goals came in the last 15 minutes, when Puskas was off the field.

Uruguay, who had conquered the mud in Berne to beat an uninspired Czech team, now exploited the firmer going in Basle to humiliate Scotland 7–0. Schiaffino, tall, pale, lean, a wonderful ball-player and strategist with a splendid understanding with his centre-forward, Miguez, tore Scotland's defence to pieces. Borges and Abbadie, the wingers, got five of the goals between them against a wretched Scottish team, which had not been helped by dissension among its officials. Andy Beattie, the team manager, had resigned after the Austrian game.

Austria, meanwhile, showed dazzling form in thrashing the Czechs 5–0, Ocwirk and the polished Gerhard Hanappi cleverly supporting an attack in which inside-forwards Probst and Stojaspal shared the goals.

But the finest match of all, perhaps the best of the whole tournament, with the exception of the Hungary–Uruguay semi-final, was Brazil's draw with Yugoslavia in Pool 1.

On the pretty Lausanne ground overlooking Lake Geneva, the Yugoslavs gave a splendid exhibition, Cjaicowski and Boskov dominating midfields with Beara superb in goal. But the only goal was by Zebec three minutes from half-time. In the second half Brazil came to life and Didi, after sustained pressure, scored the equaliser with a spectacular drive. There were no more goals in extra time.

In the play-offs, Germany, with a full team again, swamped Turkey while Italy, who had revived to beat Belgium 4–1, lost by the same score to Switzerland; a bafflingly inconsistent team. England, who had beaten the Swiss 2–0 in a dull game in Berne, were already through. They had strengthened their defence by moving Wright to centre-half in place of the injured Owen, a move which would bear abundant fruit in the years to come.

In the quarter-finals, England's 4-2 defeat by Uruguay has subsequently been put down to the goalkeeping of Merrick, as though England really deserved to win. In fact, the Uruguayans did remarkably well to defeat England, with both Varela and Andrade pulling muscles and Abbadie limping for much of the game.

England, with Matthews back in the side and shining again, did well, Lofthouse rubbing out Borges' fifth-minute goal. Varela's long-distance volley gave Uruguay a lead they did not deserve on the play – Merrick might have saved it; then after Varela had taken a free kick 'from hand', Schiaffino made it 3–1; again with a shot that could have been saved. Schiaffino's later excellence at left-half saw to it that England did not save the game. Finney's goal made it 2–3, Matthews hit the post, but at last Ambois slipped through for the fourth, and England were eliminated.

In Lausanne, Austria, again on form, won an astonishing 12-goal match with the Swiss; a score unthinkable two World Cups later! Using the speed of the Koerners down the wings and shooting, untypically, from long range, Austria had the star of the match in the classical Ocwirk. The best Swiss player was their dark inside-right, Roger Vonlanthen, who was behind most of their goals.

Meanwhile, the Brazilians met the Hungarians in what has come to be known as the Battle of Berne; a potentially great match that degenerated into a shocking display of violence.

Hungary made one of their spectacular starts, Hidegkuti scoring from a corner in the third minute, and getting his shorts ripped off for his pains. Then, five minutes later, he centred for Kocsis to head in. As the rain poured down, tackling grew ferocious. Buzansky knocked Indio down, big Djalma Santos scored from the penalty, and Hungary, without Puskas, were faltering.

A quarter of an hour after half-time, they too scored from a penalty – by Lantos, after Pinheiro had handled – but a marvellous run and shot by Julinho made it 3–2. Nilton Santos and Bozsik came to blows, and Arthur Ellis, the Halifax referee, sent both off the field. Hostilities were well and truly open. Four minutes from time, when the field resembled a boxing ring, Ellis sent off Humberto Tozzi, Brazil's inside-left, for kicking at an opponent, and in the last minute, Koscis headed the fourth for Hungary. Then the battle was transferred to the dressing-rooms...

In Geneva, Yugoslavia dominated Germany for an hour without being able to score. But the towering Horvat put past his own goalkeeper. The Slav forwards again finished poorly; Kohlmeyer kicked off the German line three times, and at last a breakaway goal by the bull-like Helmut Rahn, Germany's splendid outside-right, settled matters.

The Lausanne Hungary-Uruguay semi-final was unforgettable. Though Hungary missed Puskas, Czibor gave Hungary a 15-minute lead, from Kocsis' header, and Hidegkuti's head made it 2–0 just before half-time.

That seemed to be that, but with only a quarter of an hour left

Schiaffino put the Argentinian-born Hohberg through to make it 2-1 – and repeated the move three minutes from the end.

In the first half of extra time Hohberg was through a third time, but his shot hit the post and Hungary survived. Two splendid headers from Kocsis in the last 15 minutes gave them a wonderful match.

Germany, meanwhile, to the general astonishment, routed Austria, not least because goalkeeper Walter Zeman had a tragic game. The Germans, splendidly marshalled by their captain, Fritz Walter, backed up by his Kaiserslautern 'block', scored twice from corners, twice from centres, twice from penalties. Germany's switching, Walter's scheming and his cunning corners gave Austria a nightmare second-half, in which they conceded five goals.

In the third place match, in Zurich, Austria gained consolation. Unlike the equivalent game of 1934, they started underdogs, yet won – against a tired, demoralised Uruguay. A first-half injury to Schiaffino put the lid on it; Stojaspal emerged as the game's cleverest forward, and Ocwirk was magisterial. It was Ocwirk who shot the third goal from 25 yards in a tepid second-half.

And so to Berne, and the dramatic, unexpected final.

Hungary, with Puskas insisting that he play, might have demoralised Germany with their opening attack. After six minutes Boszik put Kocsis through, his shot was blocked, but Puskas followed up to score. Two minutes more and Czibor, on the right wing, made it 2-0.

What saved Germany was their swift reply – Morlock putting in Fritz Walter's fast centre. Rahn scored from a corner – and the game was open again. Turek, in Germany's goal, made save after dazzling save, Hidegkuti hit a post, Kocsis the bar, and Kohlemeyer kicked off the line. Then Eckel and Mai got a tighter grip on the Hungarian inside-forwards, Fritz Walter brought his wingers into the game and at last Boszik mispassed. Schaefer found Fritz Walter, the cross was pushed out – and Rahn smashed the ball in. Germany had won. When Puskas, coming to life again, raced on to Toth's pass to score, the goal was flagged offside. And when Czibor shot, Turek made another marvellous save.

Hungary, tired in body and spirit by their battles with the South Americans, may have been the moral victors, but Germany's success was none the less a memorable one.

POOL 1

Yugoslavia (1) 1, France (0) 0 (Lausanne)
Yugoslavia: Beara; Stankovic, Crnkovic; Cjaicowski I (capt), Horvat, Boskov; Milutinovic, Mitic, Vukas, Bobek, Zebec.
France: Remetter; Gianessi, Kaelbel; Penverne, Jonquet (capt), Marcel; Kopa, Glovacki, Strappe, Dereuddre, Vincent.
Scorer: Milutinovic for Yugoslavia.

Brazil (4) 5, Mexico (0) 0 (Geneva)
Brazil: Castilho; D. Santos, N. Santos; Brandaozinho, Pinheiro

(capt), Bauer; Julinho, Didi, Baltazar, Pinga, Rodriguez.
Mexico: Mota; Lopez, Gomez; Gardenas, Romo, Avalos; Torres, Naranjo (capt), Lamadrid, Balcazar, Arellano.
Scorers: Baltazar, Didi, Pinga (2), Julinho for Brazil.

France (1) 3, Mexico (0) 2 (Geneva)
France: Remetter; Gianessi, Marche (capt); Marcel, Kaelbel, Mahjoub; Kopa, Dereuddre, Strappe, Ben Tifour, Vincent.
Mexico: Carbajal; Lopez, Romo; Cardenas, Avalos, Martinez; Torres, Naranjo (capt), Lamadrid, Balcazar, Arellano.
Scorers: Vincent, Cardenas (o.g.), Kopa (pen) for France; Naranjo, Balcazar for Mexico.

Brazil (0) 1, Yugoslavia (0) 1 after extra time (Lausanne)
Brazil: Castilho; D. Santos, N. Santos; Brandaozinho, Pinheiro (capt), Bauer; Julinho, Didi, Baltazar, Pinga, Rodriguez.
Yugoslavia: Beara; Stankovic, Crnkovic; Cjaicowski I (capt), Horvat, Boskov; Milutinovic, Mitic, Zebec, Vukas, Dvornic.
Scorers: Zebec for Yugoslavia; Didi for Brazil.

	P	W	D	L	F	A	Pts
Brazil	2	1	1	0	6	1	3
Yugoslavia	2	1	1	0	2	1	3
France	2	1	0	1	3	3	2
Mexico	2	0	0	2	2	8	0

POOL 2
Hungary (4) 9, South Korea (0) 0 (Zurich)
Hungary: Grosics; Buzansky, Lantos; Bozsik, Lorant, Szojka; Budai, Kocsis, Palotas, Puskas (capt), Czibor.
South Korea: Hong; K. Park, Kang; Min (capt), Y. Park, Chu; Chung, I. Park, Sung, Woo, Choi.
Scorers: Czibor, Kocsis (3), Puskas (2), Lantos, Palotas (2) for Hungary.

West Germany (1) 4, Turkey (1) 1 (Berne)
West Germany: Turek; Laband, Kohlmeyer; Eckel, Posipal, Mai; Klodt, Morlock, O. Walter, F. Walter (capt), Schaefer.
Turkey: Turgay (capt); Ridvan, Basti; Mustafa, Cetin, Rober; Erol, Suat, Feridun, Burhan, Lefter.
Scorers: Klodt, Morlock, Schaefer, O. Walter for West Germany; Suat for Turkey.

Hungary (3) 8, West Germany (1) 3 (Basle)
Hungary: Grosics; Buzansky, Lantos; Bozsik, Lorant, Zakarias; J. Toth, Kocsis, Hidegkuti, Paskas (capt), Czibor.
West Germany: Kwiatowski; Bauer, Kohlmeyer; Posipal, Liebrich, Mebus; Rahn, Eckel, F. Walter (capt), Pfaff, Herrmann.

Scorers: Hidegkuti (2), Kocsis (4), Puskas, Toth for Hungary; Pfaff, Herrmann, Rahn for Germany.

Turkey (4) 7, South Korea (0) 0 (Geneva)
Turkey: Turgay (capt); Ridvan, Basri; Mustafa, Cetin, Rober; Erol, Suat, Necmettin, Lefter, Burhan.
South Korea: Hong; K. Park (Capt), Kang; Han, C. K. Lee, Kim, Choi, S. Lee, G. C. Lee, Woo, Chung.
Scorers: Burham (3), Erol, Lefter, Suat (2) for Turkey.

	P	W	D	L	F	A	Pts
Hungary	2	2	0	0	17	3	4
Germany	2	1	0	1	7	9	2
Turkey	2	1	0	1	8	4	2
Korea	2	0	0	2	0	16	0

Play-off
West Germany (3) 7, Turkey (1) 2 (Zurich)
West Germany: Turek; Laband, Bauer; Eckel, Posipal, Mai; Klodt, Morlock, O. Walter, F. Walter (capt), Schaefer.
Turkey: Sukru; Ridvan, Basri; Mehmet, Cetin (capt), Rober; Erol, Mustafa, Necmettin, Soskun, Lefter.
Scorers: Morlock (3), O. Walter, Schaefer (2), F. Walter for West Germany; Mustafa, Lefter for Turkey.

POOL 3
Austria (1) 1, Scotland (0) 0 (Zurich)
Austria: Schmied; Hanappi, Barschandt; Ocwirk (capt), Happel, Koller; R. Koerner, Schleger, Dienst, Probst, A. Koerner.
Scotland: Martin; Cunningham (capt), Aird; Docherty, Davidson, Cowie; McKenzie, Fernie, Mochan, Brown, Ormond.
Scorer: Probst for Austria.

Uruguay (0) 2, Czechoslovakia (0) 0 (Berne)
Uruguay: Maspoli; Santamaría, Martinez; Andrade, Varela (capt), Cruz; Abbadie, Ambrois, Miguez, Schiaffino, Borges.
Czechoslovakia: Reiman; Safranek, Novak (capt); Trnka, Hledik, Hertl; Hlavacek, Hemele, Kacani, Pazicky, Krauss.
Scorers: Miguez, Schiaffino for Uruguay.

Austria (4) 5, Czechoslovakia (0) 0, (Zurich)
Austria: Schmied; Hanappi, Barschandt; Ocwirk (capt), Happel, Koller; R. Koerner, Wagner, Stojaspal, Probst, A. Koerner.
Czechoslovakia: Stacho; Safranek, Novak (capt); Trnka, Pluskal, Hertl; Hlavacek, Hemele, Kacani, Pazicky, Krauss.
Scorers: Stojaspal (2), Probst (3) for Austria.

Uruguay (2) 7, Scotland (0) 0 (Basle)

Uruguay: Maspoli; Santamaría, Martinez; Andrade, Varela (capt), Cruz; Abbadie, Ambrois, Miguez, Schiaffino, Borges.
Scotland: Martin; Cunningham (capt), Aird; Docherty, Davidson, Cowie; McKenzie, Fernie, Mochan, Brown, Ormond.
Scorers: Borges (3), Miguez (2), Abbadie (2) for Uruguay.

	P	W	D	L	F	A	Pts
Uruguay	2	2	0	0	9	0	4
Austria	2	2	0	0	6	0	4
Czechoslovakia	2	0	0	2	0	7	0
Scotland	2	0	0	2	0	8	0

POOL 4

England (2) 4, Belgium (1) 4 after extra time (Basle)
England: Merrick; Staniforth, Byrne; Wright (capt), Owen, Dickinson; Matthews, Broadis, Lofthouse, Taylor, Finney.
Belgium: Gerneay; Dries (capt), Van Brandt; Huysmans, Carré, Mees; Mermans, Houf, Coppens, Anoul, P. Van den Bosch.
Scorers: Anoul (2), Coppens, Dickinson (o.g.) for Belgium: Broadis (2), Lofthouse (2) for England.

England (1) 2, Switzerland (0) 0 (Berne)
England: Merrick; Staniforth, Byrne; McGarry, Wright (capt), Dickinson; Finney, Broadis, Wilshaw, Taylor, Mullen.
Switzerland: Parlier; Neury, Kernen; Eggimann, Bocquet (capt), Bigler; Antenen, Vonlanthen, Meier, Ballaman, Fatton.
Scorers: Mullen, Wilshaw for England.

Switzerland (1) 2, Italy (1) 1 (Lausanne)
Switzerland: Parlier; Neury, Kernen; Flueckiger, Bocquet (capt), Casali; Ballaman, Vonlanthen, Hugi, Meier, Fatton.
Italy: Ghezzi; Vincenzi, Giacomazzi; Neri, Tognon, Nesti; Muccinell Boniperti (capt), Galli, Pandolfini, Lorenzi.
Scorers: Ballaman, Hugi for Switzerland; Boniperti for Italy.

Italy (1) 4, Belgium (0) 1 (Lugano)
Italy: Ghezzi; Magnini, Giacomazzi (capt); Neri, Tognon, Nesti; Frignani, Cappello, Galli, Pandolfini, Lorenzi.
Belgium: Gernaey; Dries (capt), Van Brandt; Huysmans, Carré, Mees; Mermans, H. Van den Bosch, Coppens, Anoul, P. Van den Bosch.
Scorers: Pandolfini (pen), Galli, Frignani, Lorenzi for Italy; Anoul for Belgium.

	P	W	D	L	F	A	Pts.
England	2	1	1	0	6	4	3
Italy	2	1	0	1	5	3	2
Switzerland	2	1	0	1	2	3	2
Belgium	2	0	1	1	5	8	1

Play-off
Switzerland (1) 4, Italy (0) 1 (Basle)
Switzerland: Parlier, Neury, Kernen; Eggimann, Bocquet (capt), Casali; Antenen, Vonlanthen, Hugi, Ballaman, Fatton.
Italy: Viola; Vincenzi, Giacomazzi (capt), Neri, Tognon, Nesti; Muccinelli, Pandolfini, Lorenzi, Segato, Frignani.
Scorers: Hugi (2), Ballaman, Fatton for Switzerland; Nesti for Italy.

QUARTER FINALS
West Germany (1) 2, Yugoslavia (0) 0 (Geneva)
West Germany: Turek; Laband, Kohlmeyer; Eckel, Liebrich, Mai; Rahn, Morlock, O. Walter, F. Walter (capt), Schaefer.
Yugoslavia: Beara; Stankovic, Crnkovic; Cjaicowski I, Horvat, Boskov; Milutinovic, Mitic (capt), Vukas, Bobek, Zebec.
Scorers: Horvat (o.g.), Rahn for West Germany.

Hungary (2) 4, Brazil (1) 2 (Berne)
Hungary: Grosics; Buzansky, Lantos; Bozsik (capt), Lorant, Zakarias; M. Toth, Kocsis, Hidegkuti, Czibor, J. Toth.
Brazil: Castilho; D. Santos, N. Santos; Brandaozinho, Pinheiro (capt), Bauer; Julinho, Didi, Indio, Tozzi, Maurinho.
Scorers: Hidegkuti (2), Kocsis, Lantos (penalty) for Hungary; D. Santos, (pen), Julinho for Brazil.

Austria (5) 7, Switzerland (4) 5 (Lausanne)
Austria: Schmied; Hanappi, Barschandt; Ocwirk (capt), Happel, Koller; R. Koerner, Wagner, Stojaspal, Probst, A. Koerner.
Switzerland: Parlier; Neury, Kernen, Eggimann, Bocquet (capt), Casali; Antenen, Vonlanthen, Hugi, Ballaman, Fatton.
Scorers: Ballaman (2), Hugi (2), Hanappi (o.g.) for Switzerland; A. Koerner (2), Ocwirk, Wagner (3), Probst for Austria.

Uruguay (2) 4, England (1) 2 (Basle)
Uruguay: Maspoli; Santamaría, Martinez; Andrade, Varela (capt), Cruz; Abbadie, Ambrois, Miguez, Schiaffino, Borges.
England: Merrick, Staniforth, Byrne; McGarry, Wright (capt), Dickinson; Matthews, Broadis, Lofthouse, Wilshaw, Finney.
Scorers: Borges, Varela, Schiaffino, Ambrois for Uruguay; Lofthouse, Finney for England.

SEMI-FINALS
West Germany (1) 6, Austria (0) 1 (Basle)
West Germany: Turek; Posipal, Kohlmeyer; Eckel, Liebrich, Mai; Rahn, Morlock, O. Walter, F. Walter (capt), Schaefer.
Austria: Zeman; Hanappi, Schleger; Ocwirk (capt), Happel, Koller; R. Koerner, Wagner, Stojaspal, Probst, A. Koerner.
Scorers: Schaefer, Morlock, F. Walter, (2 pen), O. Walter (2) for West Germany; Probst for Austria.

Hungary (1) 4, Uruguay (0) 2, after extra time (Lausanne)
Hungary: Grosics; Buzansky, Lantos; Bozsik (capt), Lorant, Zakarias; Budai, Kocsis, Palotas, Hidgekuti, Czibor.
Uruguay: Maspoli; Santamaría, Martinez; Andrade (capt), Carballo, Cruz; Souto, Ambrois, Schiaffino, Hohberg, Borges.
Scorers: Czibor, Hidegkuti, Kocsis (2) for Hungary; Hohberg (2) for Uruguay.

THIRD PLACE MATCH
Austria (1) 3, Uruguay (1) 1 (Zurich)
Austria: Schmied; Hanappi, Barschandt; Ocwirk (capt), Kollmann, Koller; R. Koerner, Wagner, Dienst, Stojaspal, Probst.
Uruguay: Mospoli; Santamaría, Martinez; Andrade (capt), Carballo, Cruz; Abbadie, Hohberg, Mendez, Schiaffino, Borges.
Scorers: Stojaspal (pen), Cruz (o.g.), Ocwirk for Austria; Hohberg for Uruguay.

FINAL
West Germany (2) 3, Hungary (2) 2 (Berne)
West Germany: Turek; Posipal, Kohlmeyer; Eckel, Liebrich, Mai; Rahn, Morlock, O. Walter, F. Walter, Schaefer.
Hungary: Groscis; Buzansky, Lantos; Bozsik, Lorant, Zakarias; Czibor, Kocsis, Hidegkuti, Puskas, J. Toth.
Scorers: Morlock, Rahn (2) for West Germany; Puskas, Czibor for Hungary.
Leading Scorer: Kocsis (Hungary) 11.

WORLD CUP 1958 – Sweden
At long last, after the disappointment of 1950 and the violent elimination of 1954, Brazil carried off the World Cup in spectacular fashion, with a performance in the final against Sweden which rivalled the greatest ever seen. There, on the rain-soaked stadium of Rasunda, the Brazilian forwards juggled, gyrated and, above all finished with marvellous, gymnastic skill. There, Garrincha, the outside-right, and Pelé, the 17-year-old inside left, together with the incomparable Didi, wrote themselves indelibly into the history of the game.

It was a World Cup which began greyly, and built up to an ultimate crescendo; a World Cup heavy with nostalgia, thanks to the return of Sweden's stars. Professionals now, the Swedes could recall Nacka Skoglund, a hero of their 1950 World Cup team, and Nils Liedholm and Gunnar Gren from their great 1948 Olympic team. They could also bring back from Italy Julli Gustavsson, their splended centre-half, and Kurt Hamrin, a dazzling little outside-right. To begin with, their supporters were pessimistic, but as round succeeded round and George Raynor's elderly team marched on to the final, nationalist feeling mounted alarmingly, culminating in the Gothenburg semi-final.

Brazil had toured Europe in 1956 without much success, but they had learned from their tour. Now they brought with them the 4-2-4 formation that was soon to sweep the world. Four defenders in line, two pivotal players in midfield, four forwards up to strike. They were established, if a little precariously, as the favourites.

England's chances had been gravely affected by the tragic air disaster at Munich, in which their Manchester United stars, Tommy Taylor, Roger Byrne, and the mighty Duncan Edwards, had perished.

The Russians, included with England, Brazil, and Austria in quite the most powerful qualifying group of all (this time, all three teams would play one another), had just drawn 1-1 with England in Moscow. This was their first World Cup, but they had won the Olympic tournament in Australia two years before, while in Lev Yachin they had one of the finest goalkeepers in the game.

Italy and Uruguay were out; Uruguay thrashed 5-0 in Asuncion by Paraguay, Italy eliminated by brave little Northern Ireland. The Irish brilliantly captained by their elegant right-half Danny Blanchflower, generalled in attack by Jimmy McIlroy, were the surprise of the eliminators. After a black game of violence in Belfast, when the referee, Hungary's Zsolt, was fog bound and the World Cup game was turned into a friendly, Chiappella of Italy was sent off and the crowd swarmed on to the pitch. The rematch saw Ireland victorious 2-1. But the Munich crash deprived them of Jackie Blanchflower, a key man at centre-half.

Wales was there on the most fragile grounds. Already eliminated, they were given a second chance when FIFA decided Israel could not qualify by forfeit alone after Uruguay had refused to come back into the competition. So Wales had the fairly easy task of eliminating Israel, which they did surprisingly well.

Scotland, who had eliminated Spain, were in mediocre form, and had been humiliated by England in Glasgow 4-0. West Germany, the holders, captained again by Fritz Walter, had the burly Helmut Rahn on the right wing, but had turned Hans Schaefer into an inside-forward. A new star was the powerful, ruthless wing-half, Horst Szymaniak. Clearly they would take some beating.

Sweden opened the tournament on 8 June in Stockholm, with an easy 3-0 win over Mexico. Two of the goals were scored by their strong, fair-haired centre-forward, Ange Simonsson, while Liedholme got the other goal from a penalty. Bror Mellberg, a 1950 World Cup man, played at inside-right.

In the same group, Hungary, shorn of Puskas, Kocsis, and Czibor, who had stayed in the West after the 1956 Revolution, were held to a 1-1 draw by Wales. Jack Kelsey, Wales' calm, strong goalkeeper, a hero of the tournament, was dazzled by the sun when Bozsik scored after four minutes, but the massive John Charles, recalled from Italy, headed the equaliser from a corner.

In Gothenburg, England and Russia had an exciting battle in which England rallied for a somewhat lucky draw. The power of Voinov and Tsarev (left-half and captain Igor Netto was injured) plus the skill of Salnikov, in midfield, the goalkeeping of Yachin and the domination of

Krijevski, enabled Russia to take a 2–0 lead. But Kevan headed in a free kick and at last Tom Finney, injured in a ruthless tackle and destined to take no further part in the competition, equalised with a penalty.

The Brazilians accounted for Austria 3–0 in Boras, but their team was still in the melting-pot. Pelé, canvassed as their *wunderkind*, was injured, and some wanted the unorthodox Garrincha on the right wing. Team manager Feola himself preferred Vavá to Mazzola at centre-forward, despite the fact that Mazzola (real name José Altafini) scored two of the three goals.

In Group 1, the brave Irish at once showed their quality by defeating the Czechs 1–0 at Halmstad, tough little Wilbur Cush, their versatile inside-right, getting the goal. Harry Gregg had a fine game in goal, but the absence of Jackie Blanchflower forced his brother Danny much deeper into defence.

At Malmö, West Germany were too strong and efficient for an Argentina side which, having brilliantly won the South American Championship the previous year, at once lost its chief stars to Italy. Their style looked old-fashioned, and they had no answer to Rahn, who added two more to his tally of World Cup goals.

No one had expected anything from the French, yet here they were in Norrköping, thrashing Paraguay 7–3, their inside-forward trio of Fontaine (who had expected to be a reserve), Kopa, back from Real Madrid and playing deep, and Piantoni doing remarkable things. Three of the goals were from Kopa. In fact the weeks in training camp at Kopparberg, under Paul Nicolas, had transformed the French morale.

Scotland, meanwhile, undeterred by the fact that Yugoslavia had recently beaten England 5–0, held them to a 1–1 draw at Vasteras. Stamina and determination saved the game after an anxious first half and a seven-minute goal by Petakovic. At right-half, the 35-year-old Eddie Turnbull was in splendid form for the Scots.

The second 'round' was full of surprises. In Gothenburg, an English defence cleverly organised to the prescription of Bill Nicholson, the team coach, held up Brazil's forwards. Howe, the right-back, played in the middle, Clamp, the right half, on the flank, while Slater marked Didi out of the game. Brazil were rather lucky not to give away a penalty in the second half when Bellini felled Kevan, but England, on the other hand, owed much to the cool elegance in goal of Colin McDonald of Burnley. There was no score.

At Boras, Russia, too, accounted for an ageing Austria.

In Group 1, Ireland had a shock 3–1 defeat by the Argentinians, who brought back 40-year-old Angel Labruna at inside-left and gave them a casual lesson in the skills of the game. The stars were Labruna and another veteran, the roving-centre-half Nestor Rossi.

West Germany, two down, rallied to draw with the Czechs, a goal going to the rejuvenated Helmut Rahn, who'd been written off between the two World Cups.

Yugoslavia, who had Branko Zebec, their Rest of Europe left-winger, at centre-half, surprised France to win with a breakaway goal three minutes from time. At Norrköping, a tired-looking Scottish team went down to Paraguay, inspired by Silvio Parodi from inside-forward. Bobby Evans, the red-haired Celtic centre-half, laboured in vain against a thrustful Paraguayan attack.

Wales, feeble in attack, were held to a draw by Mexico in Stockholm, and the following day, again at Rasunda, the Swedes rather unconvincingly beat Hungary. Hungary, with Bozsik of all people at deep centre-forward, were laboured in attack, with only the ferocious shooting of Tichy to keep them in the game. Did Tichy score in the 55th minute with a shot that beat Svensson and hit the underside of the bar? The referee thought not, and half a minute later Hamrin's lob was deflected past Grosics to make it 2–0. Tichy's goal, when it did come, was irrelevant.

The shock of the final round was Czechoslovakia's 6–1 crushing of Argentina at Halsingborg, the sequel to which was a bombardment of rubbish for the Argentina players when they got back to Buenos Aires airport. The Czechs were altogether too fast, with Borovicka and Molnar unstoppable.

Northern Ireland and West Germany drew 2–2 in one of the best matches of the competition, with Gregg superb in goal and Rahn having a superb first half but fading in the second. Peter McParland, Ireland's tough outside-left, twice gave them the lead, but Uwe Seeler, a new young star at centre-forward, equalised 11 minutes from time; so Ireland had to play off against the Czechs.

England, in Boras, stubbornly unchanged by their manager Walter Winterbottom, toiled to a mediocre draw with Austria, so they too had to replay. Haynes, the general, and Douglas, on the right wing, were plainly exhausted after the effort they had made to drag their respective clubs out of Division II; Kevan remained a blunt instrument; Finney was still injured. In Gothenburg, meanwhile, Brazil, at the plea of their own players, at last gave a chance to Garrincha, who mesmerised the Russian defence. Pelé had his first game, and the clever Zito replaced Dino as linking right-half. Russia used Netto to shadow Didi, but Didi was the dominant player of the match. Vivá, replacing Mazzola at centre-forward, scored in the third and 77th minutes, but the 2–0 score flattered Russia. Brazil had found their team, and their form.

In Group 2, France just got home against a Scottish team well served by Bill Brown, making his debut in goal, while Paraguay held the Yugoslavs to a draw. Sweden, fielding five reserves, were satisfied with a goalless draw with Wales, who thus had to meet Hungary (easy conquerors of Mexico) in the play-off.

This they bravely and surprisingly won 2–1 with John Charles back in defence. Tichy opened the score; Ivor Allchurch equalised with a superb 40-yard volley, and, five minutes later Terry Medwin intercepted Grosics' short goal kick to win the game. Sipos was sent off for kicking Hewitt, and Wales hung on to win and to qualify. A famous victory.

Equally famous was Northern Ireland's defeat of the Czechs. Peter

Doherty, once a great Irish inside-forward, now an inspirational team manager, had expressed his confidence that what they had done once, they could do again; and so they did. Injuries to Uprichard, in goal, and to Bertie Peacock did not hold them back. A goal down and forced to play half an hour's extra time, they won in the 100th minute when McParland converted Blanchflower's free kick. Again, the winger scored both goals.

England, at last making changes, throwing Peter Broadbent and Peter Brabrook in the deep end, unluckily went down to Russia in Gothenburg. Twice Brabrook hit the post, but when Russia's Ilyin hit the post, the ball went in. England were eliminated.

In the quarter-finals, the weary, depleted Irish went down 4–0 to France at Norrköping, Casey playing despite just having had four stitches in his shin and Gregg keeping goal on one leg. But theirs had been a glorious achievement.

Wales too went out, defending superbly against Brazil but falling at last to a goal by Pelé, deflected past the splendid Kelsey by the equally splendid Williams. John Charles was unfit to play, but his brother Mel was a superb centre-half and Hopkins cleverly contained Garrincha.

Sweden, with Hamrin irresistible, knocked out the Russians. The little winger headed the first goal, and made the second for Simonsson Finally, a ruthless German team knocked out the Yugoslavs in Malmö with Rahn inevitably getting the goal. As in Switzerland four years earlier, the Slavs dominated the game but just could not score.

In the semi-finals, France's luck deserted them. For 37 minutes, at the Rasunda, they held Brazil, but with the score 1–1, Jonquet, their elegant centre-half, was hurt, and that was that. Didi's 30-yard swerver gave Brazil the lead, and Pelé, at last showing his quality, got three more in the second half.

In Gothenburg, a chanting, nationalistic crowd mustered by official cheer leaders was urging Sweden on to victory against the West Germans. It was rather an unsatisfactory match in many ways. Schaefer brilliantly volleyed Germany into the lead – but Sweden equalised after Liedholm had handled with impunity. In the second half, the game turned on Juskowiak's flash of temper. He kicked Hamrin, was sent off, and the way was clear for Gren, nine minutes from time, and Hemrin himself – a wonderfully impertinent, dribbling goal – to take Sweden into the final.

France thrashed Germany 6–3 on that same ground, in the third-place match, four of the goals going to the rampant Fontaine brilliantly combining with Kopa. This was one of the finest partnerships the World Cup has seen, giving Fontaine a new scoring record for the competition.

It rained in Stockholm on the day of the final, but the crowd, its cheer leaders now properly banned, was quiet, and even Liedholm's fine, early goal, as he picked his way through the Brazilian penalty area, did not decide the game. The Brazilians, scornful of George

Raynor's forecast that if they gave away an early goal, 'they'd panic all over the show', stubbornly held on. Six minutes later, Garrincha, with marvellous swerve and acceleration, left Axbom and Parling standing and made the equaliser for Vavá. Pelé hit a post; Zagalo, always ready to drop deep, cleared from under his own bar; but it was clear that the two fullbacks Santos (with Djalma playing his first game of the tournament) had the measure of Sweden's little wingers.

After 32 minutes Garrincha repeated his astonishing *tour de force*, and Vavá scored again. In the second half, he gave way to the incredible Pelé, who coolly juggled the ball to smash in a third. Zito and Didi were immaculate now in midfield, while Zagalo had sandwiched a goal of his own between Pelé's and the Swedes' second, making it 4–2. Then came the final goal, a brilliant header from Pelé, with the Brazilian fans shouting '*Samba, samba!*' It had been a dazzling exhibition of the arts of the game, and victory at last for the team that morally deserved it.

POOL 1

West Germany (2) 3, Argentina (1) 1 (Malmö)
West Germany: Herkenrath; Stollenwerk, Juskowiak; Eckel, Erhardt, Szymaniak; Rahn, Walter, Seeler, Schmidt, Schaefer.
Argentina: Carrizo; Lombardo, Vairo; Rossi, Dellacha, Varacka; Corbatta, Prado, Menendez, Rojas, Cruz.
Scorers: Rahn (2), Schmidt for West Germany; Corbatta for Argentina.

Northern Ireland (1) 1, Czechoslovakia (0) 0 (Halmstad)
Ireland: Gregg; Keith, McMichael; Blanchflower, Cunningham, Peacock; Bingham, Cush, Dougan, McIlroy, McParland.
Czechoslovakia: Dolejsi; Mraz, Novak; Pluskal, Cadek, Masopust; Hovorka, Dvorak, Borovicka, Hartl, Kraus.
Scorer: Cush for Northern Ireland.

West Germany (1) 2, Czechoslovakia (0) 2 (Halsingborg)
West Germany: Herkenrath; Stollenwerk, Juskowiak; Schnellinger, Erhardt, Szymaniak; Rahn, Walter, Seeler, Schaefer, Klodt.
Czechoslovakia: Dolejsi; Mraz, Novak; Pluskal, Popluhar, Masopust; Hovorka, Dvorak, Molnar, Feureisl, Zikan.
Scorers: Rahn, Schaefer for West Germany; Dvorak (pen) Zikan for Czechoslovakia.

Argentina (1) 3, Northern Ireland (1) 1 (Halmstad)
Argentina: Carrizo; Lombardo, Vario; Rossi, Dellacha, Varacka; Corbatta, Avio, Menendez, Labruna, Boggio.
Northern Ireland: Gregg; Keith, McMichael; Blanchflower, Cunnham, Peacock; Bingham, Cush, Casey, McIlroy, McParland.
Scorers: Corbatta (2) (one pen), Menendez for Argentina; McParland for Northern Ireland.

West Germany (1) 2, Northern Ireland (1) 2 (Malmö)
West Germany: Herkenrath; Stollenwerk, Juskowiak; Eckel, Erhardt, Szymaniak; Rahn, Walter, Seeler, Schaefer, Klodt.
Northern Ireland: Gregg; Keith, McMichael; Blanchflower, Cunningham, Peacock; Bingham, Cush, Casey, McIlroy, McParland.
Scorers: Rahn, Seeler for West Germany; McParland (2) for Northern Ireland.

Czechoslovakia (3) 6, Argentina (1) 1 (Halsingborg)
Czechoslovakia: Dolejsi; Mraz, Novak; Dvorak, Popluhar, Masopust; Hovorka, Borovicka, Molnar, Feureisl, Zikan.
Argentina: Carrizo; Lombardo, Vario; Rossi, Dellacha, Varacka; Corbatta, Avio, Menendez, Labruna, Cruz.
Scorers: Dvorak, Zikan (2), Feureisl, Hovorka (2) for Czechoslovakia; Corbatta for Argentina.

	P	W	D	L	F	A	Pts
West Germany	3	1	2	0	7	5	4
Czechoslovakia	3	1	1	1	8	4	3
Northern Ireland	3	1	1	1	4	5	3
Argentina	3	1	0	2	5	10	2

Play-off
Northern Ireland (1) 2, Czechoslovakia (1) 1 after extra time (Malmö)
Northern Ireland: Uprichard; Keith, McMichael; Blanchflower, Cunningham, Peacock; Bingham, Cush, Scott, McIlroy, McParland.
Czechoslovakia: Dolejsi; Mraz, Novak; Bubernik, Popluhar, Masopust; Dvorak, Borovicka, Feureisl, Molnar, Zikan.
Scorers: McParland (2) for Northern Ireland; Zikan for Czechoslovakia.

POOL 2
France (2) 7, Paraguay (2) 3 (Norrköping)
France: Lemetter; Kaelbel, Lerond; Penverne, Jonquet, Marcel; Wisnieski, Fontaine, Kopa, Piantoni, Vincent.
Paraguay: Mayeregger; Arevalo, Miranda; Achucarro, Lezcano, Villalba; Aguero, Parodi, Romero, Re, Amarilla.
Scorers: Fontaine (3), Piantoni, Wisnieski, Kopa, Vincent for France; Amarilla (2) (1 pen), Romero for Paraguay.

Yugoslavia (1) 1, Scotland (0) 1 (Vasteras)
Yugoslavia: Beara; Sijakovic, Crnkovic; Krstic, Zebec, Boskov; Petakovic, Veselinovic, Milutinovic, Sekularac, Rajkov.
Scotland: Younger; Caldow, Hewie; Turnbull, Evans, Cowie; Leggat, Murray, Mudie, Collins, Imlach.
Scorers: Petakovic for Yugoslavia; Murray for Scotland.

Yugoslavia (1) 3, France (1) 2 (Vasteras)
Yugoslavia: Beara; Tomic, Crnkovic; Krstic, Zebec, Boskov; Petakovic, Veselinovic, Milutinovic, Sekularac, Rajkov.
France: Remetter; Kaelbel, Marche; Penverne, Jonquet, Lerond; Wisnieski, Fontaine, Kopa, Piantoni, Vincent.
Scorers: Petakovic, Veselinovic (2) for Yugoslavia; Fontaine (2) for France.

Paraguay (2) 3, Scotland (1) 2 (Norrköping)
Paraguay: Aguilar; Arevalo, Enhague; Achucarro, Lezcano, Villalba; Aguero, Parodi, Romero, Re, Amarilla.
Scotland: Younger; Parker, Caldow; Turnbull, Evans, Cowie; Leggat, Collins, Mudie, Robertson, Fernie.
Scorers: Aguero, Re, Parodi for Paraguay; Mudie, Collins for Scotland.

France (2) 2, Scotland (0) 1 (Cerebro)
France: Abbes; Kaelbel, Lerond; Penverne, Jonquet, Marcel; Wisnieski, Fontaine, Kopa, Piantoni, Vincent.
Scotland: Brown; Caldow, Hewie; Turnbull, Evans, Mackay; Collins, Murray, Mudie, Baird, Imlach.
Scorers: Kopa, Fontaine for France; Baird for Scotland.

Yugoslavia (2) 3, Paraguay (1) 3 (Ekilstuna)
Yugoslavia: Beara; Tomic, Crnkovic; Boskov, Zebec, Krstic; Petakovic, Velesinovic, Ognjanovic, Sekularac, Rajkov.
Paraguay; Aguilar; Arevalo, Echague; Villalba, Lezcano, Achucarro; Aguero, Parodi, Romero, Re, Amarilla.
Scorers: Ognjanovic, Veselinovic, Rajkov for Yugoslavia; Parodi, Aguero, Romero for Paraguay.

	P	W	D	L	F	A	Pts
France	3	2	0	1	11	7	4
Yugoslavia	3	1	2	0	7	6	4
Paraguay	3	1	1	1	9	12	3
Scotland	3	0	1	2	4	6	1

POOL 3
Sweden (1) 3, Mexico (0) 0 (Stockholm)
Sweden: Svensson; Bergmark, Axbom; Liedholm, Gustavsson, Parling; Hamrin, Melberg, Simonsson, Gren, Skoglund.
Mexico: Carbajal; Del Muro, Gutierrez; Cardenas, Romo, Flores; Hernandez, Reyes, Calderon, Gutierrez, Sesma.
Scorers: Simonsson (2), Liedholm (pen) for Sweden.

Hungary (1) 1, Wales (1) 1 (Sandviken)
Hungary: Grosics; Matray, Sarosi; Bozsik, Sipos, Berendi; Sandor, Tichy, Hidegkuti, Bundzsak, Fenyvesi.
Wales: Kelsey; Williams, Hopkins; Sullivan, M. Charles, Bowen; Webster, Medwin, J. Charles, Allchurch, Jones.
Scorers: Bozsik for Hungary; J. Charles, for Wales.

Wales (1) 1, Mexico (1) 1 (Stockholm)
Wales: Kelsey; Williams, Hopkins; Baker, M. Charles, Bowen; Webster, Medwin, J. Charles, Allchurch, Jones.
Mexico: Carbajal: Del Muro, Gutierrez; Cardenas, Romo, Flores; Belmonte, Reyes, Blanco, Gonzales, Sesma.
Scorers: Allchurch for Wales; Belmonte for Mexico.

Sweden (1) 2, Hungary (0) 1 (Stockholm)
Sweden: Svensson; Bergmark, Axbom; Liedholm, Gustavsson, Parling; ling; Berndtsson, Selmosson, Kaelgren, Lofgren, Skoglund.
Hungary: Grosics; Matray, Sarosi; Szojka, Sipos, Berendi; Sandor, Tichy, Bozsik, Bundzsak, Fenyvesi.
Scorers: Hamrin (2) for Sweden; Tichy for Hungary.

Sweden (0) 0, Wales (0) 0 (Stockholm)
Sweden: Svensson; Bergmark, Axbom; Boerjesson, Gustavsson, Parling; Berndtsson, Kaelgren, Lofgren, Skoglund.
Wales: Kelsey; Williams, Hopkins; Sullivan, M. Charles, Bowen; Vernon, Hewitt, J. Charles, Allchurch, Jones.

Hungary (1) 4, Mexico (0) 0 (Sandviken)
Hungary: Ilku; Matray, Sarosi; Bozsik, Sipos, Kotasz; Budai, Bencsics, Tichy, Bundzsak, Fenyvesi.
Mexico: Carbajal; Del Muro, Gutierrez; Cardenas, Sepulvedo, Flores; Belmonte, Reyes, Blanco, Gonzales, Sesma.
Scorers: Tichy (2), Sandor, Bencsics for Hungary.

	P	W	D	L	F	A	Pts
Sweden	3	2	1	0	5	1	5
Hungary	3	1	1	1	6	3	3
Wales	3	0	3	0	2	2	3
Mexico	3	0	1	2	1	8	1

Play-off
Wales (0) 2, Hungary (1) 1 (Stockholm)
Wales: Kelsey; Williams, Hopkins; Sullivan, M. Charles, Bowen; Medwin, Hewitt, J. Charles, Allchurch, Jones.
Hungary: Grosics; Matray, Sarosi; Bozsik, Sipos, Kotasz; Budai, Bencsics, Tichy, Bundzsak, Fenyvesi.
Scorers: Allchurch, Medwin for Wales; Tichy for Hungary.

POOL 4
England (0) 2, Russia (1) 2 (Gothenburg)
England: McDonald; Howe, Banks; Clamp, Wright, Slater; Douglas, Robson, Kevan, Haynes, Finney.
Russia: Yachin; Kessarev, Kuznetsov; Voinov, Krijevski, Tsarev; A. Ivanov, V. Ivanov, Simonian, Salnikov, Ilyin.
Scorers: Simonian, A. Ivanov, for Russia; Kevan, Finney (pen) for England.

Brazil (1) 3, Austria (0) 0 (Boras)
Brazil: Gilmar; De Sordi, N. Santos; Dino, Bellini, Orlando; Joel, Didi, Mazzola, Dida, Zagalo.
Austria: Szanwald; Halla, Swoboda; Hanappi, Happel, Koller; Horak, Senekowitsch, Buzek, Koerner, Schleger.
Scorers: Mazzola (2), Santos for Brazil.

England (0) 0, Brazil (0) 0 (Gothenburg)
England: McDonald; Howe, Banks; Clamp, Wright, Slater; Douglas, Robson, Kevan, Haynes, A'Court.
Brazil: Gilmar; De Sordi, N. Santos; Dino, Bellini, Orlando; Joel, Didi, Mazzola, Vavá, Zagalo.

Russia (1) 2, Austria (0) 0 (Boras)
Russia: Yachin; Kessarev, Kuznetsov; Voinov, Krijevski, Tsarev; A. Ivanov, V. Ivanov, Simonian, Salnikov, Ilyin.
Austria: Schmied; E. Kozlicek, Swoboda; Hanappi, Stotz, Koller; Horak, P. Hozlicek, Buzek, Koerner, Senekowitsch.
Scorers: Ilyin, V. Ivanov for Russia.

Brazil (1) 2, Russia (0) 0 (Gothenburg)
Brazil: Gilmar; De Sordi, N. Santos; Zito, Bellini, Orlando; Garrincha, Didi, Vavá, Pelé, Zagalo.
Russia: Yachin; Kessarev, Kuznetsov; Voinov, Krijevski, Tsarev; A. Ivanov, V. Ivanov, Simonian, Netto, Ilyin.
Scorer: Vavá (2) for Brazil.

England (0) 2, Austria (1) 2 (Boras)
England: McDonald; Howe, Banks; Clamp, Wright, Slater; Douglas, Robson, Kevan, Haynes, A'Court.
Austria: Szanwald; Kollmann, Swoboda; Hanappi, Happel, Koller; E. Kozlicek, P. Kozlicek, Buzek, Koerner, Senekowitsch.
Scorers: Haynes, Kevan for England; Koller, Koerner for Austria.

	P	W	D	L	F	A	Pts
Brazil	3	2	1	0	5	0	5
England	3	0	3	0	4	4	3
Russia	3	1	1	1	4	4	3
Austria	3	0	1	2	2	7	1

Play-off
Russia (0) 1, England (0) 0 (Gothenburg)
Russia: Yachin; Kessarev, Kuznetsov; Voinov, Krijevski, Tsarev; Apoukhtin, V. Ivanov, Simonian, Falin, Ilyin.
England: McDonald; Howe, Banks; Clayton, Wright, Slater; Brabrook, Broadbent, Kevan, Haynes, A'Court.
Scorer: Ilyin for Russia.

QUARTER-FINALS
France (1) 4, Ireland (0) 0 (Norrköping)
France: Abbes; Kaelbel, Lerond; Penverne, Jonquet, Marcel; Wisnieski, Fontaine, Kopa, Piantoni, Vincent.
Northern Ireland: Gregg; Keith, McMichael; Blanchflower, Cunningham, Cush; Bingham, Casey, Scott, McIlroy, McParland.
Scorers: Wisnieski, Fontaine (2), Piantoni for France.

West Germany (1) 1, Yugoslavia (0) 0 (Malmö)
West Germany: Herkenrath; Stollenwerk, Juskowiak; Eckel, Erhardt, Szymaniak; Rahn, Walter, Seeler, Schmidt, Schaefer.
Yugoslavia: Krivocuka; Sijakovic, Crnkovic; Kristic, Zebec, Boskov; Petakovic, Veselinovic, Milutinovic, Ognjanovic, Rajkov.
Scorer: Rahn for West Germany.

Sweden (0) 2, Russia (0) 0 (Stockholm)
Sweden: Svensson; Bergmark, Axbom; Boerjesson, Gustavsson, Parling; Hamrin, Gren, Simonsson, Liedholm, Skoglund.
Russia: Yachin; Kessarev, Kuznetsov; Voinov, Krijevski Tsarev; A. Ivanov, V. Ivanov, Simonian, Salnikov, Ilyin.
Scorers: Hamrin, Simonsson for Sweden

Brazil (0) 1, Wales (0) 0 (Gothenburg)
Brazil: Gilmar; De Sordi, N. Santos; Zito, Bellini, Orlando; Garrincha, Didi, Mazzola, Pelé, Zagalo.
Wales: Kelsey; Williams, Hopkins; Sullivan, M. Charles, Bowen; Medwin, Hewitt, Webster, Allchurch, Jones.
Scorer: Pelé for Brazil.

SEMI-FINALS
Brazil (2) 5, France (1) 2 (Stockholm)
Brazil: Gilmar; De Sordi, N. Santos; Zito, Bellini, Orlando; Garrincha, Didi, Vavá, Pelé, Zagalo.
France: Abbes; Kaelbel, Lerond; Penverne, Jonquet, Marcel; Wisnieski, Fontaine, Kopa, Piantoni, Vincent.
Scorers: Vavá, Didi, Pelé (3) for Brazil; Fontaine, Piantoni for France.

Sweden (1) 3, West Germany (1) 1 (Gothenburg)
Sweden: Svensson; Bergmark, Axbom; Boerjesson, Gustavsson, Parling; Hamrin, Gren, Simonsson, Liedholm, Skoglund.
West Germany: Herkenrath; Stollenwerk, Juskowiak; Eckel, Erhardt, Szymaniak; Rahn, Walter, Seeler, Schaefer, Cieslarczyk.
Scorers: Skoglund, Gren, Hamrin for Sweden; Schaefer for West Germany.

THIRD PLACE MATCH
France (0) 6, West Germany (0) 3 (Gothenburg)
France: Abbes; Kaelbel, Lerond; Penverne, Lafont, Marcel; Wisnieski, Douis, Kopa, Fontaine, Vincent.

West Germany: Kwiatowski; Stollenwerk, Erhardt; Schnellinger, Wewers, Szymaniak; Rahn, Sturm, Kelbassa, Schaefer, Cieslarzcyk.
Scorers: Fontaine (4) Kopa (pen), Douis for France; Cieslarczyk, Rahn, Schaefer for West Germany.

FINAL

Brazil (2) 5, Sweden (1) 2 (Stockholm)
Brazil: Gilmar; D. Santos, N. Santos; Zito, Bellini, Orlando; Garrincha, Didi, Vavá, Pelé, Zagalo.
Sweden: Svensson; Bergmark, Axbom; Boerjesson, Gustavsson, Parling; Hamrin, Gren, Simonsson, Liedholm, Skoglund.
Scorers: Vavá (2), Pelé (2), Zagalo for Brazil; Liedholm, Simonsson for Sweden.
Leading Scorer: Fontaine (France)13 (present record total).

WORLD CUP 1962 – Chile

The selection of Chile as host to the 1962 World Cup was a surprising one, determined largely by sentiment and by the pressures of Chile's representative to FIFA, the late Carlos Dittborn: 'We have nothing, that is why we must have the World Cup.' Chile had recently suffered a disastrous earthquake, but Dittborn promised all would be ready in time. Argentina, the logical choice, had a poor record in terms of loyalty to the tournament and, in fact, Chile made a good enough job of the organisation, though the insanely high prices kept out an impoverished working class and there was flagrant profiteering by hotels and agencies.

Once again, the four-pool qualifying system was employed, this time with such disastrous effects (goal average was counted) as to cast doubt not only on the system but on the whole future of the game. Manic defence, eight men in the penalty box, reduced many of the qualifying matches to farce.

Brazil and Russia were the favourites, Russia because, on their recent South American tour, they had beaten Argentina, Uruguay, and Chile. Otherwise, the field looked a mediocre one. England had just lost to Scotland in Glasgow for the first time for 25 years; Hungary, Argentina, and Italy were in decline; West Germany as tough as ever, but lacking a Fritz Walter. Chile had the great advantage of playing at home, and the experienced managership of Fernando Riera, but nobody much favoured them.

The Brazilians, after various experiments, fell back on almost exactly the team that won in 1958. Vavá and Didi had returned from Madrid, and Mauro, Bellini's understudy in Sweden, replaced him at centre-half. Zagalo, when Pelé dropped out injured after the second game, played a still deeper left wing role, turning 4–2–4 into a definite 4–3–3. The one 'revelation' was Pelé's 24-year-old replacement, Amarildo. The outstanding figure was Garrincha, adding remarkable finishing power with both feet and his head to his known gifts of swerve and acceleration.

Playing in the delightful seaside *cancha* of Viña del Mar, they began with a laborious 2-0 win over the resilient Mexicans, drew 0-0 with the well organised Czechs, losing Pelé with a severely pulled muscle, and were given a bad fright by Spain. Helenio Herrera, recalled from Milan to manage the Spaniards, made four changes and nearly did the trick. Spain led by Adelardo's goal at half-time, and only Garrincha's brilliance, making two goals for Adelardo, turned the trick for Brazil. The Czechs, though beaten by Mexico, were runners-up.

England, in the Rancagua group played on the stadium owned by the Braden Copper Company (they themselves had a remote mountain camp at Coya) came second to Hungary; their conquerors in the first match. A team based on the crossfield and through passing of Johnny Haynes was too predictable. The 21-year-old Bobby Moore, first capped in Lima on the way to Chile, did well at wing-half, but too closely resembled the other halfback Flowers for a 4-2-4 to be workable. Haynes hadn't enough creative support. These problems were compounded by Ron Springett's strange vulnerability in goal to long shots. The powerful Tichy beat him with one in the opening match, Albert brilliantly scoring the other after Flowers had equalised from a penalty. A halfback like the admirable Solymosi of Hungary was just what England needed.

They did much better against Argentina, who had won a dull, dour match 1-0 against Bulgaria. Alan Peacock of Middlesbrough made an excellent debut at centre-forward, despite the brutal attentions of Navarro. Again Flowers scored from a penalty, Bobby Charlton, admirable on the left wing, made it 2-0 before half-time, Greaves scored at third, and Sanfilippo's goal came too late to count.

Hungary overwhelmed Bulgaria then went through the motions in a draw with Argentina. England also drew 0-0 against Bulgaria in a game of unspeakable tedium, and they nearly lost when Kolev broke clear.

The Chileans, with Toro and Rojas a forceful pair in midfield, were the surprise of Group 1, which produced their notorious match against Italy. The Italians, stuffed with South Americans, were unpopular because two of their correspondents had criticised life in Santiago. At the imposing new stadium – not yet a camp for political prisoners, as it became 11 years later – Chile were provocative from the first. The Italians responded in kind and Ken Aston, the referee, much criticised for his performance, found it 'uncontrollable'. In the event, the Chileans did better. Two Italians, Ferrini and David, were sent off, while Leonel Sanchez broke the Italo-Argentinian Maschio's nose with impunity. Chile won 2-0, but lost by the same score to the parsimonious, counter-attacking Germans, themselves conquerors of the Swiss after breaking Eschmann's leg. Italy and Germany had drawn 0-0; Germany and Chile qualified.

Far up in the North, at Arica, Russia were the disappointment, Colombia the surprise. When the two met, Lev Yachin for once was out of form and the result was a remarkable 4-4 draw, Klinger, the little black Colombian inside-left, being the best man afield. The Colombians, who had held Uruguay to 2–1 in their opening match, then ran out of steam and were thrashed 5–0 by Yugoslavia.

Yachin had his only good game of the tournament in the opening match against Yugoslavia, a vicious but skilful affair in which Dubinski, the Russian fullback, had his leg broken by Mujic, who was sent home. Victor Ponedelnik engineered both goals, in the second half, scoring the second himself after hitting the bar with a free kick for Ivanov to score the first.

Dragoslav Sekularac, who had a magnificent tournament, was irrepressible, while he was better still against the Uruguayans, who carried him off the field after they'd lost 3–1. Russia, lucky to beat Uruguay, won the group, with the Yugoslavs second. But it was Yugoslavia who survived the quarter-finals.

In Santiago, they at long last beat their eternal 'bogeys', the West Germans, with a late goal by their little midfield halfback, Radakovic, playing with a bandaged head. They were much the more creative.

Brazil 'at home' in Viña del Mar, won a curious match against England, who had to take the field without the injured Peacock. Garrincha was in unstoppable form, his swerve and acceleration as irresistible as in Sweden. After 31 minutes, he showed another talent, getting up splendidly to head in a corner. England should have been two down when Flowers unaccountably passed across his own goal to Amarildo, but Springett saved brilliantly, and Hitchens equalised after Greaves' header came back from the bar.

Alas for Springett, however, he allowed Garrincha's second-half free kick to come back off his chest for Vavá to score easily, and later he was tricked by Garrincha's clever swerving long shot. Brazil were through, but they had been a little lucky.

In Arica, Chile, whose fans were growing more and more crazily excited, put out Russia. Again, Yachin had a poor game, badly placed for Leonel Sanchez's goal straight from a free kick after 10 minutes; still more at fault with Eladio Rojas' 35-yard second. Chislenko replied a couple of minutes later, but the 4–2–4 Chilean team held on to a narrow success.

Surprisingly, the Czechs beat the Hungarians 1–0 in Rancagua. For 80 minutes they were penned in their own half, while Hungary beat a tattoo on their goalposts. Schroiff, in goal, was unbeatable, and Scherer's breakaway goal in the 13th minute won the match. Tichy's 'equaliser' was ruled, disputably, offside.

In the semi-finals, Garrincha dashed Chile's hopes with another marvellous display. A magnificent 20-yard left-footer after nine minutes put Brazil ahead; a header from a corner doubled the lead. Toro, with a mighty free kick, made it 2–1, but just after half-time Vavá headed a vital goal from Garrincha's dropping corner-kick: 3–1. Leonel Sanchez made it 3–2, from a penalty, but Vavá tied up the match, heading in Zagalo's centre. Zagalo had worked with boundless stamina and decisive effect.

In a displeasing finale, Landa, Chile's centre-forward, and Garrincha were in turn sent off the field. Garrincha for kicking Rojas, Landa for a foul on Zito. As he made his way round the track, Garrincha had his head cut by a missile thrown from a frantically partisan crowd.

The Czechs, to everyone's amazement, prevailed again – over the talented Yugoslavs. At Viña del Mar, watched by a mere and miserable 5000, Schroiff was again the determining player. The Slavs had most of the game but, weak on the wings, could not turn their domination into more than Jerkovic's equalising goal. A breakaway allowed Scherer to give the Czechs the lead again; a silly handling offence by Markovic allowed the same player to decide the match from the penalty spot.

A tired Yugoslav team, with Sekularac even so the best player on the field, lost 1–0 to Chile in the third place game. Rojas' long shot, deflected, beat an excellent Soskic for the only goal of a dreary match.

In the final, Brazil once more had to play without Pelé. Playing at a slow, steady rhythm, with Kvasniak tireless and long-legged in midfield, the Czechs cleverly took the lead when Masopust ran on to Scherer's through pass. But alas for the Czechs, this was not to be a good day for Schroiff. He should have stopped Amarildo's equaliser from the narrowest of angles. In the second half, Amarildo whiplashed past his man to make a headed goal, under the bar, for Zito, and, 13 minutes from time, poor Schroiff dropped high lob into the sun by Djalma Santos and that was number three. Not a Brazilian victory to be compared with Stockholm; this was an older, more cautious team, without Pelé, with a slower Didi, with Garrincha well controlled by the experienced Czech defence. The Czechs had been distinguished losers.

GROUP 1 (Arica)
Uruguay (0) 2, Colombia (1) 1
Uruguay: Sosa; Troche, Em. Alvarez; El. Alvarez, Mendez, Gonçalves; Rocha, Perez, Langon, Sasia, Cubilla.
Colombia: Sanchez; Zaluaga, Gonzalez, Lopez, Etcheverri; Silva, Coll; Aceros, Klinger, Gamboa, Arias.
Scorers: Cubilla, Sasia for Uruguay; Zaluaga for Colombia.

Russia (0) 2, Yugoslavia (0) 0
Russia: Yachin; Dubinski, Ostrovski; Voronin, Maslenkin, Netto; Metreveli, Ivanov, Ponedelnik, Kanevski, Meschki.
Yugoslavia: Soskic; Durkovic, Jusufi; Matus, Markovic, Popovic; Mujic, Sekularac, Jerkovic, Galic, Skoblar.
Scorers: Ivanov, Ponedelnik for Russia.

Yugoslavia (2) 3, Uruguay (1) 1
Yugoslavia: Soskic; Durkovic, Jusufi; Radakovic, Markovic, Popovic; Melic, Sekularac, Jerkovic, Galic, Skoblar.
Uruguay: Sosa; Troche, Em. Alvarez, El. Alvarez, Mendez; Gonçalves, Rocha; Cubilla, Cabrera, Sasia, Perez.
Scorers: Skoblar, Galic, Jerkovic for Yugoslavia; Cabrera for Uruguay.

Russia (3) 4, Colombia (1) 4
Russia: Yachin; Tchokelli, Ostrovski; Netto, Maslenkin, Voronin; Chislenko, Ivanov, Ponedelnik, Kanevski, Meschki.
Colombia: Sanchez; L. Gonzalez, Lopez, Alzate, Etcheverri; Serrano, Coll; Aceros, Rada, Klinger, C. Gonzalez.
Scorers: Ivanov (2), Chislenko, Ponedelnik for Russia; Aceros, Coll, Rada, Klinger for Colombia.

Russia (1) 2, Uruguay (0) 1
Russia: Yachin; Tchokelli, Ostrovski; Netto, Maslenkin, Voronin; Chislenko, Ivanov, Ponedelnik, Mamikin, Hussainov.
Uruguay: Sosa; Troche, El. Alvarez, Em. Alvarez, Mendez; Gonçalves, Cortes; Cubilla, Cabrera, Sasia, Perez.
Scorers: Mamikin, Ivanov for Russia; Sasia for Uruguay.

Yugoslavia (2) 5, Colombia (0) 0
Yugoslavia: Soskic; Durkovic, Yusufi; Radakovic, Markovic, Popovic; Ankovic, Sekularac, Jerkovic, Galic, Melic.
Colombia: Sanchez; Alzate, O. Gonzalez, Lopez, Etcheverri; Serrano, Coll; Aceros, Klinger, Rada, C. Gonzalez.
Scorers: Galic, Jerkovic (3), Melic for Yugoslavia.

	P	W	D	L	F	A	Pts
Russia	3	2	1	0	8	5	5
Yugoslavia	3	2	0	1	8	3	4
Uruguay	3	1	0	2	4	6	2
Colombia	3	0	1	2	5	11	1

GROUP 2 (Santiago)
Chile (1) 3, Switzerland (1) 1
Chile: Escuti; Eyzaguirre, R. Sanchez, Contreras, Navarro; Toro, Rojas; Ramirez, Landa, Fouilloux, L. Sanchez.
Switzerland: Elsener; Morf, Schneiter, Tacchella; Grobety, Weber; Allemann, Pottier, Eschmann, Wuthrich, Antenen.
Scorers: L. Sanchez (2), Ramirez for Chile; Wuthrich for Switzerland.

West Germany (0) 0, Italy (0) 0
West Germany: Fahrian; Novak, Schnellinger; Schulz, Erhardt, Szymaniak; Sturm, Haller, Seeler, Brülls, Schaefer.
Italy: Buffon; Losi, Robotti; Salvadore, Maldini, Radice; Ferrini, Rivera, Altafino, Sivori, Menichelli.

Chile (0) 2, Italy (0) 0
Chile: Escuti; Eyzaguirre, Contreras, R. Sanchez, Navarro; Toro, Rojas; Ramirez, Landa, Fouilloux, L. Sanchez.
Italy: Mattrel; David, Robotti; Salvadore, Janich, Tumburus; Mora, Maschio, Altafini, Ferrini, Menichelli.
Scorers: Ramirez, Toro for Chile.

West Germany (1) 2, Switzerland (0) 1
West Germany: Fahrian; Novak, Schnellinger; Schulz, Erhardt, Szymaniak; Koslowski, Haller, Seeler, Brülls, Schaefer.
Switzerland: Elsener; Schneiter, Tacchella, Grobety; Wuthrich, Weber; Antenen, Vonlanthen, Allemann, Eschmann, Durr.
Scorers: Brülls, Seeler for West Germany; Schneiter for Switzerland

West Germany (1) 2, Chile (0) 0
West Germany: Fahrian; Novak, Schnellinger; Schulz, Erhardt, Giesemann; Krauss, Szymaniak, Seeler, Schaefer, Brülls.
Chile: Escuti; Eyzaguirre, Contreras, R. Sanchez, Navarro; Tobar, Rojas; Moreno, Landa, L. Sanchez, Ramirez.
Scorers: Szymaniak (pen), Seeler for West Germany.

Italy (1) 3, Switzerland (0) 0
Italy: Buffon; Losi, Robotti; Salvadore, Maldini, Radice; Mora, Bulgarelli, Sormani, Sivori, Pascutti.
Switzerland: Elsener; Schneiter, Meier, Tacchella; Grobety, Weber; Antenen, Vonlanthen, Wuthrich, Allemann, Durr.
Scorers: Mora, Bulgarelli (2) for Italy.

	P	W	D	L	F	A	Pts
West Germany	3	2	1	0	4	1	5
Chile	3	2	0	1	5	3	4
Italy	3	1	1	1	3	2	3
Switzerland	3	0	0	3	2	8	0

GROUP 3 (Viña del Mar)
Brazil (0) 2, Mexico (0) 0
Brazil: Gilmar; D. Santos, Mauro, Zozimo, N. Santos; Zito, Didi; Garrincha, Vavá, Pelé, Zagalo.
Mexico: Carbajal; Del Muro, Cardenas, Sepulveda, Villegas; Reyes, Najera; Del Aguila, Hernandez, Jasso, Diaz.
Scorers: Zagalo, Pelé for Brazil.

Czechoslovakia (0) 1, Spain (0) 0
Czechoslovakia: Schroiff; Lala, Novak; Pluskal, Popluhar, Masopust; Stibranyi, Scherer, Kvasniak, Adamec, Jelinck.
Spain: Carmelo; Rivilla, Reija; Segarra, Santamaría, Garay; Del Sol, Martinez, Puskas, Suarez, Gento.
Scorer: Stibranyi for Czechoslovakia.

Brazil (0) 0, Czechoslovakia (0) 0
Brazil: Gilmar; D. Santos, Mauro, Zozimo, N. Santos; Zito, Didi; Garrincha, Vavá, Pelé, Zagalo.
Czechoslovakia: Schroiff; Lala, Novak; Pluskal, Popluhar, Masopust; Stibranyi, Scherer, Kvasniak, Adamec, Jelinck.

Spain (0) 1, Mexico (0) 0
Spain: Carmelo; Rodri, Garcia; Verges, Santamaria, Pachin; Del Sol, Peiró, Puskas, Suarez, Gento.
Mexico: Carbajal; Del Muro, Cardenas, Sepulveda, Jauregui; Reyes, Najera; Del Aguila, H. Hernandez, Jasso, Diaz.
Scorer: Peiró for Spain.

Brazil (0) 2, Spain (1) 1
Brazil: Gilmar; D. Santos, Mauro, Zozimo, N. Santos, Zito, Didi; Garrincha, Vavá, Amarildo, Zagalo.
Spain: Araguistain; Rodri, Gracia; Verges, Echevarria, Pachin; Collar, Adelardo, Puskas, Peiró, Gento.
Scorers: Amarildo (2) for Brazil; Adelardo for Spain.

Mexico (2) 3, Czechoslovakia (1) 1
Mexico: Carbajal; Del Muro, Cardenas, Sepulveda, Jauregui; Reyes, Najera; Del Aguila, A. Hernandez, H. Hernandez, Diaz.
Czechoslovakia: Schroiff; Lala, Novak; Pluskal, Popluhar, Masopust; Stibranyi, Scherer, Kvasniak, Adamec, Masek.
Scorers: Diaz, Del Aguila, H. Hernandez (pen) for Mexico; Masek for Czechoslovakia.

	P	W	D	L	F	A	Pts
Brazil	3	2	1	0	4	1	5
Czechoslovakia	3	1	1	1	2	3	3
Mexico	3	1	0	2	3	4	2
Spain	3	1	0	2	2	3	2

GROUP 4 (Rancagua)
Argentina (1) 1, Bulgaria (0) 0
Argentina: Roma; Navarro, Baez, Sainz, Marzolini; Sacchi, Rossi; Facundo, Pagani, Sanfilippo, Belen.
Bulgaria: Naidenov; Rakarov, Kotov; Kostov, Dimitrov, Kovatchev; Diev, Velitchkov, Iliev, Yakimov, Kolev.
Scorer: Facundo for Argentina.

Hungary (1) 2, England (0) 1
Hungary: Grosics; Matrai, Sarosi; Solymosi, Meszoly, Sipos; Sandor, Rakosi, Albert, Tichy, Fenyvesi.
England: Springett; Armfield, Wilson; Moore, Norman, Flowers; Douglas, Greaves, Hitchens, Haynes, Charlton.
Scorers: Tichy, Albert for Hungary; Flowers (pen) for England.

England (2) 3, Argentina (0) 1
England: Springett; Armfield, Wilson; Moore, Norman, Flowers; Douglas, Greaves, Peacock, Haynes, Charlton.
Argentina: Roma; Capp, Baez, Navarro, Marzolini; Sacchi, Rattin; Oleniak, Sosa, Sanfilippo, Belen.
Scorers: Flowers (pen), Charlton, Greaves for England; Sanfilippo for Argentina.

Hungary (4) 6, Bulgaria (0) 1
Hungary: Ilku; Matrai, Sarosi; Solymosi, Meszoly, Sipos, Sandor, Rakosi, Alberr, Tichy, Fenyvesi.
Bulgaria: Naidenov; Rakarov, Kotov; Kostov, Dimitrov, Kovatchev; Sokolov, Velitchkov, Asparoukhov, Kolev, Dermendiev.
Scorers: Albert (3), Tichy (2), Solymosi for Hungary; Sokolov for Bulgaria.

Argentina (0) 0, Hungary (0) 0
Argentina: Dominguez; Capp, Sainz, Delgado, Marzolini; Sacchi, Pando; Facundo, Pagani, Oleniak, Gonzales.
Hungary: Grosics; Matrai, Sarosi; Solymosi, Meszoly, Sipos; Kuharszki, Gorocs, Monostroi, Tichy, Rakosi.

England (0) 0, Bulgaria (0) 0
England: Springett; Armfield, Wilson; Moore, Norman, Flowers; Douglas, Greaves, Peacock, Haynes, Charlton.
Bulgaria: Naidenov; Rakarov, Jetchev; D. Kostov, Dimitrov, Kovatchev; A. Kostov, Velitchkov, Iliev, Kolev, Yakimov.

	P	W	D	L	F	A	Pts
Hungary	3	2	1	0	8	2	5
England	3	1	1	1	4	3	3
Argentina	3	1	1	1	2	3	3
Bulgaria	3	0	1	2	1	7	1

QUARTER-FINALS

Yugoslavia (0) 1, West Germany (0) 0 (Santiago)
Yugoslavia: Soskic; Durkovic, Jusufi; Radakovic, Markovic, Popovic; Kovacevic, Sekularac, Jerkovic, Galic, Skoblar.
West Germany: Fahrian; Novak, Schnellinger; Schulz, Erhardt, Giesemann; Haller, Szymaniak, Seeler, Brülls, Schaefer.
Scorer: Radakovic for Yugoslavia.

Brazil (1) 3, England (1) 1 (Viña del Mar)
Brazil: Gilmar; D. Santos, Mauro, Zozimo, N. Santos; Zito, Didi; Garrincha, Vavá, Amarildo, Zagalo.
England: Springett; Armfield, Wilson; Moore, Norman, Flowers; Douglas, Greaves, Hitchens, Haynes, Charlton.
Scorers: Garrincha (2), Vavá for Brazil; Hitchens for England.

Chile (2) 2, Russia (1) 1 (Arica)
Chile: Escutti; Eyzaguirre, Contreras, R. Sanchez, Navarro; Toro, Rojas; Ramirez, Landa, Tobar, L. Sanchez.
Russia: Yachin; Tchokelli, Ostrovski; Voronin, Maslenkin, Netto; Chislenko, Ivanov, Ponedelnik, Mamikin, Meshki.
Scorers: L. Sanchez, Rojas for Chile; Chislenko for Russia.

Czechoslovakia (1) 1, Hungary (0) 0 (Rancagua)
Czechoslovakia: Schroiff; Lala, Novak; Pluskal, Popluhar, Masopust; Pospichal, Scherer, Kvasniak, Kadraba, Jelinek.
Hungary: Grosics; Matrai, Sorisi; Solymosi, Meszoly, Sipos; Sandor, Rakosi, Albert, Tichy, Fenyvesi.
Scorer: Scherer for Czechoslovakia.

SEMI-FINALS
Brazil (2) 4, Chile (1) 2 (Santiago)
Brazil: Gilmar; D. Santos, Mauro, Zozimo, N. Santos; Zito, Didì; Garrincha, Vavá, Amarildo, Zagalo.
Chile: Escutti; Eyzaguirre, Contreras, R. Sanchez, Rodriguez; Toro, Rojas; Ramirez, Landa, Tobar, L. Sanchez.
Scorers: Garrincha (2), Vavá (2) for Brazil; Toro, L. Sanchez (pen) for Chile.

Czechoslovakia (0) 3, Yugoslavia (0) 1 (Viña del Mar)
Czechoslovakia: Schroiff; Lala, Novak; Pluskal, Popluhar, Masupust; Pospichal, Scherer, Kvasniak, Kadraba, Jelinek.
Yugoslavia: Soskic; Durkovic, Jusufi; Radakovic, Markovic, Popovic; Sujakovic, Sekularac, Jerkovic, Galic, Skoblar.
Scorers: Kadraba, Scherer (2), for Czechoslovakia; Jerkovic for Yugoslavia.

THIRD PLACE MATCH
Chile (0) 1, Yugoslavia (0) 0 (Santiago)
Chile: Godoy; Eyzaguirre, Cruz, R. Sanchez, Rodriguez; Toro, Rojas; Ramirez, Campos, Tobar, L. Sanchez.
Yugoslavia: Soskic; Durkovic, Svinjarevic; Radakovic, Markovic, Popovic; Kovacevic, Sekularac, Jerkovic, Galic, Skoblar.
Scorer: Rojas for Chile.

FINAL
Brazil (1) 3, Czechoslovakia (1) 1 (Santiago)
Brazil: Gilmar; D. Santos, Mauro, Zozimo, N. Santos; Zito, Didì; Garrincha, Vavá, Amarildo, Zagalo.
Czechoslovakia; Schroiff; Tichy, Novak; Pluskal, Popluhar, Masopust; Pospichal, Scherer, Kvasniak, Kadraba, Jelinek.
Scorers: Amarildo, Zito, Vavá for Brazil; Masopust for Czechoslovakia.

Leading Scorers: Albert (Hungary, Ivanov (Russia), L. Sanchez (Chile), Garrincha, Vavá (Brazil), Jerkovic (Yugoslavia) each 4.

WORLD CUP 1966 – England
England, as Alf Ramsey had promised, won the World Cup. They won it, in the end, deservedly, with two fine performances in semi-final and

final, won it without Jimmy Greaves, won it despite a brutal setback in the last minute of the final itself.

Starting painfully and laboriously, their attack terribly unimpressive in the three qualifying games, England 'came good' when it was most necessary – in the ill-tempered quarter-final against Argentina (when the Argentinians went virtually berserk in the tunnel at the end). Geoff Hurst, the West Ham United player, who had looked sadly out of form as recently as the tour match against Denmark in Copenhagen, came back into the team against Argentina to become, perhaps, the decisive force in England's success. His three goals in the final established a new record.

In general terms, it was a disappointing World Cup, with no team to match the Brazilians of 1958 and 1962 or the Hungarians of 1954. England had a superb defence, but their 4–3–3 formation, generally without specialised wingers, was by no means as impressive in attack. What saved them was the eruption of Hurst, the sudden blossoming of Bobby Charlton in semi-final and final, the energy of Alan Ball against Portugal followed by his astonishing, all-round performance against the West Germans.

Brazil were shown to be clearly in decline. This time they and their manager, Feola, paid the penalty for an exaggerated reliance on old names, old faces. An injury to Pelé in the first game had an effect on them which it never had in Chile. Good young players had, it's true, been left behind, but obviously a period of retrenchment was needed.

The surprise of the tournament were the lively little North Koreans, who astonished and humiliated the listless Italians. Quick, intelligent, learning from game to game, they were wonderfully popular with the Middlesbrough crowd, and gave Portugal an enormous scare in the quarter-finals.

The Hungarians, with a novel tactical formation, played superbly against Brazil but were betrayed by poor goalkeeping. Portugal, with Eusebio the leading scorer and perhaps the outstanding player of the whole tournament, might have done better still had their defence in any way matched their attack. As for the West Germans, the runners-up, their powerful, well-balanced side, though it never lived up to its opening flourish against Switzerland, was full of talent.

Fittingly, the tournament started with that epitome of modern World Cups, a goalless draw. Uruguay went out to stop England from scoring, massed eight and nine men in defence, and succeeded with little trouble. An ingenuously chosen England team, with Ball as a pseudo-winger and the essentially destructive Stiles at linking wing-half, played into their hands. The strikers and schemers alike were impotent against the tough, rhythmic, immensely professional Uruguayans, responding as always to the challenge of a World Cup.

It was Pelé, appropriately, who scored the first goal of the tournament next day – the player who, above all others, was expected to dominate the tournament. After 14 minutes of Brazil's match at Everton with Bulgaria, he smashed in a pheonomenal right-footed free-kick. In the second half, an equally remarkable free-kick by Garrincha gave Brazil a second, but they were not over impressive. Pelé dazzlingly apart, the team often stuttered. He himself was ruthlessly marked by Zhechev.

This turned out to be the most exciting group of all. Hungary and Portugal, who would each beat Brazil and qualify, met at Old Trafford, Portugal winning thanks to a couple of errors by the Hungarian 'keeper, Szentmihalyi. The Hungarians' formation, three link-men breaking to support two strikers, was promising, however, and they came to fulfilment at Everton three days later against Brazil. Brazil severely felt the loss of Pelé; and the burden of years carried by Djalma Santos, Bellini, and Garrincha. Moreover, they left Florian Albert free to dominate the field. Bene, the little right winger, wriggled through for a lovely individual goal after only three minutes, but Brazil equalised when Tostão, making his World Cup debut, drove in the rebound from Lima's free kick. However, under pouring rain, Hungary took firm hold of the game. Albert and Bene, in the second half, made a spectacularly shot goal for Farkas, Meszöly scored the third from a penalty. It was Brazil's first World Cup defeat since 1954.

Portugal, helped by an own goal and a silly back-pass, easily beat Bulgaria at Old Trafford, then tackled Brazil at Goodison. Desperately, Brazil made nine belated changes, giving a World Cup debut to seven men. But Manga was shaky in goal. After 14 minutes, he weakly pushed out Eusebio's cross for Simões to head in, then the huge Torres nodded Coluna's free kick across for Eusebio to head a second. Pelé was back, but struggling, and a brutal, gratuitous foul by Morais put him definitively out. Late on, Rildo came up to whip home a goal, but the excellent Eusebio drove in Portugal's third after a right wing corner. Brazil were out.

England unimpressively beat Mexico and France 2-0 to win Group 2. The Mexicans staked everything on defence, but were at last breached by a marvellous right-foot goal from Bobby Charlton, Hunt scoring the second after a superb through pass by Charlton had split the defence for Greaves. Hunt scored twice more against a French team reduced to 10 by Herbin's early injury, but both midfield and defence were unconvincing. Uruguay, with minimal enterprise, beat France at the White City, drew 0–0 with Mexico, and came second.

In Group 3, West Germany unmasked the splendid Franz Beckenbauer who scored two goals against a Swiss team that suspended two leading players, Kuhn and Leimgruber, for breaking curfew. The Argentinians, elegant but ruthless, beat Spain, whose use of Suarez was harsh at Villa Park. Argentina scored twice through the opportunism of the gifted Luis Artime, well abetted by Onega. When they and the West Germans met, it was a horrid, goalless affair in which Argentina's fearsome Albrecht was sent off. Argentina then beat Switzerland, West Germany disposed of a lively Spain, and both qualified.

In Group 4, the North Koreans finished poorly, fought bravely, but were physically overwhelmed at Ayresome Park by Russia. Italy beat Chile in a bloodless reprise of the Battle of Santiago, left out Rivera, and surprisingly went down to Russia at Sunderland, Chislenko scoring a fine only goal.

So the cataclysm of a Tuesday that saw North Korea beat Italy; Brazil lose to Portugal and go out. Having drawn with Chile, North Korea ran hard and fast against a flaccid Italy, who lost Bulgarelli after 34 minutes with a damaged knee after he had fouled an opponent. Seven minutes later Pak Doo Ik scored his unforgettable goal and Italy were on their knees. Russia and North Korea went through.

England's quarter-final with Argentina at Wembley remains notorious; the match which after Alf Ramsey expressed the hope that his next opponents would not 'act as animals'. Argentina had the all-round skill to win, but preferred a policy of cynical obstruction and endless petty fouling. Herr Kreitlein, the tiny, bald West German referee, took names with manic zeal, and eventually sent off the towering Argentinian captain, Antonio Rattin, for dissent and 'the look on his face'. Still, England found it hard. Geoff Hurst, brought in to replace the injured Greaves, forced Roma to an incredible save early in the first half and at last beat him with a fine, glided header to Peter's left wing cross.

At Everton, Portugal found themselves 3-0 down to the dazzling North Koreans in 20 minutes. Then Eusebio took the game by the scruff of the neck and scored four goals (two of them penalties); a couple before half-time, a couple after. Running out of steam, the gallant Koreans lost 5-3 – and subsided anew into anonymity.

Russia surprisingly beat Hungary, betrayed again by poor goal-keeping. Gelei, fumbling a shot and failing with a cross, took blame for both Russian goals; Rakosi missed an open goal at the Russian end, and the technically superior Hungarians had to settle for Bene's goal.

At Hillsbrough, more mayhem. Two Uruguayans were sent off and West Germany beat their depleted team 4-0. Uruguay were incensed when Schnellinger seemed to handle on the line with impunity, then Held's shot was freakishly deflected home off Haller. Troche was expelled for kicking Emmerich, Silva for fouling Haller.

In the semi-finals, England took wing at last in a memorable game with Portugal, Bobby Charlton rampant; West Germany won a dismal struggle against Russia at Everton. There were cries of 'conspiracy' when it was known England would play at Wembley, accusations that Sir Stanley Rous had had his way. The truth was that Rous wanted the game played at Everton and was overruled by the World Cup committee!

England, with Stiles playing Eusebio out of the match and galvanising his defence, dominated the match, but found goals hard to score. Bobby Charlton got both. After 30 minutes, Wilson put Hunt through, Pereira couldn't hold the shot, and Charlton followed up. Eleven minutes from time, Hurst forced his way to the right hand goal-line and pulled the ball back for Charlton to score again. Three minutes later, Eusebio converted a penalty after Jackie Charlton punched

Torres' clever header, but Stiles and Banks took England safely through the difficult closing minutes.

At Everton, squalor. Sabo hurt himself early on trying to foul Beckenbauer, Chislenko had himself sent off in the second half for kicking Held soon after being badly hurt when Schnellinger went through to make the second goal. Even against nine fit men, Germany had a hard time of it, and Russia actually scored two minutes from time when Tilkowski dropped a cross. A skilful, swerving shot by Beckenbauer beat the splendid Yachin for Germany's second goal.

The third place match was equally dreary. Portugal won, for what it mattered. Khurtsilava's foolish hand-ball allowed Eusebio to score another penalty and take his total of goals to nine, highest of the tournament. Pereira's error gave Malafeev the equaliser, but Torres scored the winner when Augusto nodded down Simões' cross.

England won the dramatic final, so maintaining a 65-year-old unbeaten record against Germany. Greaves was omitted from their team, Hunt controversially stayed, missing a good chance in the first half, throwing away another with an inept pass in the second; errors that made extra time necessary. For the Germans, seemingly well beaten at 2–1, hit back in the last minute to score through Weber, on the far post, after Emmerich's free-kick; itself dubiously given against Jackie Charlton. They had opened the scoring, after 13 minutes, when Wilson uncharacteristically headed a cross straight to Haller's feet. Hurst headed in Moore's quickly taken free-kick to equalise, and Peters put England ahead in the second half when Weber blocked Hurst's shot after a corner.

At the last, it was Ball's astonishing stamina, his inextinguishable running, that gave England victory in extra time. His was the run and cross which, after 100 minutes, allowed Hurst to smash the ball in off the crossbar. Bakhramov, the Russian linesman, gave a goal that is still contested in West Germany. Perhaps we shall never be quite sure whether the ball crossed the line. In any case, Hurst, with his left foot, scored a fourth goal as England broke away in the closing seconds.

England's morale and resistance were a credit to Alf Ramsey, who unquestionably inspired this team. The Germans must still regret Helmut Schoen's decision to use Beckenbauer so negatively as the guardian of Bobby Charlton. Beckenbauer, nonetheless, was still among the best of his team, with Schultz, Held, and Seeler. But Alan Ball was the true hero of the day.

GROUP 1
England (0) 0, Uruguay (0) 0 (Wembley)
England: Banks (Leicester City); Cohen (Fulham), Wilson (Everton); Stiles (Manchester United), J. Charlton (Leeds United), Moore (West Ham United); Ball (Blackpool), Greaves (Spurs), R. Charlton (Manchester United), Hunt (Liverpool), Connelly (Manchester United).
Uruguay: Mazurkiewicz; Troche, Ubinas; Gonçalves, Manicera, Caetano; Cortes, Viera, Silva, Rocha, Perez.

France (0) 1, Mexico (0) 1 (Wembley)
France: Aubour; Djorkaeff, Budzinski, Artelesa, De Michele; Bosquier, Herbin, Bonnel; Combin, Gondet, Hausser.
Mexico: Calderon; Chaires, Pena, Nunez, Hernandez; Diaz, Mercado, Reyes; Borja, Fragoso, Padilla.
Scorers: Borja for Mexico; Hausser for France.

Uruguay (2) 2, France (1) 1 (White City)
Uruguay: Mazurkiewicz; Troche, Ubinas; Gonçalves, Manicera, Caetano; Viera, Cortes, Rocha, Sacia, Perez.
France: Aubour; Djorkaeff, Artelesa, Budzinski, Bosquier; Bonnel, Simon; Herbet, Gondet, De Bourgoing, Hausser.
Scorers: Rocha, Cortes for Uruguay; De Bourgoing (pen) for France.

England (1) 2, Mexico (0) 0 (Wembley)
England: Banks (Leicester City); Cohen (Fulham), Wilson (Everton); Stiles (Manchester United), J. Charlton, (Leeds United), Moore (West Ham United); Paine (Southampton), Greaves (Spurs), R. Charlton (Manchester United), Hunt (Liverpool), Peters (West Ham United).
Mexico: Calderon; Del Muro; Chaires, Pena Nunez, Hernandez; Diaz, Jauregui, Reyes; Borja, Padilla.
Scorers: R. Charlton, Hunt for England.

Uruguay (0) 0, Mexico (0) 0 (Wembley)
Uruguay: Mazurkiewicz; Troche; Ubinas, Gonçalves, Manicera, Caetano; Viera, Rocha, Cortes, Sacia, Perez.
Mexico: Carbajal; Chaires, Pena, Nunez, Hernandez; Diaz, Mercado; Reyes, Cisneros, Borja, Padilla.

England (1) 2, France (0) 0 (Wembley)
England: Banks (Leicester City); Cohen (Fulham), Wilson (Everton); Stiles (Manchester United), J. Charlton (Leeds United), Moore (West Ham United); Callaghan (Liverpool), Greaves (Spurs), R. Charlton (Manchester United), Hunt (Liverpool), Peters (West Ham United).
France: Aubour; Djorkaeff, Artelesa, Budzinski, Bosquier; Bonnel, Herbin, Simon; Herbet, Gondet, Hausser.
Scorer: Hunt (2) for England.

	P	W	D	L	F	A	Pts
England	3	2	1	0	4	0	5
Uruguay	3	1	2	0	2	1	4
Mexico	3	0	2	1	1	3	2
France	3	0	1	2	2	5	1

GROUP 2
West Germany (3) 5, Switzerland (0) 0 (Hillsborough, Sheffield)
West Germany: Tilkowski; Hottges, Schulz, Weber, Schnellinger; Beckenbauer, Haller; Brülls, Seeler, Overath, Held.

Switzerland: Elsener; Grobety, Schneiter; Techella, Fuhrer, Bani; Durr, Odermatt, Kunzli, Hosp, Schindelholz.
Scorers: Held, Haller (2) (1 pen), Beckenbauer 2 for West Germany.

Argentina (0) 2, Spain (0) 1 (Villa Park, Birmingham)
Argentina: Roma; Perfumo, Marzolini; Ferreiro, Rattin, Albrecht; Solari, Gonzalez, Artime, Onega, Mas.
Spain: Iribar; Sanchis, Eladio; Pirri, Gallego, Zoco; Ufarte, Del Sol, Peiro, Suarez, Gento.
Scorers: Artime (2) for Argentine; Pirri for Spain.

Spain (0) 2, Switzerland (1) 1 (Hillsborough, Sheffield)
Spain: Iribar; Sanchis, Reija; Pirri, Callego, Zoco; Amancio, Del Sol, Peiro, Suarez, Gento.
Switzerland: Elsener; Brodmann, Fuhrer; Leimgruber, Armbruster, Stierli; Bani, Kuhn, Gottardi, Hosp, Quentin.
Scorers: Sanchis, Amancio for Spain; Quentin for Switzerland.

Argentine (0) 0, West Germany (0) 0 (Villa Park Birmingham)
Argentina: Roma; Perfumo, Marzolini; Ferreiro, Rattin, Albrecht; Solari, Gonzalez, Artime, Onega, Mas.
West Germany: Tilkowski; Hottges, Schulz, Weber, Schnellinger; Beckenbauer, Haller, Brülls, Seeler, Overath, Held.

Argentina (0) 2, Switzerland (0) 0 (Villa Park, Birmingham)
Argentina: Roma; Perfumo, Marzolini; Ferreiro, Rattin, Calics; Solari, Gonzalez, Artime, Onega, Mas.
Switzerland: Eichmann; Fuhrer, Brodmann; Kuhn, Armbruster, Stierli; Bani, Kunzli, Gottardi, Hosp, Quentin.
Scorers: Artime, Onega for Argentina.

West Germany (1) 2, Spain (1) 1 (Villa Park, Birmingham)
West Germany: Tilkowski; Hottges, Schulz, Weber, Schnellinger; Beckenbauer, Overath; Kramer, Seeler, Held, Emmerich.
Spain: Iribar; Sanchis, Reija; Glaria, Callego, Zoco; Amancio, Adelardo, Marcelino, Fuste, Lapetra.
Scorers: Emmerich and Seeler for West Germany; Fuste for Spain.

	P	W	D	L	F	A	Pts
West Germany	3	2	1	0	7	1	5
Argentina	3	2	1	0	4	1	5
Spain	3	1	0	2	4	5	2
Switzerland	3	0	0	3	1	9	0

GROUP 3
Brazil (1) 2, Bulgaria (0) 0 (Goodison Park, Liverpool)
Brazil: Gilmar; D. Santos, Bellini, Altair, Paolo Henrique; Edilson, Lima; Garrincha, Pelé, Alcindo, Jairzinho.

Bulgaria: Neidenov; Chalamanov, Vutzov, Gaganelov, Penev; Kitov, Zhechev, Yakimov; Dermendjiev, Asparoukhov, Kolev.
Scorers: Pelé, Garrincha for Brazil.

Portugal (1) 3, Hungary (0) 1 (Old Trafford, Manchester)
Portugal: Carvalho; Morais, Baptista, Vicente, Hilario; Graça, Coluna; Augusto, Eusebio, Torres, Simões.
Hungary: Szentmihalyi; Matrai, Kaposzta; Sovari, Meszoly, Sipos; Bene, Nagy, Albert, Farkas, Rakosi.
Scorers: Augusto (2), Torres for Portugal; Bene for Hungary.

Hungary (1) 3, Brazil (1) 1 (Goodison Park, Liverpool)
Hungary: Gelei; Kaposzta, Matrai, Sipos, Szepesi; Mathesz, Meszoly; Bene, Albert, Farkas, Rakosi.
Brazil: Gilmar; D. Santos, Bellini, Altair, Paolo Henrique; Lima, Gerson; Garrincha, Alcindo, Tostão, Jairzinho.
Scorers: Bene, Farkas, Meszoly (pen) for Hungary; Tostão for Brazil.

Portugal (2) 3, Bulgaria (0) 0 (Old Trafford, Manchester)
Portugal: José Pereira; Festa, Germano, Vicente, Hilario; Graça, Coluna; Augusto, Eusebio, Torres, Simões.
Bulgaria: Naidenov; Chalamanov, Vutzov, Gaganelov, Penev; Zechev, Yakimov; Dermendjiev, Zhekov, Asparoukhov, Kostov.
Scorers: Vutzov (o.g.), Eusebio, Torres for Portugal.

Portugal (2) 3, Brazil (0) 1 (Goodison Park, Liverpool)
Portugal: José Pereira; Morais, Baptista, Vicente, Hilario; Graça, Coluna, Augusto; Eusebio, Torres, Simões.
Brazil: Manga; Fidelis, Brito, Orlando, Rildo; Denilson, Lima; Jair, Silva, Pelé, Parana.
Scorers: Simoes, Eusebio (2) for Portugal; Rildo for Brazil.

Hungary (2) 3, Bulgaria (1) 1 (Old Trafford, Manchester)
Hungary: Gelei; Kaposzta, Matrai, Meszoly, Sipos, Szepesi; Mathesz, Albert, Rakosi; Bene, Farkas.
Bulgaria: Simenov; Penev, Largov, Vutzov, Gaganelov; Zhechev, Dadidov; Kotkov, Asparoukhov, Yakimov, Kolev.
Scorers: Davidov (o.g.), Meszoly, Bene for Hungary; Asparoukhov for Bulgaria.

	P	W	D	L	F	A	Pts
Portugal	3	3	0	0	9	2	6
Hungary	3	2	0	1	7	5	4
Brazil	3	1	0	2	4	6	2
Bulgaria	3	0	0	3	1	8	0

GROUP 4

Russia (2) 3, North Korea (0) 0 (Middlesbrough)
Russia: Kavazashvili; Ponomarev, Chesternjiev, Khurtsilava, Ostrovski; Sabo, Schinava; Chislenko, Malafeev, Banichevski, Khusainov.
North Korea: Li Chan Myung; Pak Li Sup, Shin Yung Kyoo, Lim Zoong Sun, Kang Bong Chil; Pak Seung Din, Im Seung Hwi; Han Bong Jin, Pak Doo Ik, Kang Ryong-Woon, Kim Seung II.
Scorers: Malafeev (2), Banichevski for Russia.

Italy (1) 2, Chile (0) 0 (Sunderland)
Italy: Albertosi; Burgnich, Facchetti; Rosato, Salvadore, Lodetti; Perani, Bulgarelli, Mazzola, Rivera, Barison,
Chile: Olivares; Eyzaguirre, Cruz, Figueroa, Villanueva; Prieto, Marcos; Araya, Tobar, Fouilloux, Sanchez.
Scorers: Barison, Mazzola for Italy.

Chile (1) 1, North Korea (0) 1 (Middlesbrough)
Chile: Olivares; Valentini, Cruz; Figueroa, Villanueva, Prieto; Marcos, Fouilloux, Landa, Araya, Sanchez.
North Korea: Li Chan Myung; Pak Li Sup, Shin Yung Kyoo, Kim Joon Sun, O Yoon Kyung; Pak Seung Jin, Im Seung Hwi; Han Bong Jin, Pak Doo Ik, Ri Dong Woon, Kim Seung II.
Scorers: Marcos (pen) for Chile; Pak Sung Jin for North Korea.

Russia (0) 1, Italy (0) 0 (Sunderland)
Russia: Yachin; Ponomarev, Chesternjiev, Khurtsilava, Danilov; Sabo, Voronin; Chislenko, Malafeev, Banichevski, Khusainov.
Italy: Albertosi; Burgnich, Facchetti; Rosato, Salvadore, Leoncini; Meroni, Lodetti, Mazzola, Bulgarelli, Pascutti.
Scorer: Chislenko for Russia.

North Korea (1) 1, Italy (0) 0 (Middlesbrough)
North Korea: Li Chan Myung; Lim Zoong Sun, Shin Yung Kyoo; Ha Jung Won, O Yoon Kyung, Im Seung Hwi; Han Bong Jin, Pak Doo Ik, Pak Seung Zin, Kim Bong Hwan, Yan Sung Kook.
Italy: Albertosi; Landini, Facchetti; Guarneri, Janich, Fogli; Perani, Bulgarelli, Mazzola, Rivera, Barison.
Scorer: Pak Doo Ik for North Korea.

Russia (1) 2, Chile (1) 1 (Sunderland)
Russia: Kavazashvili; Getmanov, Chesternjiev, Afonin, Ostrovski; Voronin, Korneev; Metreveli, Serebrianikov, Markarov, Porkujan.
Chile: Olivares; Valentini, Cruz, Figueroa, Villaneuva; Marcos, Prieto; Araya, Landa, Yavar, Sanchez.
Scorers: Porkujan (2) for Russia; Marcos for Chile.

	P	W	D	L	F	A	Pts
Russia	3	3	0	0	6	1	6
North Korea	3	1	1	1	2	4	3
Italy	3	1	0	2	2	2	2
Chile	3	0	1	2	2	5	1

QUARTER-FINALS

England (0) 1, Argentina (0) 0 (Wembley)
England: Banks (Leicester City); Cohen (Fulham), Wilson (Everton); Stiles (Manchester United), J. Charlton (Leeds United), Moore (West Ham United); Ball (Blackpool), Hurst (West Ham United), R. Charlton, (Manchester United), Hunt (Liverpool), Peters (West Ham United).
Argentina: Roma; Ferreiro, Perfumo, Albrecht, Marzolini; Gonzalez, Rattin, Onega; Solari, Artime, Mas.
Scorer: Hurst for England.

West Germany (1) 4, Uruguay (0) 0 (Sheffield)
West Germany: Tilkowski; Hottges, Weber, Schulz, Schnellinger; Beckenbauer, Haller, Overath, Seeler, Held, Emmerich.
Uruguay: Mazurkiewicz; Troche; Ubinas, Gonçalves, Manicera, Caetano; Salva, Rocha; Silva, Cortez, Perez.
Scorers: Held, Beckenbauer, Seeler, Haller for West Germany.

Portugal (2) 5, *North Korea* (3) 3 (Goodison)
Portugal: José Pereira; Morais, Baptista, Vicente, Hilario; Graça, Coluna; Augusto, Eusebio, Torres, Simões.
North Korea: Li Chan Myung; Rim Yung Sum, Shin Yung Kyoo, Ha Jung Won, O Yoon Kyung; Pak Seung Jin, Im Seung Hwi; Han Bong Jin, Pak Doo Ik, Li Dong Woon, Yang Sung Kook.
Scorers: Eusebio 4 (2 pen), Augusto for Portugal; Pak Seung Jin, Yang Sung Kook, Li Dong Woon for North Korea.

Russia (1) 2, Hungary (0) 1 (Sunderland)
Russia: Yachin; Ponomarev, Chesternjiev, Voronin, Danilov; Sabo, Khusainov; Chislenko, Banichevski, Malafeev, Porkujan.
Hungary: Gelei; Matrai, Kaposzta, Meszoly, Sipos, Szepesi; Nagy, Albert, Rakosi; Bene, Farkas.
Scorers: Chislenko, Portkujan for Russia; Bene for Hungary.

SEMI-FINALS

West Germany (1) 2, Russia (0) 1 (Goodison)
West Germany: Tilkowski; Hottges, Weber, Schulz, Schnellinger; Beckenbauer, Haller, Overath; Seeler, Held, Emmerich.
Russia: Yachin; Ponomarev, Chesternjiev, Voronin, Danilov; Sabo, Khusainov; Chislenko, Banichevski, Malafeev, Porkujan.
Scorers: Haller, Beckenbauer for West Germany; Porkujan for Russia.

England (1) 2, Portugal (0) 1 (Wembley)
England: Banks (Leicester City); Cohen (Fulham), Wilson (Everton); Stiles (Manchester United), J. Charlton (Leeds United), Moore (West Ham United); Ball (Blackpool), Hurst (West Ham United), R. Charlton, (Manchester United), Hunt (Liverpool), Peters (West Ham United).
Portugal: José Pereira; Festa, Baptista, Carlos, Hilario; Graça, Coluna, Augusto; Eusebio, Torres, Simões.
Scorers: R. Charlton (2) for England; Eusebio (pen) for Portugal.

THIRD PLACE MATCH
Portugal (1) 2, Russia (1) 1 (Wembley)
Portugal: José Pereira; Festa, Baptista, Carlos, Hilario; Graça, Coluna, Augusto; Eusebio, Torres, Simões.
Russia: Yachin; Ponomarev, Khurtsilava, Korneev, Danilov; Voronin, Sichinava; Metreveli, Malafeev, Banichevski, Serebrianikov.
Scorers: Eusebio (pen), Torres for Portugal; Malafeev for Russia.

FINAL
England (1) 4, West Germany (1) 2 after extra time (Wembley)
England: Banks; Cohen, Wilson, Stiles, J. Charlton, Moore; Ball, Hurst, Hunt, R. Charlton, Peters.
West Germany: Tilkowski; Hottges, Schulz, Weber, Schnellinger; Haller, Beckenbauer, Overath; Seeler, Held, Emmerich.
Scorers: Hurst (3) Peters for England; Haller, Weber for West Germany.
Leading Scorer: Eusebio 9.

WORLD CUP 1970
For the third time in four tournaments, Brazil won the World Cup, and very properly retained the Jules Rimet Trophy in consequence. There was no doubt at all of the merits of their success, even if the Italian team they crushed 4–1 in the final could scarcely claim to be the competition's second best. Brazil won every one of their matches, including a narrow and slightly fortunate win against England – thus condemned to play their quarter final in León against West Germany.

Most teams seemed to solve the problem of altitude, but that of heat was simply insoluble. Goodness knows how much the temperatures in Guadalajara, which sometimes rose as high as 98° in a match, affected the England players. In the circumstances they acquitted themselves with honour, especially Bobby Moore, rising superbly above the dingy and unfounded charges of theft brought against him in Colombia.

From an objective point of view, the success of a Brazilian team so wholeheartedly committed to attack – and definitely porous in defence – was a splendid sign in a grey footballing world. For the next four years, one was entitled to hope, the future might at long last lie with creative rather than negative football.

Brazil's triumph was the more remarkable in that they had changed horses, or managers, rather further than mid-stream, Zagalo, a hero of their 1958 and 1962 teams, succeeding the controversial João Saldanha.

The Guadalajara group pivoted on the match between Brazil and England; the second for both of them, and one of those played in the roasting heat of noon. England's players were not helped by the fact that a yelling throng of Mexicans, unharassed by the police, laid siege to their hotel, chanting and honking till the small hours.

Without their 'slow sodium' pills, England would have wilted in the 98°F heat, each player as it was losing an average of 10 pounds during the game. Brazil clearly missed Gerson, their general, but only Banks' amazing one-handed save from Pelé's bouncing header, after Jairzinho beat Cooper and crossed from the line, kept the score goalless at half-time. England themselves missed chances through Lee and Hurst, then, after Brazil had scored, through Ball and Astle, whose was the most clamorous miss of all. The only goal came 14 minutes into the second half. Tostão held off three English defenders – literally in the case of the immaculate Moore – crossed from the left, Pelé rolled the ball on, and Jairzinho scored.

Playing with Rivelino as a 'retractable' left winger, Brazil had beaten the Czechs in their opening game, despite an early goal by the powerful Petras and a near miss. Then Brazil's wonderful control and shooting prevailed, the Czechs throwing away their last chance when Kvasniak, so much slower than in 1962, missed. Rivelino's fierce freekick, Pelé's cool virtuosity as he caught Gerson's long pass on his chest, Jairzinho's irresistable run; these brought memorable goals.

England, their players ill-treated by the brutal Mocanu, beat Romania on merit with a goal by Hurst; but made tediously hard work of defeating the Czechs, thanks to a dubious penalty, in their final game. The Brazilians won only 3–2 against Romania, for whom Dumitrache was an admirable, skilled centre-forward.

Group 1 began with a tiresome 0–0 draw – the curtain raiser – between Mexico and Russia, and produced two scandalous decisions. When Mexico beat El Salvador, they took and exploited a free-kick that had been awarded to the visitors! The penalty by which they beat Belgium had no basis in reality. Belgium, however, were a team without morale, their players bickering over football boot contracts. Russia beat them easily, finishing second on goal average to the Mexicans.

Group 2 saw Italy at their most fearful and defensive, clearly terrified of another North Korean experience A major row over the dropping of Gianni Rivera in favour of Sandro Mazzola did not help. It took Franchi, president of their Federation, to calm the waters. Ferruccio Valcareggi, the uneasy team manager, eventually found the compromise of using both players; Mazzola in the first half, Rivera in the second. All went well, particularly in the quarter- and semi-finals, till the final itself. Mazzola played too well to be replaced; Rivera came on for the last six minutes!

A goalkeeping error gave Italy a narrow win against the Swedes at Toluca. They then drew cravenly, without scoring, against Uruguay and little Israel who, also boldly forced a draw with the Swedes. Sweden beat the Uruguayans in a game overshadowed by the fact that Sir Stanley Rous took the designated referee, De Moraes, off the match at the 11th hour because of rumours that he might have been corrupted. They were never proved and turned out to have been spread by another Brazilian referee, jealous that De Moraes had been preferred to him. Uruguay made a furious protest, which was rejected. Meanwhile, they scraped through to the quarter finals on goal average.

Peru and the brilliant young black inside-left Teofilo Cubillas were the revelations of the León group, despite the blow to their morale of the appalling Peruvian earthquakes. This probably accounted for their slow start against Bulgaria, two up before Peru overhauled them. West Germany were given a fright by Morocco, who deservedly scored after 20 minutes, but were caught in the second half when Germany scored through Seeler and Müller; the two centre forwards whom Schoen had cleverly integrated by using Seeler 'deep'. The Germans, and the remarkable Müller, then got into their stride, thrashing Bulgaria then beating Peru, Müller scoring five of the eight goals. Müller's opportunism undid Peru, in the first half, and when the Germans flagged in the steamy heat, Sepp Maier's goalkeeping saved them. So they and Peru survived.

It was in León that West Germany beat England in an extraordinary quarter-final, which seemed virtually over when England made it 2–0 early in the second half. The determining factor may well have been the fact that Gordon Banks, England's fine goalkeeper, drank a bottle of beer, upset his stomach, and had to drop out of the game. Peter Bonetti, his replacement, hadn't played a match for a month, and was blamed for at least one and by some for all three of the German goals. Other critics pointed out that Alf Ramsey overworked and exhausted his overlapping fullbacks in the heat, then failed to make intelligent substitutions. Certainly the game turned when the fresh Grabowski came on at outside-right and ran rings round a weary Terry Cooper. England took the lead with a goal beautifully orchestrated then scored by Alan Mullery. Newton made the cross, as he did for Peters' goal after half-time. But Beckenbauer's shot went under Bonetti's body, a remarkable backheader from Seeler made it 2–2, and Gerd Müller volleyed the winner in extra time.

In Mexico City the Uruguayans, who had lost their star midfield player Pedro Rocha in their very first game, unexpectedly beat Russia with a disputed 'over the line' goal in the last minute of extra time, little Cubilla crossing for Esparrago to score.

Mexico's balloon burst in Toluca. They got the first, illusory goal after only 12 minutes, but a deflected shot by Domenghini made it 1–1; and when Rivera came on in the second half and Riva at last found his famous touch, the Mexicans were outclassed 4–1.

Brazil beat Peru 4–2 in an error-ridden match in Guadalajara. Gallardo, Peru's black striker, once with Milan, kept Peru within range, but Brazil, despite the manifest insufficiency of Felix, their goalkeeper, always had something in hand. Tostão restored the two-goal margin, Cubillas pulled it back to one, then Jairzinho scored the fourth, decisive goal with a fine, individual flourish.

The Italy-West Germany semi-final in Mexico City may be seen either as a classic of excitement or a comedy of errors. As one who was there, I incline towards the second. I also believe that the match was lost and won when the marvellous Beckenbauer was viciously chopped down, on the very edge of the penalty box, as he flowed through Italy's defence. Since Schoen, hoist with his own petard this time, had used both his substitutes, Beckenbauer had to play through extra time with his arm in a sling. Yamasaki was a wretchedly indulgent referee. Italy took an early lead through a left-foot shot by Boninsegna after a lucky rebound from two German defenders, and they held it, despite Germany's strong rally in the second half, till the third minute of injury time. Then the Germans, who had abandoned their *catenaccio* and brought on their 1966 World Cup final star, Held, for Patzke, equalised when Schnellinger banged in Grabowski's cross.

Extra time brought a deluge of goals. First, Poletti clumsily ran the ball away from his own goalkeeper, Müller putting the final touch. Burgnich came up to score after Rivera's free-kick, Gigi Riva pivoted to beat Schnellinger and drive in a fine left-foot cross-shot, Müller equalised in the second period when he nodded in Seeler's headed pass. And finally Boninsegna broke away, pulled the ball back, and Gianni Rivera, who had come on at half-time, scored the winner.

In Guadalajara, Uruguay surprised Brazil with a ludicrous first goal, Cubilla's narrow angled shot literally bouncing past Felix. Would Uruguay reaffirm their old hoodoo over Brazil? It seemed they might till late in the first half when Clodoaldo, growing in stature with every game, came through on the blind side to equalise. After that, Brazil were in charge, though Felix had to make one magnificent save from Cubilla's header. With 14 minutes remaining, a superb run and shot by Jairzinho put Brazil ahead at last, and in the last minute Rivelino's left foot made it 3–1. Uruguay, furious at having to play in Guadalajara rather than Mexico City, had more than justified their prestige as World Cup fighters.

Brazil found the final a much easier affair. Italy's craven tactics played into their hands; and weren't even well calculated. Gerson was given the freedom of midfield, Jairzinho constantly pulled Facchetti into the middle which, as Italy had no left winger, allowed Carlos Alberto to overlap at will and ultimately to score Brazil's fourth, exciting goal.

Pelé, again in glorious form, gave them the lead after 18 minutes, leaping to Rivelino's high left wing cross. A silly backheel by Clodoaldo, seven minutes from half-time, allowed Boninsegna to equalise, and with Mazzola dribbling beautifully there might have been a chance, had Italy been bolder. As it was, Gerson's fine left-foot goal from outside the box, after 66 minutes, stunned them, and the initiative returned to Brazil. The third goal came when Pelé touched Gerson's free-kick to the onrushing Jairzinho, and Carlos Alberto thumped in the fourth. Pure, joyous football had triumphed over negativity.

GROUP 1 (Mexico City)
Mexico (0) 0, Russia (0) 0
Mexico: Calderon; Vantolra, Pena, Guzman, Perez; Hernandez Pulido, Velarde (Munguia); Valdivia, Fragoso, Horacio Lopez.
Russia: Kavazashvili; Lovchev, Chesternjief, Kaplichni, Logofet, Serebrianikov (Pusacs), Muntijan, Asatiani; Nodia (Porkujan), Bychevetz, Evriuzhikin.

Belgium (1) 3, El Salvador (0) 0
Belgium: Piot; Heylens, Thissen; Dewalque, Dockx, Semmeling, Van Moer, Devrindt, Van Himst, Lambert, Puis.
El Salvador: Magaña; Rivas, Mariona, Osorio, Manzano; Quintanilla, Vazquez, Cabezas; Rodriguez, Martinez, Aparicio.
Scorers: Van Moer (2), Lambert (pen) for Belgium.

Russia (1) 4, Belgium (0) 1
Russia: Kavazashvili; Dzodzuashvili (Kiselev), Chesternjiev, Khurtsilava, Afonin, Kaplichni (Lovchev); Asatiani, Muntijan; Bychevetz, Evriuzhikin, Khmelnitzki.
Belgium: Piot; Heylens, Thissen, Dewalque, Jeck, Dockx, Semmeling, Van Moer, Van Himst, Puis, Lambert.
Scorers: Bychevetz (2), Asatiani, Khmelnitzki for Russia; Lambert for Belgium.

Mexico (1) 4, El Salvador (0) 0
Mexico: Calderon; Vantolra, Pena, Guzman, Perez; Gonzalez, Munguia; Valdivia, Borja (Basaguren, then Lopez), Fragoso, Padilla.
El Salvador: Magaña; Rivas, Mariona, Osorio, Cortez, (Monge); Quintanilla, Vazquez, Cabezas; Rodriguez, Martinez, Aparicio (Mendez).
Scorers: Valdivia (2), Fragoso, Basaguren for Mexico.

Russia (0) 2, El Salvador (0) 0
Russia: Kavazashvili; Dzodzuashvili, Khurtsilava, Chesternjiev, Afonin; Kiselev (Asatiani), Serebrianikov, Muntijan; Pusacs, (Evriuzhikin), Bychevetz, Khmelnitzki.
El Salvador: Magana; Rivas, Mariona, Castro, Osorio, Vazquez; Portillo, Cabezas (Aparicio), Rodriguez (Sermeno), Mendez, Monge.
Scorers: Bychevetz (2) for Russia.

Mexico (1) 1, Belgium (0) 0
Mexico: Calderon; Vantolra, Guzman, Pena, Perez; Gonzalez, Munguia, Pulido; Padilla, Fragoso, Valdivia (Basaguren).

Belgium: Piot; Heylens, Jeck, Dockx, Thissen, Dewalque, Polleunis, (Devrindt), Semmeling, Van Moer, Van Himst, Puis.
Scorer: Pena (pen) for Mexico.

	P	W	D	L	F	A	Pts
Mexico	3	2	1	0	5	0	5
Russia	3	2	1	0	6	1	5
Belgium	3	1	0	2	4	5	2
El Salvador	3	0	0	3	0	9	0

GROUP 2 (Puebla, Toluca)

Uruguay (1) 2, Israel (0) 0
Uruguay: Mazurkiewicz; Ubinas, Mujica; Montero Castillo, Ancheta, Matosas; Cubilla, Esparrago, Maneiro, Rocha (Cortes), Lozado.
Israel: Vissoker; Bello, Rosen, Daniel, Talbi (Bar), Schwager (Vollach), Rosenthal, Shum, Spiegler, Spiegel, Faygenbaum.
Scorers: Maneiro, Mujica for Uruguay.

Italy (1) 1, Sweden (0) 0
Italy: Albertosi; Burgnich, Facchetti; Cera, Niccolai (Rosato), Bertini; Domenghini, Mazzola, Boninsegna, De Sisti, Riva.
Sweden: Hellstrom; Nordqvist, Grip, Svensson, Axelsson, B. Larsson; Grahn, Eriksson (Ejderstedt), Kindvall, Kronqvist, Olsson.
Scorer: Domenghini for Italy.

Uruguay (0) 0, Italy (0) 0
Uruguay: Mazurkiewicz; Ubinas, Ancheta, Matosas, Mujica; Cortes, Montero Castillo, Maniziro; Cubilla, Esparrago, Bareno (Zubia).
Italy: Albertosi; Burgnich, Cera, Rosato, Facchetti; De Sisti, Bertini, Mazzola, Domenghini (Furino), Boninsegna, Riva.

Sweden (0) 1, Israel (0) 1
Sweden: G. Larsson; Selander, Axelsson, Grip, Svensson, B. Larsson, (Nicklasson), Nordahl, Turesson, Kindvall, Persson, Olsson.
Israel: Vissoker; Primo, Rosen, Bar, Rosenthal, Shum, Schwager, Spiegel, Vollach, Spiegler, Faygenbaum.
Scorers: Turesson for Sweden; Spiegler for Israel.

Sweden (0) 1, Uruguay (0) 0
Sweden: G. Larsson; Selander, Nordqvist, Axelsson, Grip, Svensson, B. Larsson, Eriksson, Kindvall, Nicklasson (Grahn), Persson (Turesson).
Uruguay: Mazurkiewicz; Ubinas, Ancheta, Matosas, Mujica; Montero Castillo, Maneiro, Cortes; Esparrago (Fontes), Zubia, Losada.
Scorer: Grahn for Sweden.

Italy (0) 0, Israel (0) 0
Italy: Albertosi; Burgnich, Facchetti; Cera, Rosato, Bertini; Domenghini (Rivera), Mazzola, Boninsegna, De Sisti, Riva.

Israel: Vissoker; Primo, Bello, Bar, Rosenthal, Rosen, Shum, Spiegel, Faygenbaum (Daniel), Spiegler, Schwager.

	P	W	D	L	F	A	Pts
Italy	3	1	2	0	1	0	4
Uruguay	3	1	1	1	2	1	3
Sweden	3	1	1	1	2	2	3
Israel	3	0	2	1	1	3	2

GROUP 3 (Guadalajara)
England (0) 1, Romania (0) 0
England: Banks (Stoke City); Newton (Everton) [sub. Wright (Everton)], Cooper (Leeds United); Mullery (Spurs), Labone (Everton), Moore (West Ham United); Lee (Manchester City) [sub. Osgood (Chelsea)], Ball (Everton), Charlton (Manchester United), Hurst (West Ham United), Peters (Spurs).
Romania: Adamache; Satmareanu, Lupescu, Dinu, Mocanu; Dumitru, Nunweiller VI; Dembrowski, Tataru (sub. Neagu), Dumitrache, Lucescu.
Scorer: Hurst for England.

Brazil (1) 4, Czechoslovakia (1) 1
Brazil: Felix; Carlos Alberto, Piazza, Brito, Everaldo; Clodaldo, Gerson (Paulo César), Jairzinho, Tostão, Pelé, Rivelino.
Czechoslovakia: Viktor; Dobias, Migas, Horvath, Hagara; Hrdlicka (Kvasniak), Kuna; F. Vesely (B. Vesely), Petras, Adamec, Jokl.
Scorers: Petras for Czechoslovakia; Rivelino, Pelé, Jairzinho (2) for Brazil.

Romania (0) 2, Czechoslovakia (1) 1
Romania: Adamache; Satmareanu, Lupescu, Dinu, Mocanu; Dumitru (Tataru), Nunweiller VI; Dembrowski, Neagu, Dumitrache, Lucescu (Ghergheli).
Czechoslovakia: Vencel; Dobias, Migas, Horvath, Zlocha; Kuna, Kvasniak; B. Vesely, Petras, Jurkanin (Adamec), Jokl (F. Vesely).
Scorers: Neagu, Dumitrache (pen) for Romania; Petras for Czechoslovakia.

Brazil (0) 1, England (0) 0
Brazil: Felix; Carlos Alberto, Brito, Piazza, Everaldo; Clodaldo Rivelino, Paulo César; Jairzinho, Tostão (Roberto), Pelé.
England: Banks (Stoke City); Wright (Everton), Cooper (Leeds United), Mullery (Spurs), Labone (Everton), Moore (West Ham United); Lee (Manchester City) [Astle (West Bromwich Albion)], Ball (Everton), Charlton (Manchester United) [Bell (Manchester City)], Hurst (West Ham United), Peters (Spurs).
Scorer: Jairzinho for Brazil.

Brazil (2) 3, Romania (1) 2
Brazil: Felix; Carlos Alberto, Brito, Fontana, Everaldo (Marco Antonio); Clodoaldo, Piazza; Jairzinho, Tostão, Pelé, Paulo César.
Romania: Adamache (Raducanu); Satmareanu, Lupescu, Dumitru, Mocanu; Neagu, Dinu, Nunweiller VI; Dembrowski, Dumitrache (Tataru), Lucescu.
Scorers: Jairzinho, Pelé (2) for Brazil; Dumitrache, Dembrowski for Romania.

England (0) 1, Czechoslovakia (0) 0
England: Banks (Stoke City); Newton (Everton), Cooper (Leeds United); Mullery (Spurs), J. Charlton (Leeds United), Moore (West Ham United); Bell (Manchester City), Clarke (Leeds United), Astle (West Bromwich Albion) [Osgood (Chelsea)], R. Charlton (Manchester United) [Ball (Everton)], Peters (Spurs).
Czechoslovakia: Viktor; Dobias, Migas, Hrivnak, Hagara; Pollak, Kuna; F. Vesely (Jokl), Petras, Adamec, Jan Capkovic.
Scorer: Clarke (pen) for England.

	P	W	D	L	F	A	Pts
Brazil	3	3	0	0	8	3	6
England	3	2	0	1	2	1	4
Romania	3	1	0	2	4	5	2
Czechoslovakia	3	0	0	3	2	7	0

GROUP 4 (León)
Peru (0) 3, Bulgaria (1) 2
Peru: Rubiños; Campos (J. Gonzalez), De La Torre, Chumpitaz, Fuentes; Cubillas, Mifflin, Challe, Baylon (Sotil), Perico Leon, Gallardo.
Bulgaria: Simeonov; Chalamanov, Dimitrov, Davidov, Aladjiev, Bonev (Asparoukhov), Penev, Yakimov, Popov (Maraschliev), Jekov, Dermendjiev.
Scorers: Chumpitaz, Gallardo, Cubillas for Peru; Dermendjiev, Donev for Bulgaria.

West Germany (0) 2, Morocco (1) 1
West Germany: Maier; Vogts, Schulz, Fichtel, Hottges (Loehr); Haller (Grabowski), Beckenbauer, Overath; Seeler, Müller, Held.
Morocco: Allal Abdallah; Lamrani, Moulay, Slimani; Boujema, Bamous (Faras), Maaroufi, Filali; Said, Houmane, Ghazouani (Abdelkader).
Scorers: Seeler, Müller for West Germany; Houmane for Morocco.

Peru (0) 3, Morocco (0) 0
Peru: Rubiños; P. Gonzalez, De La Torre, Chumpitaz, Fuentes; Challe, Mifflin (Cruzado), Cubillas; Sotil, Perico Leon, Gallardo (Ramirez).

Morocco: Allal Abdallah; Lamrani, Khanoussi, Slimani, Boujema (Gadili); Maaroufi, Bamous, Filali; Ghandi (Allaqui), Houmane, Fhazouani.
Scorers: Cubillas (2), Challe for Peru.

West Germany (2) 5, Bulgaria (1) 2
West Germany: Maier; Vogts, Schnellinger, Fichtel, Hottges; Beckenbauer (Weber), Overath; Libuda, Seeler, Müller, Loehr (Grabowski).
Bulgaria: Simeonov; Gaydarski, Penev, Jetchev, Gaganelov; Kolev, Bonev, Nikodimov; Dermendjiev, Asparoukhov, Maraschliev.
Scorers: Libuda, Müller (3) (1 pen), Seeler for West Germany; Nikodimov, Kolev for Bulgaria.

West Germany (3) 3, Peru (1) 1
West Germany: Maier; Vogts, Fichtel, Schnellinger, Hottges (Patzke), Beckenbauer, Seeler, Overath; Libuda (Grabowski), Müller, Loehr.
Peru: Rubiños; P. González, De La Torre, Chumpitaz, Fuentes; Mifflin, Challe (Cruzado); Sotil, Perico Leon (Ramirez), Gallardo.
Scorers: Müller (3) for West Germany; Perico Leon for Peru.

Bulgaria (1) 1, Morocco (0) 1
Bulgaria: Yordanov; Chalamanov, Gaydarski, Jetchev, Penev (Dimitrov), Popov, T. Kolev, Yakimov (Bonev), Mitkov, Asparoukhov, Nikodimov.
Morocco: Hazzaaz; Khanoussi, Slimani, Benkrif, Fadili; Maaroufi, Bamous (Choukhri), Filali; Ghandi, Allaqui (Faras), Ghazouani.
Scorers: Jetchev for Bulgaria; Ghazouani for Morocco.

	P	W	D	L	F	A	Pts
West Germany	3	3	0	0	10	4	6
Peru	3	2	0	1	7	5	4
Bulgaria	3	0	1	2	5	9	1
Morocco	3	0	1	2	2	6	1

QUARTER-FINALS
West Germany (0) 3, England (1) 2 after extra time (León)
West Germany: Maier; Schnellinger, Vogts, Hottges (Schulz); Beckenbauer, Overath, Seeler; Libuda (Grabowski), Müller, Loehr.
England: Bonetti (Chelsea); Newton (Everton), Cooper (Leeds United); Mullery (Spurs), Labone (Everton,) Moore (West Ham United); Lee (Manchester City), Ball (Everton), Hurst (West Ham United), Charlton (Manchester United) [Bell (Manchester City)], Peters (Spurs) [Hunter (Leeds United)].
Scorers: Beckenbauer, Seeler, Müller for West Germany; Mullery, Peters for England.

Brazil (2) 4, Peru (1) 2 (Guadalajara)
Brazil: Felix; Carlos Alberto, Brito, Piazza, Marco Antonio; Clodoaldo, Gerson (Paulo César); Jairzinho (Roberto), Tostão, Pelé, Rivelino.

Peru: Rubiños; Campos, Fernandez, Chumpitaz, Fuentes; Mifflin, Challe; Baylon (Sotil), Perico Leon (Eladio Reyes), Cubillas, Gallardo.
Scorers: Rivellino, Tostão (2), Jairzinho for Brazil; Gallardo, Cubillas for Peru.

Italy (1) 4, Mexico (1) 1 (Toluca)
Italy: Albertosi; Burgnich, Cera, Rossato, Facchetti; Bertini, Mazzola (Rivera), De Sisti; Domenghini (Gori), Boninsegna, Riva.
Mexico: Calderon; Vantolra, Pena, Guzman, Perez; Gonzales (Borja), Pulido, Munguia (Diaz); Valdivia, Fragoso, Padilla.
Scorers: Domenghini, Riva (2), Rivera for Italy; Gonzalez for Mexico.

Uruguay (0) 1, Russia (0) 0 after extra time (Mexico City)
Uruguay: Mazurkiewicz; Ubinas, Ancheta, Matosas, Mujica; Maneiro, Cortes, Montero Castiloo; Cubilla, Fontes (Gomez), Morales (Esparrago).
Russia: Kavazashvili; Dzodzuashvili, Afonin, Khurtsilava (Logofet), Chesternjiev; Muntijan, Asatiani (Kiselev), Kaplichni; Evriuzhkinzin, Bychevetz, Khmelnitzki.
Scorer: Esparrago for Uruguay.

SEMI-FINALS
Italy (1) 4, West Germany (0) 3 after extra time (Mexico City)
Italy: Albertosi; Cera; Burgnich, Bertini, Rosato, (Poletti) Facchetti; Domenghini, Mazzola (Rivera), De Sisti; Boninsegna, Riva.
West Germany: Maier; Schnellinger; Vogts, Schulz, Beckenbauer Patzke (Held); Seeler, Overath; Grabowski, Müller, Loehr (Libuda).
Scorers: Boninsegna, Burgnich, Riva, Rivera for Italy; Schnellinger, Müller (2) for West Germany.

Brazil (1) 3, Uruguay (1) 1 (Guadalajara)
Brazil: Felix; Carlos Alberto, Brito, Piazza, Everaldo; Clodoaldo, Gerson; Jairzinho, Tostão, Pelé, Rivelino.
Uruguay: Mazurkiewicz; Ubinas, Ancheta, Matosas, Mujica; Montero Castillo, Cortes, Fontes; Cabilla, Maneiro (Esparrago), Morales.
Scorers: Clodoaldo, Jairzinho, Rivelino for Brazil; Cubilla for Uruguay.

THIRD PLACE MATCH
West Germany (1) 1, Uruguay (0) 0 (Mexico City)
West Germany: Wolter; Schnellinger (Lorenz); Patzke, Fichtel, Weber, Vogts; Seeler, Overath; Libuda (Loehr), Müller, Held.
Uruguay: Mazurkiewicz; Ubinas, Ancheta, Matosas, Mujica; Montero Castillo, Cortes, Fontes (Sandoval); Cubilla, Maneiro (Esparrago) Morales.
Scorer: Overath for West Germany.

FINAL
Brazil (1) 4, Italy (1) 1 (Mexico City)
Brazil: Felix; Carlos Alberto, Brito, Piazza, Everaldo; Clodoaldo, Gerson; Jairzinho, Tostão, Pelé, Rivelino.
Italy: Albertosi; Cera; Burgnich, Bertini, (Juliano), Rosato, Facchetti; Domenghini, Mazzola, De Sisti; Boninsegna (Rivera), Riva.
Scorers: Pelé, Gerson, Jairzinho, Carlos Alberto for Brazil; Boninsegna for Italy.

Leading Scorer: Müller (West Germany) 10.

CHAPTER THIRTEEN

The European Football Championship

This was initiated in 1958 as a home and away knockout tournament, with the semi-finals and final to be played in one country, along the lines of the World Cup. The title of the tournament was changed from the European Nations Cup to the European Football Championship for the 1966–68 episode.

EUROPEAN NATIONS CUP 1958–60

The first tournament dragged on till 1960 and a somewhat anti-climactic finish in Paris. Russia won it, but they had been favoured by the withdrawal of Spain, whom they were due to meet in the quarter-final. No British country competed. The final rounds were notable for the superb form of Russia's goalkeeper, Lev Yachin.

Preliminary Round
Eire 2, Czechoslovakia 0
Czechoslovakia 4, Eire 0
Czechoslovakia 5, Denmark 1
Poland 2, Spain 4
Spain 3, Poland 0

First Round
France 7, Greece 1
Greece 1, France 1
Russia 3, Hungary 1
Hungary 0, Russia 1
Romania 3, Turkey 0
Turkey 2, Romania 0
Norway 0, Austria 1
Austria 5, Norway 2
Yugoslavia 2, Bulgaria 0
Bulgaria 1, Yugoslavia 1
Portugal 2, East Germany 0
East Germany 2, Portugal 3
Denmark 2, Czechoslovakia 2

Quarter-finals
Portugal 2, Yugoslavia 1
Yugoslavia 5, Portugal 1
France 5, Austria 2
Austria 2, France 0
Romania 0, Czechoslovakia 2
Czechoslovakia 3, Romania 0
Russia beat Spain who withdrew

Semi-finals
Yugoslavia 5, France 4 (Paris)
Russia 3, Czechoslovakia 0 (Marseilles)

Final Paris, 10 July 1960
Russia 2, Yugoslavia 1 after extra time
Russia: Yachin; Tchekeli, Kroutikov; Voinov, Maslenkin, Netto; Metreveli, Ivanov, Ponedelnik, Bubukin, Meshki.
Yugoslavia: Vidinic; Durkovic, Jusufi; Zanetic, Miladinovic, Perusic; Sekularac, Jerkovic, Galic, Matus, Kostic.
Scorers: Metreveli, Ponedelnik for Russia; Netto (o.g.) for Yugoslavia.

EUROPEAN NATIONS CUP 1962–64

This time, England, Northern Ireland, and Wales competed, but Scotland inexcusably and inexplicably stayed out. England's performance was far from glorious. After struggling to draw with France at Sheffield, they played the return during the bitter winter of 1963, took a floundering team to Paris, poorly selected (no scheming inside-forward) and with a goalkeeper out of practice and form, to lose 5–2.

Northern Ireland did better, playing gallantly to beat Poland, and exceedingly well to hold Spain to a draw away. For the return, however, Spain recalled their Italian-based stars, Del Sol and Suarez, and just squeezed through in Belfast. The Welsh, meanwhile, had already gone out to Hungary. Spain did not need Del Sol and Suarez to put out Eire, which they did with ease, while Hungary surprised France in Paris; a revitalised team.

The closing rounds, played in Spain, not surprisingly saw the home team prevail, though not without infinite trouble. After narrowly prevailing against Hungary, Spain ran up against a packed Russian defence, scored in five minutes, let in an eighth-minute equaliser, then inspired by Suarez had enough of the play for Marcellino to give them the game with a brilliant opportunist goal. The Russians used Kornaev as an extra defender. Hungary took third place with a laborious win over Denmark.

Third Place Match
Hungary 3, Denmark 1 after extra time

Final Madrid, 21 June 1964
Spain (1) 2, Russia (1) 1
Spain: Iribar; Rivilla, Calleja; Fuste, Olivella, Zoco; Amancio, Pereda, Marcellino, Suarez, Lapetra.
Russia: Yachin; Chustikov, Mudrik; Voronin, Chesternjiev, Anitchkine; Chislenko, Ivanov, Ponedelnik, Kornaev, Khusainov.
Scorers: Pereda, Marcellino for Spain; Khusainov for Russia.

EUROPEAN FOOTBALL CHAMPIONSHIP 1966–68

Italy won a most unsatisfactory final series, on their own soil. In the semi-finals, they drew with Russia after extra time at Naples and won the toss: a competition rule which properly met with bitter criticism. In the final, a late goal from a free kick gave them a lucky draw against the superior Yugoslav side. The replay, two days later, found

Yugoslavia exhausted, Italy reinforced by capable reserves, and the Italians won with some ease. Previously, in a brutally hard match, Yugoslavia had put out England in Florence through a late goal by Dzajic.

England had qualified for the quarter-finals by winning the home international championship. Beaten at Wembley by Scotland, they drew the vital match at Hampden in February 1968. The Scots threw away points against weaker opposition. England went on to eliminate Spain in the quarter-finals, playing specially well in Madrid.

The competition was this time divided into eight qualifying groups, in which the results were as follows:

Group I
Eire 0, Spain 0
Eire 2, Turkey 0
Spain 2, Eire 0
Turkey 0, Spain 0
Turkey 2, Eire 1
Eire 0, Czechoslovakia 2
Spain 2, Turkey 0
Czechoslovakia 1, Spain 0
Spain 2, Czechoslovakia 1
Czechoslovakia 4, Turkey 0
Turkey 0, Czechoslovakia 0
Czechoslovakia 1, Eire 2

Group II
Norway 0, Bulgaria 2
Portugal 1, Sweden 2
Bulgaria 0, Norway 2
Sweden 1, Portugal 1
Norway 1, Portugal 2
Sweden 0, Bulgaria 2
Norway 3, Sweden 1
Sweden 5, Norway 1
Bulgaria 3, Sweden 0
Portugal 2, Norway 1
Bulgaria 1, Portugal 0
Portugal 0, Bulgaria 0

Group III
Finland 0, Austria 0
Greece 2, Finland 1
Finland 1, Greece 1
Russia 4, Austria 3
Russia 2, Finland 0
Finland 2, Russia 5
Austria 2, Finland 1
Greece 4, Austria 0

Austria 1, Russia 0
Greece 0, Russia 1
Austria 1, Greece 1
Russia 4, Greece 1

Group IV
Albania 0, Yugoslavia 2
West Germany 6, Albania 0
Yugoslavia 1, West Germany 0
West Germany 3, Yugoslavia 1
Yugoslavia 4, Albania 0
Albania 0, West Germany 0

Group V
Netherlands 2, Hungary 2
Hungary 6, Denmark 0
Netherlands 2, Denmark 0
East Germany 4, Netherlands 3
Hungary 2, Netherlands 1
Denmark 0, Hungary 2
Denmark 1, East Germany 1
Netherlands 1, East Germany 0
Hungary 3, East Germany 1
Denmark 3, Netherlands 2
East Germany 3, Denmark 2
East Germany 1, Hungary 0

Group VI
Cyprus 1, Romania 5
Romania 4, Switzerland 2
Italy 3, Romania 1
Cyprus 0, Italy 2
Romania 7, Cyprus 0
Switzerland 7, Romania 1
Italy 5, Cyprus 0
Switzerland 5, Cyprus 0
Switzerland 2, Italy 2

Italy 4, Switzerland 0
Cyprus 2, Switzerland 1
Romania 0, Italy 1

Group VII
Poland 4, Luxembourg 0
France 2, Poland 1
Luxembourg 0, France 3
Luxembourg 0, Belgium 5
Luxembourg 0, Poland 0
Poland 3, Belgium 1
Belgium 2, France 1
Poland 1, France 4
Belgium 2, Poland 4
France 1, Belgium 1
Belgium 3, Luxembourg 0
France 3, Luxembourg 1

Group VIII
Northern Ireland 0, England 2
Wales 1, Scotland 1
England 5, Wales 1
Scotland 2, Northern Ireland 1
Northern Ireland 0, Wales 0
England 2, Scotland 3
Wales 0, England 3

Northern Ireland 1, Scotland 0
England 2, Northern Ireland 0
Scotland 3, Wales 2
Scotland 1, England 1
Wales 2, Northern Ireland 0

Quarter-finals
England 1, Spain 0
Spain 1, England 2
Bulgaria 3, Italy 2
Italy 2, Bulgaria 0
France 1, Yugoslavia 1
Yugoslavia 5, France 1
Hungary 2, Russia 0
Russia 3, Hungary 0

Semi-finals (Italy)
Yugoslavia 1, England 0
Italy 0, Russia 0, Italy won toss

Third-place match (Rome)
England 2, Russia 0

Final (Rome)
Italy 1, Yugoslavia 1

Replayed Final Rome, 10 June 1968
Italy (2) 2, Yugoslavia (0) 0
Italy: Zoff; Burgnich, Facchetti; Rosato, Guarneri, Salvadore; Domenghini, Mazzola, Anastasi, De Sisti, Riva.
Yugoslavia: Pantelic; Fazlagic, Damjanovic; Pavlovic, Paunovic, Holcer; Hosic, Acimovic, Musemic, Trivic, Dzajic.
Scorers: Riva, Anastasi for Italy.

EUROPEAN FOOTBALL CHAMPIONSHIP 1970-72

This tournament was won gloriously by West Germany, a team excitingly dedicated to attack in the style of 'total football'. Franz Beckenbauer played in his favourite role as a mobile sweeper, magnificently abetted by Günter Netzer in midfield and the opportunism of the prolific Gerd Müller. It was a total departure from the old German school of physical football.

England, ineptly choosing a team with no midfield half-back to confront Netzer, were thrashed 3-1 at Wembley, though they gained a futile draw with harsh, negative tactics in Berlin; an odd aberration by Sir Alf Ramsey.

The West Germans then beat Belgium in the semi-final in Antwerp in an exciting game, while Russia got the better of Hungary in Brussels, a game watched by only a few thousand because the other was televised. In the final, West Germany outplayed the heavy Russians, and had it not been for the goalkeeping of Rudakov they would have won much more easily than 3–0.

Group I
Czechoslovakia 1, Finland 1
Romania 3, Finland 0
Wales 0, Romania 0
Wales 1, Czechoslovakia 3
Finland 0, Wales 1
Czechoslovakia 1, Romania 0
Finland 0, Czechoslovakia 4
Finland 0, Romania 4
Wales 3, Finland 0
Czechoslovakia 1, Wales 0
Romania 2, Czechoslovakia 1
Romania 2, Wales 0

Group II
Norway 1, Hungary 3
France 3, Norway 1
Bulgaria 1, Norway 1
Hungary 1, France 1
Bulgaria 3, Hungary 0
Norway 1, Bulgaria 4
Norway 1, France 3
Hungary 2, Bulgaria 0
France 0, Hungary 2
Hungary 4, Norway 0
France 2, Bulgaria 1
Bulgaria 2, France 1

Group III
Greece 0, Switzerland 1
Malta 1, Switzerland 2
Malta 0, England 1
England 3, Greece 0
Switzerland 5, Malta 0
England 5, Malta 0
Malta 1, Greece 1
Switzerland 1, Greece 0
Greece 2, Malta 0
Switzerland 2, England 3
England 1, Switzerland 1
Greece 0, England 2

Group IV
Spain 3, Northern Ireland 0
Cyprus 0, Northern Ireland 3
Northern Ireland 5, Cyprus 0
Cyprus 1, Russia 3
Cyprus 0, Spain 2
Russia 2, Spain 1
Russia 6, Cyprus 1
Russia 1, Northern Ireland 0
Northern Ireland 1, Russia 1
Spain 0, Russia 0
Spain 7, Cyprus 0
Northern Ireland 1, Spain 1

Group V
Denmark 0, Portugal 1
Scotland 1, Denmark 0
Belgium 2, Denmark 0
Belgium 3, Scotland 0
Belgium 3, Portugal 0
Portugal 2, Scotland 0
Denmark 1, Scotland 0
Portugal 5, Denmark 0
Denmark 1, Belgium 2
Scotland 2, Portugal 1
Scotland 1, Belgium 0
Portugal 1, Belgium 1

Group VI
Eire 1, Sweden 1
Sweden 1, Eire 0
Austria 1, Italy 2
Italy 3, Eire 0
Eire 1, Italy 2
Eire 1, Austria 4
Sweden 1, Austria 0
Sweden 0, Italy 0
Austria 1, Sweden 0
Austria 6, Eire 0
Italy 2, Austria 2
Italy 3, Sweden 0

GROUP VII
Netherlands 1, Yugoslavia 1
East Germany 1, Netherlands 0
Luxembourg 0, East Germany 5
Yugoslavia 2, Netherlands 0

East Germany 2, Luxembourg 1
Netherlands 6, Luxembourg 0
Luxembourg 0, Yugoslavia 2
Netherlands 3, East Germany 2
East Germany 1, Yugoslavia 2
Yugoslavia 0, East Germany 0
Luxembourg 0, Netherlands 8
Yugoslavia 2, Luxembourg 0

Group VIII
Poland 3, Albania 0
West Germany 1, Turkey 1
Turkey 2, Albania 1
Albania 0, West Germany 1
Turkey 0, West Germany 3
Albania 1, Poland 1
West Germany 2, Albania 0
Poland 5, Turkey 1
Poland 1, West Germany 3
Albania 3, Turkey 0

West Germany 0, Poland 0
Turkey 1, Poland 0

Quarter-Finals
England 1, West Germany 3
West Germany 0, England 0
Italy 0, Belgium 0
Belgium 2, Italy 1
Hungary 1, Romania 1
Romania 2, Hungary 2
Hungary 2, Romania 1
Yugoslavia 0, Russia 0
Russia 3, Yugoslavia 0

Semi-finals (Belgium)
Belgium 1, West Germany 2
 (Antwerp)
Russia 1, Hungary 0 (Brussels)

Third Place Match (Liège)
Belgium 2, Hungary 1

Final Brussels, 18 June 1972
West Germany (1) 3, Russia (0) 0
West Germany: Maier; Hottges, Breitner, Beckenbauer, Schwarzenbeck, Wimmer, Heynckes, Hoeness, Müller, Netzer, Kremer.
Russia: Rudakov; Dzodzuashvili, Khurtsilava, Kaplichnyi, Istomine, Troshkine, Kolotov, Baidnachyi, Konkov (Dolmatov), Banichevski (Kozinkevich), Onishenko.
Scorers: Müller (2), Wimmer for West Germany.

CHAPTER FOURTEEN

World Club Championship History

These matches began in 1960 – originally without the blessing of FIFA – between the winners of the European Cup and the winners of the more recently innovated South American Cup. They were to play one another at home and away, the championship to be decided not on goal average but on actual results. That is to say, were each team to win one match a play-off would be necessary, and that play-off would take place immediately, on the ground of the team playing at home in the second leg. Clearly this was monstrously unjust to the team playing away, and even a later change of the rules to put the replay on a neutral ground – but still in the same continent as the second match – was by no means satisfactory.

In 1960 there was no need for such a play-off. Real Madrid, having drawn 0–0 in Montevideo on a day of pouring rain, easily crushed Peñarol in Madrid – two full months later – though Peñarol suffered from the lack of their brilliant linking halfback, Gonçalvez.

In 1961, Peñarol had their revenge. Beaten 1–0 in Lisbon by Benfica, they thrashed the Portuguese club 5–0 in the return, although Benfica had to play without their two key men, Germano, centre-half, and Aguas, centre-forward. For the third match, they flew out the 19-year-old coloured inside-forward, Eusebio. He scored a brilliant goal, but again Peñarol prevailed.

In 1962, it was the turn of Santos. Once more, Benfica were the losers. There was nothing they could do against the astounding brilliance of Pelé who, if he was superb in the first leg in Brazil, reached supreme heights of virtuosity in Lisbon.

In 1963, Milan, who had already beaten Santos 4–0 earlier in the year in the Milan City Cup, beat them again 4–2 in the first leg, Amarildo, their new Brazilian star, playing superbly and scoring twice. But they fell badly to pieces in the return, after being two goals up, at the Maracana. Santos' recovery was all the more remarkable in that they lacked Zito and Pelé. Almir, who took Pelé's place, was their star.

The decider, a couple of days later, was bad tempered and violent. Two players were sent off, Maldini of Milan – who gave away the penalty that won the match – and Ismael of Santos. There could scarcely have been a better example of the competition's misbegotten rules.

In 1964, it was Inter who beat Independiente in a third match; played in Madrid.

In 1965, for the second year in succession, Internazionale defeated Independiente of Buenos Aires; but this time, there was no need for a third match. In Milan, Inter majestically overwhelmed an Independiente side foolishly committed to playing them at their own game, of defence and breakaway. Inter demonstrated that they knew how to attack and express themselves, just as well as defend.

In Buenos Aires, by contrast, they rose above intimidation in the streets and on the field – Herrera and at least four players were struck by missiles – to cling to the draw they had come for.

In 1966, Peñarol and Real Madrid met for the title, the Uruguayan club scoring two surprisingly decisive victories. Just as in their meeting seven years earlier, it rained heavily in Montevideo, but this time Peñarol scored twice, each time through Spencer, their coloured centre-forward from Ecuador, to win. In the return, their fine defence and dazzling breakaways were too much for Real. With Leczano, of Paraguay, sweeping-up, the veteran Abbadie in midfield, Joya, from Peru, and Spencer brilliant strikers, they again won 2–0, the first goal coming from a penalty, Joya making the second with a clever backheel, for Spencer.

The finals of 1967 were a disgrace to the game. Violently provoked by the tactics of Racing Club of Buenos Aires, Glasgow Celtic eventually matched brutality with brutality, in the third game in Montevideo.

In Glasgow, they'd won a dull, bruising match through McNeill's header at a corner. Before the return, in Buenos Aires, could even begin, Ronnie Simpson, the goalkeeper, was hit by a stone on the back of the head, and had to leave the field. Cardenas scored the game's winning goal three minutes after half-time.

In Montevideo, disgraceful scenes took place, involving culprits on both sides. Four Celtic and two Racing players were sent off. Celtic, on their return, fined each of their players £250. Racing gave theirs a new car. The only goal of the play-off was scored with a strong, high shot by Cardenas, in the second half.

The 1968 finals were scarcely an improvement. Again, the disgraceful behaviour of an Argentinian team was at the root of it; this time, Estudiantes de la Plata. The first leg, in Buenos Aires, was preceded by an almost hysterical campaign against the little Manchester United and England halfback, Nobby Stiles. In the event, he was sent off for a mere gesture of disgust at a linesman who gave him wrongly offside; this after he himself had been deliberately back-headed in the face early in the game, cutting his eye, while Bobby Charlton had to have three stitches in his shin after being brutally kicked by Pachamé. No wonder such famous forwards as Law and Best stood virtually apart from the proceedings; won 1–0 by Estudiantes through a goal headed from a corner-kick by Conigliaro.

The return, in Manchester, was predictably rough and ill tempered. A good goal headed by Veron, from a free kick after only five minutes, virtually decided matters. Best and Medina were sent off for brawling; Morgan eventually though uselessly equalised.

The following year, Estudiantes surpassed themselves. Their conduct was bad enough when they were well beaten in Milan, but it passed all bounds in the return in Buenos Aires. Aguirre Suarez broke Nestor Combin's nose with a vicious blow of the elbow, while Poletti, the goalkeeper, kicked Prati in the back while he was on the ground having treatment. General Ongania, the Argentinian President, imprisoned both Estudiantes players, and Madero. Later all three were suspended from international competition, Poletti for life, though he was later reinstated.

Though Milan duly won the trophy on goal aggregate – providentially, the first time this had been possible – their season was gravely compromised.

Much the same thing happened to Feyenoord the following year. The first game, in Buenos Aires, passed over more or less without incident, perhaps because the Estudiantes players felt Big Brother was watching them, but the behaviour of the Argentinians in the return game was so cynical that Feyenoord said afterwards that had they not won, they would have refused to engage in a play-off.

The decisive goal in Rotterdam was scored by the young, bespectacled forward Van Deale, sent on because Feyenoord feared for the safety of their veteran left-winger, Coen Moulijn. The notorious Pachamé contrived to break Van Deale's glasses so that he could not see for the rest of the game, but Feyenoord held on to win.

By now the competition was exposed as a shabby, violent affair of little value to European clubs, of vital economic importance to the impoverished Argentinian and Uruguayan clubs. Thus in 1971, Ajax refused to play Nacional, giving specious medical reasons for a decision clearly taken on somewhat different physical grounds. Disgracefully, the European Union (UEFA) threatened them with sanctions, instead of supporting them, and eventually deputed Panathinaikos, the runners-up, to play.

Panathinaikos paid the penalty, not only losing the tie, but losing their right-back Tomaras with a leg broken viciously by the Uruguayan left-winger Morales in Athens. Nacional drew there, then won in Montevideo, all their goals being scored by their astonishing veteran centre-forward, the Argentinian Luis Artime, enjoying a notable Indian summer.

The greed of their players moved Ajax foolishly to change their minds and compete, in 1972, against Independiente. Again, it was costly. Johan Cruyff received a severe ankle injury when he was kicked by Mircoli in Buenos Aires, where Ajax drew, after leading through Cruyff's goal at half-time. Despite more harsh usage, they won 3-0 in Amsterdam, their hero the blond, young striker Johnny Rep, who came on as substitute, scored twice, and thereafter held his place, going on to score the only goal of the European Cup final, against Juventus.

1960
Montevideo, 3 July
Peñarol (0) 0, Real Madrid (0) 0
Peñarol: Maidana; Martinez, Aguerre; Pino, Salvador, Gonçalvez; Cubilla, Linazza, Hohberg, Spencer, Borges.
Real Madrid: Dominguez; Marquitos, Pachin; Vidal, Santamaria, Zarraga; Canario, Del Sol, Di Stefano, Puskas, Bueno.
Madrid, 4 September
Real Madrid (4) 5, Peñarol (0) 1
Real Madrid: Dominguez; Marquitos, Pachin; Vidal, Santamaria, Zarraga; Herrera, Del Sol, Di Stefano, Puskas, Gento.
Peñarol: Maidana; Pino, Mayewki, Martinez; Aguerre, Salvador; Cubilla, Linazza, Hohberg, Spencer, Borges.
Scorers: Puskas (2), Di Stefano, Herrera, Gento for Real; Borges for Peñarol.

1961
Lisbon, 4 September
Benfica (0) 1, Peñarol (0) 0
Benfica: Costa Pereira; Angelo, Joao; Neto, Saraiva, Cruz; Augusto, Santana, Aguas, Coluña, Cavem.
Peñarol: Maidana; Gonzales, Martinez, Aguerre; Cano, Gonçalvez; Cubilla, Spencer, Cabrera, Sasia, Ledesma.
Scorer: Coluña for Benfica.

Montevideo, 17 September
Peñarol (4) 5, Benfica (0) 0
Peñarol: Maidana; Gonzales, Martinez, Aguerre; Cano, Gonçalvez; Cubilla, Ledesma, Sasia, Spencer, Joya.
Benfica: Costa Pereira; Angelo, Joao; Neto, Saraiva, Cruz; Augusto, Santana, Mendes, Coluña, Cavem.
Scorers: Sasia (pen), Joya (2), Spencer (2) for Peñarol.

Montevideo, 19 September
Peñarol (2) 2, Benfica (1) 1
Peñarol: Maidana; Gonzales, Martinez, Aguerre; Cano, Gonçalvez; Cubilla, Ledesma, Sasia, Spencer, Joya.
Benfica: Costa Pereira; Angelo, Cruz; Neto, Humberto, Coluña; Augusto, Eusebio, Aguas, Cavem, Simões.
Scorers: Sasia (2) (1 pen) for Peñarol; Eusebio for Benfica.

1962

Rio, 19 September
Santos (1) 3, Benfica (0) 2
Santos: Gilmar; Lima, Calvet; Zito, Mauro, Dalmo; Dorval, Mengalvio, Coutinho, Pelé, Pepe.
Benfica: Costa Pereira; Jacinto, Raul, Humberto, Cruz; Cavem, Coluña; Augusto, Santana, Eusebio, Simões.
Scorers: Pelé (2), Coutinho for Santos; Santana (2) for Benfica.

Lisbon, 11 October
Benfica (0) 2, Santos (2) 5
Benfica: Costa Pereira; Jacinto, Raul, Humberto, Cruz; Cavem, Coluna; Augusto, Santana, Eusebio, Simões.
Santos: Gilmar; Olavo, Calvet; Dalmo, Mauro, Lima; Dorval, Zito, Coutinho, Pelé, Pepe.
Scorers: Pelé (3), Coutinho, Pepe for Santos; Eusebio, Santana for Benfica.

1963

Milan, 16 October
Milan (2) 4, Santos (0) 2
Milan: Ghezzi; David, Trebbi; Pelagalli, Maldini, Trapattoni; Mora, Lodetti, Altafini, Rivera, Amarildo.
Santos: Gilmar; Lima, Haroldo, Calvet, Geraldino; Zito, Mengalvio; Dorval, Coutinho, Pelé, Pepe.
Scorers: Trapattoni, Amarildo (2), Mora for Milan; Pelé (2) (1 pen) for Santos.

Rio, 14 November
Santos 4, Milan 2 (0–2)
Santos: Gilmar; Ismael, Dalmo, Mauro, Haroldo; Lima, Mengalvio; Dorval, Coutinho, Almir, Pepe.
Milan: Ghezzi; David, Trebbi; Pelagalli, Maldini, Trapattoni; Mora, Lodetti, Altafini, Rivera, Amarildo.
Scorers: Pepe (2), Almir, Lima for Santos; Altafini, Mora for Milan.

Rio, 16 November
Santos (1) 1, Milan (0) 0
Santos: Gilmar; Ismael, Dalmo, Mauro, Haroldo; Lima, Mengalvio; Dorval, Coutinho, Almir, Pepe.
Milan: Balzarini (Barluzzi); Pelagalli, Trebbi; Benitez, Maldini, Trapattoni; Mora, Lodetti, Altafini, Amarildo, Fortunato.
Scorer: Dalmo (pen) for Santos.

1964
Buenos Aires, 9 September
Independiente (0) 1, Internazionale (0) 0
Independiente: Santoro; Ferreiro, Rolan; Acevedo, Guzman, Maldonado; Bernao, Mura, Prospitti, Rodriguez, Savoy.
Internazionale: Sarti; Burgnich, Facchetti; Tagnin, Guarneri, Picchi; Jair, Mazzola, Peiró, Suarez, Corso.
Scorer: Rodriguez for Independiente.

Milan, 23 September
Internazionale (2) 2, Independiente (0) 0
Internazionale: Sarti; Burgnich, Facchetti; Malatrasi, Guarneri, Picchi; Jair, Mazzola, Milani, Suarez, Corso.
Independiente: Santoro; Acevedo, Decaria; Maldonado, Ferreiro, Paflik; Suarez, Mura, Prospitti, Rodriguez, Savoy.
Scorers: Mazzola, Corso for Inter.

Madrid, 26 September
Internazionale (0) 1, Independiente (0) 0 after extra time
Internazionale: Sarti; Malatrasi, Facchetti; Tagnin, Guarneri, Picchi; Domenghini, Peiró, Milani, Suarez, Corso.
Independiente: Santoro; Guzman, Decaria; Acevedo, Paflik, Maldonado; Bernao, Prospitti, Suarez, Rodriguez, Savoy.
Scorer: Corso for Inter.

1965
Milan, 8 September
Internazionale (2) 3, Independiente (0) 0
Internazionale: Sarti; Burgnich, Facchetti; Bedin, Guarneri, Picchi; Jair, Mazzola, Peiró, Suarez, Corso.
Independiente: Santoro; Pavoni, Navarro; Acevedo, Guzman, Ferreiro; Bernao, De La Mata, Avallay, Rodriguez, Savoy.
Scorers: Peiró, Mazzola (2) for Internazionale.

Buenos Aires, 15 September
Independiente (0) 0, Internazionale (0) 0
Independiente: Santoro; Navarro, Pavoni; Rolan, Guzman, Ferreiro; Bernao, Mura, Avallay, Mori, Savoy.
Internazionale: Sarti; Burgnich, Facchetti; Bedin, Guarneri, Picchi; Jair, Mazzola, Peiró, Suarez, Corso.

1966

Montevideo, 12 October
Peñarol (1) 2, Real Madrid (0) 0
Peñarol: Mazurkiewicz; Forlan, Gonzales; Gonçalvez, Lezcano, Varela; Abbadie, Cortes, Spencer, Rocha, Joya.
Real Madrid: Betancort; Pachin, Sanchis; Ruiz, De Felipe, Zoco; Serena, Amancio, Pirri, Velázquez, Bueno.
Scorer: Spencer (2) for Peñarol.

Madrid, 26 October
Real Madrid (0) 0, Peñarol (2) 2
Real Madrid: Betancort; Calpe, Sanchis; Pirri, De Felipe, Zoco; Serena, Amancio, Grosso, Velázquez, Gento.
Peñarol: Mazurkiewicz; Gonzales, Caetano; Gonçalves, Lezcano, Varela: Abbadie, Cortes, Spencer, Rocha, Joya.
Scorers: Rocha (pen), Spencer for Peñarol.

1967

Glasgow, 18 October
Celtic (0) 1, Racing Club (0) 0
Celtic: Simpson; Craig, Gemmell; Murdoch, McNeill, Clark; Johnstone, Lennox, Wallace, Auld, Hughes.
Racing: Cejas; Perfumo, Diaz; Martin, Mori, Basile; Raffo, Rulli, Cardenas, Rodriguez, Maschio.
Scorer: McNeill for Celtic.

Buenos Aires, 1 November
Racing Club (1) 2, Celtic (1) 1
Racing: Cejas; Perfumo, Chabay; Martin, Rulli, Basile; Raffo, Cardoso, Cardenas, Rodriguez, Maschio.
Celtic: Fallon; Craig, Gemmell; Murdoch, McNeill, Clark; Johnstone, Wallace, Chalmers, O'Neill, Lennox.
Scorers: Raffo, Cardenas for Racing; Gemmell (pen) for Celtic.

Montevideo, 4 November
Racing Club (0) 1, Celtic (0) 0
Racing: Cejas; Perfumo, Chabay; Martin, Rulli, Basile; Raffo, Cardoso, Cardenas, Rodriguez, Maschio.
Celtic: Fallon; Craig, Gemmell; Murdoch, McNeill, Clark; Johnstone, Lennox, Wallace, Auld, Hughes.
Scorer: Cardenas for Racing.

1968

Buenos Aires, 25 September
Estudiantes (1) 1, Manchester United (0) 0
Estudiantes: Poletti; Malbernat, Suarez, Madero, Medina; Bilardo, Pachame, Togneri; Ribaudo, Conigliaro, Veron.
Manchester United: Stepney; Dunne, Burns; Crerand, Foulkes, Stiles; Morgan, Sadler, Law, Charlton, Best.
Scorer: Conigliaro for Estudiantes.

Manchester, 16 October
Manchester United (0) 1, Estudiantes (1) 1
Manchester United: Stepney; Dunne, Brennan; Crerand, Foulkes, Sadler; Morgan, Kidd, Charlton, Law (Sartori), Best.
Estudiantes: Poletti; Malbernat, Suarez, Madero, Medina; Bilardo, Pachame, Togneri; Ribaudo, Conigliaro, Veron (Echecopar).
Scorers: Morgan for Manchester United; Veron for Estudiantes.
1969
Milan, 8 October
Milan (2) 3, Estudiantes (0) 0
Milan: Cudicini; Malatrasi; Anquilletti, Rosato, Schnellinger; Lodetti, Rivera, Fogli; Sormani, Combin (Rognoni), Prati.
Estudiantes: Poletti; Aguirre Suarez, Manera, Madero, Malbernat; Bilardo, Togneri, Echecopar; Flores, Conigliaro, Veron.
Scorers: Sormani (2), Combin for Milan.
Buenos Aires, 22 October
Estudiantes (2) 2, Milan (1) 1
Estudiantes: Poletti; Manera, Aguirre Suarez, Madero, Malbernat; Bilardo (Echecopar), Romeo, Togneri; Conigliaro, Taverna, Veron.
Milan: Cudicini; Malatrasi (Fogli); Anquilletti, Maldera, Rosato, Schnellinger; Lodetti, Rivera; Sormani, Combin, Prati (Rognoni).
Scorers: Aguirre Suarez, Conigliaro for Estudiantes; Rivera for Milan.
Milan, under the new dispensation whereby goal aggregate is decisive, won by 4 goals to 2.
1970
Buenos Aires, 26 August
Estudiantes (2) 2, Feyenoord (1) 2
Estudiantes: Errea; Pagnanini, Spadaro, Togneri, Malbernat, Bilardo, (Solari), Pachame, Echecopar (Rudzki), Conigliaro, Flores, Veron.
Feyenoord: Treytel; Romeyn, Israel, Laseroms, Van Duivenbode, Hasil, Jansen, Van Hanegem (Boskamp), Wery, Kindvall, Moulijn.
Scorers: Echecopar, Veron for Estudiantes; Kindvall, Van Hanegem for Feyenoord.
Rotterdam, 9 September
Feyenoord (0) 1, Estudiantes (0) 0
Feyenoord: Treytel; Romeyn, Israel, Laseroms, Van Duivenbode, Hasil (Boskamp), Van Hanegem, Jansen, Wery, Kindvall, Moulijn (Van Deale).
Estudiantes: Pezzano; Malbernat, Spadaro, Togneri, Medina (Pagnanini), Bilardo, Pachame, Romeo, Conigliaro (Rudzki), Flores, Veron.
Scorer: Van Deale for Feyenoord.
1971
Athens, 15 December
Panathinaikos (0) 1, Nacional (1) 1
Panathinaikos: Ikonomopoulos; Tomaras (Vlahos), Kapsis, Sourpis, Athanassopoulos, Eleftherakiss, Filakouris, Dimitrou, Kouvos, Antoniadis, Domazos.

Nacional: Manga; Masnik, Maneiro, Montero Castillo, Blanco, Ubinas Esparrago, Cubilla, Artime, Brunel, Morales.
Scorers: Filakouris for Panathinaikos; Artime for Nacional.
Montevideo, 29 December
Nacional (1) 2, Panathinaikos (0) 1
Nacional: Manga; Ubinas, Brunel, Masnik, Blanco, Montero Castillo, Maneiro, Esparrago, Cubilla (Mujica), Artime, Mamelli (Bareno).
Panathinaikos: Ikonomopoulos; Mitropoulos, Kapsis, Sourpis, Athanassopoulos, Kamaras (Filakouris), Domazos, Eleftherakis, Dimitrou, Antoniadis, Koudas.
Scorers: Artime (2) for National; Filakouris for Panathinaikos.

1972
Buenos Aires, 6 September
Independiente (0) 1, Ajax (1) 1
Independiente: Santoro; Commisso, Lopez, Sa, Pavoni, Semenewiecz, Pastoriza, Raimundo (Bulla), Balbuena, Maglioni, Mircoli.
Ajax: Stuy; Suurbier, Hulshoff, Blankenburg, Krol, Neeskens, Haan, G. Muhren, Swart, Cruyff, (A. Muhren), Keizer.
Scorers: Sa for Independiente; Cruyff for Ajax.
Amsterdam, 28 September
Ajax (1) 3, Independiente (0) 0
Ajax: Stuy; Suurbier, Hulshoff, Blankenburg, Krol, Neeskens, Haan, G. Muhren, Swart (Rep), Cruyff, Keizer.
Independiente: Santoro; Commisso, Lopez, Sa, Pavoni, Pastoriza, Garisto (Magan), Semenewiecz, Balbuena, Maglioni, Mircoli (Bulla).
Scorers: Neeskens, Rep (2) for Ajax.

CHAPTER FIFTEEN

The European Cup History

The European Cup was the brainchild of the veteran French journalist, selector and international player, Gabriel Hanot, and his Parisian newspaper, *L'Equipe*. Confined to clubs which have won their national League championship (though the holders' country may enter a second team), matches preceding the Final are decided on a home and away goal aggregate basis.

Though Scotland entered at once when the tournament began in 1955, England did not. The Football League refused Chelsea, then the English champions, permission to take part, and the following season advised Manchester United not to enter. Fortunately United would have no truck with such negative counsel, and duly took part, but in 1958, when the organisers generously invited them to take part again, as a token of sympathy for the Munich air crash disaster, they were meanly frustrated. The League forbade them to enter, maintaining that this was a competition for national champions, and United had not won the League title (thus claiming to make UEFA's rules for them). United appealed successfully to the Football Association but the League, in turn, were upheld in their decision by a joint F.A.–F.L. body. It was a thoroughly shabby episode.

The feature of the first five European Cups was the extraordinary dominance of Real Madrid. Off the field, the credit belonged to their vigorous President, Santiago Bernabeu; but on it, to the great Argentinian centre-forward, Alfredo Di Stefano. Long before the coming of Puskas, Di Stefano had inspired his team to bestride Europe. Not until 1960–61 did Barcelona at last become the first team to knock Real out of the European Cup.

EUROPEAN CUP 1955–56

With no entry from England, Hibernian of Edinburgh were the sole representatives of Britain and they reached the semi-finals with an excellent team which included Tommy Younger in goal, and a forward-line of Gordon Smith, Combe, Reilly, Turnbull, and Ormond. A brilliant 4–0 away win against Rot Weiss Essen took them through the first round; Djurgarden of Sweden were twice beaten on Scottish soil in the second, but Reims proved too strong for them in the semi-final. The return match, at Easter Road, was a brilliant one, with Kopa and Bob Jonquet in splendid form for Reims, but Hibernian having most of the play – and failing to score.

The final, in Paris, provided a splendid match between Reims and Real, in which Di Stefano and Kopa reached great heights of technique and organisation. Leblond and Templin gave Reims a 2–0 lead in the first ten minutes, it was 2–2 at half time, Hidalgo restored the lead for Reims, but a remarkable individual goal by the Real centre-half Marquitos equalised, and Rial, the Argentinian-born inside-left scored the winner, 11 minutes from time.

First Round
Sporting Lisbon 3, Partizan Belgrade 3
Partizan Belgrade 5, Sporting Lisbon 2
Voros Logobo 6, Anderlecht 3
Anderlecht 1, Voros Logobo 4
Servette Geneva 0, Real Madrid 2
Real Madrid 5, Servette 0
Rot Weiss Essen 0, Hibernian 4
Hibernian 1, Rot Weiss Essen 1
Aarhus 0, Reims 2
Reims 2, Aarhus 2
Rapid Vienna 6, Eindhoven 1
Eindhoven 1, Rapid 0

Djurgarden 0, Gwardia Warsaw 0
Gwardia 1, Djurgarden 4
AC Milan 3, Saarbrücken 4
Saarbrücken 1, AC Milan 4

Quarter-finals
Hibernian 3, Djurgarden 1
Djurgarden 0, Hibernian 1
  (*in Edinburgh*)
Reims 4, Voros Logobo 2
Voros Logobo 4, Reims 4
Real Madrid 4, Partizan Belgrade 0
Partizan Belgrade 3, Real Madrid 0

Rapid Vienna 1, Milan 1 Hibernian 0, Reims 1
Milan 7, Rapid Vienna 2 Real Madrid 4, Milan 2
　　　　　　　　　　　　　Milan 2, Real Madrid 1

Semi-finals
Reims 2, Hibernian 0

Final Paris, 13 June 1956
Real Madrid (2) 4, Reims (2) 3
Real: Alonso; Atienza, Lesmes; Munoz, Marquitos, Zarraga; Joseito; Marchal, Di Stefano, Rial, Gento.
Reims: Jacquet; Zimny, Giraudo; Leblond, Jonquet, Siatka; Hidalgo, Glovacki, Kopa, Bliard, Templin.
Scorers: Leblond, Templin, Hidalgo for Reims, Di Stefano, Rial (2), Marquitos for Real Madrid.

EUROPEAN CUP 1956-57

Manchester United now entered the lists for England, and put up an excellent performance, reaching the semi-finals with a dazzling young team among whose stars were Roger Byrne, Duncan Edwards and Tommy Taylor – all to die at Munich. Their ten-goal win over Anderlecht, at Maine Road, was a remarkable one. Denis Viollet, their inside-left, scored four of the goals. The third round, in Bilbao, saw United beaten 5–3 on a very heavy pitch, but they recovered for a splendid 3–0 victory in the return, and went through to the semi-finals, where the power of Real was just too much for them.

Rangers, Scotland's entry, went out ingloriously to Nice.

In the final, Italy's gifted Fiorentina side, which had splendid South American forwards in Julinho and Montuori, succumbed to Real, on Real's own ground.

First Round (Preliminary)
Dortmund Borussia 4, Spora Luxemburg 3
Spora Luxemburg 2, Dortmund Borussia 1
Dortmund Borussia 7, Spora Luxemburg 0
Dynamo Bucharest 3, Galatasaray 1
Galatasaray 2, Dynamo Bucharest 1
Slovan Bratislava 4, CWKS Warsaw 0
CWKS Warsaw 2, Slovan Bratislava 0
Anderlecht 0, Manchester United 2
Manchester United 10, Anderlecht 0
Aarhus 1, Nice 1
Nice 5, Aarhus 1
Porto 1, Atlético Bilbao 2
Atlético Bilbao 3, Porto 2
Byes: *Real Madrid, CDNA Sofia, Grasshoppers, Rangers, Rapid Vienna, Rapid Heerlen, Red Star Belgrade, Fiorentina, Norrköping, Honved.*

First Round Proper
Manchester United 3, Dortmund Borussia 2
Dortmund Borussia 0, Manchester United 0
CDNA Sofia 8, Dynamo Bucharest 1
Dynamo Bucharest 3, CDNA Sofia 2

Slovan Bratislava 1, Grasshoppers 0
Grasshoppers 2, Slovan Bratislava 0
Rangers 2, Nice 1
Nice 2, Rangers 1
Rangers 1, Nice 3
Real Madrid 4, Rapid Vienna 2
Rapid Vienna 3, Real Madrid 1
Real Madrid 2, Rapid Vienna 0
Rapid Juliana 3, Red Star Belgrade 4
Red Star Belgrade 2, Rapid Juliana 0
Fiorentina 1, Norrköping 1
Norrköping 0, Fiorentina 1
Atlético Bilbao 3, Honved 2
Honved 3, Atlético Bilbao 3

Quarter-finals
Atlético Bilbao 5, Manchester United 3
Manchester United 3, Atlético Bilbao 0
Fiorentina 3, Grasshoppers 1
Grasshopers 2, Fiorentina 2
Red Star 3, CDNA Sofia 1
CDNA Sofia 2, Red Star 1
Real Madrid 3, Nice 0
Nice 2, Real Madrid 3
Semi-finals
Red Star 0, Fiorentina 1
Fiorentina 0, Red Star 0
Real Madrid 3, Manchester United 1
Manchester United 2, Real Madrid 2

Final Madrid, 30 May 1957
Real Madrid (0) 2, *Fiorentina* (0) 0
Real: Alonso; Torres, Lesmes; Munoz, Marquitos, Zarraga; Kopa, Mateos, Di Stefano, Rial, Gento.
Fiorentina: Sarti; Magnini, Cervato; Scaramucci, Orzan, Segato; Julinho, Gratton, Virgili, Montuori, Bizzarri.
Scorers: Di Stefano (pen), Gento for Real Madrid.

EUROPEAN CUP 1957–58

For British football, this was the European Cup which was cruelly overshadowed by the Munich disaster, when the Elizabethan carrying Manchester United back from their match in Belgrade crashed on take-off, killing seven players. United had already qualified for the semi-finals, and their patched-up team made a brave show against Milan, winning the first leg in Manchester 2–1, Ernie Taylor getting the winner from a penalty, but losing the return 4–0. Rangers, who knocked out St Etienne, had been comfortably despatched by Milan in the eighth-finals.

Real, who now had Santamaria at centre-half, were lucky to get the better of Milan in a really thrilling final. Real survived when a shot by Cucchiaroni hit the bar, and went on to win in extra-time with a 107th-minute goal by Gento. It was a fine day for the Milan inside-forwards, Nils Liedholm and Argentina's Ernesto Grillo.

Preliminary Round
Rangers 3, St Etienne 1
St Etienne 2, Rangers 1
CNDA Sofia 2, Vasas Budapest 1
Vasas Budapest 6, CNDA Sofia 1
Red Star Belgrade 5, Stade Dudelange 0
Stade Dudelange 1, Red Star Belgrade 9
Aarhus 0, Glenavon 0

Glevavon 0, Aarhus 3
Gwardia Warsaw 3, Wismut
  Karl-Marx-Stadt 1
Wismut Karl-Marx-Stadt 2,
  Gwardia Warsaw 0
Wismut Karl-Marx-Stadt 1,
  Gwardia Warsaw 1 (*Wismut
  won the toss*)
Seville 3, Benfica 1
Benfica 0, Seville 0
Shamrock Rovers 0, Manchester
  United 6
Manchester United 3, Shamrock
  Rovers 2
Milan 4, Rapid Vienna 1
Rapid Vienna 5, Milan 2
Milan 4, Rapid Vienna 2
Byes: *Antwerp, Real Madrid,
  Norrköping, Ajax Amsterdam,
  Dukla Prague, Young Boys
  Berne, Borussia Dortmund,
  CCA Bucharest.*

First Round Proper
Antwerp 1, Real Madrid 2
Real Madrid 6, Antwerp 0
Norrköping 2, Red Star 2
Red Star 2, Norrköping 1
Wismut Karl-Marx-Stadt 1,
  Ajax Amsterdam 3
Ajax Amsterdam 1, Wismut
  Karl-Marx-Stadt 0

Manchester United 3, Dukla
  Prague 0
Dukla Prague 1, Manchester
  United 0
Young Boys Berne 1, Vasas 1
Vasas 2, Young Boys Berne 1
Rangers 1, Milan 4
Milan 2, Rangers 0
Seville 4, Aarhus 0
Aarhus 2, Seville 0
Dortmund Borussia 4, CCA
  Bucharest 2
CCA Bucharest 3, Dortmund
  Borussia 1
Dortmund Borussia 3, CCA
  Bucharest 1

Quarter-finals
Manchester United 2, Red Star 1
Red Star 3, Manchester United 3
Real Madrid 8, Seville 0
Seville 2, Real Madrid 2
Ajax Amsterdam 2, Vasas 2
Vasas 4, Ajax Amsterdam 0
Dortmund Borussia 1, Milan 1
Milan 4, Dortmund Borussia 1

Semi-finals
Real Madrid 4, Vasas Budapest 0
Vasas 2, Real Madrid 0
Manchester United 2, Milan 1
Milan 4, Manchester United 0

Final Brussels, 28 May 1958
Real Madrid (0) 3, Milan (0) 2 after extra time
Real Madrid: Alonso; Atienza, Lesmes; Santisteban, Santamaria, Zarraga; Kopa, Joseito, Di Stefano, Rial, Gento.
Milan: Soldan; Fontana, Beraldo; Bergamaschi, Maldini, Radice; Danova, Liedholm, Schiaffino, Grillo, Cucchiaroni.
Scorers: Schiaffino, Grillo for Milan; Di Stefano, Rial, Gento for Real Madrid.

EUROPEAN CUP 1958–59
After the champagne of Manchester United, the rather flat beer of the Wolves, who were put out, somewhat obscurely, by Schalke 04 in the first round. As for Hearts, the coloured Liège centre-forward, quaintly named Bonga-Bonga, tore their defence to shreds. Real proved more majestic than ever, especially in the crushing of Wiener Sport-

klub. But the all-Madrid semi-final with Atlético turned out to be a frighteningly close affair, in which Atlético (led by Brazil's Vavá) fought with magnificent spirit, forcing a third match. The final, against Reims, was anti-climax; a dull match which Real won despite an injury to Kopa, playing against his old club.

Preliminary Round
Boldklub Copenhagen 3, Schalke 04 0
Schalke 04 5, Boldklub Copenhagen 2
Schalke 04 3, Boldklub Copenhagen 1
Standard Liège 5, Hearts 1
Hearts 2, Standard Liège 1
Dynamo Zagreb 2, Dukla Prague 2
Dukla Prague 2, Dynamo Zagreb 1
Jeunesse Esch 1, Gothenburg 2
Gothenburg 0, Jeunesse Esch 1
Gothenburg 5, Jeunesse Esch 1
Wismut Karl-Marx-Stadt 4, Petrolul Ploesti 2
Petrolul Ploesti 2, Wismut Karl-Marx-Stadt 0
Wismut Karl-Marx-Stadt 4, Petrolul Ploesti 0
Polonia Bytom 0, MTK Budapest 3
MTK Budapest 3, Polonia Bytom 0
Atlético Madrid 8, Drumcondra 0
Drumcondra 1, Atlético Madrid 5
DSO Utrecht 3, Sporting Lisbon 4
Sporting Lisbon 2, DSO Utrecht 1
Ards 1, Reims 4
Reims 6, Ards 2
Juventus 3, Wiener SK 1
Wiener SK 7, Juventus 0
Byes: *Real Madrid, CDNA Sofia, Wolverhampton Wanderers, Palloseura Helsinki.* Walk-overs: *Young Boys Berne, Besiktas.*

First Round Proper
Sporting Lisbon 2, Standard Liège 3
Standard Liège 2, Sporting Lisbon 0
MTK 1, Young Boys Berne 2
Young Boys Berne 4, MTK 1
Wiener SK 3, Dukla Prague 1
Dukla Prague 1, Weiner SK 0
Atletico Madrid 2, CDNA Sofia 1
CDNA Sofia 1, Atlético Madrid 0
Atlético Madrid 3, CDNA Sofia 1 after extra time
Gothenburg 2, Wismut Karl-Marx-Stadt 2
Wismut Karl-Marx-Stadt 4, Gothenburg 0
Wolverhampton Wanderers 2, Schalke 04 2
Shalke 04 2, Wolverhampton Wanderers 1
Real Madrid 2, Besiktas Istanbul 0
Besiktas Istanbul 1, Real Madrid 1
Reims 4, Palloseura Helsinki 0
Reims 3, Palloseura Helsinki 0

Quarter-finals
Standard Liège 2, Reims 0
Reims 3, Standard Liège 0
Atlético Madrid 3, Schalke 04 0
Schalke 04 1, Atlético Madrid 1
Wiener SK 0, Real Madrid 0
Real Madrid 7, Wiener SK 1
Young Boys 2, Wismut Karl-Marx-Stadt 2
Wismut Karl-Marx-Stadt 0, Young Boys 0
Young Boys 2, Wismut Karl-Marx-Stadt 1

Semi-finals
Young Boys 1, Reims 0
Reims 3, Young Boys 0
Real Madrid 2, Atlético Madrid 1
Atlético Madrid 1, Real Madrid 0
Real Madrid 2, Atlético Madrid 1

Final Stuttgart, 2 June 1959
Real Madrid (1) 2, *Reims* (0) 0
Real Madrid: Dominguez; Marquitos, Zarraga; Santisteban, Santamaria, Ruiz; Kopa, Mateos, Di Stefano, Rial, Gento.
Reims: Colonna; Rodzik, Giraudo; Penverne, Jonquet, Leblond; Lamartine, Bliard, Fontaine, Piantoni, Vincent.
Scorers: Mateos, Di Stefano for Real Madrid.

EUROPEAN CUP 1959-60

The year 1960 produced one of the finest and most spectacular finals, a match in which Real – who now had the great Puskas in the side, with tireless Del Sol at inside-right – easily rode an early goal by Eintracht, to crush them 7-3. The immense Hampden crowd gave them a memorable ovation after the match. Di Stefano and Puskas were peerlessly brilliant, Puskas getting four of the goals, his left foot as ferocious as ever, with Di Stefano, tirelessly inventive, scoring the other three.

But Eintracht must not be written off; their progress to the final was splendid, not least their contemptuous home and away thrashing of Rangers. Their veteran inside-left, Pfaff, was a major star.

Nor must one forget the virtuosity of Barcelona and their polyglot team, under the flamboyant Herrera – who was abused by fans and sacked, after the elimination by Real in two awe-inspiring matches. Previously, they had killed the legend that Continentals cannot play in thick mud by humiliating Wolves on just such a pitch at Molineux. Of all the European Cups played, this was so far the most exciting and glittering.

Preliminary Round
Nice 3, Shamrock Rovers 2
Shamrock Rovers 1, Nice 1
CDNA Sofia 2, Barcelona 2
Barcelona 6, CDNA Sofia 2
Linfield 2, IFK Gothenburg 1
IFK Gothenburg 6, Linfield 1
Jeunesse Esch 5, Lodz 1
Lodz 2, Jeunesse Esch 1
Wiener SK 0, Petrolul Ploesti 0
Petrolul Ploesti 1, Wiener SK 2
Olympiakos 2, Milan 2
Milan 3, Olympiakos 1
Fenerbahce 1, Csepel 1
Fenerbahce 3, Csepel 2
Rangers 5, Anderlecht 2
Anderlecht 0, Rangers 2
Red Star Bratizlava 2, Porto 1
Porto 0, Red Star Bratislava 2
Vorwaerts Berlin 2,
  Wolverhampton Wanderers 1

Wolverhampton Wanderers 2,
  Vorwaerts Berlin 0
Byes: *Real Madrid, Odense BK09, Young Boys Berne, Sparta Rotterdam, Red Star Belgrade.* Walkover: *Eintracht Frankfurt.*

First Round
Real Madrid 7, Esch 0
Esch 2, Real Madrid 5
Odense BK 09 0, Weiner SK 3
Weiner SK 2, Odense BK 09 2
Sparta Rotterdam 3, IFK
  Gothenburg 1
IFK Gothenburg 3, Sparta
  Rotterdam 1
Sparta Rotterdam 3, IFK
  Gothenburg 1
Milan 0, Barcelona 2
Barcelona 5, Milan 1

Young Boys Berne 1, Eintracht
 Frankfurt 4
Eintracht Frankfurt 1, Young
 Boys Berne 1
Red Star Belgrade 1,
 Wolverhampton Wanderers 1
Wolverhampton Wanderers 3,
 Red Star Belgrade 0
Rangers 4, Red Star Bratislava 3
Red Star Bratislava 1, Rangers 1
Fenerbahce 2, Nice 1
Nice 2, Fenerbahce 1
Nice 5, Fenerbahce 1

Quarter-finals
Nice 3, Real Madrid 2

Real Madrid 4, Nice 0
Barcelona 4, Wolverhampton
 Wanderers 0
Wolverhampton Wanderers 2,
 Barcelona 5
Eintracht 2, Wiener SK 1
Wiener SK 1, Eintracht 1
Rangers 3, Sparta 2
Sparta 1, Rangers 0
Rangers 3, Sparta 2

Semi-finals
Eintracht 6, Rangers 1
Rangers 3, Eintracht 6
Real Madrid 3, Barcelona 1
Barcelona 1, Real Madrid 3

Final Glasgow, 18 May 1960
Real Madrid (3) 7, *Eintracht Frankfurt* (1) 3
Real Madrid: Dominguez; Marquitos, Pachin; Vidal, Santamaria, Zarraga; Canario, Del Sol, Di Stefano, Puskas, Gento.
Eintracht: Loy; Lutz, Hoefer; Wellbaecher, Eigenbrodt, Stinka; Kress, Lindner, Stein, Pfaff, Meier.
Scorers: Di Stefano (3), Puskas (4) for Real; Kress, Stein (2) for Eintracht.

EUROPEAN CUP 1960-61

At long last, the reign of Real Madrid was brought to an end. But the team that eliminated them – Barcelona, taking revenge for the previous year – did not win the Cup. Instead, it went, against all expectation, to Benfica, the Portuguese club, managed with immense shrewdness by the veretan Hungarian, Bela Guttmann. Benfica may have had a little luck in the final, when the sun dazzled Ramallets, and he let in a couple of simple goals, but they undoubtedly had a splendid team. Germano, the centre-half, was the best and most mobile in Europe, Coluna a superb midfield player, and Aguas a mature centre forward.

Burnley, England's representatives, played skilful football, but failed badly against Hamburg in their return quarter-final, when they had enough of the play to have won. Hearts were unfortunate enough to meet Benfica in the first round.

Preliminary Round
Frederikstadt 4, Ajax
 Amsterdam 3
Ajax Amsterdam 0,
 Frederikstadt 0
Limerick 0, Young Boys Berne 6
Young Boys Berne 4, Limerick 2

Kamraterna 1, IFK Malmö 3
IFK Malmö 2, Kamraterna 1
Reims 6, Jeunesse Esch 1
Jeunesse Esch 0, Reims 5
Rapid Vienna 4, Besiktas
 Istanbul 0
Besiktas Istanbul 1, Rapid
 Vienna 0

Juventus 2, CDNA Sofia 0
CDNA Sofia 4, Juventus 1
Aarhus GF 3, Legia Warsaw 0
Legia Warsaw 1, Aarhus GF 0
Red Star Belgrade 1, Ujpest
  Dozsa 2
Ujpest Dozsa 3, Red Star
  Belgrade 0
Barcelona 2, Lierse SK 0
Lierse SK 0, Barcelona 3
Hearts 1, Benfica 2
Benfica 3, Hearts 0
CCA Bucharest 0, Spartak
  Kralove 3
Forfeited *Glenavon and CCA Bucharest*
Byes: *Real Madrid, Panathinaikos SV Hamburg, Burnley*. Walk-over: *Wismut Karl-Marx-Stadt*.

First Round
Aarhus GF 3, Frederikstadt 0
Frederikstadt 0, Aarhus GF 1
IFK Malmö 1, CDNA Sofia 0
CDNA Sofia 1, IFK Malmö 1
Young Boys 0, SV Hamburg 5
SV Hamburg 3, Young Boys 3
Spartak Kralove 1,
  Panathinaikos 0
Panathinaikos 0, Spartak
  Kralove 0

Final Berne, 31 March 1961
Benfica (2) 3, *Barcelona* (1) 2

Benfica 6, Ujpest 2
Ujpest 2, Benfica 1
Real Madrid 2, Barcelona 2
Barcelona 2, Real Madrid 1
Rapid Vienna 3, Wismut
  Karl-Marx-Stadt 1
Wismut Karl-Marx-Stadt 2,
  Rapid Vienna 0
Rapid Vienna 1, Wismut
  Karl-Marx-Stadt 0
Burnley 2, Reims 0
Reims 3, Burnley 2

Quarter-finals
Burnley 3, Hamburg 1
Hamburg 4, Burnley 1
Barcelona 4, Spartak Kralove 0
Spartak Kralove 1, Barcelona 1
Benfica 3, Aarhus 1
Aarhus 2, Benfica 4
Rapid Vienna 2, IFK Malmö 0
IFK Malmö 0, Rapid Vienna 2

Semi-finals
Barcelona 1, Hamburg 0
Hamburg 2, Barcelona 1
Barcelona 1, Hamburg 0
Benfica 3, Rapid Vienna 0
Rapid Vienna 1, Benfica 1

Benfica: Costa Pereira; Joao, Angelo; Netto, Germano, Cruz; Augusto, Santana, Aguas, Coluna, Cavem.
Barcelona: Ramallets; Foncho, Gracia; Verges, Garay, Gensana; Kubala, Kocsis, Evaristo, Suarez, Czibor.
Scorers: Aguas, Ramallets (own goal), Coluna for Benfica; Kocsis, Czibor for Barcelona.

EUROPEAN CUP 1961–62

It was now the turn of the brilliant Spurs team to represent England. They played some memorable matches, not least the one in which they crushed Gornik of Poland 8–1 in a frenzied atmosphere of partisan passion, after losing the first leg. But over-emphasis on defence in Lisbon, mistakes by the backs, and a little bad luck in a frenetic return, against Benfica, cost them the semi-finals. Benfica went on to win a marvellous final against Real, in Amsterdam, proving that their success the season before had been no fluke. They survived a fine early goal worked out by Di Stefano and Puskas, and the shooting in this match from Puskas, Coluna, Eusebio, and Cavem really had to be seen to be believed.

Rangers, once again representing Scotland, had a creditable passage, but failed sadly and surprisingly in Liège against Standard.

Preliminary Round
Nuremberg 5, Drumcondra 0
Drumcondra 1, Nuremberg 4
Vorwaerts 3, Linfield 0
(*Linfield gave Vorwaerts a walkover in the second leg when the East Germans were refused visas*).
Spora Luxemburg 0, Odense BK 09 6
Odense BK 09 9, Spora Luxemburg 2
Monaco 2, Rangers 3
Rangers 3, Monaco 2
Vasas Budapest 0, Real Madrid 2
Real Madrid 3, Vasas Budapest 1
CDNA Sofia 4, Dulka 4
Dulka 2, CDNA Sofia 1
Standard Liège 2, Frederikstadt 1
Frederikstadt 0, Standard Liège 2
IFK Gothenburg 0, Feyenoord 3
Feyenoord 8, IFK Gothenburg 2
Servette 5, Valetta 0
Valetta 1, Servette 2
Gornik Zabrze 4, Tottenham Hotspur 2
Tottenham Hotspur 8, Gornik Zabrze 1
Sporting Lisbon 1, Partizan Belgrade 1
Partizan Belgrade 2, Sporting Lisbon 0
Panathinaikos 1, Juventus 1
Juventus 2, Panathinaikos 1
Bucharest 0, FK Austria 0
FK Austria 2, Bucharest 0
Byes: *Benfica, Valkeakosken, Fenerbahce.*

First Round
Odense BK 09 0, Real Madrid 3
Real Madrid 9, Odense BK 09 0
Fenerbahce 1, Nuremberg 2
Nuremberg 1, Fenerbahce 0
Standard Liège 5, Valkeakosken 1
Valkeakosken 0, Standard Liège 2
FK Austria 1, Benfica 1
Benfica 5, FK Austria 1
Servette 4, Dukla 3
Dukla 2, Servette 0
Feyenoord 1, Tottenham Hotspur 3
Tottenham Hotspur 1, Feyenoord 1
Partizan 1, Juventus 2
Juventus 5, Partizan 1
Vorwaerts Berlin 1, Rangers 2
Rangers 4, Vorwaerts Berlin 1

Quarter-finals
Nuremberg 3, Benfica 1
Benfica 6, Nuremberg 0
Standard Liège 4, Rangers 1
Rangers 2, Standard Liège 0
Dukla 1, Tottenham Hotspur 0
Tottenham Hotspur 4, Dukla 1
Juventus 0, Real Madrid 1
Real Madrid 0, Juventus 1
Real Madrid 3, Juventus 1

Semi-finals
Benfica 3, Tottenham Hotspur 1
Tottenham Hotspur 2, Benfica 1
Real Madrid 4, Standard Liège 0
Standard Liège 0, Real Madrid 2

Final Amsterdam, 2 May 1962
Benfica (2) 5, *Real Madrid* (3) 3
Benfica: Costa Pereira; Joao, Angelo; Cavem, Germano, Cruz; Augusto, Eusebio, Aguas, Coluna, Simoes.

Real Madrid: Araquistain; Cassado, Miera; Felo, Santamaria, Pachin; Tejada, Del Sol, Di Stefano, Puskas, Gento.
Scorers: Puskas (3) for Real Madrid; Aguas, Cavem, Coluna, Eusebio (2) for Benfica.

EUROPEAN CUP 1962-63

For the third successive time, Benfica reached the final, but this one was to end in their defeat. Milan beat them at Wembley in a slightly disappointing game. Managed now by the Chilean, Riera, instead of Guttmann, Benfica had gone over to 4-2-4 and a more defensive outlook, partly dictated by the loss of Germano through injury, Aguas through form. Milan, well generalled by the precocious young Rivera, hit back with two goals by Brazil's Altafini (the second of which looked offside) after Eusebio had put Benfica ahead. But an injury to Coluna who had to go off in the second half, badly affected them.

Ipswich, England's representatives, and Dundee both went out to Milan. Ipswich floundered in heavy rain in Milan, played more briskly in the return – and won – but Dundee were a revelation. Clever breakaway tactics and a defence splendidly marshalled by Ian Ure enabled them to become the dark horse of the tournament. For Real, knocked out in Belgium by a goal from Jef Jurion, this was a season of relative twilight.

Preliminary Round
Linfield 1, Esbjerg 2
Esbjerg 0, Linfield 0
Real Madrid 3, Anderlecht 3
Anderlecht 1, Real Madrid 0
Floriana Malta 1, Ipswich Town 4
Ipswich Town 10, Floriana Malta 0
Dundee 8, Cologne 1
Cologne 4, Dundee 0
Shelbourne 0, Sporting Lisbon 2
Sporting Lisbon 5, Shelbourne 1
Vorwaerts 0, Dukla Prague 3
Dukla Prague 1, Vorwaerts 0
Norrköping 9, Partizan Tirana 2
Partizan Tirana 1, Norrköping 1
Dynamo Bucharest 1, Galatasaray 1
Galatasaray 3, Dynamo Bucharest 0
Servette Geneva 1, Feyenoord 3
Feyenoord 1, Servette Geneva 3
Servette Geneva 1, Feyenoord 3
Polonia 2, Panathinaikos 1
Panathinaikos 1, Polonia 4
Frederikstadt 1, Vasas Budapest 4
Vasas Budapest 7, Frederikstadt 0
FK Austria 5, Kamraterna Helsinki 3
Kamraterna Helsinki 0, FK Austria 2
CDNA Sofia 2, Partizan Belgrade 1
Partizan Belgrade 1, CDNA Sofia 4
Milan 8, US Luxemburg 0
US Luxemburg 0, Milan 6
Byes: *Benfica, Reims*

First Round
FK Austria 3, Reims 2
Reims 5, FK Austria 0
Sporting Lisbon 1, Dundee 0
Dundee 4, Sporting Lisbon 1
Norrköping 1, Benfica 1
Benfica 5, Norrköping 1
Galatasaray 4, Polonia Bytom 1
Polonia Bytom 1, Galatasaray 0
Esbjerg 0, Dukla 0
Dukla 5, Esbjerg 0
Feyenoord 1, Vasas 1
Vasas 2, Feyenoord 2

Feyenoord 1, Vasas 0
Milan 3, Ipswich Town 0
Ipswich Town 2, Milan 1

Dukla 0, Benfica 0
Reims 0, Feyenoord 1
Feyenoord 1, Reims 1

Quarter-finals
Anderlecht 1, Dundee 4
Dundee 2, Anderlecht 1
Galatasaray 1, Milan 3
Milan 5, Galatasaray 0
Benfica 2, Dukla 1

Semi-finals
Milan 5, Dundee 1
Dundee 1, Milan 0
Benfica 3, Feyenoord 1
Feyenoord 0, Benfica 0

Final Wembley Stadium, 22 May 1963
Milan (0) 2, Benfica (1) 1
Milan: Ghezzi; David, Trebbi; Benitez, Maldini, Trapattoni; Pivatelli, Sani, Altafini, Rivera, Mora.
Benfica: Costa Pereira; Cavem, Cruz; Humberto, Raul, Coluna; Augusto, Santana, Torres, Eusebio, Simões.
Scorers: Eusebio for Benfica; Altafini (2) for Milan.

EUROPEAN CUP 1963–64

Britain's challenge disappeared with depressing speed. Rangers, somewhat unlucky to lose to a late goal by Puskas in a breakaway at Ibrox, were torn apart in Madrid, where Puskas showed much of his old form. It must be said in Rangers' defence that they lacked several experienced forwards. Everton were baffled by the reinforced Inter defence at Goodison, though many feel they did breach it, when a goal by Vernon was narrowly judged offside. In Milan, they themselves employed massive defence, and it was only a freak goal from near the by-line, scored by Jair, which beat them.

Benfica, lacking Costa Pereira and Eusebio, were thrashed in their return match with Borussia Dortmund who went on to eliminate Dukla. A superb display in Madrid enabled Real to eliminate Milan, while Inter's massive defence and breakaway attacks accounted for Monaco, Partizan, and Borussia. In the final, Inter left out their extra defender, Szymaniak, gambled on a genuine leader in Milani, blotted out Real's attack, and exploited the mistakes of their defence. Mazzola scored from long range just before half-time. Poor goalkeeping gave Milani a second, Felo headed in from a corner, but an incredible blunder by Santamaria presented Mazzola with the third.

Preliminary Round
Galatasary 4, Ferencvaros 0
Ferencvaros 2, Galatasaray 0
Partizan Belgrade 3, Anorthosis 0
Anorthosis 1, Partizan Belgrade 3
Dundalk 0, FC Zürich 3
FC Zürich 1, Dundalk 2
Lyn Oslo 2, Borussia
 Dortmund 4

Borussia Dortmund 3, Lyn Oslo 1
Dukla Prague 6, Valetta 0
Valetta 0, Dukla Prague 2
Everton 0, Internazionale 0
Internazionale 1, Everton 0
Gornik Zabrze 1, FK Austria 0
FK Austria 1, Gornik Zabrze 0
Gornik Zabrze 2, FK Austria 1
Monaco 7, AEK Athens 2

Müller smashes home Kapelmann's long cross from the left to put Bayern Munich two up in the replayed European Cup final against Atlético Madrid.

The men who put Leeds United at the top of British football – Billy Bremner and Don Revie. Will the 1974–75 season see them conquerors of Europe?

A storybook ending to a season that had its stormy moments for Liverpool manager Bill Shankly and his former captain Tommy Smith (centre), whose crosses led to two of Liverpool's three goals in the FA Cup final.

Jackie Charlton won't forget the 1973–74 season for a long time.
In his first season as a manager he took Middlesbrough back into
the First Division and was named Manager of the Year.

The old brigade, the new brigadier. The England's caretaker manager Joe Mercer is flanked by his predecessor's two lieutenants, Harold Shepherdson (left) and Les Cocker.

England are out of the World Cup. Norman Hunter covers his face following England's elimination by Poland, while a dejected Emlyn Hughes is comforted by Harold Shepherdson.

Manchester's moment of shame. As a result of this invasion by fans during a United – City derby, Manchester United were ordered to erect fences at Old Trafford – the first time this has happened in Britain.

Billy McNeill, yet again a tower of strength in Celtic's 'double' team, is challenged by Dundee United's Gray during the 1974 Scottish Cup final.

AEK Athens 1, Monaco 1
Dynamo Bucharest 2, Motor
 Jena 0
Motor Jena 0, Dynamo
 Bucharest 1
Valkeakosken 4, Jeunesse Esch 1
Jeunesse Esch 4, Valkaekosken 0
Standard Liège 1, Norrköping 0
Norrköping 2, Standard Liège 0
Tirania 1, Spartak Plovdiv 0
Spartak Plovdiv 3, Tirania 1
Eindhoven 7, Esbjerg 1
Esbjerg 3, Eindhoven 4
Distillery 3, Benfica 3
Benfica 5, Distillery 0
Rangers 0, Real Madrid 1
Real Madrid 6, Rangers 0
Bye: *Milan*

First Round
Benfica 2, Borussia Dortmund 1
Borussia Dortmund 5, Benfica 0
Internazionale 1, Monaco 0
Monaco 0, Internazionale 3
Norrköpping 1, Milan 1
Milan 5, Norrköpping 2
FC Zürich 3, Galatasaray 0
Galatasaray 2, FC Zürich 0
Gornik 2, Dukla 0
Dukla 4, Gornik 1

Jeunesse Esch 2, Partizan
 Belgrade 1
Partizan Belgrade 6, Heunesse
 Esch 2
Spartak Plovdiv 0, Eindhoven 1
Eindhoven 0, Spartak Plovdiv 0
Dynamo Bucharest 1, Real
 Madrid 3
Real Madrid 5, Dynamo
 Bucharest 3

Quarter-finals
Real Madrid 4, Milan 1
Milan 2, Real Madrid 0
Partizan Belgrade 0,
 Internazionale 3
Internazionale 2, Partizan
 Belgrade 1
Eindhoven 1, FC Zürich 0
FC Zürich 3, Eindhoven 1
Dukla 0, Borussia Dortmund 4
Borussia Dortmund 1, Dukla 3

Semi-finals
Borussia Dortmund 2,
 Internazionale 2
Internazionale 2, Borussia
 Dortmund 0
FC Zürich 1, Real Madrid 2
Real Madrid 6, FC Zürich 0

Final Vienna, 27 May 1964
Internazionale 3, Real Madrid 1
Internazionale: Sarti; Burgnich, Facchetti; Tagnin, Guarneri, Picchi; Jair, Mazzola, Milani, Suarez, Corso.
Real Madrid: Vicente; Isidro, Pachin; Muller, Santamaria, Zoco; Amancio, Felo, Di Stefano, Puskas, Gento.
Scorers: Mazola (2), Milani for Internazionale; Felo for Real Madrid.

EUROPEAN CUP 1964–65
Once again, Inter won the tournament, though not without considerable difficulty, on the way. Much of this was gallantly provided by Liverpool who, three days after a bruising Cup final, involving extra time, and playing without two key men, brilliantly defeated them at Anfield. Inter, however, recovered to win in Milan, though Peiró's gaol, after a challenge on goalkeeper Lawrence, which is still a subject of dispute. Previously, Liverpool had had a notable success against an Anderlecht team till then in splendid form. A clever tactical plan, using

Smith as a second centre-half, was their chief weapon, but they were very lucky indeed to win the toss in Rotterdam against a brave 10-man Cologne team, which fought back from 0–2.

Rangers also did well, and might have done better still, had not Jim Baxter broken a leg, while helping materially to get them through, in Vienna.

In the final, Inter won laboriously and unconvincingly against a brave Benfica side, naturally reluctant to play it on Inter's own ground. Benfica lost Costa Pereira, their goalkeeper, half-an-hour from time, but the score remained unchanged. And the goal, by Jair, was really a result of the appalling, rainy conditions, for his shot slipped under Costa Pereira's body.

Preliminary Round
Anderlecht 1, Bologna 0
Bologna 2, Anderlecht 1
Anderlecht 0, Bologna 0 (*in Barcelona*)
(Anderlecht *won toss*)
Rangers 3, Red Star Belgrade 1
Red Star Belgrade 4, Rangers 2
Rangers 3, Red Star Belgrade 1 (*at Highbury*)
Chemie Leipzig 0, Vasas Gyor 2
Vasas Gyor 4, Chemie Leipzig 2
Dukla Prague 4, Gornik Zabrze 1
Gornik Zabrze 3, Dukla Prague 0
Gornik Zabrze 0, Dukla Prague 0 (*in Duisberg*)
(Dukla *won toss*)
Reipas Lahti 2, Lyn Oslo 1
Lyn Oslo 3, Reipas Lahti 0
Partizan Tirana 0, Cologne 0
Cologne 2, Partizan Tirana 0
St Eteinne 2, Chaux de Fonds 2
Chaux de Fonds 2, St Etienne 1
Glentoran 2, Panathinaikos 2
Panathinaikos 3, Glentoran 2
Odense BK 09 2, Real Madrid 5
Real Madrid 4, Odense BK 09 0
Aris 1, Benfica 5
Benfica 5, Aris 1
DWS Amsterdam 3, Fenerbahce 0
Fenerbahce 0, DWS Amsterdam 1
Rapid Vienna 3, Shamrock Rovers 0
Shamrock Rovers 0, Rapid Vienna 2
Lokomotiv Sofia 8, Malmö 3
Malmö 2, Lokomotiv Sofia 0
Reykjavic 0, Liverpool 5
Liverpool 6, Reykjavic 1
Dynamo Bucharest 5, Sliema Wanderers 0
Sliema Wanderers 0, Dynamo Bucharest 2
Bye: *Internazionale*

First Round
Panathinaikos 1, Cologne 1
Cologne 2, Panathinaikos 1
Internazionale 6, Dynamo Bucharest 0
Dynamo Bucharest 0, Internazionale 1
Vasas Gyor 5, Lokomotiv Sofia 3
Lokomotiv Sofia 4, Vasas Gyor 3
Rangers 1, Rapid Vienna 0
Rapid Vienna 0, Rangers 2
Real Madrid 4, Dukla 0
Dukla 2, Real Madrid 2
Liverpool 3, Anderlecht 0
Anderlecht 0, Liverpool 1
DWS Amsterdam 5, Lyn 0
Lyn 1, DWS Amsterdam 3
Chaux de Fonds 1, Benfica 1
Benfica 5, Chaux de Fonds 0

Quarter-finals
Cologne 0, Liverpool 0
Liverpool 0, Cologne 0
Liverpool 2, Cologne 2 (*in Rotterdam*)
Liverpool *won toss*

Internazionale 3, Rangers 1
Rangers 1, Internazionale 0
Benfica 3, Real Madrid 1
Real Madrid 2, Benfica 1
DWS Amsterdam 1, Vasas
  Gyor 1
Vasas Gyor 1, DWS
  Amsterdam 0

Semi-finals
Vasas Gyor 0, Benfica 1
Benfica 4, Vasas Gyor 0
Liverpool 3, Internazionale 1
Internazionale 3, Liverpool 0

Final Milan, 27 May 1965
Internazionale (1) 1, Benfica (0) 0
Internazionale: Sarti; Burgnich, Facchetti; Bedin, Guarneri, Picchi; Jair, Mazzola, Peiró, Suarez, Corso.
Benfica: Costa Pereira; Cavem, Cruz; Netto, Germano, Raul; Augusto, Eusebio, Torres, Coluna, Simões.
Scorer: Jair for Inter.

EUROPEAN CUP 1965–66

Once again, Manchester United reached the semi-finals – and folded up. Once again Real Madrid, for the sixth time in their history, took the Cup. The virtual final was composed by their two matches against Inter, the holders and favourites, who made the mistake of fielding a defensive formation against them in the first leg of the semi-finals, in Madrid. Real got through by the only goal and, at San Siro, virtually settled matters when they took the lead through Amancio. Inter equalised, but never seemed likely to win.

In the final, Real, a young, vigorous side with none of the high quality of the Di Stefano days, duly beat Partizan, the Belgrade dark horses, despite falling behind to a goal by Vasovic 10 minutes after half-time.

Previously, Partizan had beaten a sloppy Manchester United side in Belgrade, and held them to a single, rather lucky, goal by Stiles, at Old Trafford, where United were without Best, Partizan without their midfield schemer, Kovacevic – and without Galic, doing his military service but recalled for the final, in Brussels. United had the consolation of putting up perhaps the finest display of the competition, when they brilliantly thrashed Benfica in Lisbon, in the return leg of the quarter-finals. George Best, irresistible, scored the two opening goals in the first 12 minutes.

Preliminary Round
Lyn 5, Derry City 3
Derry City 5, Lyn 1
Feyenoord 2, Real Madrid 1
Real Madrid 5, Feyenoord 0
Kevflavik 1, Ferencvaros 4
Ferencvaros 9, Kevflavik 1
Fenerbahce 0, Anderlecht 0
Anderlecht 5, Fenerbahce 1
Tirania 0, Kilmarnock 0
Kilmarnock 1, Tirania 0
Djurgarden 2, Levski 1
Levski 6, Djurgarden 0
Drumcondra 1, Vorwaerts
  Berlin 0
Vorwaerts Berlin 2,
  Drumcondra 0
Linz 1, Gornik Zabrze 3

Gornik Zabrze 2, Linz 1
Partizan Belgrade 2, Nantes 0
Nantes 2, Partizan Belgrade 2
HJK Helsinki 2, Manchester
 United 3
Manchester United 6,
 HJK Helsinki 0
Lausanne 0, Sparta Prague 0
Sparta Prague 4, Lausanne 0
Dundelange 0, Benfica 8
Benfica 10, Dundelange 0
Panathinaikos 4, Sliema 1
Sliema 1, Panathinaikos 0
Hapoel Nicosia 0, Werder
 Bremen 5 (Bremen)
Werder Bremen 5, Hapoel
 Nicosia 0
Dynamo Bucharest 4, Odense
 BK 09 0
Odense BK 09 2, Dynamo
 Bucharest 3
Bye: *Internazionale*

Kilmarnock 2, Real Madrid 2
Real Madrid 5, Kilmarnock 1
Vorwaerts 0, Manchester
 United 2
Manchester United 3,
 Vorwaerts 1
Sparta 3, Gornik 0
Gornik 1, Sparta 2
Dynamo Bucharest 2,
 Internazionale 1
Internazionale 2, Dynamo
 Bucharest 0
Anderlecht 9, Derry City 0
(*no return match*)

Second Round
Manchester United 3, Benfica 2
Benfica 1, Manchester United 5
Anderlecht 1, Real Madrid 0
Real Madrid 4, Anderlecht 2
Sparta 4, Partizan 1
Partizan 5, Sparta 0
Internazionale 4, Ferencvaros 0
Ferencevaros 1, Internazionale 1

First Round
Partizan 3, Werder Bremen 0
Werder Bremen 1, Partizan 0
Levski 2, Benfica 2
Benfica 3, Levski 2
Ferencvaros 0, Panathinaikos 0
Panathinaikos 1, Ferencvaros 3

Semi-finals
Partizan 2, Manchester United 0
Manchester United 1, Partizan 0
Real Madrid 1, Internazionale 0
Internazionale 1, Real Madrid 1

Final Brussels, 11 May 1966
Real Madrid (0) 2, Partizan (0) 1
Real Madrid: Araquistain; Pachin, Sanchis; Pirri, De Felipe, Zoco; Serena, Amancio, Grosso, Velasquez, Gento.
Partizan: Soskic; Jusufi, Milhailovic; Becejac, Rasovic, Vasovic; Bakic, Kovacevic, Hasanagic, Galic, Primajer.
Scorers: Amancio and Serena for Real; Vasovic for Partizan.

EUROPEAN CUP 1966-67
To the general surprise, and delight, the Cup was won by a Celtic team competing in it for the first time; one, moreover, which overwhelmed a weary and pathetically negative Inter in the final, at Lisbon. Shrewdly and forcefully managed by their old centre-half, Jock Stein, Celtic's football was (with the exception of a cautious holding action away to Dukla) fast, muscular, and attacking. Gemmell overlapped powerfully at left-back, scoring a magnificent, half-volleyed goal in the final, Auld was a fine midfield player, little Johnstone a superb outside-right.

Inter reached their zenith in the quarter-finals, when they took an ample revenge on Real Madrid for the previous year's elimination. Cappellini, then, looked an impressive new centre-forward. Then the bubble burst, and they made pitifully heavy weather disposing, in three matches, of the honest, modest CSKA Sofia, previously much troubled by Linfield.

Liverpool were thrashed by a splendid Ajax forward-line, in Amsterdam; finely led by Cruyff; but Dukla knew too much for Ajax. Torpedo, Russia's first entrants, put up a sturdy fight against Inter, in Milan, but went out by the only goal – Voronin's own goal – of the tie.

In the final, Inter, without their midfield general Suarez, and with Mazzola not fully fit, took the lead from a penalty when, in the eighth minute, Craig tripped Cappellini, then bolted back into defence, to be besieged for the rest of the game. Gemmell equalised after 63 minutes, and Chalmers got the winner five minutes from time.

Preliminary Round
Sliema Wanderers 1, CSKA
 Sofia 2
CSKA Sofia 4, Sliema
 Wanderers 0
Waterford 1, Vorwaerts Berlin 6
Vorwaerts Berlin 6, Waterford 0

First Round
Reykjavik 2, Nantes 3
Nantes 5, Reykjavik 2
Aris Bonnevoie 3, Linfield 3
Linfield 6, Aris Bonnevioe 1
Admira 0, Vojvodina 1
Vojvodina 0, Admira 0
Anderlecht 10, Valkeakovski 1
Valkeakovski 0, Anderlecht 2
 (*in Brussels*)
Munich 1860 8, Nicosia 0
Nicosia 1, Munich 1860 2
 (*in Munich*)
Liverpool 2, Petrolul Ploesti 0
Petrolul Ploesti 3, Liverpool 1
Liverpool 2, Petrolul Ploesti 0
 (*in Brussels*)
Celtic 2, Zürich 0
Zürich 0, Celtic 3
Malmö 0, Atlético Madrid 2
Atletico Madrid 3, Malmö 1
Esbjerg 0, Dukla Prague 2
Dukla Prague 4, Esbjerg 0
Ajax Amsterdam 2, Besiktas 0
Besiktas 1, Ajax Amsterdam 2

Vasas Budapest 5, Sporting
 Lisbon 0
Sporting Lisbon 0, Vasas
 Budapest 2
CSKA 3, Olimpiakos Piraeus 1
Olimpiakos Piraeus 1, CSKA 0
Gornik Zabrze 2, Vorwaerts 1
Vorwaerts 2, Gornik Zabrze 1
Gornik Zabrze 2, Vorwaerts 1
 (*in Budapest*)
Internazionale 1, Torpedo 0
Torpedo 0, Internazionale 0
Bye: *Real Madrid*. Walk-over:
 Valerengen

Second Round
Valerengen Oslo 1, Linfield 4
Linfield 1, Valerengen Oslo 1
Inter 2, Vasas 1
Vasas 0, Inter 2
Dukla 4, Anderlecht 1
Anderlecht 1, Dukla 2
Munich 1860 1, Real Madrid 0
Real Madrid 3, Munich 1860 1
CSKA 4, Gornik 1
Gornik 3, CSKA 0
Vojvodina 3, Atéltico Madrid 1
Atlético Madrid 2, Vojvodina 3
 (*in Madrid*)
Nantes 1, Celtic 3
Celtic 3, Nantes 1
Ajax 5, Liverpool 1
Liverpool 2, Ajax 2

Quarter-finals	Celtic 2, Vojvodina 0
Inter 1, Real Madrid 0	
Real Madrid 0, Inter 2	**Semi-finals**
Linfield 2, CSKA 2	Celtic 3, Dukla 1
CSKA 1, Linfield 0	Dukla 0, Celtic 0
Ajax 1, Dukla 1	Inter 1, CSKA 1
Dukla 2, Ajax 1	CSKA 1, Inter 1
Vojvodina 1, Celtic 0	Inter 1, CSKA 0 (*in Bologna*)

Final Lisbon, 25 May 1967
Celtic (0) 2, Internazionale (1) 1
Celtic: Simpson; Craig, Gemmell; Murdoch, McNeill, Clark; Johnstone, Wallace, Chalmers, Auld, Lennox.
Inter: Sarti; Burgnich, Facchetti; Bedin, Guarneri, Picchi; Bicicli, Mazzola, Cappellini, Corso, Domenghini.
Scorers: Gemmell, Chalmers for Celtic, Mazzola (pen) for Inter.

EUROPEAN CUP 1967–68

For the first time, the European Cup was won by an English club; most fittingly, Manchester United, who had been semi-finalists on three previous occasions. The final, at Wembley, was remarkable. United dominated the first half, but couldn't turn their advantage into goals, flagged badly late in the second half, when Benfica equalised Charlton's goal, and were ultimately galvanised by a superb goal, early in extra time, scored by George Best.

Previously, they'd had little trouble with the Maltese – though they surprisingly drew 0–0 in Malta – had overcome a rough, determined Sarajevo, and beaten Real Madrid after an astonishing revival at Bernabeu Stadium, centre-half Foulkes getting the equaliser. There was also a memorable quarter-final versus Gornik, who were defied by brilliant goalkeeping at Old Trafford. United then managed to keep the score down to 1–0 on an impossibly Arctic pitch, in Poland.

Celtic, the holders, surprisingly went out to Dynamo Kiev in the first round. Bychevetz was their destroyer in Glasgow, but they were rather unlucky in the return, when Murdoch was sent off, and fighting broke out late in the game. Glentoran, the Irish champions, gave Benfica a terrible fright in the same round, going out only on the newly and dubiously introduced rule whereby away goals, in case of equality, count double. Benfica did not really find form and recover from manager Riera's resignation till the semi-finals, when Vasas were overcome. At Wembley, they lost many friends with their rough treatment of Best.

This was the first European Cup to be seeded.

First Round

Glentoran 1, Benfica 1	Rapid Vienna 3, Besiktas 0
Benfica 0, Glentoran 0	Celtic 1, Dynamo Kiev 2
Besiktas 0, Rapid Vienna 1	Dynamo Kiev 1, Celtic 1

Olimpiakos Piraeus 0,
Juventus 0
Juventus 2, Olimpiakos
Piraeus 0
Dundalk 0, Vasas Budapest 1
Vasas Budapest 8, Dundalk 1
Manchester United 4, Hibernian
(Malta) 0
Hibernian (Malta) 0, Manchester
United 0
St Etienne 2, Kuopio 0
Kuopio 3, St Etienne 0
Karl-Marx-Stadt 1, Anderlecht 3
Anderlecht 2, Karl-Marx-Stadt 1
Basel 1, Hvidovre 2
Hvidovre 3, Basel 3
Skeid Oslo 0, Sparta Prague 1
Sparta Prague 1, Skied Oslo 1
Olympiakos Nicosia 2,
Sarajevo 2
Sarajevo 3, Olympiakos
Nicosia 1
Ajax 1, Real Madrid 1
Real Madrid 2, Ajax 1
Valur 1, Jeunesse Esch 1
Jeunesse Esch 3, Valur 3
Gornik Zabrze 3, Djurgarden 0
Djurgarden 0, Gornik Zabrze 0
Plovdiv Traka 2, Rapid
Bucharest 0
Rapid Bucharest 3, Plovdiv
Traka 0
Walk-over: *Eintracht Brunswick*

Second Round
Sarajevo 0, Manchester United 0
Manchester United 2, Sarajevo 1
Hvidovre 2, Real Madrid 2
Real Madrid 4, Hvidovre 1
Rapid Vienna 1, Eintracht
Brunswick 0
Eintracht Brunswick 2, Rapid
Vienna 0
Benfica 2, St Etienne 0
St Etienne 1, Benfica 0
Vasas 6, Reykjavik 0
Reykjavik 1, Vasas 5
Dynamo Kiev 1, Gornik 2
Gornik 1, Dynamo Kiev 1
Juventus 1, Rapid Bucharest 0
Rapid Bucharest 0, Juventus 0
Sparta Prague 3, Anderlecht 2
Anderlecht 2, Sparta Prague 3

Quarter-finals
Eintracht Brunswick 3, Juventus 2
Juventus 1, Eintracht Brunswick 0
(*play-off*)
Manchester United 2, Gornik 0
Gornik 1, Manchester United 0
Real Madrid 3, Sparta Prague 0
Sparta Prague 2, Real Madrid 1
Vasas 0, Benfica 0
Benfica 3, Vasas 0

Semi-finals
Manchester United 1, Real
Madrid 0
Real Madrid 3, Manchester
United 3
Benfica 0, Juventus 0
Juventos 0, Benfica 1

Final Wembley Stadium, 29 May 1968
Manchester United (0) (1) 4, Benfica (0) (1) 1 (after extra time).
Manchester United: Stepney; Brennan, Dunne; Crerand, Foulkes, Stiles; Best, Kidd, Charlton, Sadler, Aston.
Benfica: Henrique; Adolfo, Humberto, Jacinto, Cruz; Graça, Coluna; Augusto, Eusebio, Torres, Simões.
Scorers: Charlton (2), Best, Kidd for Manchester United; Graça for Benfica.

EUROPEAN CUP 1968–69

Milan won their second European Cup, gathering strength and momentum as the competition progressed, knocking out both Celtic and Manchester United, and finally overwhelming Ajax in a one-sided final. Pierino Prati established himself as one of the game's most dangerous finishers, ruthlessly exploiting a slip by McNeill at a throw-in to put out Celtic in Glasgow, and scoring three times, with much help from Gianni Rivera, in the final, in Madrid.

Mistaken selection and sloppy defensive play helped to put out Manchester United, after they had comfortably accounted for Rapid – Best showing superb form. Surprisingly in the first leg of the quarter-final in Milan, they chose the veteran Foulkes for centre-half; Sormani was thus allowed his best game for months. The inexperienced Rimmer played in goal. United lost 2–0, and though they won an ill-tempered return in Manchester – during which Cudicini was felled by a missile from the notorious Stretford End – they properly went out; once again gifted but maddening.

Ajax, with Cruyff a dazzling centre-forward, were first astonished by Benfica, before astonishing them in their turn. A poor first game by Spartak Trnava's goalkeeper assisted their passage into the final, but there, they were simply outclassed.

All the Iron Curtain teams but the Czech withdrew in protest against a decision to re-draw the First Round.

First Round
St Etienne 2, Celtic 0
Celtic 4, St Etienne 0
Waterford 1, Manchester United 3
Manchester United 7, Waterford 1
Manchester City 0, Fenerbahce 0
Fenerbahce 2, Manchester City 1
Anderlecht 3, Glentoran 0
Glentoran 2, Anderlecht 2
AEK Athens 3, Jeunesse Esch 0
Jeunesse Esch 3, AEK Athens 2
Nuremberg 1, Ajax 1
Ajax 4, Nuremberg 0
Malmö 2, Milan 1
Milan 4, Malmö 1
Steaua Bucharest 3, Spartak Trnava 1
Spartak Trnava 4, Steaua Bucharest 0
Zurich 1, AB Copenhagen 3
AB Copenhagen 1, Zurich 2
Trondheim 1, Rapid Vienna 3
Rapid Vienna 3, Trondheim 3
Valetta 1, Repias Lahti 1
Reipas Lahti 2, Valetta 0
Real Madrid 6, Limassol 0
Real Madrid 6, Limassol 0
(*in Madrid*)
Valur Reykjavik 0, Benfica 0
Benfica 8, Valur Reykjavik 0
Byes: *Milan, Benfica*

Second Round
Manchester United 3, Anderlecht 0
Anderlecht 3, Manchester United 1
Celtic 5, Red Star 1
Red Star 1, Celtic 1
Rapid Vienna 1, Real Madrid 0
Real Madrid 2, Rapid Vienna 1
Reipas Lahti 1, Spartak Trnava 9
Spartak Trnava 7, Reipas Lahti 1
AEK 0, AB Copenhagen 0
AB Copenhagen 0, AEK 2
Ajax 2, Fenerbahce 0
Fenerbahce 0, Ajax 2

Quarter-finals
Ajax 1, Benfica 3
Benfica 1, Ajax 3
Ajax 3, Benfica 0
Milan 0, Celtic 0
Celtic 0, Milan 1
Manchester United 3,
   Rapid Vienna 0
Rapid Vienna 0, Manchester
   United 0

Spartak Trnava 2, AEK 1
AEK 1, Sparta Trnava 1

Semi-finals
Milan 2, Manchester United 0
Manchester United 1, Milan 0
Ajax 3, Spartak Trnava 0
Spartak Trnava 2, Ajax 0

Final Madrid, 28 May 1969
Milan (2) 4, Ajax Amsterdam (0) 1
Milan: Cudicini; Anquilletti, Schnellinger; Maldera, Rosato, Trapattoni; Hamrin, Lodetti, Sormani, Rivera, Prati.
Ajax: Blas, Suurbier (Nuninga), Vasovic, Van Duivenbode, Hulshoff; Pronk, Groot; Swart, Cruyff, Danielsson, Keizer.
Scorers: Prati 3, Sormani for Milan; Vasovic (pen) for Ajax.

EUROPEAN CUP 1969-70

Feyenoord, the second consecutive Dutch team to reach the final of the European Cup, most unexpectedly won it with a fine victory over Celtic. Their superiority in the second half in Milan was such that the game should never have gone to extra time, let alone the closing minutes of extra time when Kindvall got away to score the winner. Feyenoord's performance was all the more meritorious in that it included a deserved victory over the holders, Milan, admittedly much scarred by their harsh encounters with Estudiantes in the world club championship.

The peak of Celtic's achievement was their splendid double over Leeds United, whom they deservedly beat in the semi-finals at Elland Road with an early, deflected goal by Connelly, then overwhelmed in front of an immense, frenzied crowd at Hampden Park, despite Bremner's early goal against the play. Leeds, however, were tired and depleted by their efforts in three major competitions.

Feyenoord's performance in Milan was a marvel of flexibility, severe *catenaccio* modulating in the second half to lively attack, with Hasil brilliant in midfield. Gemmell gave Celtic a rather fortunate lead with a pulverising free kick. From another free kick, Israel, Feyenoord's sweeper, came up to head the equaliser. Kindvall's belated winner followed a break down the left when McNeill misjudged and handled the ball. It was a curiously flaccid and disappointing performance by Celtic, a dazzling one by Feyenoord, accompanied by a myriad of honking Dutch horns.

Preliminary Round
Turku Palloseura 0, KB
   Copenhagen 1

KB Copenhagen 3, Turku
   Palloseura 0

First Round
Milan 5, Avenir Beggen 0
Avenir Beggen 0, Milan 3
Leeds United 10, Lyn Oslo 0
Lyn Oslo 0, Leeds United 6
Red Star Belgrade 8, Linfield 0
Linfield 2, Red Star Belgrade 4
Basel 0, Celtic 0
Celtic 2, Basel 0
Hibernian (Malta) 2, Spartak Trnava 2
Spartak Trnava 4, Hibernian (Malta) 0
Galatasaray 2, Waterford 0
Waterford 2, Galatasaray 3
CSKA Sofia 2, Ferencvaros 1
Ferencvaros 4, CSKA Sofia 1
Arad 1, Legia Warsaw 2
Legia Warsaw 8, Arad 0
Vorwaerts 2, Panathinaikos 0
Panathinaikos 1, Vorwaerts 1
Bayern Munich 2, St Etienne 0
St Etienne 3, Bayern Munich 0
Standard Liège 3, Nendori Tirana 0
Nendori Tirana 1, Standard Liège 1
Feyenoord 12, Reykjavik 0
Reykjavik 0, Feyenoord 4
FK Austria 1, Dynamo Kiev 2
Dynamo Kiev 3, FK Austria 1
Fiorentina 1, Oester 0
Oester 1, Fiorentina 2
Benfica 0, KB Copenhagen 0
KB Copenhagen 2, Benfica 3
Real Madrid 8, Olympiakos Nicosia 0
Olympiakos Nicosia 1, Real Madrid 6

Second Round
Leeds United 3, Ferencvaros 0
Ferencvaros 0, Leeds United 3
Celtic 3, Benfica 0
Benfica 3, Celtic 0
 (*Celtic won toss*)
Dynamo Kiev 1, Fiorentina 2
Fiorentina 0, Dynamo Kiev 0
Milan 1, Feyenoord 0
Feyenoord 2, Milan 0
Spartak Trnava 1, Galatasaray 0
Galatasaray 1, Spartak Trnava 0
 (*Galatasaray won toss*)
Legia Warsaw 2, St Etienne 1
St Etienne 0, Warsaw 1
Vorwaerts 2, Red Star 1
Red Star 3, Vorwaerts 2
Standard Liège 1, Real Madrid 0
Real Madrid 2, Standard Liège 3

Quarter-finals
Standard Liège 0, Leeds United 1
Leeds United 1, Standard Liège 0
Celtic 3, Fiorentina 0
Fiorentina 1, Celtic 0
Galatasaray 1, Legia Warsaw 1
Legia Warsaw 2, Galatasaray 0
Vorwaerts 1, Feyenoord 0
Feyenoord 2, Vorwaerts 0

Semi-finals
Leeds United 0, Celtic 1
Celtic 2, Leeds United 1
Legia Warsaw 0, Feyenoord 0
Feyenoord 2, Legia Warsaw 0

Final San Siro, Milan, 6 May 1970
Feyenoord (1) 2, Celtic (1) 1 after extra time
Feyenoord: Pieters Graafland; Romeyn (Haak), Israel, Laseroms, Jansen, Van Duivenbode; Hasil, Van Hanegem; Wery, Kindvall, Moulijn.

Celtic: Williams; Hay, Gemmell; Murdoch, McNeill, Brogan; Johnstone, Wallace, Hughes, Auld (Connelly), Lennox.
Scorers: Gemmell for Celtic; Israel, Kinvall for Feyenoord.

EUROPEAN CUP 1970-71

Ajax of Amsterdam became the second consecutive Dutch club to win the European Cup, thus making up for their defeat in the 1969 Final. Though they disappointingly shut up shop at Wembley in the second half against Panathinaikos, they were an admirable side, with a dazzling centre-forward in Johan Cruyff.

Panathinaikos, under the managership of Ferenc Puskas, were remarkable dark horses. They eliminated Everton, forcing a draw at Goodison – indeed, they only lost their early lead in the closing seconds, after resisting heavy pressure – then held them again in Athens and qualified through their away goal. Their methods were often ruthless, yet their achievement in turning a 4-1 deficit into ultimate qualification against Red Star in the semi-finals was extraordinary, and in the final, their conduct was largely good.

Perhaps Red Star would have gone through, had Dragan Dzajic, their star forward, not been controversially suspended for four games, after being sent off in the quarter-finals in Jena.

Celtic reached the quarter-finals but, clearly in a transitional period, were crushed in Amsterdam. Ajax closed their ranks to lose the return by only 1-0, going down by the same score to Atlético in Madrid, but again winning the home leg 3-0 to reach the final.

At Wembley, Van Dijk headed a simple goal from the clever Piet Keizer's centre after only five minutes, and despite Domazos' undoubted skill, the die was cast. Kamaras missed the Greek's best chance just before half-time, and in the second half, Ajax brought on two substitutes, one of whom, Haan, got their second goal by way of a Greek defender, three minutes from the end of a now dull game.

Preliminary Round
Levski-Spartak 3, FK Austria 1
FK Austria 3, Levski-Spartak 0

First Round
Everton 6, Keflavik 2
Keflavik 0, Everton 3
Celtic 9, Kokkola 0
Kokkola 0, Celtic 5
Glentoran 1, Waterford 3
Waterford 1, Glentoran 0
Cagliari 3, St Etienne 0
St Etienne 1, Cagliari 0
Slovan Bratislava 2, BK Copenhagen 1
BK Copenhagen 2, Slovan Bratislava 2
Nenduri Tirana 2, Ajax Amsterdam 2
Ajax Amsterdam 2, Nenduri Tirana 0
IFK Gothenburg 0, Legia Warsaw 4
Legia Warsaw 2, IFK Gothenburg 1
Ujpest 2, Red Star 0
Red Star 4, Ujpest 0
Rosenborg 0, Standard Liège 2
Standard Liège 5, Rosenborg 0
Borussia Mönchengladbach 6 EP Larnax (Cyprus) 0
(*at Augsberg*)
Borussia Mönchengladbach 10 EP Larnax 0
Spartak Moscow 3, Basel 2
Basel 2, Spartak Moscow 1
Feyenoord 1, UT Arad 1
UT Arad 0, Feyenoord 0
Atlético Madrid 2, FK Austria 0
FK Austria 1, Atlético Madrid 2
Jeunesse Esch 1, Panathinakios 2
Panathinaikos 5, Jeunesse Esch 0

203

Fenerbahce 0, Carl Zeiss Jena 4
Carl Zeiss Jena 1, Fenerbahce 0
Sporting Lisbon 5, Floriana 0
Floriana 0, Sporting Lisbon 4

Second Round
Borussia Mönchengladbach 1,
   Everton 1
Everton 1, Borussia
   Mönchengladbach 1
(Everton qualify on new
   penalty-kicks rule)
Waterford 0, Celtic 7
Celtic 3, Waterford 2
Red Star Belgrade 3, UT Arad 0
UT Arad 1, Red Star Belgrade 3
Carl Zeiss Jena 2, Sporting
   Lisbon 1
Sporting Lisbon 1, Carl Zeiss
   Jena 2
Panathinaikos 3, Slovan
   Bratislava 0
Slovan Bratislava 2,
   Panathinaikos 1
Standard Liège 1, Legia Warsaw 0
Legia Warsaw 2, Standard Liège 0
Cagliari 2, Atlético Madrid 1

Atlético Madrid 3, Cagliari 0
Ajax Amsterdam 3, Basel 0
Basel 1, Ajax Amsterdam 2

Quarter-finals
Everton 1, Panathinaikos 1
Panathinaikos 0, Everton 0
Ajax Amsterdam 3, Celtic 0
Celtic 1, Ajax Amsterdam 0
Atlético Madrid 1, Legia
   Warsaw 0
Legia Warsaw 2, Atlético
   Madrid 1
Carl Zeiss Jena 3, Red Star
   Belgrade 2
Red Star Belgrade 4, Carl Zeiss
   Jena 0

Semi-finals
Red Star Belgrade 4,
   Panathinaikos 1
Panathinaikos 3, Red Star
   Belgrade 0
Atlética Madrid 1, Ajax
   Amsterdam 0
Ajax Amsterdam 3, Atlético
   Madrid 0

Final Wembley Stadium, 2 June 1971
Ajax Amsterdam (1) 2, Panathinaikos (0) 0
Ajax: Stuy; Neeskens, Vasovic, Hulshoff, Suurbier; Rijnders (Blankenburg), Muhren; Swart (Haan), Cruyff, Van Dijk, Keizer.
Panathinaikos: Oeconomopoulos; Tomaras, Vlahos, Eleftherakis, Kamaras, Sourpis, Grammos, Filakouris, Antoniadis, Domazos, Kapsis.
Scorers: Van Dijk, Haan for Ajax.

EUROPEAN CUP 1971–72
Gathering stature and flexibility, now under the managership of the Romanian Stefan Kovacs, and playing 'total football' with a mobile sweeper, Ajax won more convincingly than in 1971. The final, against Inter in Rotterdam, was the old, sterile *catenaccio* pitted against the dynamic new, which won hands down. Inter's negativity inevitably produced a dour, one-sided game, and it wasn't until the second half that a defensive muddle gave Cruyff a remarkably easy first goal. Later, he headed a second.

Arsenal were put out by Ajax in the quarter-finals; overplayed in

Amsterdam and losing by an unlucky own goal at Highbury. Celtic, improving by the round, did very well to reach the semi-finals, which ended with stalemate against Inter. The Italians prevailed on penalties, after extra time, 'Dixie' Deans missing the first of Celtic's. Inter were rather lucky to be there at all, their 7–1 defeat by Borussia Mönchengladbach having been annulled because Boninsegna was hit by a beer can.

Preliminary Round
Valencia 3, US Luxembourg 1
US Luxembourg 0, Valencia 1
First Round
Olympique Marseilles 2, Gornik Zabrze 1
Gornik Zabrze 1, Olympique Marseilles 1
Galatasaray 1, CSKA Moscow 1
CSKA Moscow 3, Galatasaray 0
Akranes 0, Sliema Wanderers 4
Sliema Wanderers 0, Akranes 0
Ujpest Dozsa 4, Malmö 0
Malmö 1, Ujpest Dozsa 0
CSKA Sofia 3, Partizan Tirana 0
Partizan Tirana 0, CSKA Sofia 1
Stromsgodset 1, Arsenal 3
Arsenal 4, Stromsgodset 0
BK 1903 Copenhagen 2, Celtic 1
Celtic 3, BK 1903 0
Standard Liège 2, Linfield 0
Linfield 2, Standard Liège 3
Valencia 0, Hajduk Split 0
Hajduk 1, Valencia 1
Internazionale 4, AEK Athens 1
AEK Athens 3, Internazionale 2
Reipas Lahti 1, Grasshoppers 1
Grasshoppers 8, Reipas Lahti 0
Ajax 2, Dynamo Dresden 0
Dynamo Dresden 0, Ajax 0
Wacker Innsbruk 0, Benfica 4
Benfica 3, Wacker Innsbruck 1
Feyenoord 8, Olympiakos Nicosia 0
Feyenoord 9, Olympiakos Nicosia 0
Dynamo Bucharest 0, Spartak Trnava 0
Spartak Trnava 2, Dynamo Bucharest 2

Cork Hibernians 0, Borussia Mönchengladbach 5
Borussia Mönchengladbach 2, Cork Hibernians 1

Second Round
Grasshoppers 0, Arsenal 2
Arsenal 3, Grasshoppers 0
Celtic 5, Sliema Wanderers 0
Sliema Wanderers 1, Celtic 2
Internazionale 4, Borussia Mönchengladbach 2
Borussia Mönchengladbach 0, Internazionale 0
Dynamo Bucharest 0, Feyenoord 3
Feyenoord 2, Dynamo Bucharest 0
Valencia 0, Ujpest 1
Ujpest 2, Valencia 1
CSKA Moscow 1, Standard Liège 0
Standard Liège 2, CSKA Moscow 0
Olympique Marseilles 1, Ajax 2
Ajax 4, Olympique Marseilles 1
Benfica 2, CSKA Sofia 1
CSKA 0, Benfica 0

Quarter-finals
Ajax 2, Arsenal 1
Arsenal 0, Ajax 1
Ujpest 1, Celtic 2
Celtic 1, Ujpest 1
Internazionale 1, Standard Liège 0
Standard Liège 2, Internazionale 1
Feyenoord 1, Benfica 0
Benfica 5, Feyenoord 1

Semi-finals   (*Inter won on penalties* 5–4)
Internazionale 0, Celtic 0   Ajax 1, Benfica 0
Celtic 0, Internazionale 0   Benfica 0, Ajax 0

Final Rotterdam, 31 May 1972
Ajax (0) 2, Internazionale (0) 0
Ajax: Stuy; Suurbier, Hulshoff, Blankenburg, Krol; Haan, Neeskens, G. Muhren; Swart, Cruyff, Keizer.
Internazionale: Bordon; Bellugi, Burgnich, Giubertoni (Bertini), Facchetti; Oriali, Mazzola, Bedin, Jair (Pellizzaro), Boninsegna, Frustalupi.
Scorer: Cruyff (2) for Ajax.

EUROPEAN CUP 1972–73

Ajax won their third successive title, again beating an Italian club, Juventus, in the final; a very dull match after Ajax's fine beginning, which brought a quick, determining goal headed by Rep from Blankenburg's left wing centre.

Derby County, competing for the first time, did well to reach the semi-finals, where Juventus' expertise proved too much for them. Lacking key players in both matches, they were beaten 3–1 in Turin, largely through Altafini's opportunism, and held 0–0 at Derby. But they had fine home victories over Spartak Trnava and Benfica. Celtic went out to clever Ujpest, who very nearly eliminated Juventus, too. Ajax, however, were once again head and shoulders above the field, their tactics exciting, Cruyff remarkable.

First Round
Derby County 2, Zeljeznicar Sarajevo 0
Zeljezinicar 1, Derby County 2
Celtic 2, Rosenborg 1
Rosenborg 1, Celtic 3
Real Madrid 3, Keflavik 0
Keflavik 0, Real Madrid 1
Anderlecht 4, Vejle 2
Vejle 0, Anderlecht 3
Ujpest 2, Basle 0
Basle 2, Ujpest 3
Galatasaray 1, Bayern Munich 1
Bayern Munich 6, Galatasaray 0
Olympique Marseilles 1, Juventus 0
Juventus 3, Olympique Marseilles 0
Malmö 1, Benfica 0
Benfica 4, Malmö 1
T-S Innsbruck 0, Dynamo Kiev 1
Dynamo Kiev 2, T-S Innsbruck 0

CSKA Sofia 2, Panathinaikos 1
Panathinaikos 0, CSKA Sofia 2
Sliema Wanderers 0, Gornik 5
Gornik 5, Sliema Wanderers 0
Magdeburg 6, Turun Palloseura 0
Turun Palloseura 1, Magdeburg 3
Aris 0, Arges Pitesti 2
Arges Pitesti 4, Aris 0
Waterford 0, Omonia Nicosia 1
Omonia Nicosia 2, Waterford 0
Byes: *Ajax Amsterdam, Spartak Trnava*

Second Round
Derby County 3, Benfica 0
Benfica 0, Derby County 0
Omonia Nicosia 0, Bayern Munich 9
Bayern Munich 4, Omonia Nicosia 0
Celtic 2, Ujpest 1
Ujpest 3, Celtic 0

Dynamo Kiev 2, Gornik 0
Gornik 2, Dynamo Kiev 1
Juventus 1, Magdeburg 0
Magdeburg 0, Juventus 1
Arges Pitesti 2, Real Madrid 1
Real Madrid 3, Arges Pitesti 1
CSKA Sofia 1, Ajax 3
Ajax 3, CSKA 0
Spartak Trnava 1, Anderlecht 0
Anderlecht 0, Spartak Trnava 1

Quarter-finals
Spartak Trnava 1, Derby
   County 0
Derby County 2, Spartak
   Trnava 0
Dynamo Kiev 0, Real Madrid 0
Real Madrid 3, Dynamo Kiev 0
Ajax 4, Bayern Munich 0
Bayern Munich 2, Ajax 1
Juventus 0, Ujpest 0
Ujpest 2, Juventus 2

Semi-finals
Juventus 3, Derby County 1
Derby County 0, Juventus 0
Ajax 2, Real Madrid 1
Real Madrid 0, Ajax 1

Final Belgrade, 30 May 1973
Ajax (1) 1 Juventus (0) 0
Ajax: Stuy; Suurbier, Hulshoff, Blankenburg, Kroll; Neeskens, Haan, G. Muhren; Rep, Cruyff, Keizer.
Juventus: Zoff; Longobucco, Marchetti, Furino, Morini, Salvadore, Causio (Cuccureddu), Altafini, Anastasi, Capello, Bettega (Haller).
Scorer: Rep for Ajax.

CHAPTER SIXTEEN

The European Cup-Winners' Cup History

This Cup is something of a poor relation to the European Cup, if only because relatively few countries have a *bona fide* Cup competition. Italy, who play theirs off obscurely in midweek, are a notable instance. On the other hand, the decisive matches have often drawn mammoth crowds and evinced huge enthusiasm, while Tottenham's performance in winning the 1963 tournament was of high quality.

EUROPEAN CUP-WINNERS' CUP 1960–61
This was really Glasgow Ranger's finest hour to date in a European competition. Their appetite whetted by the European Cup, their fans took wholeheartedly to the new tournament, and virtually invaded Wolverhampton on the occasion of the floodlit tie there.

In the final, however, Fiorentina were a little too well balanced and experienced. Above all, they had in Kurt Hamrin, their Swedish international outside-right, one of the greatest match winners in Europe.

Qualifying Round
Vorwaerts Berlin 2, Red Star Brno 1
Red Star Brno 2, Vorwaerts Berlin 0
Rangers 4, Ferencvaros 2
Ferencvaros 2, Rangers 1

Quarter-finals
Red Star Brno 0, Dynamo Zagreb 0
Dynamo Zagreb 2, Red Star Brno 0
FK Austria 2, Wolverhampton Wanderers 0

Wolverhampton Wanderers 5, FK Austria 0
Borussia Dusseldorf 0, Rangers 3
Rangers 8, Borussia Dusseldorf 0
Lucerne 0, Fiorentina 3
Fiorentina 6, Lucerne 2

Semi-finals
Fiorentina 3, Dynamo Zagreb 0
Dynamo Zagreb 2, Fiorentina 1
Rangers 2, Wolverhampton Wanderers 0
Wolverhampton Wanderers 1, Rangers 1

Final
1st Leg. Glasgow, 17 May 1961
Rangers (0) 0, Fiorentina (1) 2
Rangers: Ritchie; Shearer, Caldow; Davis, Paterson, Baxter; Wilson, McMillan, Scott, Brand, Hume.
Fiorentina: Albertosi; Robotti, Castelletti; Gonfiantini, Orzan, Rimbaldo; Hamrin, Micheli, Da Costa, Milan, Petris.
Scorer: Milan (2) for Fiorentina.

2nd Leg. Florence, 27 May, 1961
Fiorentina (1) 2, Rangers (1) 1
Fiorentina: Albertosi; Robotti, Castelletti; Gonfiantini, Orzan, Rimbaldo; Hamrin, Micheli, Da Costa, Milan, Petris.
Rangers: Ritchie; Shearer, Caldow; Davis, Paterson, Baxter; Scott, McMillan, Millar, Brand, Wilson.
Scorers: Milan, Hamrin for Fiorentina, Scott for Rangers.

EUROPEAN CUP-WINNERS' CUP 1961–62

Leicester City took the place of Spurs, who had beaten them in the final but, having also won the League, were committed to the European Cup. Spain, entering for the first time in the imposing shape of Atlético Madrid, won the tournament, beating Leicester on the way and ultimately defeating Fiorentina in a replayed final – no longer a two-legged affair.

Preliminary Round
Glenavon 1, Leicester City 4
Leicester City 3, Glenavon 1
Dunfermline Ath. 4, St Patrick's 1
St Patrick's 0, Dunfermline Ath. 4
Swansea Town 2, Motor Jena 2
Motor Jena 5, Swansea Town 1

Chaux de Fonds 6, Leixoes 2
Leixoes 5, Chaux de Fonds 0
Sedan 2, Atlético Madrid 3
Atlético Madrid 4, Sedan 1
Rapid Vienna 0, Spartak Varna 0
Spartak Varna 2, Rapid Vienna 5
Floriana 2, Ujpest Dozsa 5
Ujpest Dozsa 10, Floriana 2

Byes: *Fiorentina, Vardar, Werder, Bremen, Aarhus, Ajax, Olympiakos Piraeus, Dynamo Zilina, Progresul, Allianet Dudelange*

First Round
Fiorentina 3, Rapid Vienna 1
Rapid Vienna 2, Fiorentina 6
Leicester City 1, Atlético Madrid 1
Atlético Madrid 2, Leicester City 0
Dunfermline Ath. 5, Vardar 2
Vardar 2, Dunfermline Ath. 0
Werder Bremen 2, Aarhus 0
Aarhus 2, Werder Bremen 3
Ajax 2, Ujpest 1
Ujpest 3, Ajax 1
Olympiakos Piraeus 2, Dynamo Zilina (Czech.) 3
Dynamo Zilina 1, Olympiakos Piraeus 0
Leixoes (Portugal) 1, Progresul 1
Progresul 0, Leixoes 1
Motor Jena 7, Alliance Dudelange 0
Alliance Dudelange 2, Motor Jena 2

Quarter-finals
Atlético Madrid 3, Werder Bremen 1
Werder Bremen 1, Atlético Madrid 1
Ujpest 4, Dunfermline 3
Dunfermline 0, Ujpest 1
Fiorentina 2, Dynamo Zilina 3
Dynamo Zilina 0, Fiorentina 2
Motor Jena 1, Leixoes 1
Leixoes 1, Motor Jena 3

Semi-finals
Fiorentina 2, Ujpest 0
Ujpest 0, Fiorentina 1
Atlético Madrid 1, Motor Jena 0
Motor Jena 0, Atlético Madrid 4

Final Glasgow, 10 May 1962
Fiorentina (1) 1, Atlético Madrid (1) 1
Scorers: Peiro for Atlético Madrid, Hamrin for Fiorentina.
Replay Stuttgart, 5 September 1962
Atlético Madrid (2) 3, Fiorentina (0) 0

Atlético Madrid: Madinabeytia; Rivilla, Calleja; Ramirez, Griffa, Glaria; Jones, Adelardo, Mendonça, Peirò, Collar.
Fiorentina: Albertosi; Robotti, Castelletti; Malatrasi, Orzan, Marchesi; Hamrin, Ferretti, Milani, Dell'Angelo, Petris.
Scorers: Jones, Mendonça, Peirò for Atlético Madrid.
Same teams for both matches.

EUROPEAN CUP-WINNERS' CUP 1962–63

This was most impressively won by Spurs. Invincible at home, they played brilliant football to humiliate Rangers, and recovered impressively after a poor performance in Bratislava. OFK, after losing in Belgrade, never had much of a chance of survival. In the final, though robbed at the last moment of the dynamic Mackay with a stomach injury, Spurs played some magnificent football to defeat Atlético Madrid, dominating the first half, surviving a sticky patch at the beginning of the second, and at last turning the game with a surprising long-range goal by outside-left Terry Dyson.

One must not leave this Cup without recording the brave achievement of the little Welsh non-League club, Bangor City, who actually beat the expensive Naples team and forced them to a third, decisive, game.

Preliminary Round
Lausanne 3, Sparta 0
Sparta 4, Lausanne 2
St Etienne 1, Vitoria 1
Vitoria 0, St Etienne 3
Alliance Dudelange 1, Odense 1
Odense 8, Alliance Dudelange 1
Rangers 4, Seville 0
Seville 2, Rangers 0
OFK Belgrade 2, Chemie 0
Chemie 3, OFK Belgrade 3
Steaua 3, Botev 2
Botev 5, Steaua 1
Ujpest Dozsa 5, Zaglebie 0
Zaglebie 0, Ujpest Dozsa 0
Bangor City 2, Naples 0
Naples 3, Bangor City 1
Naples 2, Bangor City 1
 (*at Highbury*)
Byes: *Nuremburg, Atlético Madrid, Hibernian Malta, Shamrock Rovers, Graz, Tottenham Hotspur, Portadown, Slovan Bratislava*

First Round
St Etienne 0, Nuremburg 0
Nuremburg 3, St Etienne 0
Atlético Madrid 4, Hibernian Malta 0
Hibernian Malta 0, Atlético Madrid 1
Botev 4, Shamrock Rovers 0

Shamrock Rovers 0, Botev 1
Graz 1, Odense BK 09 1
Odense BK 09 5, Graz 3
Tottenham Hotspur 5, Rangers 2
Rangers 2, Tottenham Hotspur 3
OFK Belgrade 5, Portadown 1
Portadown 3, OFK Belgrade 2
Lausanne 1, Slovan Bratislava 1
Slovan Bratislava 1, Lausanne 0
Ujpest 1, Naples 1
Naples 1, Ujpest 1
Naples 3, Ujpest 1

Quarter-finals
Slovan 2, Tottenham Hotspur 0
Tottenham Hotspur 6, Slovan 0
Odense 0, Nuremburg 1
Nuremburg 6, Odense 0
Botev 1, Atlético Madrid 1
Atlético Madrid 6, Botev 0
OFK Belgrade 2, Naples 0
Naples 3, OFK Belgrade 1
Play off OFK Belgrade 3, Naples 1

Semi-finals
OFK Belgrade 1, Tottenham Hotspur 2
Tottenham Hotspur 3, OFK Belgrade 1
Nuremburg 2, Atlético Madrid 1
Atlético Madrid 2, Nuremburg 0

Final Rotterdam, 15 May 1963
Tottenham Hotspur (2) 5, Atlético Madrid (0) 1
Spurs: Brown; Baker, Henry; Blanchflower, Norman, Marchi; Jones, White, Smith, Greaves, Dyson.
Atlético Madrid: Madinabeytia; Rivilla, Rodrigues; Ramiro, Griffa, Glaria; Jones, Adelardo, Chuzo, Mendonça, Collar.
Scorers: Greaves (2), White, Dyson (2) for Spurs, Collar (pen) for Atlético Madrid.

EUROPEAN CUP-WINNERS' CUP 1963-64
Tottenham's success in 1963 meant that England were able to enter two teams, and as luck would have it, Spurs and Manchester United

were quickly drawn together. A dour first leg at Tottenham saw Spurs get through with great difficulty, 2–0. But in the return the unhappy Mackay fractured a leg, and Manchester United took the game 4–1 and qualified. It was the first time the holders had been eliminated before the final. United, who should have had a bigger lead in their first leg against Sporting, lost the return in Lisbon a few days after an exhausting FA Cup semi-final. Glasgow Celtic were the splendid surprise of the tournament. Qualified only because Rangers, the Scottish Cupholders, were in the European Cup, they sailed through Europe, before falling to MTK in the semi-final. Celtic put up a brave fight, but were overwhelmed in the replay when MTK got their international stars, Sandor and Nagy, back. Sporting won a tremendously tight semi-final series in a third, deciding match; Lyon had a man sent off in the second half. In the final, the opportunism of Sandor enabled MTK to hold their own in Vienna, but the better-balanced Sporting team defeated them in Antwerp. The winning goal was scored by Morais, direct from a corner, in the twentieth minute.

Preliminary Round
Fenerbahce 4, Petrolul 1
Petrolul 1, Fenerbahce 0
Basel 1, Celtic 5
Celtic 5, Basel 0
Tilburg Holland 1, Manchester United 1
Manchester United 6, Tilburg 1
SV Hamburg 4, US Luxemburg 0
US Luxemburg 2, SV Hamburg 3
Olympiakos Piraeus 2, Zaglebie 1
Zaglebie 1, Olympiakos Piraeus 0
Olympiakos Piraeus 2, Zaglebie 0
Shelbourne 0, Barcelona 2
Barcelona 3, Shelbourne 1
Lyon 3, Odense 1
Odense 1, Lyon 3
MTK Budapest 1, Slavia 0
Slavia 1, MTK Budapest 1
Linz 1, Dynamo Zagreb 0
Dynamo Zagreb 1, Linz 0
Dynamo Zagreb 1, Linz 1
(*Dynamo Zagreb won the toss*)
Sliema Wanderers 0, Borough United 0
Borough United 2, Sliema Wanderers 0
Atlanta 2, Sporting Lisbon 0
Sporting Lisbon 3, Atlanta 1
Apoel (Cyprus) 6, Gjoevik (Norway) 0
Gjoevik 1, Apoel 0
Palloseura Helsinki 1, Slovan Bratislava 4
Slovan Bratislava 8, Palloseura Helsinki 1
Byes: *Tottenham Hotspur, Linfield, Motor Zwickau*

First Round
Tottenham Hotspur 2, Manchester United 0
Manchester United 4, Tottenham Hotspur 1
Fenerbahce 4, Linfield 1
Linfield 2, Fenerbahce 0
Barcelona 4, SV Hamburg 4
SV Hamburg 0, Barcelona 0
SV Hamburg 3, Barcelona 2
Sporting Lisbon 16, Apoel 1
Apoel 0, Sporting Lisbon 2
Lyon 4, Olympiakos 1
Olympiakos 2, Lyon 1
Motor Zwickau 1, MTK Budapest 0
MTK Budapest 2, Motor Zwickau 0
Celtic 3, Dynamo Zagreb 0
Dynamo Zagreb 2, Celtic 1

Borough United 0, Slovan
Bratislava 1
Slovan Bratislava 3, Borough
United 0

Celtic 1, Slovan Bratislava 0
Slovan Bratislava 0, Celtic 1
Fenerbahce 1, MTK Budapest 1
MTK Budapest 1, Fenerbahce 0

Quarter-finals
Manchester United 4, Sporting
Lisbon 1
Sporting Lisbon 5, Manchester
United 0
SV Hamburg 1, Lyon 1
Lyon 2, SV Hamburg 0

Semi-finals
Celtic 3, MTK Budapest 0
MTK Budapest 4, Celtic 0
Lyon 0, Sporting Lisbon 0
Sporting Lisbon 1, Lyon 1
Lyon 0, Sporting Lisbon 1

Final Brussels, 13 May 1964
MTK Budapest 3, Sporting Lisbon 3 after extra time (full-time 3–3)
MTK Budapest: Kovalik; Keszei, Dansky; Jenei, Nagy, Kovaks; Sandor, Vasas, Kuti, Bodor, Halapi.
Sporting Lisbon: Carvalho; Gomez, Peridis; Baptista, Carlos, Geo; Mendes, Oswaldo, Mascarenhas, Figueiredo, Morais.
Scorers: Sandor (2), Kuti for MTK Budapest; Figueiredo (2), Dansky (o.g.) for Sporting Lisbon.

Replay Antwerp, 15 May 1964
MTK Budapest 0, Sporting Lisbon 1
Scorer: Morais for Sporting Lisbon.

EUROPEAN CUP-WINNERS' CUP 1964–65

For the second time in three years, a London team was the winner, and West Ham's splendid performance at Wembley, in an exciting final, was a memorable one. The Hammers' achievement was the more impressive as they had lost Johnny Byrne, their outstanding forward, injured while playing for England against Scotland. This caused him to miss the second leg of the semi-final, in Saragossa, and the final itself. Saragossa were probably the second best team in the competition, with outstanding forwards in Lapetra, on the left wing, and the centre-forward, Marcelino. Mention must also be made of the astonishing achievement of Cardiff City, a Second Division club, in knocking out the holders, Sporting Lisbon. They did almost as well by pulling back two goals to draw in Saragossa, but a defensive slip cost them the return match.

Munich 1860 were a physically strong, direct, intelligent side, thwarted in the final by Standen's splendid goalkeeping. Late in the game, after a rash of missed chances, Alan Sealey scored twice for West Ham, to settle the match.

Preliminary Round
Admira Vienna 1, Legia Warsaw 3
Legia Warsaw 1, Admira Vienna 0
Lausanne 2, Honved 0

Honved 1, Lausanne 0
US Luxemburg 0, Munich 1960 4
Munich 1860 6, US Luxemburg 0

Valetta 0, Saragossa 3
Saragossa 5, Valetta 1
AEK Athens 2, Dynamo Zagreb 0
Dynamo Zagreb 3, AEK Athens 0
Dynamo Bucharest 3, Derry City 0
Derry City 0, Dynamo Bucharest 2
Magdeburg 1, Galatasaray 1
Galatasaray 1, Magdeburg 1
Magdeburg 1, Galatasaray 1
  (*in Vienna*)
(*Galatasarya won toss*)
Esbjerg 0, Cardiff City 0
Cardiff City 1, Esbjerg 0
Skeid Oslo 1, Haka Finland 0
Haka Finland 2, Skeid Oslo 0
Porto 3, Lyon 0
Lyon 0, Porto 1
Sparta Prague 10, St Anorthosis
  (Cyprus) 0
St Anorthosis 0, Sparta 6
La Gantoise 0, West Ham
  United 1
West Ham United 1, La
  Gantoise 1
Torino 3, Fortuna Geelen 1
Fortuna Geelen 2, Torino 2
Slavia Sofia 1, Cork Celtic 1
Cork Celtic 0, Slavia Sofia 2
Byes: *Sporting Lisbon, Dundee*

Legia 2, Galatasaray 1
Galatasaray 2, Legia 1
Legia 2, Galatasaray 1
West Ham United 2, Sparta 0
Sparta 2, West Ham United 1
Porto 0, Munich 1860 1
Munich 1860 1, Porto 1
Dynamo Bucharest 1, Dynamo
  Zagreb 1
Dynamo Zagreb 2, Dynamo
  Bucharest 0
Sporting Lisbon 1, Cardiff
  City 2
Cardiff City 0, Sporting Lisbon 0
Torino 5, Haka 0
Haka 0, Torino 1

Quarter-finals
Saragossa 2, Cardiff City 2
Cardiff City 0, Saragossa 1
Legia 0, Munich 1860 4
Munich 1860 0, Legia 0
Torino 1, Dynamo Zagreb 1
Dynamo Zagreb 1, Torino 2
Lausanne 1, West Ham United 2
West Ham United 4, Lausanne 3

First Round
Dundee 2, Saragossa 2
Saragossa 2, Dundee 1
Slavia 1, Lausanne 0
Lausanne 2, Slavia 1
Lausanne 3, Slavia 2
  (*in Rome*)

Semi-finals
West Ham United 2, Saragossa 1
Saragossa 1, West Ham United 1
Torino 2, Munich 1860 0
Munich 1860 3, Torino 1
Munich 1860 2, Torino 0
  (*in Zurich*)

Final Wembley Stadium, 19 May 1965
West Ham United (0) 2, Munich 1860 (0) 0
West Ham United: Standen; Kirkup, Burkett; Peters, Brown, Moore; Sealey, Boyce, Hurst, Dear, Sissons.
Munich 1860: Radenkovic; Wagner, Kohlars; Bena, Reich, Luttrop; Heiss, Kuppers, Brunnenmeier, Grosser, Rebele.
Scorer: Sealey (2) for West Ham United.

EUROPEAN CUP-WINNERS' CUP 1965–66
Despite getting three of their four entrants into the semi-finals, Britain failed to retain the Cup, which went to Borussia and Germany – on merit. The Dortmund team, astoundingly fit and very incisive, broke

wonderfully well from defence, despite the fact that they used Paul as sweeper-up behind four backs. Sigi Held, later to play so well in the World Cup, was a splendid striker, powerfully abetted by the Bundesliga's top scorer, Lothar Emmerich, the nominal left-winger.

Defending powerfully and breaking rapidly, Borussia surprisingly took all West Ham, the holders, could hurl at them at Upton Park and won on a couple of counter-attacks. In the final, they deserved to beat a disappointing Liverpool team, terribly vulnerable through the middle and lucky to equalise when the ball had so clearly crossed the goal line. Celtic, beaten by Liverpool in the semi-final, had an excellent run, and showed how their manager and former centre-half, Jock Stein, had tempered them for major competition.

First Round
Reykjavik 1, Rosenberg Trondheim 3
Rosenberg Trondheim 3, Reykjavik 1
Wiener Neustadt 0, Stintza Cluj 1
Stintza Cluj 2, Wiener Neustadt 0
Reipas Lahti 2, Honved 10
Honved 6, Reipas Lahti 0
Coleraine 1, Dynamo Kiev 6
Dynamo Kiev 4, Coleraine 0
Sion 5, Galatasaray 1
Galatasaray 2, Sion 1
Alético Madrid 4, Dynamo Zagreb 0
Dynamo Zagreb 0, Atlético Madrid 1
Dukla Prague 2, Rennes 0
Rennes 0, Dukla Prague 0
SC Magdeburg 1, Spora 0
Spora 0, SC Magdeburg 2
Go Ahead Deventer 0, Celtic 6
Celtic 1, Go Ahead Deventer 0
Juventus 1, Liverpool 0
Liverpool 2, Juventus 0
Limerick 1, CSKA Sofia 2
CSKA Sofia 2, Limerick 0
Floriana 1, Borussia Dortmund 5
Borussia Dortmund 8, Floriana 0
Omonia Nicosia 0, Olympiakos 1
Olympiakos 1, Omonia Nicosia 1
Aarhus 2, Vitoria Setubal 1
Vitoria Setubal 1, Aarhus 2
Bye: *West Ham United*

Second Round
Dukla 2, Honved 3
Honved 1, Dukla 2
Honved won on away goals rule
Borussia Dortmund 3, CSKA 0
CSKA 4, Borussia Dortmund 2
SC Magdeburg 8, Sion 1
Sion 2, SC Magdeburg 2
Stintza Cluj 0, Atlético Madrid 2
Atlético Madrid 4, Stantza Cluj 0
Aarhus 0, Celtic 1
Celtic 2, Aarhus 0
West Ham United 4, Olympiakos Piraeus 0
Olympiakos Piraeus 2, West Ham United 2
Liverpool 3, Standard Liège 1
Standard Liège 1, Liverpool 2
Rosenberg 1, Dynamo Kiev 4
Dynamo Kiev 2, Rosenberg 0

Quarter-finals
Celtic 3, Dynamo Kiev 0
Dynamo Kiev 1, Celtic 1
Atlético Madrid 1, Borussia Dortmund 1
Borussia Dortmund 1, Atlético Madrid 0
Honved 0, Liverpool 0
Liverpool 2, Honved 0
West Ham United 1, SC Magdeburg 0
SC Magdeburg 1, West Ham United 1

Semi-finals

West Ham United 1, Borussia Dortmund 2
Borussia Dortmund 3, West Ham United 1

Celtic 1, Liverpool 0
Liverpool 2, Celtic 0

Final Glasgow, 5 May 1966
Borussia Dortmund (0) 2, Liverpool (0) 1
Borussia: Tilkowski; Cyliax, Redder; Kurrat, Paul, Assauer; Libuda, Schmidt, Held, Sturo, Emmerich.
Liverpool: Lawrence; Lawler, Byrne; Milne, Yeats, Stevenson; Callaghan, Hunt, St John, Smith, Thompson.
Scorers: Held, Yeats (o.g.) for Borussia; Hunt for Liverpool.

EUROPEAN CUP-WINNERS' CUP 1966–67

After a fine passage to their second Cup-Winners' Cup Final, Rangers found the luck of the (German) venue and Bayern's all-round accomplishment just too much for them.

The competition was played under the highly suspect dispensation of away goals counting double, in the event of two teams finishing level on aggregate. Rangers put out the holders, Borussia Dortmund, beating them in Glasgow more easily than the score suggests, and holding them in Munich, despite an injury to Watson. But they were lucky to get through against Saragossa, on the toss of a coin. Bayern scraped through against a brave Shamrock Rovers, and recovered from defeat in Vienna to beat Rapid in a rough second leg, to take the other semi-final. Müller, their young centre-forward, scored the winner in extra time.

In the final, played at Nuremberg, Rangers dominated the first half, Bayern the second and extra time was again needed. It produced the decisive goal, by Roth.

Preliminary Round

Valur Reykjavik 1, Standard Liège 1
Standard Liège 8, Valur Reykjavik 1

First Round

Skeid Oslo 3, Saragossa 2
Saragossa 3, Skeid Oslo 1
Rapid Vienna 4, Galatasaray 0
Galatasaray 3, Rapid Vienna 5
Servette Geneva 1, Kamraterna Turku 1
Kamraterna Turku 1, Servette Geneva 2
Glentoran 1, Rangers 1
Rangers 4, Glentoran 0
Swansea Town 1, Slavia Sofia 1
Slavia Sofia 4, Swansea Town 0
Tatan Presov 1, Bayern Munich 1
Bayern Munich 3, Tatan Presov 2
AEK Athens 0, Braga (Portugal) 1
Braga 3, AEK Athens 2
Shamrock Rovers 4, Spora Luxemburg 0
Spora 1, Shamrock Rovers 4
Aalborg 0, Everton 0
Everton 2, Aalborg 1
OFK Belgrade 1, Spartak Moscow 3
Spartak Moscow 3, OFK Belgrade 0
Fiorentina 1, Vasas Gyor 0
Vasas Gyor 4, Fiorentina 2
Chemie Leipzig 3, Legia Warsaw 0
Legia Warsaw 2, Chemie Leipzig 2

Strasbourg 1, Steaua Bucharest 0
Steaua Bucharest 1, Strasbourg 1
Floriana Valetta 1, Sparta
  Rotterdam 1
Sparta Rotterdam 6, Floriana
  Valetta 0
Standard Liège 5, Limassol 1
Limassol 0, Standard Liège 1
Bye: *Borussia Dortmund*
Second Round
Saragossa 2, Everton 0
Everton 1, Saragossa 0
Shamrock Rovers 1, Bayern
  Munich 1
Bayern Munich 3, Shamrock
  Rovers 2
Vasas Gyor 3, Sporting Braga 0
Sporting Braga 2, Vasas Gyor 0
Spartak Moscow 1, Rapid
  Vienna 1
Rapid Vienna 1, Spartak
  Moscow 0
Servette 2, Sparta Rotterdam 0
Sparta Rotterdam 1, Servette 0
Rangers 2, Borussia Dortmund 1
Borussia Dortmund 0, Rangers 0

Strasbourg 1, Slavia Sofia 0
Slavia Sofia 2, Strasbourg 0
Chemie Liepzig 2, Standard
  Liège 1
Standard Liège 1, Chemie
  Leipzig 0

Quarter-finals
Rapid Vienna 1, Bayern
  Munich 0
Bayern Munich 2, Rapid
  Vienna 0
Rangers 2, Saragossa 0
Saragossa 2, Rangers 0
Vasas Gyor 2, Standard Liège 1
Standard Liège 2, Vasas Gyor 0
Servette 1, Slavia Sofia 0
Slavia Sofia 3, Servette 0

Semi-finals
Bayern Munich 2, Standard
  Liège 0
Standard Liège 1, Bayern
  Munich 3
Slavia Sofia 0, Rangers 1
Rangers 1, Slavia Sofia 0

Final Nuremberg, 31 May 1967
Bayern Munich (0) 1, Rangers (0) 0
Bayern: Maier; Nowak, Kupferschmidt; Roth, Beckenbauer, Olk; Nafziger, Ohlhauser, Muller, Koulmann, Brenninger.
Rangers: Martin; Johansen, Provan; Jardine, McKinnon, Greig; Henderson, A. Smith, Hynd, D. Smith, Johnstone.
Scorer: Roth after extra time.

EUROPEAN CUP-WINNERS' CUP 1967–68

AC Milan, who in the meantime were comfortably carrying off the Italian Championship, added to it the European Cup-Winners' Cup on their first appearance in the tournament. Their victory over Hamburg in the final, at Rotterdam, was a mere canter. Both goals were scored by the veteran Swedish right-winger, Kurt Hamrin, the second a brilliant individual affair. It was far easier for Milan than their painfully hard qualifications against Vasas Gyor and Standard Liège.

Cardiff City were Britain's most impressive competitors, doing wonderfully well. Shamrock Rovers and Breda were no great problem, and in the quarter-finals they belied recent poor League form by knocking out Torpedo Moscow. They won at home with a fine, late headed goal by Barrie Jones, went down 1–0 in Tashkent then, with five reserves, won the play-off, in Augsburg, 1–0, Toshack heading down for Dean to score. In the semi-finals, still fighting relegation in the League, they held Hamburg (without Seeler and Schulz) to an away draw, then lost unluckily at home.

Spurs went out feebly to Lyon, after a brawl in the away match, and some dismal defence at home. Aberdeen went down to Standard Liège, though they played well at home in the return leg. Standard went on to draw twice with Milan, but lost the play-off. Milan then knocked out the holders, Bayern, in the semi-finals.

First Round

FK Austria 0, Steaua Bucharest 2
Steaua Bucharest 2, FK Austria 1
Hamburg 5, Randers Freja 3
Randers Freja 0, Hamburg 2
AC Milan 5, Levski 1
Levski 1, AC Milan 1
Hajduk Split 0, Tottenham Hotspur 2
Tottenham Hotspur 4, Hajduk Split 3
Shamrock Rovers 1, Cardiff City 1
Cardiff City 2, Shamrock Rovers 0
Lausanne Sports 3, Spartak Trnava 2
Spartak Trnava 2, Lausanne Sports 0
Aberdeen 10, Reykjavik 0
Reykjavik 1, Aberdeen 4
Valencia 4, Crusaders 0
Crusaders 2, Valencia 4
Torpedo Moscow 0, Motor Zwickau 0
Motor Zwickau 0, Torpedo Moscow 1
Izmir 2, Standard Liège 3
Standard Liège 0, Izmir 0
Aris Bonnevoie 0, Lyon 3
Lyon 2, Aris Bonnevoie 1
Fredrikstadt 1, Vitoria Setubal 5
Vitoria Setubal 2, Fredrikstadt 1
Vasas Gyor 5, Apollon Limassol 0
Apollon Limassol 0, Vasas Gyor 4
Bayern Munich 5, Panathinaikos 0
Panathinaikos 1, Bayern Munich 2
JHK Helsinki 1, Wislaw Cracow 4
Wislaw Cracow 4, JHK Helsinki 0
Floriana Malta 1, NAC Breda 2
NAC Breda 1, Floriana Malta 0

Second Round

Bayern Munich 6, Vitoria Setubal 2
Vitoria Setubal 1, Bayern Munich 1
Wislaw 0, Hamburg 1
Hamburg 4, Wislaw 0
NAC Breda 1, Cardiff City 1
Cardiff City 4, NAC Breda 1
Vasas Gyor 2, AC Milan 2
AC Milan 1, Vasas Gyor 1
Lyon 1, Tottenham Hotspur 0
Tottenham Hotspur 4, Lyon 3
Standard Liège 3, Aberdeen 0
Aberdeen 2, Standard Liège 0
Torpedo Moscow 3, Spartak Trnava 1
Spartak Trnava 1, Torpedo Moscow 3
Steaua Bucharest 1, Valencia 0
Valencia 3, Steaua Bucharest 0

Quarter-finals

SV Hamburg 2, Lyon 0
Lyon 2, SV Hamburg 0
SV Hamburg 2, Lyon 0
Standard Liège 1, AC Milan 1
AC Milan 1, Standard Liège 1
AC Milan 2, Standard Liège 0
Torpedo Moscow 1, Cardiff City 0
Cardiff City 1, Torpedo Moscow 0
Valencia 1, Bayern Munich 1
Bayern Munich 1, Valencia 0

217

Semi-finals
SV Hamburg 1, Cardiff City 1   AC Milan 2, Bayern Munich 0
Cardiff City 2, SV Hamburg 3   Bayern Munich 0, AC Milan 0

Final Rotterdam, 23 May 1968
AC Milan (2) 2, SV Hamburg (0) 0
AC Milan: Cudicini; Anquilletti, Schnellinger; Trappatoni, Rosato, Scala; Hamrin, Lodetti, Sormani, Rivera, Prati.
SV Hamburg: Ozcan; Sondemann, Kurbjohn; Dieckemann, Horst, H. Schulz; Dorfel II, Kramer, Seeler, Hornig, Dorfel I.
Scorer: Hamrin (2) for Milan.

EUROPEAN CUP-WINNERS' CUP 1968–69

For the first time, one of the two major European club competitions was won by an Eastern European country; more precisely by the Czech team, Slovan Bratislava. The Soviet invasion of Czechoslovakia the previous summer had led to a refusal by many Western European clubs to play against Eastern clubs. This in turn had led to the 'zoning' of the first round, and all Eastern clubs except Slovan had withdrawn in protest. Slovan's victory was peculiarly appropriate under the circumstances.

Dunfermline, cleverly managed by the old Blackpool goalkeeper, George Farm, did best of the British entry, surviving until the semifinal. After a rough second leg, in which they had a player sent off, they protested at the way they were treated in Bratislava.

West Bromwich Albion, the FA Cup holders, were surprisingly among Dunfermline's victims. After conceding a draw at home, Dunfermline adjusted better to the icy circumstances at The Hawthorns, and won by Gardner's headed goal, scored after only 90 seconds.

Barcelona, if anybody, looked favourites for the final, especially after their fine 4–1 victory over Cologne in the second leg of the semifinals. But for the second time they lost a European final on Swiss soil. Cvetler, Slovan's clever winger, put them ahead in the second minute, and by half-time discomfited Barcelona were 3–1 behind. Though Rexach proceeded to score straight from a corner kick, the Czechs held on to win.

Cardiff, veterans of so many brave battles in this tournament, alas went out at the first hurdle.

First Round
Bruges 3, West Bromwich Albion 1
West Bromwich Albion 2, Bruges 0
Dunfermline Ath. 10, Apoel Nicosia 1
Apoel Nicosia 0, Dunfermline Ath. 2
Crusaders 2, Norrköping 2
Norrköping 4, Crusaders 1
Cardiff City 2, Porto 2
Porto 2, Cardiff City 1
Bordeaux 2, Cologne 1
Cologne 3, Bordeaux 0
Slovan Bratislava 3, Bor 0
Bor 2, Slovan Bratislava 0
Partizan Tirana 1, Torino 0

Torino 3, Partizan Tirana 1
Rumelange 2, Sliema Malta 1
Sliema Malta 1, Rumelange 0
Izmir 3, Lyn Oslo 1
Lyn Oslo 4, Izmir 1
Freja 1, Shamrock Rovers 0
Shamrock Rovers 1, Freja 2
Lugano 0, Barcelona 1
Barcelona 3, Lugano 0
Olympiakos Piraeus 2, Frem
  Reykjavik 0
Frem Reykjavik 0, Olympiakos
  Piraeus 2
ADO The Hague 4, Graz 1
Graz 0, ADO The Hague 2
Walk-over: *Dynamo Bucharest*

Second Round
Dynamo Bucharest 1, West
  Bromwich Albion 1
West Bromwich Albion 4,
  Dynamo Bucharest 0
Dunfermline 4, Olympiakos 0
Olympiakos 3, Dunfermline 0
Porto 1, Slovan Bratislava 0
Slovan Bratislava 4, Porto 0

Randers Freja 6, Sliema Malta 0
Sliema Malta 0, Randers Freja 2
ADO 0, Cologne 1
Cologne 3, ADO 0
Byes: *Torino, Barcelona*

Quarter-finals
Barcelona 3, Lyn Oslo 2
Barcelona 2, Lyn Oslo 2
  (*in Barcelona*)
Cologne 2, Randers Freja 1
Randers Freja 0, Cologne 3
Torino 0, Slovan Bratislava 1
Slovan Bratislava 2, Torino 1
Dunfermline 0, West Bromwich
  Albion 0
West Bromwich Albion 0,
  Dumfermline 1

Semi-finals
Dunfermline 1, Slovan
  Bratislava 1
Slovan Bratislava 1,
  Dunfermline 0
Cologne 2, Barcelona 2
Barcelona 4, Cologne 1

Final Basel, 21 May 1969
Slovan Bratislava (3) 3, Barcelona (1) 2
Slovan: Vencel; Filo, Hrivnak; Jan Zlocha, Horvarth, Hrdlicka;
Cvetler, Moder, Josef Capkovic, Jokl, Jan Capkovic.
Barcelona: Sadurni; Franch, Eladio; Rife, Olivella, Zabalza; Pelicer,
Castro, Zaldua, Fuste, Rexach, subs: Pereda, Mendonça.
Scorers: Cvetler, Hrivnak, Jan Capkovic for Slovan; Zaldua, Rexach
for Barcelona.

EUROPEAN CUP-WINNERS' CUP 1969–70
Manchester City added the Cup-Winners' Cup to the various honours
they had won since 1968, decisively beating Gornik in the final despite
some rough treatment by the Polish defenders. On their way to Vienna,
they beat Atlético Bilbao in the first round, after being at one stage
3–1 down in the first leg, in Spain, but rallying to draw 3–3. Their
League form in mid-season was poor, but they were always able to
produce something extra for their Cup-Winners' Cup matches.
Slovan, the holders, went out in the very first round, to Dynamo
Zagreb. Lierse were thoroughly thrashed in the second round by
Manchester City, Academica Coimbra narrowly beaten in the third.
Schalke won the first leg of the semi-final thanks to a characteristic

individualist goal by Libuda, but City annihilated them at Manchester. Francis Lee, Colin Bell, and Mike Summerbee, till he was hurt, were ebullient.

Gornik beat Roma to reach the final on the toss of a coin. In heavy rain, Lee had another fine match, and City comfortably overcame the loss of Doyle, through injury. Gornik's goal, made by Lubanski for Oslizlo, came too late to matter. Young and Lee – a penalty when Young was fouled – got City's goals.

Preliminary Round
Rapid Vienna 0, Torpedo Moscow 0
Torpedo Moscow 1, Rapid Vienna 1

First Round
Atlético Bilbao 3, Manchester City 3
Manchester City 3, Atlético Bilbao 0
Ards 0, Roma 0
Roma 3, Ards 1
Rangers 2, Steaua Bucharest 0
Steaua Bucharest 0, Rangers 0
Mjoendalen 1, Cardiff City 7
Cardiff City 5, Mjoendalen 1
Shamrock Rovers 2, Schalke 04 1
Schalke 04 3, Shamrock Rovers 0
Magdeburg 1, MTK Budapest 0
MTK Budapest 1, Magdeburg 1
Dukla Prague 1, Marseilles 0
Marseilles 2, Dukla Prague 0
Rapid Vienna 1, PSV Eindhoven 2
PSV Eindhoven 4, Rapid Vienna 2
Frem Copenhagen 2, St Gallen 1
St Gallen 1, Frem Copenhagen 0
Norrköping 5, Sliema 1
Sliema 1, Norrköping 0
Dynamo Zagreb 3, Slovan Bratislava 0
Slovan Bratislava 0, Dynamo Zagreb 0
Lierse 10, Apoel Cyprus 0
Apoel Cyprus 0, Lierse 1
Olympiakos Piraeus 2, Gornik Zabrze 2
Gornik Zabrze 5, Olympiakos Piraeus 0
Goeztepe Izmir 3, Union Luxemburg 0
Union Luxemburg 2, Goeztepe Izmir 3
IBV Reykjavik 0, Levski Sofia 4
Levski Sofia 4, IBV Reykjavik 0
Academica 0, Palloseura 0
Palloseura 0, Academica 1

Second Round
Lierse 0, Manchester City 3
Manchester City 5, Lierse 0
Gornik 3, Rangers 1
Rangers 1, Gornik 3
Goeztepe Izmir 3, Cardiff City 0
Cardiff City 1, Goeztepe Izmir 0
Roma 1, PSV 0
PSV 1, Roma 0
(*Roma won toss*)
Norrköping 0, Schalke 04 0
Schalke 04 1, Norrköping 0
Levski 4, St Gallen 0
St Gallen 0, Levski 0
Magdeburg 1, Academica 0
Academica 2, Magdeburg 0
Marseilles 1, Dynamo Zagreb 1
Dynamo Zagreb 0, Marseilles 0

Quarter-finals
Academica 0, Manchester City 0
Manchester City 1, Academica 0
Roma 2, Goeztepe Izmir 0
Goeztepe Izmir 0, Roma 0
Levski 3, Gornik 2
Gornik 2, Levski 1
Dyanamo Zagreb 1, Schalke 04 3
Schalke 04 1, Dynamo Zagreb 0

Semi-finals
Schalke 04 1, Manchester City 0
Manchester City 5, Schalke 04 1
Roma 1, Gornik 1

Gornik 2, Roma 2
Gornik 1, Roma 1
(*at Strasbourg Gornik won toss*)

Final Vienna, 29 April 1970
Manchester City (2) 2, Gornik (0) 1
Manchester City: Corrigan; Book, Booth, Heslop, Pardoe; Doyle (Bowyer), Oakes, Towers; Bell, Lee, Young.
Gornik: Kostka; Gorgon, Oslizlo, Latocha, Florenski (Deja), Olek, Szoltysik, Wilczek (Skowronck), Banas, Lubanski, Szarynski.
Scorers: Young, Lee for Manchester City; Oslizlo for Gornik.

EUROPEAN CUP-WINNERS' CUP 1970–71

Chelsea kept the trophy in England, defeating Real Madrid in a replayed final in Athens, having knocked out the holders, Manchester City, in the semi-finals. Injuries seriously afflicted City's hopes of retaining the Cup. Chelsea's victory in Athens owed much to the splendid form in midfield of the unpredictable Charlie Cooke, on this occasion displaying the full range of his exceptional talent.

Cardiff City yet again gave an excellent account of themselves in this competition, thrashing Nantes and giving Real Madrid a good run for their money.

After a shaky beginning against Linfield, Manchester City got into their stride, defeating Honved and Gornik (in a play-off) and revealing such fine new, locally developed players as the slim Mellor and the powerfully versatile Jeffries. The absence of both wing-halves, Doyle and Oakes, and above all the splendid Colin Bell, however, ruined their chances against Chelsea. These semi-final games had, absurdly, to be fitted in with the Easter programme, and were something of a fiasco. Chelsea, themselves without Peter Osgood, made heavy weather of beating City at Stamford Bridge, the South African Derek Smethurst at last getting the only goal from Webb's pass. Lee was the best player on the field. Chelsea also won the return against what amounted to a reserve City side, their young goalkeeper, Healey, carrying Weller's indirect free kick over his own line for the only goal.

But Chelsea, who had previously and convincingly beaten Aris, CSKA Sofia and Bruges, were not be undervalued. In the final, in Athens, still without the thrustful Hutchinson, and with Hollins and Osgood patched up for the fray, they took the lead ten minutes after half-time through Osgood; later obliged to hobble off. Real, largely the better side, equalised when Dempsey miskicked and Zoco seized the chance. Webb and Bonetti kept Real out in extra time.

Switching boldly to 4–2–4 in the replay, Chelsea owed much to Bonetti's goalkeeping, Cooke's skill, and Baldwin's thrust. He made the second goal for Osgood, Dempsey having got the first after a corner. Fleitas scored a fine goal for Real 15 minutes from time, but Real, with Pirri nursing his injured arm, had nobody to match Cooke.

Preliminary Round
Bohemians 1, Gottwaldov 2
Gottwaldov 2, Bohemians 1

First Round
Aberdeen 3, Honved 1
Honved 3, Aberdeen 1
(*Honved won on penalties*)
Cardiff City 8, Larnaca Cyprus 0
Larnaca 0, Cardiff City 0
Aris Salonika 1, Chelsea 1
Chelsea 5, Aris Salonika 1
Manchester City 1, Linfield 0
Linfield 2, Manchester City 1
Hibernians Malta 0, Real Madrid 0
Real Madrid 5, Hibernians Malta 0
Gottwaldov 2, PSV Eindhoven 1
PSV Eindhoven 1, Gottwaldov 0
Olympic Ljubljana 1, Benfica 1
Benfica 8, Olympic Ljubljana 1
Stromsgodset 0, Nantes 5
Nantes 2, Stromsgodset 3
Wacker Innsbruck 3, Partizan Tirana 2
Partizan Tirana 1, Wacker Innsbruck 2
CSKA Sofia 9, Valkeakosken 0
Valkeakosken 1, CSKA Sofia 2
Vorwearts 0, Bologna 0
Bologna 1, Vorwearts 1
Offenbach Kickers 2, Bruges 1
Bruges 2, Offenbach Kickers 0
Goeztepe Izmir 5, US Luxemburg 0
US Luxemburg 1, Goeztepe Izmir 0
Aalborg 0, Gornik 1
Gornik 8, Aalborg 0
Akureyri Iceland 1, Zurich 7
Zurich 7, Akureyri 0
Steaua Bucharest 1, Karpaty Lvov 0
Karpaty Lvov 0, Steaua Bucharest 1

Second Round
CSKA Sofia 0, Chelsea 1
Chelsea 1, CSKA Sofia 0
Honved 1, Manchester City 0
Manchester City 2, Honved 0
Goztepe Izmir 0, Gornik 1
Gornik 3, Goztepe Izmir 0
PSV Eindhoven 4, Steaua Bucharest 0
Steaua Bucharest 0, PSV Eindhoven 3
Benfica 2, Vorwaerts 0
Vorwaerts 2, Benfica 0
Vorwaerts won on penalties
Bruges 2, Zurich 0
Zurich 3, Bruges 2
Cardiff City 5, Nantes 1
Nantes 1, Cardiff City 2
Real Madrid 0, Wacker Innsbruck 1
Wacker Innsbruck 0, Real Madrid 2

Quarter-finals
Cardiff City 1, Real Madrid 0
Real Madrid 2, Cardiff City 0
Bruges 2, Chelsea 0
Chelsea 4, Bruges 0
Gornik 2, Manchester City 0
Manchester City 2, Gornik 0
Manchester City 3, Gornik 1
PSV Eindhoven 2, Vorwaerts 0
Vorwearts 1, PSV Eindhoven 0

Semi-finals
Chelsea 1, Manchester City 0
Manchester City 0, Chelsea 1
PSV Eindhoven 0, Real Madrid 0
Real Madrid 2, PSV Eindhoven 1

Final (Replay)
Athens, 21 May 1971
Chelsea (2) 2, Real Madrid (0) 1
Chelsea: Bonetti; Boyle, Harris; Cooke, Dempsey, Webb; Weller, Baldwin, Osgood (Smethurst), Hudson, Houseman.

Real Madrid: Borja; José Luis, Zunzunegui; Pirri, Benito, Zoco; Fleitas, Amancio, Grosso, Velazquez, (Gento), Bueno (Grande).
Scorers: Dempsey, Osgood for Chelsea; Fleitas for Real.

EUROPEAN CUP-WINNERS' CUP 1971–72

A notable if somewhat Pyrrhic victory for Rangers, playing their third and first successful final in the competition. They duly defeated Moscow Dynamo, first Iron Curtain team to reach a major European final, in Barcelona, but such were the drunken excesses of their supporters in the stadium afterwards that they were banned by UEFA from defending it. A severe penalty indeed.

Rangers had a strange shock at Lisbon in the second round when, having clearly qualified on away goals, the referee obliged both teams to take penalties after extra time; and Sporting 'won'. Rangers appealed; and prevailed. In Turin, they played an exaggeratedly defensive game and drew, then beat Torino in the return more comfortably than the 1–0 score suggests. Their victory over Bayern Munich, their conquerors in the 1967 final, was splendid. Drawing a little fortunately in Munich, they overwhelmed the Germans at Ibrox, where Parlane made a spectacular debut at centre-forward, scoring the second goal. In the final, Rangers' rhythm was too much for Dynamo, who went 3–0 down before a late rally brought them two goals.

Preliminary Round
BK 69 Odense 4, FK Austria 2
FK Austria 2, BK 69 Odense 0
Fram Reykjavik 0, Hibernians Malta 3
Hibernians 2, Fram 0

First Round
Dynamo Berlin 1, Cardiff City 1
Cardiff City 1, Dynamo Berlin 1
Dynamo won on penalties
Jeunesse Hautcharage 0 Chelsea 8
Chelsea 13 Jeunesse Hautcharage 0
Rennes 1 Rangers 1
Rangers 1, Rennes 0
Servette 2, Liverpool 1
Liverpool 2, Servette 0
Distillery 1, Barcelona 3
Barcelona 4, Distillery 0
Sporting Lisbon, 4, Lyn Oslo 0
Lyn Oslo 0, Sporting Lisbon 3
Olympiakos Piraeus 0, Moscow Dynamo 2
Moscow Dynamo 1, Olympiakos Piraeus 2
Banyasz 2, Red Star Belgrade 7
Red Star 1, Banyasz 2
Dynamo Tirana 1, FK Austria 1
FK Austria 1, Dynamo Tirana 0
Zaglebie Sosnowicz 3, Atvidaberg 4
Atvidaberg 1, Zaglebie 1
Mikkeli 0, Eskisehirspor 0
Eskisehirspor 4, Mikkeli 0
Limerick 0, Torino 1
Torino 4, Limerick 0
Skoda Pilsen 0, Bayern Munich 1
Bayern Munich 1, Skoda Pilsen 1
Levski Sofia 1, Sparta Rotterdam 1
Sparta Rotterdam 2, Levski Sofia 0
Beerschot 7 Famagusta 0
Famagusta 0 Beerschot 1
Hibernians Malta 0 Steaua Bucharest 0
Steaua 1, Hibernians Malta 0

Second Round
Rangers 3, Sporting Lisbon 2
Sporting Lisbon 4, Rangers 3

Sparta Rotterdam 1, Red Star Belgrade 1
Red Star 2, Sparta 1
Atvidaberg 0, Chelsea 0
Chelsea 1, Atvidaberg 1
Torino 1, FK Austria 0
FK Austria 0, Torino 0
Liverpool 0, Bayern Munich 0
Bayern Munich 3, Liverpool 1
Beerschot 1, Dynamo Berlin 3
Dynamo Berlin 3, Beerschot 1
Eskisehirspor 0, Moscow Dynamo 1
Moscow Dynamo 1, Eskisehirspor 0
Barcelona 0, Steaua Bucharest 1
Steaua Bucharest 2, Barcelona 1

Quarter Finals
Torino 1, Rangers 1
Rangers 1, Torino 0

Steaua Bucharest 1, Bayern Munich 1
Bayern Munich 0, Steaua Bucharest 0
Atvidaberg 0, Dynamo Berlin 2
Dynamo Berlin 2, Atvidaberg 2
Red Star Belgrade 1, Moscow Dynamo 2
Moscow Dynamo 1, Red Star Belgrade 1

Semi Finals
Bayern Munich 1, Rangers 1
Rangers 2, Bayern Munich 0
Dynamo Berlin 1, Moscow Dynamo 1
Moscow Dynamo 1, Dynamo Berlin 1
Moscow Dynamo won on penalties

Final Barcelona, 24 May 1972
Rangers (2) 3, Moscow Dynamo (0) 2
Rangers: McCloy; Jardine, Mathieson; Greig, Johnstone, Smith, McLean, Conn, Stein, MacDonald, Johnston.
Moscow Dynamo: Pilgui; Basalacev, Dolmatov, Zikov, Dolbonosov, Zukov, Baidazhnyi, Jakobik (Eschtrekov), Sabo, Mahovikov, Evriuschkin.
Scorers: Stein, Johnston (2) for Rangers; Eschtrekov, Mahovikov for Moscow Dynamo.

EUROPEAN CUP-WINNERS' CUP 1972–73
If ever a team was entitled to raise the old boxing manager's cry of 'We was robbed!' it was surely Leeds United. So deplorably biased was the refereeing of the ill-tempered final in Salonica by the Greek Michas that he was suspended by UEFA and his own Federation. Yet no enquiry followed to determine *why* he had been so inept. The darkest suspicions were thus given apparent justification.

Leeds lost the final to an early goal from a free-kick by Chiarugi, but might themselves have had at least a couple of penalties. Leeds had reached the final with increasing power and efficiency. The Turks of Ankaragucu put up a bruising resistance at Elland Road, and Hajduk of Split proved hard opponents in the semi-final, but Leeds' defence gave away only a couple of goals until the final; of which, despite the vital lack of their midfield generals Bremner and Giles and their striker Clarke, they were unquestionably the moral victors. A tournament that left a bad taste; though Third Division Wrexham proved notable giantkillers.

First Round
Bastia 0, Atlético Madrid 0
Atlético Madrid 2, Bastia 1
Floriana 1, Ferencvaros 0
Ferencvaros 6, Floriana 0
Schalke 04 2, Slavia Sofia 1
Slavia Sofia 3, Schalke 04 1
Standard Liège 1, Sparta Prague 0
Sparta Prague 4, Standard Liège 2
Spartak Moscow 1, Den Haag 0
Den Haag 0, Spartak Moscow 0
Vikingur Reykjavik 0, Legia
 Warsaw 2
Legia Warsaw 9, Vikingur
 Reykjavik 0
Ankaragucu 1, Leeds United 1
Leeds United 1, Ankaragucu 0
Hajduk Split 1, Frederikstad 0
Frederikstad 0, Hajduk 1
Rapid Vienna 0, POAK
 Salonica 0
POAK Salonica 2, Rapid
 Vienna 2
Zurich 1, Wrexham 1
Wrexham 2, Zurich 1
Sporting Lisbon 2, Hibernian 1
Hibernian 6, Sporting Lisbon 1
Rapid Bucharest 3, Landskrona 0
Landskrona 1, Rapid Bucharest 0
Pesoporikos Larna 1, Cork
 Hibernian 2
Cork Hibernian 4, Pesoporikos
 Larna 1
Fremad 1, Besa 1
Besa 0, Fremad 0
Carl Zeiss Jena 6, Mikkelin 1
Mikkelin 3, Carl Zeiss Jena 2
Red Boys Differdange 1,
 Milan 4
Milan 3, Red Boys 0

Second Round
Rapid Vienna 1, Rapid
 Bucharest 1
Rapid Bucharest 3, Rapid
 Vienna 1
Carl Zeiss Jena 0, Leeds United 0
Leeds United 2, Carl Zeiss Jena 0
Wrexham 3, Hajduk Split 1
Hajduk 2, Wrexham 0
Cork Hibernian 0, Schalke 04 0
Schalke 04 3, Cork Hibernian 0
Atlético Madrid 3, Spartak
 Moscow 4
Spartak Moscow 1, Atlético
 Madrid 2
Hibernian 7, Besa 1
Besa 1, Hibernian 1
Ferencvaros 2, Sparta Prague 0
Sparta Prague 4, Ferencvaros 1
Legia Warsaw 1, Milan 1
Milan 2, Legia Warsaw 1

Quarter-Finals
Leeds United 5, Rapid
 Bucharest 1
Rapid Bucharest 1,
 Leeds United 3
Hibernian 4, Hadjuk Split 2
Hajduk Split 3, Hibernian 0
Schalke 04 2, Sparta Prague 1
Sparta Prague 3, Schalke 04 0
Spartak Moscow 0, Milan 1
Milan 1, Spartak Moscow 1

Semi-Finals
Leeds United 1, Hajduk Split 1
Hajduk Split 0, Leeds United 0
Milan 1, Sparta Prague 0
Sparta Prague 0, Milan 1

Final Salonika, 16 May 1973
Milan (1) 1, Leeds United (0) 0
Milan: Vecchi; Sabadini, Zignoli, Anquilletti, Turone, Rosato (Dolci), Sogliano, Benetti, Bigon, Rivera, Chiarugi.
Leeds United: Harvey; Reaney, Cherry; Bates, Madeley, Hunter; Lorimer, Jordan, Jones, F. Gray, Yorath (McQueen).
Scorer: Chiarugi for Milan.

CHAPTER SEVENTEEN

The European Inter-Cities Fairs and UEFA Cup History

This competition, which made a creaking start, taking an unconscionable time a-playing, has since gathered prestige and popularity. It was nominally open to cities which put on trade fairs, and initially, London entered a representative team, later falling into line and putting out club sides. Home and away aggregate decides. In 1971 it became the European Union (UEFA) Cup.

1955–58
London eliminated Basel, Frankfurt, and Lausanne, but lost in the final to Barcelona. Birmingham City knocked out Inter and Zagreb, but lost (4–3, 0–1, 1–2 at Basel) to Barcelona.
London 2, Barcelona 2 (Chelsea)
Scorers: Greaves, Langley (pen) for London; Tejada, Martínez for Barcelona.
Barcelona 6, London 0
Scorers: Suarez (2), Martínez, Evaristo (2), Verges for Barcelona.

1958–60
Chelsea, representing London, went out in the second round (1–0, 1–4) to Belgrade. Birmingham eliminated Cologne (2–2, 2–0), Zagreb (2–0 3–3) and Union St Gilloise (4–2, 4–2) but lost to Barcelona in the final.
Birmingham 0, Barcelona 0
Barcelona 4, Birmingham 1
Scorers: Martínez, Czibor (2), Coll for Barcelona, Hooper for Birmingham.

1960–61
By now the competition had been properly stabilised, and played off within one season. Hibernian, representing Scotland, put out Barcelona in the second round. The decisive match at Edinburgh produced violent scenes, as the Barcelona players ran riot. Hibernian, having drawn 4–4 in Barcelona, won this second leg 3–2.

Birmingham City eliminated BK Copenhagen (4–4, 5–0), having previously put out Ujpest of Hungary, while Hibernian had a walkover against Lausanne.

In the semi-finals, Birmingham maintained their fine record in this contest by defeating Inter 2–1 both at home and away. But Hibernian, having drawn 2–2 and 3–3 with Roma, crashed 6–0 in the play-off.

In the final, Roma beat Birmingham.
Birmingham City 2, Roma 2
Scorers: Hellawell, Orritt for Birmingham; Manfredini (2) for Roma.
Roma 2, Birmingham City 0
Scorers: Farmer (o.g.), Pestrin for Roma.

1961–62

The Spaniards now succeeded in getting the entry temporarily increased to three clubs per country; and one of their own clubs, Valencia, was successful.

Of the British clubs, Sheffield Wednesday knocked out Lyon and Roma, but were eliminated by Barcelona 4–3 on aggregate, in the quarter-finals. Valencia crushed Nottingham Forest 7–1 on aggregate in the first round, but Hearts eliminated Union St Gilloise (5–1 on aggregate). In the next round, however, Inter put them out 5–0 on aggregate.

In the final, Valencia, having accounted for Inter in the quarter-finals, convincingly won an all-Spanish clash with Barcelona.

Valencia 6, Barcelona 2
Scorers: Not known for Valencia, Kocsis (2) for Barcelona.
Barcelona 1, Valencia 1
Scorers: Kocsis for Barcelona, Guillot for Valencia.

1962–63

Valencia, their teeth now well into this trophy, won it again. Everton, coming in for the first time, were surprisingly knocked out (1–0 and 0–2) by the compact Dunfermline side. Hibernian had another excellent run, beating Staevnet of Copenhagen 4–0 and 3–2, Utrecht of Holland 1–0 and 2–1, and finally going out, 0–5, 2–1, to Valencia, who had beaten Dunfermline in a third match decider in the second round. Dunfermline lost away, 4–0, but won gallantly at home, 6–2.

Dynamo Zagreb 1, Valencia 2
Scorers: Zambata for Dynamo; Waldo, Urtiaga for Valencia.
Valencia 2, Dynamo Zagreb 0
Scorers: Mañó, Núñez for Valencia.

1963–64

In an all-Spanish final at Barcelona, Saragossa narrowly got home against Valencia.

First Round
(Results of British teams only)
Staevnet Copenhagen 1, Arsenal 7
Arsenal 2, Staevnet Copenhagen 3
Utrecht 1, Sheffield Wednesday 4
Sheffield Wednesday 4, Utrecht 1
Glentoran 1, Partick Thistle 4
Partick Thistle 3, Glentoran 0
Lausanne 2, Hearts 2
Hearts 2, Lausanne 2
Lausanne 3, Hearts 2

Second Round
Cologne 3, Sheffield Wednesday 2
Sheffield Wednesday 1, Cologne 2
Arsenal 1, Liège 1
Liège 3, Arsenal 1
Partick Thistle 3, Spartak Brno 2
Spartak Brno 4, Partick Thistle 0
Lausanne 1, Saragossa 2
Saragossa 3, Lausanne 0
Juventus 1, Atlético Madrid 0
Atlético Madrid 1, Juventus 2
Juventus 1, Atlético Madrid 0
Atlético Madrid 1, Juventus 2
Valencia 0, Rapid Vienna 0
Rapid Vienna 2, Valencia 3

Ujpest Dozsa 0, Lokomotiv
  Plovdiv 0
Lokomotive Plovdiv 1, Ujpest
  Dozsa 3

Quarter-finals
Roma 3, Cologne 1
Cologne 4, Roma 0
Saragossa 3, Juventus 2
Juventus 0, Saragossa 0
Liège 2, Spartak Brno 0

Spartak Brno 2, Liège 0
Liège 1, Spartak Brno 0
Valencia 5, Ujpest 2
Ujpest 3, Valencia 1

Semi-finals
Valencia 4, Cologne 1
Cologne 2, Valencia 0
Liège 1, Saragossa 0
Saragossa 2, Liège 0

Final
Saragossa 2, Valencia 1
Scorers: Villa, Marcelino for Saragossa; Urtiaga for Valencia.

EUROPEAN INTER-CITIES FAIRS CUP 1964–65

A tournament surprisingly and meritoriously won by Ferencvaros of Budapest – very much the outsiders from the semi-finals onward, despite a forward-line which included the internationals Albert, Rakosi, and Fenyvesi, whose goal beat Juventus in the final. Manchester United, England's hopes, who had won an all-English clash with Everton on the the way, slipped badly in the semi-finals, confirming the fears of those who believed their organisation hardly matched their talent. The first of their two matches in Budapest, won by Ferencvaros with a disputed penalty, was bad tempered and unpleasant; a man from each side was sent off. Juventus, after making a very laborious way to the semi-final, suddenly found some form and recovered against Atlético Madrid, but in the end went down at home to Ferencvaros – and Dr Fenyvesi.

Preliminary Round
Eintracht Frankfurt 3,
  Kilmarnock 0
Kilmarnock 5, Eintracht
  Frankfurt 1
Wiener Sportklub 2, Lokomotiv
  Leipzig 1
Lokomotiv Leipzig 0, Wiener
  Sportklub 1
Strasbourg 2, Milan 0
Milan 1, Strasbourg 0
Basel 2, Spora Luxemburg 0
Spora Luxemburg 0, Basel 1
Atlético Bilbao 2, OFK Belgrade 2
OFK Belgrade 0, Atlético Bilbao 2
Ferencvaros 2, Spartak Brno 0
Spartak Brno 1, Ferencvaros 0

Goztep Smyrna 0, Petrolol
  Ploesti 1
Petrolul Ploesti 2, Goztep
  Smyrna 1
Odense BK 1913 1, VfB
  Stuttgart 3
VfB Stuttgart 1, Odense BK
  1913 0
Betis Seville 1, Stade Français 1
Stade Français 2, Betis Seville 0
Dynamo Zagreb 3, Grazer AK 2
Grazer AK 0, Dynamo Zagreb 6
Borussia Dortmund 4, Bordeaux 1
Bordeaux 2, Borussia Dortmund 0
Union St Gilloise 0, Juventus 1
Juventus 1, Union St Gilloise 0
Valencia 1, Liège 1

Liège 3, Valencia 1
Vojvodina 1, Lokomotiv
 Plovdiv 1
Lokomotiv Plovdiv 1,
 Vojvodina 1
Lokomotiv Plovdiv 2,
 Vojvodina1 (Sofia)
Djugaarden 1, Manchester
 United 1
Manchester United 6,
 Djugaarden 1
Valerenger 2, Everton 5
Everton 4, Valerenger 2
Leixoes 1, Celtic 1
Celtic 3, Leixoes 0
Barcelona 0, Fiorentina 1
Fiorentina 0, Barcelona 2
Aris 0, Roma 0
Roma 3, Aris 0
Belenenses 1, Shelbourne 1
Shelbourne 0, Belenenses 0
Shelbourne 2, Belenenses 1
 (Dublin)
Dunfermline Ath. 4, Oergryte 2
Oergryte 0, Dunfermline Ath. 0
Hertha Berlin 2, Antwerp 1
Antwerp 2, Hertha Berlin 0
BK Copenhagen 3, DOS
 Utrecht 4
DOS 2, BK Copenhagen 1
Servette 2, Atlético Madrid 2
Atlético Madrid 6, Servette 1
First Round
Dynamo Zagreb 1, Roma 1
Roma 1, Dynamo Zagreb 0
Stade Français 0, Juventus 0
Juventus 1, Stade Français 0
Basel 0, Strasbourg 1
Strasbourg 5, Basel 2
Kilmarnock 0, Everton 2
Everton 4, Kilmarnock 1
Petrolul 1, Lokomotiv Plovdiv 0
Lokomotiv Plovdiv 2, Petrolul 0
Borussia Dortmund 1,
 Manchester United 6
Manchester United 4,
 Borussia Dortmund 0
Dunfermline 1, VfB Stuttgart 0

VfB Stuttgart 0, Dunfermline 0
Atlético Bilbao 2, Antwerp 0
Antwerp 0, Atlético Bilbao 1
Barcelona 3, Celtic 1
Celtic 0, Barcelona 0
Utrecht 0, Liège 2
Liège 2, Utrecht 0
Ferencvaros 1, Weiner SK 0
Wiener SK 0, Ferencvaros 0
Shelbourne 0, Atlético Madrid 1
Atlético Madrid 1, Shelbourne 0

Second Round
Strasbourg 0, Barcelona 0
Barcelona 2, Strasbourg 2
Barcelona 0, Strasbourg 0
 (Barcelona)
 Strasbourg won toss
Manchester United 1, Everton 1
Everton 1, Manchester United 2
Juventus 1, Lokomotiv Plovdiv 1
Lokomotiv Plovdiv 1, Juventus 1
Juventus 2, Lokomotiv 1 (Turin)
Atlético Bilbao 1, Dunfermline 0
Dunfermline 1, Atlético Bilbao 0
Atlético Bilbao 2, Dunfermline 1
 (Bilbao)
Roma 1, Ferencvaros 2
Ferencvaros 1, Roma 0
Liège 1, Atlético Madrid 0
Atlético Madrid 2, Liège 0

Quarter-finals
Ferencvaros 1, Atlético Bilbao 0
Atlético Bilbao 1, Ferencvaros 0
Ferencvaros 3, Atlético Bilbao 0
 (Budapest)
Strasbourg 0, Manchester
 United 5
Manchester United 0,
 Strasbourg 0
Byes: *Juventus: Atletico Madrid*

Semi-finals
Manchester United 3,
 Ferencvaros 2
Ferencvaros 1, Manchester
 United 0

Ferencvaros 2, Manchester
  United 1 (Budapest)
Atlético Madrid 3, Juventus 1

Juventus 3, Atlético Madrid 1
Juventus 3, Atlético Madrid 1
  (Turin)

Final Turin
Juventus (0) 0, Ferencvaros (0) 1
M. Fenyvesi

EUROPEAN INTER-CITIES FAIRS CUP 1965–66

A tournament which produced a rash of violent matches ended in anticlimax, the two Spanish finalists being ordered by their Federation to postpone the two-legged final till the following season. When it was at last played, it turned out to be thoroughly dramatic. Winning on Barcelona's ground, Saragossa proceeded to lose on their own, three of Barcelona's goals being scored by a young newcomer to the attack, Pujol.

Chelsea's young team did well, none better than the brilliant young forward, Peter Osgood. Their three ties with Milan were memorable, above all the game at Stamford Bridge, when Schnellinger gave a performance for Milan which was matchlessly combative. Memorable for more sisnister reasons was the previous round's game in Rome, where the players were bombarded with missiles. Leeds' home game against Valencia gave rise to a disgraceful brawl. But it was Saragossa who eventually eliminated them, with surprising ease, in a decider played at Leeds.

First Round
Union Luxembourg 0, Cologne 4
Cologne 13, Union Luxembourg 0
Hibernian 2, Valencia 0
Valencia 2, Hibernian 0
Valencia 3, Hibernian 0
Liège 1, Dynamo Zagreb 0
Dynamo Zagreb 2, Liège 0
Red Star Belgrade 0,
  Fiorentina 4
Fiorentina 3, Red Star
  Belgrade 1
Stade Français 0, Porto 0
Porto 1, Stade Français 0
Malmö 0, Munich 1860 3
Munich 1860 4, Malmö 0
Bordeaux 0, Sporting Lisbon 4
Sporting Lisbon 6, Bordeaux 1
Milan 1, Strasbourg 0
Strasbourg 2, Milan 1
Milan 1, Strasbourg 1
(Milan won toss)
Chelsea 4, Roma 1
Roma 0, Chelsea 0
Spartak Brno 2, Lokomotiv
  Plovdiv 0
Lokomotiv Plovdiv 1, Spartak
  Brno 0
Nuremberg 1, Everton 1
Everton 1, Nuremberg 0
Antwerp 1, Glentoran 0
Glentoran 3, Antwerp 3
Wiener SK 6, PAOK Salonika 0
PAOK Salonika 2, Wiener SK 1
Leeds United 2, Torino 1
Torino 0, Leeds United 0
DSO Utrecht 0, Barcelona 0
Barcelona 7, DSO Utrecht 1
Alk Stockholm 3, Daring
  Brussels 1
Daring Brussels 0, Alk
  Stockholm 0
Byes: *Hanover 96, Español Barcelona, Red Flag Brasov, Goeztepe*

Izmir, Servette Geneva, CUF Setubal, Lokomotiv Leipzig, Basle, Aris Salonika, Ujpest Dozsa, BK Copenhagen, Dunfermline Ath., Hearts, Valerengen, Shamrock Rovers, Saragossa.

Second Round
Aris Salonika 2, Cologne 1
Cologne 2, Aris Salonika 0
Goeztepe Izmir 2, Munich 1860 1
Munich 1860 9, Goeztepe Izmir 1
Ujpest 3, Everton 0
Everton 2, Ujpest 1
Dunfermline 5, BK Copenhagen 0
BK Copenhagen 2, Dunfermline 4
Hanover 96 5, Porto 0
Porto 2, Hanover 96 1
Sporting Lisbon 2, Español Barcelona 1
Español Barcelona 4, Sporting Lisbon 3
Español Barcelona 2, Sporting Lisbon 1
Dynamo Zagreb 2, Red Flag Brasov 2
Red Flag Brasov 1, Dynamo Zagreb 0
Antwerp 2, Barcelona 1
Barcelona 2, Antwerp 0
Shamrock Rovers 1, Saragossa 1
Saragossa 2, Shamrock Rovers 1
Wiener SK 1, Chelsea 0
Chelsea 2, Wiener SK 0
Lokomotiv Leipzig 1, Leeds United 2
Leeds United 0, Lokomotiv Leipzig 0
CUF Setubal 2, Milan 0
Milan 2, CUF Setubal 0
Milan 1, CUF Setubal 0
Basel 1, Valencia 3
Valencia 5, Basel 1
Fiorentina 2, Spartak Brno 0
Spartak Brno 4, Fiorentina 0
Alk Stockholm 2, Servette Geneva 1
Servette Geneva 4, Alk Stockholm 1
Hearts 1, Valerengen 0
Valerengen 1, Hearts 3

Third Round
Hearts 3, Saragossa 3
Saragossa 2, Hearts 2
Saragossa 1, Hearts 0
Leeds United 1, Valencia 1
Valencia 0, Leeds United 1
Hanover 96 2, Barcelona 1
Barcelona 1, Hanover 96 0
Hanover 96 1, Barcelona 1
(Barcelona won toss)
Cologne 3, Ujpest 2
Ujpest 4, Cologne 0
Dunfermline 2, Spartak Brno 0
Spartak Brno 0, Dunfermline 0
Español 3, Red Flag Brasov 1
Red Flag Brasov 4, Español 2
Español 1, Red Star Brasov 0
Milan 2, Chelsea 1
Chelsea 2, Milan 1
Milan 1, Chelsea 1
(Chelsea won toss)
Servette Geneva 1, Munich 1860 1
Munich 1860 4, Servette Geneva 1

Fourth Round
Leeds United 4, Ujpest 1
Ujpest 1, Leeds United 1
Munich 1860 2, Chelsea 2
Chelsea 1, Munich 1860 0
Dunfermline 1, Saragossa 0
Saragossa 4, Dunfermline 2
Barcelona 1, Español 0
Español 0, Barcelona 1

Semi-finals
Saragossa 1, Leeds United 0
Leeds United 2, Saragossa 1
Leeds United 1, Saragossa 3
Barcelona 2, Chelsea 0
Chelsea 2, Barcelona 0
Barcelona 5, Chelsea 0

Final
Barcelona 0, Saragossa 1
Scorer: Canario for Saragossa.
Saragossa 2, Barcelona 4
Scorers: Marcelino (2) for Saragossa; Pujol (3), Zaballa for Barcelona.

EUROPEAN INTER-CITIES FAIRS CUP 1966–67
Postponed for the second time until the following season, the final of the 1966–67 competition was ultimately won by Dynamo Zagreb, at the expense of Leeds United. In Zagreb, they deservedly won, both goals being scored by their 18-year-old outside-right, Cercek. At Elland Road, their defence, with Skoric excellent in goal, massed to keep out the Leeds attack. Two other well-known internationals, Belin, the right-half, and Zambata, the striker, also increased their reputations.

Barcelona, the holders, had gone out to Dundee United only a matter of weeks after winning the postponed 1966 final. United shocked them by beating them on their own ground, Seemann and Persson, their Scandinavian wingers, playing splendidly. Juventus, however, were too strong for them in the Third Round, even though United won the return in Dundee.

Burnley had a very good run, beating VfB Stuttgart, Lausanne, and Naples – where, in the return match, they had to survive a short and vicious riot, involving Naples players and spectators.

Burnley's own robust tactics provoked a brawl late in the home game against Eintracht, which they surprisingly lost – thus going out of the competition.

Leeds United did very well to beat Valencia away from home, got through against Bologna on the toss of a coin, and competently disposed of Kilmarnock on their way to the final. But Benfica, on their first appearance in the tournament, surprisingly went out to Leipzig in the Third Round. Dynamo Zagreb had a splendid 3–0 home win to put out Juventus in the quarter finals, then turned a 3–0 deficit into a 4–3 aggregate win over Eintracht in the semis.

First Round
Juventus 5, Aras Salonika 0
Aris Salonika 0, Juventus 2
Olympija Ljubljana 3, Ferencvaros 3
Ferencvaros 3, Olympija Ljubjana 0
DOS Utrecht 2, Basel 1
Basel 2, DOS Utrecht 2
Vfb Stuttgart 1, Burnley 1
Burnley 2, VfB Stuttgart 0
Frigg Oslo 1, Dunfermline Ath. 3
Dunfermline Ath. 3, Frigg Oslo 1
Red Star Belgrade 4, Atlético Bilbao 0
Atlético Bilbao 2, Red Star Belgrade 0
Valencia 2, Nuremberg 1
Nuremberg 0, Valencia 2
Drumcondra 0, Eintracht Frankfurt 2
Eintracht Frankfurt 5, Drumcondra 1
Naples 3, Wiener SK 1
Wiener SK 1, Naples 2
Porto 2, Bordeaux 1

Bordeaux 2, Porto 1
(Bordeaux won toss)
Nice 2, Oergryte Gothenburg 2
Oergryte Gothenberg 2, Nice 1
Djurgaarden 1, Lokomotiv Leipzig 3
Lokomotiv Leipzig 2, Djurgaarden 1
Dynamo Pitesti 2, Seville 0
Seville 2, Dynamo Pitesti 2
Spartak Brno 2, Dynamo Zagreb 0
Dynamo Zagreb 2, Spartak Brno 0
(Dynamo won toss)
US Luxemberg 0, Antwerp 1
Antwerp 4, US Luxemberg 0
Bologna 3, Goeztepe 1
Goeztepe 1, Bologna 2
Byes: *Toulouse, Barcelona, Dundee United, Vitoria Setubal, Odense BK 09, Lausanne, BK Copenhagen, La Gantoise, Kilmarnock, Spartak Plovdiv, Benfica, Liege, Sparta Prague, West Bromwich Albion, DWS Amsterdam, Leeds United.*

Second Round
DWS 1, Leeds United 3
Leeds United 5, DWS 1
Lokomotiv Leipzig 0, Liège 0
Liège 1, Lokomotiv Leipzig 2
Lausanne 1, Burnley 3
Burnley 5, Lausanne 0
La Gantoise 1, Bordeaux 0
Bordeaux 0, La Gantoise 0
Oergryte 0, Ferencvaros 0
Ferencvaros 7, Oergryte 1
Toulouse 3, Dynamo Pitesti 0
Dynamo Pitesti 5, Toulouse 1
Dunfermline 4, Dynamo Zagreb 2
Dynamo Zagreb 2, Dunfermline 0
Barcelona 1, Dundee United 2
Dundee United 2, Barcelona 0
Odense BK 09 1, Naples 4
Naples 2, Odense BK 09 1
Antwerp 1, Kilmarnock 1
Kilmarnock 7, Antwerp 2
Valencia 1, Red Star Belgrade 0
Red Star Belgrade 1, Valencia 2
Sparta Prague 2, Bolgona 2
Bologna 2, Sparta Prague 1
Spartak Plovdiv 1, Benfica 1
Benfica 2, Spartak Plovdiv 0
DOS Utrecht 1, West Bromwich Albion 1
West Bromwich Albion 5, DOS Utrecht 2
Juventus 3, Setubal 1
Setubal 0, Juventus 2
Eintracht 5, BK Copenhagen 1
BK Copenhagen 2, Eintracht 2

Third Round
Lokomotiv Leipzig 3, Benfica 1
Benfica 2, Lokomotiv Leipzig 1
Kilmarnock 1, La Gantoise 0
La Gantoise 1, Kilmarnock 2
Burnley 3, Naples 0
Naples 0, Burnley 0
Leeds United 1, Valencia 1
Valencia 0, Leeds United 2
Bologna 3, West Bromwich Albion 0
West Bromwich Albion 1, Bologna 3
Juventus 3, Dundee United 0
Dundee United 1, Juventus 0
Dynamo Zagreb 1, Dynamo Pitesti 0
Dynamo Pitesti 0, Dynamo Zagreb 0
Eintracht 4, Ferencvaros 1
Ferencvaros 2, Eintracht 1

Quarter-finals
Bologna 1, Leeds United 0
Leeds United 1, Bologna 0
(Leeds won toss)
Juventus 2, Dynamo Zagreb 2
Dynamo Zagreb 3, Juventus 0
Eintracht 1, Burnley 1
Burnley 1, Eintracht 2,
Lokomotiv Leipzig 1, Kilmarnock 0
Kilmarnock 2, Lokomotiv Leipzig 0

Semi-finals

Leeds United 4, Kilmarnock 2	Eintracht 3, Dynamo Zagreb 0
Kilmarnock 0, Leeds United 0	Dynamo Zagreb 4, Eintracht 0

Final 30 August 1967
Dynamo Zagreb (1) 2, Leeds United (0) 0
Scorer: Cercek (2) for Dynamo Zagreb.
6 September 1967
Leeds United (0) 0, Dynamo Zagreb (0) 0

EUROPEAN INTER-CITIES FAIRS CUP 1967–68

This time, Leeds United, in another postponed final – or finals – consoled themselves for the previous year's disappointment by defeating Ferencvaros to win. They were two hard games, each on the same pattern; an away team clamming up in defence and allowing the home team to come at them. Leeds won the first game and scored the only goal of the finals in controversial circumstances; Jackie Charlton stood on the goal line at a corner and blocked the goalkeeper's path while Jones thumped the ball home.

On their way to the final, Leeds had tough opposition from Partizan Belgrade and Hibernian – who had rallied superbly in their return match with Naples, winning 5–0 after losing 4–1 away – but didn't concede a goal against Rangers.

Ferencvaros, winners of the trophy in 1965, played beautiful football at Liverpool, where Munich had crashed – and were cheered off the field by the Kop. Bologna pushed them very hard in the semi-finals.

Dundee had a splendid run into the semi-finals, but Leeds were again too good for them, defeating a Scottish side for the third time in the competition. The return match at Elland Road was played during an accumulation of postponed matches and won by an Eddie Gray goal nine minutes from time.

First Round

Spora Luxemburg 0, Leeds United 9	Bologna 2, Lyn Oslo 0
Leeds United 7, Spora Luxemburg 0	Lyn Oslo 0, Bologna 0
	Nice 0, Fiorentina 1
PAOK Salonika 0, Liège 2	Fiorentina 4, Nice 0
Liège 3, PAOK Salonika 2	Dresden Dynamo 1, Rangers 1
Wiener SK 0, Atletico Madrid 5	Rangers 2, Dresden Dynamo 1
Atletico Madrid 2, Wiener SK 1	Argesul Pitesti 3, Ferencvaros 1
St Patrick's Athletic 1, Bordeaux 3	Ferencvaros 4, Argesul Pitesti 0
	Malmö 0, Liverpool 2
Bordeaux 6, St. Patrick's Athletic 3	Liverpool 2, Malmö 1
	Hibernian 3, Porto 0
DOS Utrecht 3, Saragossa 2	Porto 3, Hibernian 1
Saragossa 3, DOS Utrecht 1	Eintracht Frankfurt 0, Nottingham Forest 1
Naples 4, Hanover 96 0	
Hanover 96 1, Naples 1	Nottingham Forest 4, Eintracht Frankfurt 0

Dynamo Zagreb 5, Petrolul
 Ploesti 0
Petrolul Ploesti 2, Dynamo
 Zagreb 0
Servette Geneva 2, Munich 1860 2
Munich 1860 4, Servette Geneva 2
Bruges 0, Sporting Lisbon 0
Sporting Lisbon 2, Bruges 1
Frem Copenhagen 0, Atlético
 Bilbao 1
Atlético Bilbao 3, Frem
 Copenhagen 2
Zurich 3, Barcelona 1
Barcelona 1, Zurich 0
Lokomotiv Leipzig 5, Linfield 1
Linfield 1, Lokomotiv Leipzig 0
DWS Amsterdam 2, Dundee 1
Dundee 3, DWS Amsterdam 0
Partizan 5, Lokomotiv Plovdiv 1
Lokomotiv Plovdiv 1, Partizan 1
Vojvodina 1, CUF 0
CUF 1, Vojvodina 3
Cologne 2, Slavia Prague 0
Slavia Prague 2, Cologne 2
Royal Antwerp 1, Goeztepe
 Izmir 2
Goetzepe Izmir 0, Royal
 Antwerp 0

Second Round
Nottingham Forest 2, Zurich 1
Zurich 1, Nottingham Forest 0
Bordeaux 1, Atlético Bilbao 3
Atlético Bilbao 1, Bordeaux 0
Dundee 3, Liège 1
Liège 1, Dundee 4
Vojvodina 0, Lokomotiv Leipzig 0
Lokomotiv Leipzig 0, Vojvodina 2
Saragossa 2, Ferencvaros 1
Ferencvaros 3, Saragossa 0

Final
Leeds United 1, Ferencvaros 0
Scorer: Jones for Leeds United.
Ferencvaros 0, Leeds United 0

Liverpool 8, Munich 1860 0
Munich 1860 2, Liverpool 1
Rangers 3, Cologne 0
Cologne 3, Rangers 1
Bologna 0, Dynamo Zagreb 0
Dynamo Zagreb 1, Bologna 2
Naples 4, Hibernian 1
Hibernian 5, Naples 0
Partizan 1, Leeds United 2
Leeds United 1, Partizan 1
Fiorentina 1, Sporting Lisbon 1
Sporting Lisbon 2, Fiorentina 1

Third Round
Ferencvaros 1, Liverpool 0
Liverpool 0, Ferencvaros 1
Leeds United 1, Hibernian 0
Hibernian 1, Leeds United 1
Vojvodina 1, Goeztepe Izmir 0
Goeztepe Izmir 0, Vojvodina 1
Zurich 3, Sporting Lisbon 0
Sporting Lisbon 1, Zurich 0
Byes: *Atlético Bilbao, Dundee, Rangers, Bologna*

Quarter-finals
Ferencvaros 2, Bilbao 1
Bilbao 2, Ferencvaros 2
Rangers 0, Leeds United 0
Leeds United 2, Rangers 0
Dundee 1, F.C. Zurich 0
F.C. Zurich 0, Dundee 1
Bologna 0, Vojvodina 0
Vojvodina 0, Bologna 2

Semi-finals
Dundee 1, Leeds United 1
Leeds United 1, Dundee 0
Ferencvaros 3, Bologna 2
Bologna 2, Ferencvaros 2

EUROPEAN INTER-CITIES FAIRS CUP 1968–69

For the second successive year, an English club won the Fairs Cup; surprisingly and laudably it was Newcastle United, on their first entry into European competition. After a somewhat erratic beginning, in which they played irresistibly at home and indifferently away, they reached a brilliant crescendo in the two-legged final against Ujpest – conquerors of the holders, Leeds United.

Having soundly beaten them at Gallowgate, thanks to two goals by their normally defensive half-back, Bobby Moncur, they rode a two-goal deficit in Budapest to win dramatically, 3–2.

Leeds might have done rather better had they not become so intensely engaged with the League Championship. They put out Standard Liège, were lucky to eliminate Naples on the iniquitous toss of a coin (Naples must be getting used to it; a similar expedient decided the 1960 Olympic semi-final and the 1968 European Nations semi-final, at Fuorigrotta), annihilated Hanover, but were well beaten, home and away, by Ujpest.

Newcastle overcame Feyenoord, Sporting Lisbon, Saragossa, Vitoria Setubal, then Rangers. 'Away goals' allowed them to scrape through against the Spanish team, but Rangers couldn't score a goal against them. Their failure provoked a barbaric invasion of the Newcastle pitch by Rangers' fans, and a prolonged stoppage of the game.

Thus to the final, in which Moncur got yet another fine goal in Budapest, and young Foggon, coming on as substitute, raced splendidly through alone to score the winner.

First Round
Chelsea 5, Morton 0
Morton 3, Chelsea 4
Newcastle United 4, Feyenoord 0
Feyenoord 2, Newcastle United 0
Slavia Sofia 0, Aberdeen 0
Aberdeen 2, Slavia Sofia 0
Atlético Bilbao 2, Liverpool 1
Liverpool 2, Atlético Bilbao 1
Atlético won the toss
Rangers 2, Vojvodina 0
Vojvodina 1, Rangers 0
Ljubjana 0, Hibernian 3
Hibernian 2, Ljubjana 1
OFK Belgrade 6, Rapid Bucharest 1
Rapid Bucharest 3, OFK Belgrade 1
Wiener Sportklub 1, Slavia Prague 0
Slavia Prague 5, Weiner Sportklub 0
Skeid Oslo 1, AIK Stockholm 1
AIK Stockholm 2, Skeid Oslo 1
Trakia Plovdiv 3, Real Saragossa 1
Real Saragossa 2, Trakia Plovdiv 0
Dynamo Zagreb 1, Fiorentina 1
Fiorentina 2, Dynamo Zagreb 1
Legia Warsaw 6, Munich 1860 0
Munich 1860 2, Legia Warsaw 3
Daring Brussels 2, Panathinaikos 1
Panathinaikos 2, Daring Brussels 0
Wacker Innsbruck, 2 Eintracht Frankfurt 2
Eintracht Frankfurt 3, Wacker Innsbruck 0
Sporting Lisbon 4, Valencia 0
Valencia 4, Sporting Lisbon 1
Bologna 4, Basel 1
Basel 1, Bologna 2
Aris Salonika 1, Hibernian Malta 0

Hibernian Malta 0, Aris
　Salonika 6
DOS Utrecht 1, Dundalk 1
Dundalk 2, DOS Utrecht 1
Hansa Rostock 3, OGC Nice 0
OGC Nice 2, Hansa Rostock 1
Atlético Madrid 2, Waregem 1
Waregem 1, Atlético Madrid 0
Goeztepe Izmir 2, Marseilles 0
Marseilles 2, Goeztepe Izmir 0
Goeztepe won the toss
Metz 1, Hamburg SV 4
Hamburg SV 3, Metz 2
Lyon 1, Coimbra Academica 0
Coimbra Academica 1, Lyon 0
Lyon won the toss
Lausanne 0, Juventus 2
Juventus 2, Lausanne 0
Beerschot 1, DWS Amsterdam 1
DWS Amsterdam 2, Beerschot 1
Odense BK 09 1, Hanover 96 3
Hanover 96 1, Odense BK 09 0
Vitoria Setubal 3, Linfield 0
Linfield 1, Vitoria Setubal 3
Standard Liège 0, Leeds United 0
Leeds United 3, Standard Liège 2
Naples 3, Grasshoppers 1
Grasshoppers 1, Naples 0
Byes: *Argesul Pitesti, Lokomotiv Leipzig, Ujpest Dozsa*

Second Round
Hibernian 3, Lokomotiv Leipzig 1
Lokomotiv 0, Hibernian 1
Leeds United 2, Naples 0
Naples 2, Leeds United 0
Leeds won the toss
Rangers 6, Dundalk 1
Dundalk 0, Rangers 3
Aberdeen 2, Real Saragossa 1
Real Saragossa 3, Aberdeen 0
Chelsea 0, DWS Amsterdam 0
DWS Amsterdam 0, Chelsea 0
DWS won the toss
Sporting Lisbon 1, Newcastle
　United 1
Newcastle United 1, Sporting
　Lisbon 0
Vitoria Setubal 5, Lyon 0

Lyon 1, Vitoria Setubal 2
Goeztepe Izmir 3, Argesul Pitesti 0
Argesul Pitesti 3, Goeztepe Izmir 2
Hansa Rostock 3, Fiorentina 2
Fiorentina 2, Hansa Rostock 1
Hamburg SV 4, Slavia Prague 1
Slavia Prague 3, Hamburg SV 1
Panathinaikos 0, Atlético
　Bilbao 0
Bilbao Atlético 1,
　Panathinaikos 0
OFK Belgrade 1, Bologna 0
Bologna 1, OFK Belgrade 1
Aris Salonika 1, Ujpest 2
Ujpest 9, Aris Salonika 1
AIK Stockholm 4, Hanover 96 2
Hanover 96 5, AIK Stockholm 2
Juventus 0, Eintracht Frankfurt 0
Eintracht Frankfurt 1, Juventus 0
Waragem 1, Legia Warsaw 0
Legia Warsaw 2, Waragem 0
Third Round
Leeds United 5, Hanover 96 1
Hanover 96 1, Leeds United 2
Hamburg SV 1, Hibernian 0
Hibernian 2, Hamburg SV 1
Legia Warsaw 0, Ujpest 1
Ujpest 2, Legia Warsaw 2
Real Saragossa 3, Newcastle
　United 2
Newcastle United 2, Real
　Saragossa 1
OFK Belgrade 3, Goeztepe Izmir 1
Goeztepe Izmir 2, OFK Belgrade 0
Eintracht Frankfurt 1, Atlético
　Bilbao 1
Atlético Bilbao 1, Eintracht
　Frankfurt 0
DWS Amsterdam 0, Rangers 2
Rangers 2, DWS Amsterdam 1
DWS won the toss
Vitoria Setubal 3, Fiorentina 0
Fiorentina 2, Vitoria Setubal 1
Quarter-finals
Newcastle United 5, Vitoria
　Setubal 1
Vitoria Setubal 3, Newcastle
　United 1

Rangers 4, Atlético Bilbao 1
Atlético Bilbao 2, Rangers 0
Leeds United 0, Ujpest 1
Ujpest 2, Leeds United 0
Goztepe Izmir *v.* Hamburg SV
   Hamburg withdrew

Semi-finals
Goeztepe Izmir 1, Ujpest 4
Ujpest 4, Goeztepe Izmir 0
Rangers 0, Newcastle United 0
Newcastle United 2, Rangers 0

Final
Newcastle United (0) 3, Ujpest (0) 0
Scorers: Moncur (2), Scott for Newcastle United.
Ujpest (2) 2, Newcastle United (0) 3
Scorers: Bene, Gorocs for Ujpest; Moncur, Arentoft, Foggon for Newcastle.
Newcastle United's team in both matches: McFaul; Craig, Clark, Gibb, Burton, Moncur, Scott, Robson, Davies, Arentoft, Sinclair.
Substitute in each match: Foggon.

EUROPEAN FAIRS CUP 1969-70

Yet again, this now bloated, slightly amorphous competition had an English winner. Though there were moments in the course of the tournament when an Arsenal victory seemed the unlikeliest of outcomes, the North London club finally and impressively prevailed, to win their first major honour since 1953.

They began modestly, actually losing to Glentoran in the first round's return leg. A flaccid Sporting Lisbon team were easily crushed at Highbury, while a hardly more impressive Rouen side gave a startling amount of trouble.

In the quarter-finals, Newcastle United, the holders, were bitterly unlucky to be squeezed out by Anderlecht on a late away goal, while Arsenal thrashed Dynamo Bacau. In the semi-finals, they played vigorously to trounce Ajax 3-0 at home, Cruyff and all, lost the return only 1-0, and so met the powerful Anderlecht in the final.

The Belgians, who had rallied surprisingly to beat Inter at San Siro, after losing at home, were much too good for Arsenal in Brussels. But again Arsenal proved formidable at home, breaking down Anderlecht's defence with a marvellous first half goal by young Kelly, and scoring two more in the second half.

First Round
Arsenal 3, Glentoran 0
Glentoran 1, Arsenal 0
Dundee United 1, Newcastle
   United 2
Newcastle United 1, Dundee
   United 0
Liverpool 10, Dundalk 0
Dundalk 0, Liverpool 4
Partizan 2, Ujpest Dozsa 1
Ujpest Dozsa 2, Partizan 0

Sabadel 2, Bruges 0
Bruges 5, Sabadel 1
Las Palmas 0, Hertha Berlin 0
Hertha Berlin 1, Las Palmas 0
Wiener Sportklub 4, Ruch
   Chorzow 2
Ruch Chorzow 4, Wiener
   Sportklub 1
Rouen 2, Twente Enschede 0
Twente Enschede 1, Rouen 0

Vitoria Guimaraes 1, Banik Ostrava 0
Banik Ostrava 1, Vitoria Guimaraes 1
Sporting Lisbon 4, Linz ASK 0
Linz ASK 2, Sporting Lisbon 2
Carl Zeiss Jena 1, Altay Izmir 0
Altay Izmir 0, Carl Zeis Jena 0
Lausanne 1, Vasas Györ 2
Vasas Györ 2, Lausanne 1
Rosenborg Trondheim 1, Southampton 0
Southampton 2, Rosenborg Trondheim 0
Hansa Rostok 3, Panionios Athens 0
Panionios Athens 2, Hansa Rostock 0
Dynamo Bacau 6, Floriana 0
Floriana 0, Dynamo Bacau 1
Slavia Sofia 2, Valencia 0
Valencia 1, Slavia Sofia 1
Internazionale 2, Sparta Prague 0
Sparta Prague 0, Internazionale 1
Juventus 3, Lokomotiv Plovdiv 1
Lokomotiv Plovdiv 1, Juventus 2
VfB Stuttgart 3, Plazs Malmo 0
Plazs Malmo 1, VfB Stuttgart 1
Hanover 96 1, Ajax 0
Ajax 3, Hanover 96 0
Aris Salonika 1, Cagliari 0
Cagliari 3, Aris Salonika 0
Metz 1, Naples 1
Naples 2, Metz 1
Barcelona 4, Odense BK 09 0
Odense BK 09 0, Barcelona 2
Gwardia Warsaw 1, Vojvodina 0
Vojvodina 1, Gwardia Warsaw 1
Dunfermline 4, Bordeaux 1
Bordeaux 2, Dunfermline 0
Zurich 3, Kilmarnock 2
Kilmarnock 3, Zurich 1
Munich 1860 2, Skied Oslo 2
Skeid Oslo 2, Munich 1860 1
Valur Reykjavik 0, Anderlecht 6
Anderlecht 2, Valur Reykjavik 0
Charleroi 2, FNK Zagreb 1
FNK Zagreb 1, Charleroi 3
Hvidovre Copenhagen 1, Porto 2
Porto 2, Hvidovre Copenhagen 0
Jeunesse d'Esch 3, Coleraine 2
Coleraine 4, Jeunesse d'Esch 0
Vitoria Setubal 3, Rapid Bucharest 1
Rapid Bucharest 1, Vitoria Setubal 4

Second Round
Sporting Lisbon 0, Arsenal 0
Arsenal 3, Sporting Lisbon 0
Anderlecht 6, Coleraine 1
Coleraine 3, Anderlecht 7
Vitoria Setubal 1, Liverpool 0
Liverpool 3, Vitoria Setubal 2
Porto 0, Newcastle United 0
Newcastle United 1, Porto 0
Ajax 7, Ruch Chorzow 0
Ruch Chorzow 1, Ajax 2
Hansa Rostock 2, Internazionale 1
Internazionale 3, Hansa Rostock 0
Carl Zeiss Jena 2, Cagliari 0
Cagliari 0, Carl Zeiss Jena 1
Hertha Berlin 3, Juventus 1
Juventus 0, Hertha Berlin 0
Vasas Györ 2, Barcelona 3
Barcelona 2, Vasas Györ 1
VfB Stuttgart 0, Naples 0
Naples 1, VfB Stuttgart 0
Kilmarnock 4, Slavia Sofia 1
Slavia Sofia 2, Kilmarnock 0
Bruges 5, Ujpest 2
Ujpest 3, Bruges 0
Skeid Oslo 0, Dynamo Bacau 1
Dynamo Bacau 2, Skeid Oslo 0
Charleroi 3, Rouen 1
Rouen 2, Charleroi 0
Vitoria Guimaraes 3, Southampton 3
Southampton 5, Vitoria Guimaraes 1
Dunfermline 2, Gwardia Warsaw 1
Gwardia Warsaw 0, Dunfermline 1

Third Round
Newcastle United 0, Southampton 0
Southampton 1, Newcastle United 1
Anderlecht 1, Dunfermline 0
Dunfermline 3, Anderlecht 2
Rouen 0, Arsenal 0
Arsenal 1, Rouen 0
Kilmarnock 1, Dynamo Bacau 1
Dynamo Bacau 2, Kilmarnock 0
Carl Zeiss Jena 1, Ujpest 0
Ujpest 0, Carl Zeiss Jena 3
Barcelona 1, Internazionale 2
Internazionale 1, Barcelona 1
Vitoria Setubal 1, Hertha Berlin 1
Hertha Berlin 1, Vitoria Setubal 0
Naples 1, Ajax 0
Ajax 4, Naples 0

Quarter-finals
Carl Zeiss Jena 3, Ajax 1
Ajax 5, Carl Zeiss Jena 1
Hertha Berlin 1, Internazionale 0
Internazionale 2, Hertha Berlin 0
Anderlecht 2, Newcastle United 0
Newcastle United 3, Anderlecht 1
Dynamo Bacau 0, Arsenal 2
Arsenal 7, Dynamo Bacau 1

Semi-finals
Anderlecht 0, Internazionale 1
Internazionale 0, Anderlecht 2
Arsenal 3, Ajax 0
Ajax 1, Arsenal 0

Final Brussels, 22 April 1970
Anderlecht (2) 3, Arsenal (0) 1
Anderlecht: Trappeniers; Heylens, Velkeneers, Kialunda, Cornelis (Peeters), Desengher, Nordahl; Devrindt, Mulder, Van Himst, Puis.
Arsenal: Wilson; Storey, McNab; Kelly, McLintock, Simpson; Armstrong, Sammels, Radford, George, Graham.
Scorers: Devrindt, Mulder (2) for Anderlecht; Kennedy (sub) for Arsenal.

Highbury, 28 April 1970
Arsenal (1) 3, Anderlecht (0) 0
Arsenal: Wilson; Storey, McNab; Kelly, McLintock, Simpson; Armstrong, Sammels, Radford, George, Graham.
Anderlecht: Trappeniers; Heylens, Velkeneers, Kialunda, Martens; Nordahl, Desanghere; Devrindt, Mulder, Van Himst, Puis.
Scorers: Kelly, Radford, Sammels for Arsenal.

EUROPEAN FAIRS CUP 1970–71
This, the last of the Fairs Cups – it would now change its name to the UEFA Cup – was won for the fourth consecutive time by an English club: Leeds United, who themselves had won it three years earlier and were appearing in their third final. Their success was well deserved, crowning a season beset by injury to key players, but it was ironic that they should overcome the fine young Juventus side in the final without beating them in either leg. The absurdity of away goals counting double

gave them the trophy. The games were drawn 2-2 in Turin, 1-1 at Elland Road, and excellent games they both were.

On their way to the final, Leeds eliminated Sarpsborg, Dynamo Dresden – on away goals – Sparta Prague, Vitoria Setubal, and Liverpool – with a goal at Anfield by the returning Billy Bremner. Liverpool, who'd thrashed Beckenbauer's Bayern Munich at home in the previous round, had been favoured to win.

Juventus, clearly taking the competition much more seriously than Italian teams are wont to, defeated Barcelona twice, came back powerfully at Enschede to eliminate Twente in the quarter final, then accounted for Cologne. Arsenal, the holders, paid the penalty for a moment's carelessness by their goalkeeper – Bob Wilson let a corner by Cologne at Highbury straight into goal – and some wretched finishing by their own attack.

After their first attempt to play the first leg of the final in Turin was frustrated by rain, Leeds were twice behind to Juventus. But, with Giles in fine form, they twice equalised, thanks to Madeley and Bates. The second goal came after Piloni bungled Giles' cross.

At Elland Road, in the return, Clarke scored after twelve minutes, putting Leeds in an impregnable position on aggregate. 'Juve' scored a fluent equaliser through Anastasi before half-time, but by the interval seemed to have resigned themselves. Cooper had one of his best attacking games for Leeds.

First Round

AEK Athens 0, Twente Enschede 1
Twente Enschede 3, AEK Athens 0
Zeleznicar 3, Anderlecht 4
Anderlecht 5, Zeleznicar 4
La Gantoise 0, Hamburg 1
Hamburg 7, La Gantoise 1
Liverpool 1, Ferencvaros 0
Ferencvaros 1, Liverpool 1
Sarpsborg 0, Leeds United 0
Leeds United 5, Sarpsborg 0
Coleraine 1, Kilmarnock 1
Kilmarnock 2, Coleraine 3
Dundee United 3, Grasshoppers 2
Grasshoppers 0, Dundee United 0
Lazio 2, Arsenal 2
Arsenal 2, Lazio 0
GKS Katowice 0, Barcelona 1
Barcelona 3, GKS Katowice 2
Wiener Sportklub 0, Beveren 2
Beveren 3, Wiener Sportklub 0
Ilves 4, Sturm Graz 2
Sturm Graz 3, Ilves 0
Juventus 7, Rumelange 0
Rumelange 0, Juventus 4
Seveille 1, Eskisehirsport 0
Eskisehirsport 3, Seville 1
Vitoria Guimaraes 3, Angouleme 0
Angouleme 3, Vitoria Guimaraes 1
Hajduk Split 3, Slavia Sofia 0
Slavia Sofia 1, Hajduk Split 0
Nykoeping 2, Hertha Berlin 4
Hertha Berlin 4, Nykoeping 1
Partizan Belgrade 0, Dynamo Dresden 0
Dynamo Dresden 6, Partizan Belgrade 0
Barreirense 2, Dynamo Zagreb 0
Dynamo Zagreb 6, Barreirense 1
Ruch Chorzow 1, Fiorentina 1
Fiorentina 2, Ruch Chorzow 0
Sparta Prague 2, Atlético Bilbao 0
Atlético Bilbao 1, Sparta Prague 1
AB Copenhagen 7, Sliema Wanderers 0

Sliema Wanderers 2, AB
  Copenhagen 3
Dynamo Bucharest 5, PAOK
  Salonika 0
PAOK Salonika 1, Dynamo
  Bucharest 0
Lausanne 0, Vitoria Setubal 2
Vitoria Setubal 2, Lausanne 1
Cologne 5, Sedan 1
Sedan 1, Cologne 0
Internazionale 1, Newcastle
  United 1
Newcastle United 2,
  Internazionale 0
Spartak Trnava 2, Olympique
  Marseilles 0
Olympique Marseilles 2, Spartak
  Trnava 0
Trnava qualified on penalties
Bayern Munich 1, Rangers 0
Rangers 1, Bayern Munich 1
Cork Hibernian 0, Valencia 3
Valencia 3, Cork Hibernian 1
Hibernian 6, Malmo 0
Malmo 2, Hibernian 3
Universitatea Craiova 2,
  Pecsi Dosza 1
Pecsi Dosza 3, Universitatea
  Craiova 0
Trakia Plovdiv 1, Coventry
  City 4
Coventry City 2, Trakia
  Plovdiv 0
Sparta Rotterdam 6, IA
  Akranes 0
IA Akranes 0, Sparta
  Rotterdam 9

Second Round
Sturm Graz 1, Arsenal 0
Arsenal 2, Sturm Graz 0
Sparta Rotterdam 2,
  Coleraine 0
Coleraine 1, Sparta
  Rotterdam 2
Leeds United 1, Dynamo
  Dresden 0
Dynamo Dresden 2, Leeds
  United 1

Liverpool 3, Dynamo Bucharest 0
Dynamo Bucharest 1, Liverpool 1
Newcastle United 2, Pecsi
  Dosza 0
Pecsi Dosza 2, Newcastle
  United 0
Pesci qualified on penalties
Bayern Munich 6, Coventry
  City 1
Coventry City 2, Bayern
  Munich 1
Sparta Prague 3, Dundee
  United 1
Dundee United 1, Sparta
  Prague 0
Hibernian 2, Vitoria
  Guimaraes 0
Vitoria Guimaraes 2,
  Hibernian 1
Eskisehirsport 3, Twente 2
Twente 6, Eskisehirsport 1
AB Copenhagen 1, Anderlecht 3
Anderlecht 4, AB Copenhagen 0
Valencia 0, Baveren 0
Beveren 1, Valencia 1
Hertha Berlin 1, Spartak
  Trnava 0
Spartak Trnava 3, Hertha
  Berlin 1
Barcelona 1, Juventus 2
Juventus 2, Barcelona 1
Dynamo Zagreb 4, Hamburg 0
Hamburg 1, Dynamo Zagreb 0
Vitoria Setubal 2, Hajduk 0
Hajduk 2, Vitoria Setubal 1
Fiorentina 1, Cologne 2
Cologne 1, Fiorentina 0

Third Round
Arsenal 4, Beveren 0
Beveren 0, Arsenal 0
Leeds United 6, Sparta Prague 0
Sparta Prague 2, Leeds United 3
Spartak Trnava 0, Cologne 1
Cologne 3, Spartak Trnava 0
Bayern Munich 2, Sparta
  Rotterdam 1
Sparta Rotterdam 1, Bayern
  Munich 3

Dynamo Zagreb 2, Twente 2
Twente 1, Dynamo Zagreb 0
Hibernian 0, Liverpool 1
Liverpool 2, Hibernian 0
Pecsi Dosza 0, Juventus 1
Juventus 2, Pecsi Dosza 0
Anderlecht 2, Vitoria Setubal 1
Vitoria Setubal 3, Anderlecht 1

Arsenal 2, Cologne 1
Cologne 1, Arsenal 0
Liverpool 3, Bayern Munich 0
Bayern Munich 1, Liverpool 1
Vitoria Setubal 1, Leeds United 1
Leeds United 2, Vitoria Setubal 1

Semi-finals
Liverpool 0, Leeds United 1
Leeds United 0, Liverpool 0
Cologne 1, Juventus 1
Juventus 2, Cologne 0

Quarter-finals
Juventus 2, Twente 0
Twente 2, Juventus 2

Final Turin, 29 May 1971
Juventus (1) 2   Leeds United (0) 2
Juventus: Piloni, Spinosi, Salvadore, Marchetti, Morini, Furino, Haller, Capello, Causio, Anastasi (Novellini), Bettega.
Leeds United: Sprake; Reaney, Cooper; Bremner, Charlton, Hunter; Lorimer, Clarke, Jones (Bates), Giles, Madeley.
Scorers: Bettega, Capello for Juventus; Madeley, Bates for Leeds.

Leeds, 3 June 1971
Leeds United (1) 1   Juventus (1) 1
Leeds United: Sprake; Reaney, Cooper; Bremner, Charlton, Hunter; Lorimer, Clarke, Jones, Giles, Madeley (Bates).
Juventus: Tancredi; Spinosi, Salvadore, Marchetti; Morini, Furino, Haller, Capello, Causio, Anastasi, Bettega.
Scorers: Clarke for Leeds; Anastasi for Juventus.
Leeds won on 'away' goals.

UEFA CUP 1971–72
This time, Football League clubs went one better than before, providing not only the winners but the runners-up, Spurs beating Wolves in the final. It was the first edition of the European Union Cup, previously and misleadingly named the Fairs Cup, since it had long strayed far from its initial basis. Tottenham's finest achievement was probably their win over a ruthless Milan team in the semi-final, though Milan would not have lost at Tottenham had they not been so defensive after taking the lead. Two shots by Steve Perryman when the ball came out of the box duly sank them, while Alan Mullery, recalled from loan to Fulham to play splendidly, scored in a 1–1 draw at San Siro.

Big Martin Chivers' opportunism won the first leg of the final at Molineux against a Wolves team that had previously played very well to draw away to Juventus and to knock out Ferencvaros, the experienced Hungarians. The second leg, at White Hart Lane, was a hard, fast bruising draw – in which Mullery once again scored the Spurs goal.

First Round
Glentoran 0, Eintracht
  Brunswick 1
Eintracht Brunswick 6,
  Glentoran 1
Keflavik 1, Tottenham Hotspur 6
Tottenham Hotspur 9, Keflavik 0
Lierse 0, Leeds United 2
Leeds United 0, Lierse 4
Dundee 4, AB Copenhagen 2
AB Copenhagen 0, Dundee 1
SV Hamburg 2, St Johnstone 1
St Johnstone 2, SV Hamburg 0
Southampton 2, Atlético Bilbao 1
Atlético Bilbao 2, Southampton 0
Milan 4, Morphou 0
Morphou 0, Milan 3
Fenerbahce 1, Ferencvaros 1
Ferencvaros 3, Fenerbahce 1
Rosenborg 3, IFK Helsinki 0
IFK Helsinki 0, Rosenborg 0
Lugano 1, Legia Warsaw 3
Legia Warsaw 0, Lugano 0
Bologna 1, Anderlecht 1
Anderlecht 0, Bologna 2
Naples 1, Rapid Bucharest 0
Rapid Bucharest 2, Naples 0
Basle 1, Real Madrid 2
Real Madrid 2, Basle 1
Vasas 1, Shelbourne 0
Shelbourne 1, Vasas 1
Celta Vigo 0, Aberdeen 2
Aberdeen 1, Celta Vigo 0
Vitoria Setubal 1, Nimes 0
Nimes 2, Vitoria Setubal 1
Porto 0, Nantes 2
Nantes 1, Porto 1
ADO (Netherlands) 5, Aris 0
Aris 2, ADO (Netherlands) 2
Hertha 3, Elfsborg 1
Elfsborg 1, Hertha 4
Carl Zeiss Jena 3, Lokomotiv
  Plovdiv 0
Lokomotive Plovdiv 3, Carl
  Zeiss Jena 1
Chemie Halle 0, PSV
  Eindhoven 0
(*No return played*)
Zaglebie 1, Union Teplice 0
Union Teplice 1, Zaglebie 3
Marsa Malta 0, Juventus 6
Juventus 5, Marsa Malta 0
UT Arad 4, Austria Salzburg 1
Austria Salzburg 3, UT Arad 1
Atlético Madrid 2, Panionios 1
Panionios 1, Atlético Madrid 0
Rapid Vienna walkover Vlaznija
  Alb scr.
Dynamo Zagreb 6, Botev 1
Botev 1, Dynamo Zagreb 2
Zeljeznicar Sarajevo 3, Brugeois 0
Brugeois 3, Zeljeznicar 1
Saint Etienne 1, Cologne 1
Cologne 2, St Etienne 1
Wolverhampton Wanderers 3,
  Academica Coimbra 0
Academica Coimbra 1,
  Wolverhampton Wanderers 4
Spartak Moscow 2, Kosice 0
Kosice 2, Spartak Moscow 1
OFK Belgrade 4, Djurgarden 1
Djurgarden 2, OFK Belgrade 2
Second Round
ADO 1, Wolverhampton
  Wanderers 3
Wolverhampton Wanderers 4,
  ADO 0
Nantes 0, Tottenham Hotspur 0
Tottenham Hotspur 1, Nantes 0
St Johnstone 2, Vasas 0
Vasas 1, St Johnstone 0
Juventus 2, Aberdeen 0
Aberdeen 1, Juventus 1
Cologne 2, Dundee 1
Dundee 4, Cologne 2
Zeljeznicar 1, Bologna 1
Bologna 2, Zeljeznicar 2
Milan 4, Hertha 2
Hertha 2, Milan 1
Ferencvaros 6, Panionios 0
Panionios expelled for unruly
  conduct
Rosenborg 4, Lierse 1
Lierse 3, Rosenborg 0
Rapid Bucharest 4, Legia
  Warsaw 0

Legia Warsaw 2, Rapid Bucharest 0
Spartak Moscow 0, Vitoria Setubal 0
Vitoria Setubal 4, Spartak Moscow 0
OFK Belgrade 1, Carl Zeiss Jena 1
Carl Zeiss Jena 4, OFK Belgrade 0
Real Madrid 3, PSV Eindhoven 1
PSV Eindhoven 2, Real Madrid 0
Zaglebie 1, UT Arad 1
UT Arad 2, Zaglebie 1
Eintracht Brunswick 2, Atlético Bilbao 1
Atlético Bilbao 2, Eintracht Brunswick 2
Dynamo Zagreb 2, Rapid Vienna 2
Rapid Vienna 0, Dynamo Zagreb 0

Third Round
Carl Zeiss Jena 0, Wolverhampton Wanderers 1
Wolverhampton Wanderers 3, Carl Zeiss Jena 0
St Johnstone 1, Zeljeznicar 0
Zeljeznicar 5, St Johnstone 0
Milan 3, Dundee 0
Dundee 2, Milan 0
Tottenham Hotspur 3, Rapid Bucharest 0

Rapid Bucharest 0, Tottenham Hotspur 2
UT Arad 3, Vitoria Setubal 0
Vitoria Setubal 1, UT Arad 0
Rapid Vienna 0, Juventus 1
Juventus 4, Rapid Vienna 1
PSV Eindhoven 1, Lierse 0
Lierse 4, PSV Eindhoven 0
Eintracht Brunswick 1, Ferencvaros 1
Ferencvaros 5, Eintracht Brunswick 2

Quarter-finals
UT Arad 0, Tottenham Hotspur 2
Tottenham Hotspur 1, UT Arad 1
Milan 2, Lierse 0
Lierse 1, Milan 1
Juventus 1, Wolverhampton Wanderers 1
Wolverhampton Wanderers 1, Juventus 0
Ferencvaros 1, Zeljeznicar 2
Zeljeznicar 1, Ferencvaros 2
Ferencvaros won on penalties

Semi-finals
Tottenham Hotspur 2, Milan 1
Milan 1, Tottenham Hotspur 1
Ferencvaros 2, Wolverhampton Wanderers 2
Wolverhampton Wanderers 2, Ferencvaros 1

Final
Molineux (Wolverhampton), 3 May 1972
Wolverhampton Wanderers (0) 1   Tottenham Hotspur (0) 2
Wolverhampton: Parkes; Shaw, Taylor; Hegan, Munro, McAlle; McCalliog, Hibbitt, Richards, Dougan, Wagstaffe.
Tottenham: Jennings; Kinnear, Knowles; Mullery, England, Beal, Gilzean, Perryman, Chivers, Peters, Coates (Pratt).
Scorers: McCalliog for Wolverhampton; Chivers 2 for Tottenham.

White Hart Lane (London), 17 May 1972
Tottenham Hotspur (1) 1, Wolverhampton Wanderers (1) 1
Tottenham: Unchanged; no subs.
Wolverhampton: Unchanged. Subs: Bailey for Hibbitt, Curran for Dougan.
Scorers: Mullery for Tottenham; Wagstaffe for Wolverhampton.

UEFA CUP 1972-73

Liverpool won their first European trophy, after a decade of effort, beating Borussia Mönchengladbach in the final. They had already knocked out Spurs, the holders, in the semi-final thanks to a slice of luck in the tie at White Hart Lane where they lost 2-1 and survived on the 'Away' goal.

The final was a strange affair. The first attempt to play the Liverpool leg was defeated by rain; but not before Liverpool had seen the vulnerability of Borussia in the air. This enabled them to bring in the tall John Toshack in the replayed match next day and his heading powers were decisive. Günter Netzer played a curiously passive game at Anfield as a kind of sweeper, but in Mönchengladbach he was back to his true form and place in midfield; quite irresistible. Liverpool lost, but narrowly hung on to a winning margin on aggregate.

First Round

Aberdeen 2, Borussia Mönchengladbach 3
Borussia Mönchengladbach 6, Aberdeen 3
Atvidaberg 3, Bruges 5
Bruges 1, Atvidaberg 2
Manchester City 2, Valencia 2
Valencia 2, Manchester City 1
Lyn Oslo 3, Tottenham Hotspur 6
Tottenham Hotspur 6, Lyn Oslo 0
Cologne 2, Bohemians 1
Bohemians 0, Cologne 3
Honved 1, Partick Thistle 0
Partick Thistle 0, Hovend 3
Viking Stavanger 1, Vastmannejar 0
Vastmannejar 0, Viking Stavanger 0
Feyenoord 9, Rumelange 0
Rumelange 0, Feyenoord 12
Liverpool 2, Eintracht 0
Eintracht 0, Liverpool 0
Grasshoppers 2, Nimes 1
Nimes 1, Grasshoppers 2
Vitoria Setubal 6, Zaglebie Sosnowiec 1
Zaglebie Sosnowiec 1, Vitoria Setubal 0
Stoke City 3, Kaiserslautern 1
Kaiserslautern 4, Stoke City 0
Racing White 0, CUF Barreirense 1
CUF Barreirense 2, Racing White 0
Torino 0, Las Palmas 0
Las Palmas 4, Torino 0
Sochaux 1, Frem 3
Frem 2, Sochaux 1
Olympiakos Piraeus 2, Cagliari 1
Cagliari 0, Olympiakos 1
Angers 1, Dynamo Berlin 1
Dynamo Berlin 2, Angers 1
Porto 3, Barcelona 1
Barcelona 0, Porto 1
Universitatea Cluj 4, Levski Sofia 1
Levski Sofia 5, Universitatea Cluj 1
Red Star Belgrade 5, Lausanne 1
Lausanne 3, Red Star Belgrade 2
Internazionale 6, Valetta 1
Valetta 0, Internazionale 1
Beroe Stara 7, FK Austria 0
FK Austria 1, Beroe Stara 3
UT Arad 1, Norrköping 2
Norrköping 2, UT Arad 0
Larna 0, Ararat Erevan 1
Ararat Erevan 1, Larna 0
AEK Athens 3, Salgotarjan 1
Salgotarjan 1, AEK Athens 1
Eskisehirspor 1, Fiorentina 2
Fiorentina 3, Eskisehirspor 0

Dukla 2, OFK Belgrade 2
OFK Belgrade 3, Dukla 1
Slovan Bratislava 6, Vojvodina 0
Vojvodina 1, Slovan Bratislava 2
Dynamo Tbilisi 3, Twente 2
Twente 2, Dynamo Tbilisi 0
Ruch Chorzow 3, Fenerbahce 0
Fenerbahce 1, Ruch Chorzow 0
Dynamo Dresden 2, Vöest Linz 0
Vöest Linz 2, Dynamo Dresden 2
Bye: *Hvidovre Copenhagen*

Second Round
Dynamo Berlin 3, Levski Sofia 0
Levski Sofia 2, Dynamo Berlin 0
Borussia Mönchengladbach 3, Hvidovre 0
Hvidovre 1, Borussia Mönchengladbach 3
Porto 3, Bruges 0
Bruges 3, Porto 2
Tottenham Hotspur 4, Olympiakos 0
Olympiakos 1, Tottenham Hotspur 0
Red Star Belgrade 3, Valencia 0
Valencia 0, Red Star Belgrade 1
Internazionale 2, Norrköping 2
Norrköping 0, Internazionale 2
Viking Stavanger 1, Cologne 0
Cologne 9, Viking Stavanger 0
Beroe Stara 3, Honved 0
Honved 1, Boroe Stara 0
Feyenoord 4, OFK Belgrade 3
OFK Belgrade 2, Feyenoord 1
Liverpool 3, AEK Athens 0
AEK 1, Liverpool 3
Vitoria Setubal 1, Fiorentina 0
Fiorentina 2, Vitoria Setubal 1
Grasshoppers 1, Ararat Erevan 3
Ararat Erevan 4, Grasshoppers 2
CUF Barreirense 1, Kaiserslautern 3
Kaiserslautern 0, CUF Barreirense 1
Las Palmas 2, Slovan Bratislava 2
Slovan Bratislava 0, Las Palmas 1
Ruch Chorzow 0, Dynamo Dresden 1
Dynamo Dresden 3, Ruch Chorzow 0
Frem 0, Twente 5
Twente 4, Frem 0

Third Round
Ararat Erevan 2, Kaiserslautern 0
Kaiserslautern 2, Ararat Erevan 0
Kaiserslautern won on penalties
Cologne 0, Borussia Mönchengladbach 0
Borussia Mönchengladbach 5, Cologne 0
Dynamo Berlin 0, Liverpool 0
Liverpool 3, Dynamo Berlin 1
Tottenham Hotspur 2, Red Star Belgrade 0
Red Star Belgrade 1, Tottenham Hotspur 0
Twente 3, Las Palmas 0
Las Palmas 2, Twente 1
Vitoria Setubal 2, Internazionale 1
Internazionale 1, Vitoria Setubal 0
OFK Belgrade 0, Beroe Stara 0
Beroe Stara 1, OFK Belgrade 3
Porto 1, Dynamo Dresden 2
Dynamo Dresden 1, Porto 0

Quarter-finals
Tottenham Hotspur 1, Vitoria Setubal 0
Vitoria Setubal 2, Tottenham Hotspur 1
Liverpool 2, Dynamo Dresden 0
Dynamo Dresden 0, Liverpool 1
Kaiserslautern 1, Borussia Mönchengladbach 2
Borussia Mönchengladbach 7, Kaiserslautern 1
OFK Belgrade 3, Twente 2
Twente 2, OFK Belgrade 0

Semi-finals

Liverpool 1, Tottenham Hotspur 0

Tottenham Hotspur 2, Liverpool 1

Borussia Mönchengladbach 3, Twente 0

Twente 1, Borussia Mönchengladbach 2

Final
Liverpool, 10 May 1973
Liverpool 3, Borussia Möchengladbach 0
Liverpool: Clemence; Lawler, Lindsay; Smith, Lloyd, Hughes; Keegan, Cormach, Toshack, Heighway (Hall), Callaghan.
Borussia: Kleff; Netzer, Danner, Michallik, Vogts, Bonhof, Kulik, Jensen, Wimmer, Rupp (Simonsen), Heynckes.
Scorers: Keegan (2), Lloyd for Liverpool.
Mönchengladbach, 23 May 1973
Borussia Mönchengladbach 2, Liverpool 0
Borussia: Kleff; Vogts, Surau, Netzer, Bonhof, Danner, Wimmer, Kulik, Jensen, Rupp, Heynckes.
Liverpool: Clemence; Lawler, Lindsay; Smith, Lloyd, Hughes; Keegan, Cormack, Heighway (Boersma), Toshack, Callaghan.
Scorer: Heynckes (2) for Burussia Möchengladbach.

CHAPTER EIGHTEEN

South American Championship and Libertadores' Cup History

CHAMPIONSHIP

		Winners	Runners-up
1917	Montevideo	Uruguay	Argentina
1919	Rio	Brazil	Uruguay
1920	Valparaiso	Uruguay	Argentina
1921	Buenos Aires	Argentina	Brazil
1922	Rio	Brazil	Paraguay
1923	Montevideo	Uruguay	Argentina
1924	Montevideo	Uruguay	Argentina
1925	Buenos Aires	Argentina	Brazil
1926	Santiago	Uruguay	Argentina
1927	Lima	Argentina	Paraguay
1929	Buenos Aires	Argentina	Uruguay
1937	Buenos Aires	Argentina	Paraguay
1939	Lima	Peru	Brazil
1942	Montevideo	Uruguay	Argentina
1947	Guayaquil	Argentina	Paraguay
1949	Rio	Brazil	Paraguay
1953	Lima	Paraguay	Brazil

1955	Santiago	Argentina	Chile
1957	Lima	Argentina	Brazil
1959	Buenos Aires	Argentina	Brazil
1963	La Paz	Bolivia	Paraguay
1967	Montevideo	Uruguay	Argentina

LIBERTADORES' CUP

The South American Cup, or *Copa de Los Libertadores*, was founded in 1960 to provide a South American team to play the winners of the European Cup, for the unofficial championship of the world. It was initially confined, like the European Cup, to champions of various countries – Brazil organized a new cup tournament to find one – but when, in the later 1960s, it was enlarged to include two teams per country, Brazilian and Argentinian clubs objected and, on various occasions, withdrew. Thus, no Brazilian clubs competed in 1965, 1969 or 1970, a year in which Argentina were represented only by the South American Cup-holders and world champions, Estudiantes. The clubs now qualify in 'mini-league' groups, in two stages, for a final played at home and away, with goal average irrelevant.

1960
Penarol 1, Olimpia Paraguay 0
Olimpia Paraguay 0, Penarol 0

1961
Penarol 1, Palmeiras 0
(Sao Paulo)
Palmeiras 1, Penarol 1

1962
Santos 2, Penarol 1
Penarol 3, Santos 2
Santos 3, Penarol 0

1963
Santos 3, Boca Juniors 2
Boca Juniors 1, Santos 2

1964
Nacional 0, Independiente 0
Independiente 1, Nacional 0

1965
Independiente 1, Penarol 0
Penarol 3, Independiente 1
Independiente 4, Penarol 1

1966
Penarol 2, River Plate 0
River Plate 3, Penarol 2
Penarol 4, River Plage 2

1967
Racing Club 0, Nacional 0
Nacional 0, Racing Club 0
Racing Club 2, Nacional 1

1968
Estudiantes 3, Palmeiras 1
Palmeiras 3, Estudiantes 1
Estudiantes 2, Palmeiras 0

1969
Nacional 0, Estudiantes 1
Estudiantes 2, Nacional 0

1970
Estudiantes 1, Penarol 0
Penarol 0, Estudiantes 0

1971
Estudiantes 1, Nacional 0
Nacional 1, Estudiantes 0
Nacional 2, Estudiantes 0

1972
Universitario 0, Independiente 0
Independiente 2, Universitario 1

1973
Independiente 1, Colo Colo 1
Colo Colo 0, Independiente 0
Independiente 2, Colo Colo 1

CHAPTER NINETEEN

Olympic Football

The Olympic Games football tournament, a knock-out affair, goes back to the London Olympics of 1908, and has been held at every subsequent Olympiad except Los Angeles, in 1932. Beyond doubt, its most brilliant and notable winners were the Uruguayan teams of 1924 and 1928, at a time when Uruguayan football was quite new to Europe. Indeed, it remained unknown to Britain for another twenty-five years. Even then, the thin, sometimes non-existent, line between amateurism and professionalism flawed the tournament, and in 1924 Britain withdrew over the question of 'broken time' payments, not to return until 1936.

Though frequently interesting, this blemish has made the competition increasingly unsatisfactory, as the amateur footballer – at high level – became more and more a figure of the past. Several members of the alleged 'student' team with which Italy won in Berlin, in 1936, went straight into the full national side. Indeed, the full-backs, Foni and Rava, were the World Cup final pair two years later.

In the 1960 Olympic football tournament, no player who had taken part in the 1958 World Cup was allowed to be chosen, a rule which still exists, with dubious effect. On that occasion it led to the elimination of Russia (who had reached the 1958 finals and could not field their full international team) and by Bulgaria, who could. Italy got round the problem, and still do, by deciding that, since their players could not *officially* be professional till 21, they must in the meantime be amateurs. Thus they were able to field a brilliant young side, almost every member of which has since been fully capped.

The 1908 tournament was won by a very powerful United Kingdom side, including the Rev. K. R. G. Hunt, of Wolves, and the brilliant Spurs and England inside-forward ,Vivian Woodward. France entered two teams in a knock-out tournament, each of which was annihilated, but the Swedes, Dutch and, above all, the Danes, greatly impressed, Denmark, in fact, lost only by 2–0 to the United Kingdom in the final. and had more of the play.

In 1912, at Stockholm, the United Kingdom again beat Denmark in the final 4–2, but the Danes were reduced to ten men by injury.

In 1920, in Antwerp, Britain surprisingly went out 3–1 to Norway in the first round. The Belgians won the tournament, after the Czechs walked off the field in the final in protest against the sending off of one of their players. Thus, second position was awarded to the rising Spanish team, who had beaten Denmark.

The year 1924 saw the first triumph of Uruguay, bringing such brilliant forwards to Paris as Petrone and Scarone. A crowd of 60,000 watched Uruguay beat Switzerland in the final. Four years later, in Amsterdam, Argentina entered for the first time, losing 2–1 to Uruguay in a replayed final.

In 1936 a less powerful field, in Berlin, saw the victory of the Italians. Britain, with Bernard Joy at centre-half, beat China 2–0 then lost 4–5 to Poland. The Italians won the final, 2–1, against Austria, who were coached by Jimmy Hogan.

The 1948 tournament, again held in London, was a fine one. The Swedish, Danish, and Yugoslav teams were among the strongest of the day, while the British amateur side put up a very fine display. After beating the powerful Dutch team in a gruelling match at Highbury, they knocked out France 1–0 at Fulham, with a goal by Bob Hardisty; lost in the semi-final to the powerful Yugoslavs; and again – with honour – in the third match with Denmark.

The Swedes, who beat Yugoslavia 3–1 at Wembley in the final, included all three famous Nordahl brothers, and had Nils Leidholm, Gunnar Gren, and Garvis Carlsson in attack.

The year 1952 saw the entry into the lists of a still greater team – Puskas and his Hungarians. Britain were ingloriously knocked out 4–5 in the first match by little Luxemburg. Russia competed, coming out of splendid isolation, and fought out a remarkable 5–5 draw with Yugoslavia, after being four behind, but lost the replay 3–1. In the Helsinki final, Hungary beat the Slavs 2–0, but not without hard labour.

In 1956 it was Russia's turn. Britain, though knocked out in the eliminators, were invited to Australia to make up the complement, but, without their regular goalkeeper, were thrashed by Bulgaria. The Russians (who had to replay to beat the Indonesians) plodded to an unsatisfying success against the Yugloslavs. India were the surprise, taking fourth place.

In 1960, the Yugoslavs at last had their victory, in Rome, but it was a lucky one; they won their Naples semi-final against Italy on the toss of a coin. A fine Danish team, having knocked out Hungary, played wearily in the final and went down 3–1, even though the Slav forward, Galic, was sent off.

In 1964 Britain, after eliminating Iceland, were defeated by Greece, 5–3 on aggregate, thus failing to qualify for Tokyo. Hungary, with Bene superb, beat the Czechs 2–1 in a splendid final.

The Mexican tournament, in 1968, was convincingly won by Hungary, even though the over-rigorous officiating of Diego De Leo, the referee, reduced the final to farce, three Bulgarians and a Hungarian being sent off. By and large, the sea level teams adapted themselves very well to the high altitude; three of them, France, Bulgaria and Japan, in fact defeated Mexico. The Japanese, their attack superbly led by Kamamoto, were the revelation of the tournament.

The 1972 tournament, in West Germany, saw Hungary beaten, for a change, in the final by a clever Polish team, both of whose goals were scored by their clever midfield player Deyna. The Hungarians were handicapped by an injury to Antal Dunai, a star of their 1968 team. Once again, the Iron Curtain countries fielded complete international sides, the rest a mélange of amateurs and young professionals.

OLYMPIC WINNERS
1908 London: Great Britain 2, Denmark 0: 3rd, Holland
1912 Stockholm: Great Britain 4, Denmark 2: 3rd, Holland
1920 Antwerp: Belgium 2, Czechoslovakia 0 (match abandoned) 2nd place awarded to Spain
1924 Paris: Uruguay 3, Switzerland 0: 3rd, Sweden
1928 Amsterdam: Uruguay 2, Argentina 1 (after 1–1 draw): 3rd, Italy
1936 Berlin: Italy 2, Austria 1 (after extra time): 3rd, Norway
1948 London: Sweden 3, Yugoslavia 1: 3rd Denmark
1952 Helsinki: Hungary 2, Yugoslavia 0: 3rd, Sweden
1956 Melbourne: USSR 1, Yugoslavia 0: 3rd, Bulgaria
1960 Rome: Yugoslavia 3, Denmark 1: 3rd, Italy
1964 Tokyo: Hungary 2, Czechoslovakia 1: 3rd, E. Germany
1968 Mexico City: Hungary 4, Bulgaria 1: 3rd, Japan
1972 Munich: Poland 2, Hungary 1 3rd: USSR and East Germany.

CHAPTER TWENTY

England and Great Britain versus The Rest

26 October 1938. *Arsenal Stadium*
England (2) 3, Rest of Europe (0) 0
England: Woodley (Chelsea); Sproston (Spurs), Hapgood (Arsenal); Willingham (Huddersfield Town), Cullis (Wolves), Copping (Arsenal); Matthews (Stoke), Hall (Spurs), Lawton (Everton), Goulden (West Ham), Boyes (Everton).
Europe: Olvieri; Foni, Rava (Italy); Kupfer (Germany), Andreolo (Italy), Kitzinger (Germany); Aston (France), Braine (Belgium), Piola (Italy), Szengeller (Hungary), Brustad (Norway).
Scorers: Hall, Goulden, Lawton for England.

10 May 1947, *Hampden Park, Glasgow*
Great Britain (4) 6, Rest of Europe (1) 1

Britain: Swift (England); Hardwick (England), Hughes (Wales); Macaulay (Scotland), Vernon (Ireland), Burgess (Wales); Matthews (England), Mannion (England), Lawton (England), Steel (Scotland), Liddell (Scotland).
Europe: Da Rui (France); Peterson (Denmark), Steffen (Switzerland); Carey (Ireland), Parola (Italy), Ludl (Czechoslovakia); Lambrecht (Belgium), Gren (Sweden), Nordahl (Sweden), Wilkes (Holland), Praest (Denmark).
Scorers: Mannion (2), Lawton (2), Steel, Parola (own goal) for Britain; Nordahl for Europe.

21 October 1953 *Wembley*
England (2) 4, Rest of Europe (FIFA) (3) 4
England: Merrick (Birmingham); Ramsey (Spurs), Eckersley (Blackburn R.); Wright (Wolves), Ufton (Charlton Athletic), Dickinson (Portsmouth); Matthews (Blackpool), Mortensen (Blackpool), Lofthouse (Bolton Wanderers), Quixall (Sheffield Wednesday), Mullen (Wolves).
Fifa: Zemen (Austria), [Beara (Yugoslavia)]; Navarro (Spain), Hanappi (Austria); Cjaicowski (Yugoslavia), Posipal (Germany), Ocwirk (Austria); Boniperti (Italy), Kubala (Spain), Nordahl (Sweden), Vukas, Zebec (Yugoslavia).
Scorers: Mullen (2), Mortensen, Ramsey (penalty) for England; Boniperti (2), Kubala (2) (1 penalty) for FIFA.

15 August 1955. *Belfast*
Great Britain (1) 1, Rest of Europe (1) 4
Great Britain: Kelsey (Wales); Sillett (England), McDonald (Scotland); Blanchflower (Ireland), Charles (Wales), Peacock (Ireland); Matthews (England), Johnstone (Scotland), Bentley (England), McIlroy (Ireland), Liddell (Scotland).
Europe: Buffon (Italy); Gustavsson (Sweden), Van Brandt (Belgium); Ocwirk (Austria), Jonquet (France), Boskov (Yugoslavia); Soerensen, (Denmark), Vukas (Yugoslavia), Kopa (France), Travassos (Portugal), Vincent (France).
Scorers: Johnstone for Britain; Vincent, Vukas (3) for Europe.

23 October 1963. *Wembley*. Centenary International
England (0) 2, Rest of the World (0) 1
England: Banks (Leicester City); Armfield (Blackpool), Wilson (Huddersfield Town); Milne (Liverpool), Norman (Spurs), Moore (West Ham United); Paine (Southampton), Greaves (Spurs), Smith, R. (Spurs), Eastham (Arsenal), Charlton (Manchester United).
Fifa: Yachin (Russia), [Soskic (Yugoslavia)]; Santos, D. (Brazil), [(Eyzaguirre (Chile)]; Schnellinger (Germany); Pluskal, Popluhar (Czechoslovakia), Masopust (Czechoslovakia) [Baxter (Scotland)]; Kopa (France) [Seeler (Germany)), Law (Scotland), Di Stefano (Spain), Eusebio (Portugal) [Puskas (Spain)], Gento (Spain).
Scorers: Paine, Greaves for England; Law for FIFA.

CHAPTER TWENTYONE

UEFA And The Lobo Affair

On 21 April, 1974, in the *Sunday Times*, my colleague Keith Botsford and I disclosed the attempt of a Hungarian refugee, Deszo Solti, to bribe the Portuguese referee, Francisco Lobo, to favour Juventus against Derby County. The offer was of $5,000 and a car; Lobo was to come to Turin as Solti's guest to see the first leg European Cup semifinal between the teams, so he could appreciate how 'rough' English football was. He would then espouse Juventus' interests in the return match on 25 April at the Baseball Ground, Derby.

Unfortunately for Solti – a notorious figure in European football, for years established in Milan, and a close if unofficial confidant of the great Milanese football clubs – Lobo is an honest man. He consulted his referees' association, strung Solti along, and finally delivered evidence, including a taped telephone call, to UEFA, the European Union.

It is now that the plot deplorably thickens. UEFA's Disciplinary Committee met on 20 June – two months after Lobo had impeccably refereed the Derby game, a goalless draw. They convened in the Atlantis Hotel, Zurich, where Lobo and Solti were present at the same time. Yet although a farcical 'identity parade' was held for Lobo, with officials of Juventus, he was never presented with Solti!

Solti told the Disciplinary Committee he was there in Lisbon 'as a tourist'. The Committee, not quite as green as that, recommended to their Executive Committee that he be declared *persona non grata* to all their members. Nine days later, meeting in Glasgow, the Executive Committee limply decided that there was insufficient evidence to do that without fear of legal reprisal. They would, however, circularise all their members of what Solti had done; or tried to do. This, too, was never implemented. The Union did, however, find time, on 5 July, to send a letter to Juventus, thanking them for their cooperation and giving them total absolution! Solti, it seemed, had been acting alone. Why? A question neither posed nor answered.

The lame reason given by Artemio Franchi, president not only of UEFA but, be it noted, of FIGC, the Italian Federation, for failing to act was that UEFA were advised it might be legally dangerous. But when the *Sunday Times* exposed Solti, he promptly disappeared!

Franchi promised the *Sunday Times*, in Florence, that he would reopen the enquiry, withdrew his promise at a Press conference in Brussels on the day of the European Cup final, then renewed it the following week at UEFA's congress in Edinburgh; where he was reelected unopposed to the presidency. A two-man commission would, he promised, be appointed.

The whole sordid affair was the climax of 10 years of dubious activity by Italian clubs and their agents. Some of the most notable instances were:

1964. European Cup semi-final between Internazionale of Milan and Borussia Dortmund; second leg at San Siro. Suarez, Inter inside-forward, kicked a German halfback in the stomach, obliging him to leave the field, but was not sent off. The following summer, a Yugoslav tourist found Tesanic, the Yugoslav referee, holidaying on the Italian coast at the expense of Inter.

1965. European Cup semi-final, between Internazionale and Liverpool; second leg at San Siro. Liverpool, 3-1 ahead after the first leg went down 3-0, with two highly dubious goals allowed by the Spanish referee, Ortiz de Mendibil. Solti later turned up in Vienna on the occasion of the European Cup final with a suitcase full of gold watches, which he distributed, apparently on behalf of Inter.

1973. European Cup semi-final between Derby County and Juventus; first leg in Turin. Derby were incensed by the fact that Helmut Haller, a West German international, should be in the dressing-room of the West German referee, Schulenberg, before the game, and should try to speak to him at half-time; precipitating a scuffle with Derby's assistant manager, Peter Taylor. Schulenberg booked two Derby players, Gemmill and McFarland, who were thus unable to play in the return game, but was oddly permissive towards the aggressive Juventus halfback, Furino.

1973. European Cup-Winners' Cup final between Leeds United and Milan; in Salonica. The disgracefully biased refereeing of the Greek, Michas, in favour of Milan led to his suspension by UEFA; but, mysteriously, no inquiry. Greek papers bitterly attacked Franchi. It emerges that members of the Greek Federation strongly opposed the choice of Michas as referee on the grounds that he was a client of the Italians.

1974. European Cup-Winners' Cup semi-final between Borussia Mönchengladbach and Milan; second leg in Dusseldorf. The one-sided refereeing of the Spaniard, Martinez, in favour of Milan precipitated an attack by the crowd and at least one player after the match. There were bitter protests from the German club and Press.

All in all, a sorry record, leading one to ask the seemingly rhetorical question: are UEFA fit to administer European football?